S0-AAG-757

THAILAND'S INDUSTRIALIZATION AND ITS CONSEQUENCES

STUDIES IN THE ECONOMIES OF EAST AND SOUTH-EAST ASIA

General Editors: Peter Nolan, Lecturer in the Faculty of Economics and Politics, University of Cambridge, and Fellow and Director of Studies in Economics, Jesus College, Cambridge, England; and Malcolm Falkus, Professor of Economic History, University of New England, Armidale, New South Wales, Australia

In the last decades of the twentieth century the small and medium-sized nations of East and South-East Asia have begun a process of potentially enormous political and economic transformation. Explosive growth has occurred already in many parts of the region, and the more slowly growing countries are attempting to emulate this vanguard group. The impact of the region upon the world economy has increased rapidly and is likely to continue to do so in the future.

In order to understand better economic developments within this vast and diverse region, this series aims to publish books on both contemporary and historical issues. It includes works both by Western scholars and by economists from countries within the region.

Published titles include:

Rajeswary Ampalavanar Brown
INDIAN CAPITAL AND THE ECONOMIC TRANSFORMATION OF MODERN SOUTH-EAST ASIA

John Butcher and Howard Dick (*editors*)
THE RISE AND FALL OF REVENUE FARMING

Mark Cleary and Shuang Yann Wong
OIL, DEVELOPMENT AND DIVERSIFICATION IN BRUNEI DARUSSALAM

Yujiro Hayami and Toshihiko Kawagoe
THE AGRARIAN ORIGINS OF COMMERCE AND INDUSTRY

Medhi Krongkaew (*editor*)
THAILAND'S INDUSTRIALIZATION AND ITS CONSEQUENCES

Rajah Rasiah
FOREIGN CAPITAL AND INDUSTRIALIZATION IN MALAYSIA

Thailand's Industrialization and its Consequences

Edited by

Medhi Krongkaew
Faculty of Economics
Thammasat University, Bangkok and
Senior Research Fellow
Research School of Pacific and Asian Studies
Canberra, Australia

St. Martin's Press

First published in Great Britain 1995 by
MACMILLAN PRESS LTD
Houndmills, Basingstoke, Hampshire RG21 2XS
and London
Companies and representatives
throughout the world

A catalogue record for this book is available
from the British Library.

ISBN 0–333–62519–6

10 9 8 7 6 5 4 3 2 1
04 03 02 01 00 99 98 97 96 95

Printed and bound in Great Britain by
Antony Rowe Ltd
Chippenham, Wiltshire

First published in the United States of America 1995 by
Scholarly and Reference Division,
ST. MARTIN'S PRESS, INC.,
175 Fifth Avenue,
New York, N.Y. 10010

ISBN 0–312–12458–9

Library of Congress Cataloging-in-Publication Data
Thailand's industrialization and its consequences / edited by Medhi Krongkaew.
p. cm. — (Studies in the economies of East and South-East Asia Asia)
An outgrowth of the conference, "The Making of a Fifth Tiger? Thailand's Industrialisation and Its Consequences," held at the Australian National University on 7–9 December 1992.
Includes bibliographical references and index.
ISBN 0–312–12458–9
1. Industrialization—Thailand—Congresses. 2. Thailand—Economic conditions—Congresses. 3. Thailand—Social conditions—Congresses.
I. Medhi, Krongkaew. II. Series.
HC445.T454 1995
338.9593—dc20 94–33766
CIP

Contents

List of Figures and Tables

Figures

Tables

Notes on the Contributors

Chai-Anan Samudavanija is Professor of Political Science, Chulalongkorn University, and Director, Institute of Public Policy Studies. His past positions include Senator in the Thai Senate, President of the Sukhothai Thammathirat Open University and President of the Social Sciences of Thailand. Professor Chai-Anan received his PhD in political science from the University of Wisconsin at Madison.

Direk Patmasiriwat is Research Fellow at the Thailand Development Research Institute. Having gained a PhD in economics from the University of Georgia, Dr Direk has taught at various universities in Thailand, including Kasetsart University, the National Institute of Development Administration, Chiang Mai University and Naresuan University. He is also currently the Secretary General of the Economic Society of Thailand.

Malcolm Falkus is Professor of Economic History and Director of Centre for Asian Studies, University of New England, New South Wales, Australia. Before moving to Australia Professor Falkus taught for 25 years at the London School of Economics. He has published widely on European and Asian economic history.

Kraiyudht Dhiratayakinant is Professor of Economics and Director of Social Research Institute, Chulalongkorn University. He was formerly Managing Director of Chulalongkorn University Press. Professor Kraiyudht studied economics at the University of Wisconsin (Madison) and the University of California at Los Angeles, where he received his PhD in economics.

Medhi Krongkaew is Senior Research Fellow, Department of Economics, Research School of Pacific and Asian Studies, the Australian National University. Dr Medhi, a former Dean of Economics and Director of the Thai Khadi Research Institute at Thammasat University, has been on leave from Thammasat University to work at the ANU since 1990.

Naris Chaiyasoot is Dean of the Faculty of Economics, Thammasat University. Since graduating with a PhD in economics from the

University of Hawaii, Dr Naris has had an active career in teaching, research and administration at Thammasat University. His immediate past position was Vice President of Planning, Thammasat University.

Nipon Poapongsakorn is Director of the Sectoral Economics Programme at the Thailand Development Research Institute (TDRI). After gaining a PhD in economics from the University of Hawaii, Dr Nipon taught for more than 20 years at the Faculty of Economics, Thammasat University before joining the TDRI.

Pranee Tinakorn is Associate Professor at the Faculty of Economics, Thammasat University. A King's Scholarship student, Dr Pranee received her PhD in economics from the University of Pennsylvania and worked as a young professional at the World Bank before joining Thammasat University.

Peter J. Rimmer is Head of the Department of Human Geography, Research School of Pacific and Asian Studies, Australian National University. Since gaining a PhD in geography from the University of Canterbury in Christchurch, New Zealand, Dr Rimmer has conducted extensive research and written widely on urbanization, human settlements and transportation in the Asia-Pacific region.

Helen Ross is Fellow at the Centre for Resource and Environmental Studies, Australian National University. She has a PhD from the London School of Economics, and worked for many years at the Australian Department of Aboriginal Affairs before joining the ANU.

Makoto Sakurai is Director General and Chief Economist of the Mitsui Marine Research Institute in Tokyo. He has a masters degree in economics from the University of Tokyo and is currently a PhD candidate there. Mr Sakurai worked for many years at the Export–Import Bank of Japan before assuming his present position.

Sirilaksana Khoman is Associate Professor and Director of the International Bachelor of Economics Programme at the Faculty of Economics, Thammasat University. She has a PhD in economics from the University of Hawaii. Dr Sirilaksana has extensively researched the educational and health systems of Thailand, and has frequently been asked to give advice to the government on those issues.

Somchai Ratanakomut is Associate Professor, Faculty of Economics, Chulalongkorn University, and formerly Deputy Director of the Social

Research Institute of that University. He received a PhD in economics from University of Utah.

Suntaree Komin is Deputy Director of the Training Center, the National Institute of Development Administration (NIDA). She has a PhD in social psychology from the University of Hawaii, and has lectured and published widely in the areas of Thai culture and value systems.

Suphat Suphachalasai is Director of Graduate Programmes, Faculty of Economics, Thammasat University. He has received a PhD in economics from the Australian National University and has published widely in the international trade of Thailand and world trading systems.

Suthiphand Chirathivat is Director of the Center for International Economic Studies at the Faculty of Economics, Chulalongkorn University. He has a PhD in economics from the University of Sorborne in Paris. Dr Suthiphand taught at Kasetsart University before recently joining Chulalongkorn University.

Suwattana Thadaniti is Deputy Director of the Social Research Institute of Chulalongkorn University. She was Head of the Department of Urban and Regional Planning, Faculty of Architecture, Chulalongkorn University prior to joining the Social Research Institute. She received her PhD in Town and Country Planning from the Technical University of Cracow in Poland.

Notes on Thai Names and Units of Measurement

In Thailand people are known both formally and informally by their first names, and all written records are entered first names first and surnames last. The adoption of Western tradition of writing the surname first followed by the initial letter of the first name to identify a Thai person often confuses Thai readers because people are not normally known or referred to by such names in Thailand. In order to avoid confusion on the use of Thai names this book lists Thai names by their first names first.

The currency unit of Thailand, the baht, was equivalent to about four US cents or slightly more than 25 baht per US$1 in the middle of 1994. The daily rate of exchange between Thai baht and other currencies fluctuates according to the basket of currencies determined by the Bank of Thailand.

Land area in Thailand is measured in *rai*. One rai is equivalent to 0.4 acre, or 2.5 rai to 1 acre.

Preface

This book is an outgrowth of a conference held at the Australian National University on 7–9 December 1992. The title of the conference, 'The Making of A Fifth Tiger? Thailand's Industrialization and Its Consequences', reflected my feeling and perception of the extraordinary events surrounding the development of Thailand since the mid-1980s. These events included the successful structural adjustments in the economy after the debilitating oil price increase in the early 1980s, the surge in Thai manufactured exports starting in 1986, the influx of direct foreign investment especially from Japan, and the boom in the tourist industry following 'Visit Thailand Year' in 1987. By early 1990 Thailand was a much changed country economically, so much so that it could claim to be a fifth member of the so-called the 'four tigers' of Asia; so much so that it gave me an irresistible urge to explore the process of this economic transformation further, and to share such knowledge and understanding with others. The quickest way to do this was to organize a conference of experts and publish their specific contributions.

Two other extraordinary events took place in 1991 and 1992, when the conference was under preparation, which put the question mark in its title. In February 1991 the army seized power from the democratically elected civilian government, and in May 1992 the new, army-controlled government ordered a brutal crackdown of pro-democracy demonstrators in Bangkok. These political events threatened to dash Thailand's hope of joining the ranks of newly industrialized countries in Asia because they adversely affected the economic optimism of the country. But this was not to be. The Thais have quickly managed to return the country and its economy to normalcy. By the end of 1992 Thailand was back on its high economic growth path, and the conference was held as planned.

This book aims to cover as much ground as possible on the salient characteristics of Thai industrialization and its economic and non-economic consequences. Due to time and space limitations, it may not succeed in all aspects but at least it should provide some balanced treatment of issues facing the economic transformation of Thailand. It is hoped that the book will be useful not only to students of the Thai economy but to all students of Thai development and Thailand in general.

In organizing the conference and preparing this volume I received help from numerous people and organizations. First of all, I would like to thank Professor Ross Garnaut, Head of the Department of Economics, Research School of Pacific and Asian Studies, Australian National University, who encouraged the conference and agreed to provide basic financial and other necessary departmental support. I also thank Dr Varakorn Samakoses, Dean of the Faculty of Economics, Thammasat University, who helped organize the conference on the Thai side, especially the crucial selection and contacting of Thai contributors. Further financial assistance for the conference came from the Australian International Development Assistance Bureau (AIDAB), the National Thai Studies Centre at the ANU, His Excellency Mr John McCarthy, the Australian Ambassador to Thailand, FAIR, Japan, the Thai Glass Industries, and STA Travel in Bangkok. I offer my thanks to these important sponsors.

I am very grateful to all those who have contributed to this volume, and to all my friends and colleagues at the ANU who chaired the conference sessions and commented on earlier drafts of the papers. I am especially grateful to Professor Malcolm Falkus, who not only wrote the overview chapter to this volume and gave me moral support during the whole endeavour, but also helped me with the editing of the book and facilitated my contact with the publisher. Without his support and assistance this book might not have been possible.

I humbly dedicate this book to the Australian National University, a great university where I have spent some fruitful years as a research fellow.

Canberra MEDHI KRONGKAEW

Introduction: The Making of the Fifth Tiger – Thailand's Industrialization and Its Consequences

Medhi Krongkaew

Thailand has provided an interesting case study for various scholars. To a modern historian studying the formation of nation states in East and South-East Asia, the non-colonisation of Thailand by Western powers in the latter part of the nineteenth century remains an intriguing story reflecting, in a large part, the consummate diplomacy of the Thai leaders. To a political scientist, the Thai political system may not differ much from other developing systems where experiments with democracy are often interrupted by military coups d'etat. Yet despite many undemocratic political changes in the last two or three decades, politically Thailand remains one of the most stable and most open countries in East and South-East Asia. To a cultural sociologist and anthropologist, the Thais exhibit certain traditional customs of societal obligations and tolerance that contribute to a smooth and harmonious way of life, free of religious and ethnic strife.

Economically Thailand also exhibits unique characteristics. Consider the following:

- In the three decades since the early 1960s, Thailand has been and is still the only one net food exporter in East and South-East Asia.
- Thailand has not experienced a negative economic growth rate in the last 30 years of its modern economic development. The growth in Thailand in the last three years of the 1980s averaged about 11.8 per cent in real terms, one of the highest in the world.
- Economic changes in Thailand took place in a situation where the labour force was still predominantly agricultural, where the secondary school attainment was one of the lowest in Asia, and where the primacy of its capital city, Bangkok, increased with development, effectively dominating all other cities in the kingdom.

- The voluntary family planning programme in Thailand is regarded as one of the most successful in the world, and helps explain the fast increase in its per capita GNP.

The above phenomena have their roots in the early 1960s when Thailand began to industrialize. As industrialization is recognized as an important indicator of economic development, or a means by which economic development could be attained, this book seeks to analyze the salient nature and characteristics of the industrialization process in Thailand and to assess the impact of this process upon various sectors of the economy. The following are some of the characteristics and questions that make the analysis and assessment of industrialization in Thailand interesting.

- In comparison with other East or South-East Asian countries, industrial development in Thailand has involved relatively little direct government intervention. This fact sets it apart from those countries whose governments often 'pick the winners', or behave in a 'father-knows-best' fashion. However the government has provided various indirect policy supports.
- The industrial development of Thailand is believed to have extracted large sacrifices from its agricultural sector. At one time rice was the most highly taxed commodity in the country, and food prices were often kept artificially low for urban workers. Over the last two decades the industrial value added as percentage of GDP increased from about 26 per cent to about 38 per cent, but the share of industrial employment only increased from about 8 per cent to about 12 per cent.
- The service sector has also benefited greatly from the process of development. In fact the banking and finance subsector has been the fastest-growing subsector of the whole economy in the last 30 years.
- The industrial concentration in and around the Greater Bangkok area, coupled with the slowdown in public investment in basic infrastructure in the last few years, has created development bottlenecks unmatched in many countries of the world.

This book is divided into four parts. Part I contains an overview chapter plus five chapters on the various characteristics and nature of Thai industrialization. Part II discusses certain economic impacts of the industrialization process, while Part III discusses impacts on social and political structures and governance, and on the environment and social values. Finally, Part IV looks at Thai industrialization from regional and international perspectives.

Malcolm Falkus begins Chapter 1 by noting the three important elements of Thai industrialization: its recentness, its rapidness and its unexpectedness. Industrialization has been almost entirely a product of the years since 1960. Before this Thailand was overwhelmingly an agricultural country, with some 90 per cent of the population engaged in agriculture and around half of the national income deriving from this source. From the early 1960s industrial growth developed at a rapid pace, with sharp acceleration after 1985. In the process, both the agricultural and manufacturing sectors in the Thai economy have become greatly diversified and increasingly outward-looking. Unexpectedly, this industrialization has been accompanied by relatively low rates of inflation and a continued increase in investment from domestic as well as foreign sources. There have been adverse effects of this industrialization, such as environmental damage, traffic congestion, AIDS, and an increasing income gap between regions and between people.

Chapter 2 by Medhi Krongkaew on the contribution of agriculture to Thai industrialization, traces the development of modern Thai agriculture from the early 1960s to the early 1990s. During this period, Thai agriculture helped the budding industrial sector by supplying the food, labour, market outlets, savings and foreign exchange necessary for industrialization. In so doing the agricultural sector has been subject to government taxation and various other extractions that have benefited the industrial sector and industrial workers. Only from the mid-1980s onward, when the industrial growth was sustained at a high level did the agricultural sector begin to receive net returns from the industrial sector. Still the future of agriculture in industrialized Thailand is uncertain, but it seems that increased productivity and diversification through mechanization and technological changes could provide some solutions.

Chapters 3 and 4, by Suphat Suphachalasai and Somchai Ratanakomut, respectively, tackle what are considered the most important factors behind the recent success of Thailand's economic development and industrialization: export growth, growth in direct foreign investment, and growth in service activities, especially tourism. Suphat provides a brief background to the various stages of industrialization in Thailand before discussing the growth and direction of manufactured exports. Major manufactured exports now include textile products, integrated circuits, jewellery and processed food, especially canned tuna and pineapple. He discusses in some detail the use of tariff protection and other trade policies to help import-substitution industrialization before the major change to export promotion in the early 1980s. In addition to export growth, the growth in direct investment in the manufacturing sector, especially that from foreign sources, has been responsible for the increase in industrial activity and the subsequent economic growth of the economy.

Somchai provides a supporting account by emphasizing the important role of the service sector in the Thai economy. He points out that the service sector's share in gross domestic product was almost 50 per cent while that of agriculture was only about 12.4 per cent in 1990. Out of these service activities, tourism is the largest item, contributing more than 110 billion baht to the economy in 1990. Important service activities also include financial services, of which Somchai proposes further liberalization to make them a more competitive and efficient contributor to future growth.

In Chapter 5, Kraiyudht Dhiratayakinant concentrates on the role of the public sector and its interaction with the private sector in promoting economic development and industrialization. In the Thai setting, Kraiyudht believes that the public sector took an active role in industrial-policy formulation during the first decade of industrialization in the early 1960s. However, with the rise in dynamism of the private sector in the second decade of industrialization (1970s), the role of the public sector in industrial-policy formulation began to erode, and in the 1980s a role switch took place. The private sector, through the creation of the Joint Public-Private Consultative Committee (JPPCC), has begun to exert its influence in industrial-policy formulation. It appears that this new form of relationship, whereby private entrepreneurs are given substantial incentives and the economic freedom to operate in the economy, will lead to further economic success in the future.

The last chapter in Part I, Chapter 6 by Nipon Poapongsakorn, considers rural industries. Nipon begins by stressing the concentration of industrial activities in Bangkok and surrounding areas, and suggests that the economics of urban agglomeration, which gives rise to economies of scope both on the input side and the output (market) side, is a major reason for such concentration in Bangkok. He notes, though, that the recent surge in land and building prices in Bangkok has pushed industrial establishments into the fringe areas of Bangkok, turning them into fast-growing industrial areas. But the situation in provincial areas remains unchanged and rural industrialization is still very limited. According to Nipon, factors retarding the growth of rural industries include, among other things, the continued expansion of agricultural land through encroachment into reserved forests, preventing the establishment of new and stable urbanized communities; the low income base in rural areas due to poverty; the lack of input supplies and necessary infrastructure; and the bias of the central government against local decentralization. It is recommended, therefore, that the future of rural industrialization lies in greater reliance upon market forces, market size and agglomeration economies, and availability of infrastructure facilities and amenities. The abolition of policy measures that bias against the rural sector, such as highly centralized fiscal policy, could provide additional help to rural industrialization.

Part II starts with Chapter 7, an analysis by Direk Patmasiriwat of the impact of industrialization on government finance. Direk establishes that the government revenue of Thailand moves procyclically with the general economic activity of the country. When the Thai economy experienced an economic boom during the second half of the 1980s government revenue also jumped. Major contributing sources of revenue were business tax, excise taxes, import duties, and personal and corporate income tax. When government revenue increased, so did government expenditure – after a lag of about two years. Expenditure on infrastructure became marked, but only after a lapse of several years due to a shortage of public funds. The government may continue to adopt fiscal policies that are conducive to stimulating industrial development. The recent success in tax collection, especially through the new value added tax (VAT) should stimulate further reforms in the tax system, which might include a greater role for the legislative branch in fiscal-policy formulation, greater fiscal autonomy for local governments, and reforms in property taxes.

From fiscal policy we move to monetary policy. In Chapter 8 Naris Chaiyasoot summarizes the development of monetary policy in Thailand over the last three decades. The major emphasis of monetary policy in Thailand as practised by the Bank of Thailand, has always been on financial and monetary stability. The bank constantly monitors the money supply and attempts to adjust its growth rate and liquidity to assure healthy economic growth without debilitating inflation. Naris also discusses the development of financial institutions, emphasizing various reforms that could have extensive repercussions upon future financial development. Such monetary measures as the liberalization of commercial and other financial institutions, the lifting of interest-rate ceiling, and the relaxation of regulations on the holding of commercial bank deposits are discussed at some length. External finance also receives attention, while the author analyzes the response of financial markets to the liberalization of the financial and exchange systems. The financial reforms discussed in this chapter are expected to mobilize domestic savings as well as to enhance the ability of domestic financial institutions to cope with global competition as Thailand becomes more industrialized.

In Chapter 9 Peter Rimmer looks at the impact of industrialization on the economy from another angle. He emphasizes the effect of rapid industrialization on rural-urban configurations, particularly on the urbanization process. Urban areas and populations grew rapidly in the 1980s, when Thailand's industrialization accelerated. Nowhere have the effects of recent economic growth been more keenly felt than in Bangkok. It is only natural that the present and future growth and industrialization of the Thai economy should pay special attention to the change in the role of Bangkok as the most important production and service centre of Thailand. Rimmer focuses upon this, and concentrates on the transport problems of Bangkok, mentioning several policy packages that have been advocated to help solve the problems. He also discusses a number of privatization plans for public enterprises to make them more efficient and able to cope with industrialized Thailand. Finally, the author stresses the new regional-development strategy, which puts Bangkok in the wider perspective of a regional-development corridor linking Chiang Mai with Bali. In this context the development of Bangkok has transcended national boundaries and, through transport and telecommunications networks, made Thailand a true part of the global economy.

Part II ends with Chapter 10 by Pranee Tinakorn, who asks how poverty and income distribution in Thailand are affected by past and present industrialization processes. Pranee describes the trends in functional as well as size distribution of income among Thai households and the incidence of poverty. She shows clearly that increased economic development and industrialization have brought about a much more unequal income distribution, but that growth has resulted in a decline in the overall proportion of the population and households classified as poor to around 21 per cent. However the rate of poverty decline has slowed in the last few years, and more than 11 million of the total 55 million were still living in poverty in the late 1980s. She attributes the growing income inequality and the small reduction in absolute poverty to industrial policies that have favoured large-scale capital-intensive firms over small-scale labour-intensive firms, and manufactured products over agricultural products, resulting in reduced welfare for workers in the agricultural sector. A future policy change should redress these policy biases to ensure that the benefits of industrialization are more equally shared and distributed.

Parts I and II form the core of the analysis of Thailand's industrialization and its economic consequences. In Part III we go on to discuss some non-economic impacts. Chapter 11 by Chai-Anan Samudavanija, addresses the relationship between economic development and democratization in the Thai context. Chai-Anan first identifies the major players in public policy making in the Thai democratic system, including state bureaucrats and technocrats, the military, businessmen, politicians, and the population at large. He then argues that increasing industrialization has brought about intersectoral conflict, especially conflict between the business sector and the agricultural sector. State bureaucrats and the military have increasingly aligned themselves with businessmen to promote capitalistic industrial development against the interests of the agricultural masses. When this occurs, the situation can develop into something of an impasse because rural people are still regarded as majority in the democratic system. Politicians (members of the legislature) are weak in the present system of governance, and remain peripheral to the issues of public policy making. At times the military have seized power and asked a group of technocrats to run the country. Many good economic policies have been made in this way, but such a process is undemocratic, and when democracy returns, different conflicts take place.

Therefore, Chai-Anan calls the present system in Thailand 'ungovernable' or 'institutionalized anarchy', where the players mentioned earlier act as opposing forces. There is no single dominant power centre, not even the most powerful military. However above the military is the monarchy, which is still considered the foundation of legitimacy. As long as the monarchy continues to be legitimate and strong, it can act as the force that holds these opposing factions together. Despite these complexities, Chai-Anan believes that Thailand will remain dynamic, will maintain its record of self-organization and will not fall into political decay

In Chapter 12 Suntaree Komin looks at the impact of industrialization on certain social values and institutions. She also touches on the democratisation process, where egalitarianism has become a rising trend in the post-industrialization scenario. But in the meantime such issues as female and child labour, and sex stratification in the job market still require close and immediate attention. On other social issues, Suntaree discusses the increasing trend towards secularization in the religious practices of Thailand, the trend towards the nuclear family (notwithstanding continuing traditional concern about the ageing population), the changing role of women and their greater participation in the labour force, the increasing commercialization of life-style, impersonalization, and the greater role of the mass media and communications technology in the lives of ordinary people. In a way the changes that are taking place in Thailand are following events that have already occurred in other industrialized societies, but in order to avoid the social instability that rapid industrialization could bring to Thai society we may need to be more alert to these social changes.

The important issue of the environmental costs of industrialization warrants a separate chapter. In Chapter 13 Helen Ross and Suwattana Thadaniti consider the types of ecosystem that have been affected by Thailand's economic growth and industrialization, looking at general forests, eucalyptus plantations, mangrove forests, water resources, tourism and mining. The discussion highlights the environmental damage that occurs as a result of economic development, such as soil erosion and devastating floods following massive deforestation; water and air pollution following manufacturing and mining activities, and so on. Bangkok is again used as an example to illustrate the environmental cost of rapid development. All the relevant problems are discussed: traffic congestion, water pollution, flooding, air pollution and land subsidence. After demonstrating the folly of development that neglects its environmental components, Ross and Suwattana suggest policy measures that should bring about a sustainable pattern of development, such as conservation of the earth's vitality and diversity, the minimization of non-renewable-resources depletion, the maintenance of the earth's carrying capacity, the provision of a national framework for integrating development and conservation, and so on.

The last chapter in Part III, Chapter 14 by Sirilaksana Khoman, assesses the implications of Thailand's industrialization upon health, education, and science and technology. This is a very broad area, but Sirilaksana is able to identify a few important issues that are crucial to an understanding of the topic. The first issue is the relationship between industrialization and health, and the author stresses the danger that hazardous industrial waste presents to the environment, such as that from sugar and pulp and paper factories. Hazardous waste may also lead to occupational health hazards, as demonstrated by several cases of lead poisoning among workers in battery plants. The threat of AIDS as a major health problem in the service industries is again focused upon. On education, Sirilaksana points out the apparent paradox between industrialization and low secondary enrolment in Thailand. Until recently industrialization has not brought about a significant increase in enrolment for secondary education. There are many reasons for this and one determinant is the wealth and income position of the household. Other reasons include the unlikelihood of gaining employment in the formal sector, large family size and poor-quality secondary teaching. Finally, on science and technology (S&T), Sirilaksana believes that S&T manpower is important for the productivity and competitiveness of services and agriculture, and is vital for Thailand's export industries. At present there are serious shortages in the local supply of S&T manpower, especially engineers and technicians. Facilities for skill upgrading are also inadequate at present. Future policy, therefore, should call for greater public investment and involvement in the area of education and skill training, where the market often fails to provide an adequate supply. Health and the environment are also public-goods-type concerns that call for greater government intervention and support.

Part IV deals with the role of newly industrializing Thailand in regional and international communities, and with Thailand's industrialization from an external perspective. It was hoped originally to compare the industrialization of Thailand with that of some of its Asian neighbours who have already reached the industrialized or newly industrialized stage, but time and space allows only one view – from Japan.

In his chapter on external economic influence, regional cooperation, and the role of Thailand as a newly industrializing country (Chapter 13), Suthiphand Chirathivat emphasizes the importance of the external sector to the industrialization and economic development of Thailand, particularly through export growth and direct foreign investment. The contributions of the external sector cannot be overemphasized. However the focus of this chapter is on the expectation of Thailand becoming a member of the Asian 'tigers' in its trade relations with other developed trading partners. Thailand is likely to face the trend towards increasing trade protection, loss of specialized trade preferences, the deeper regionalization of the Asia-Pacific economy including the expanding trade relations within ASEAN itself, and intensification of worldwide competition in trade and investment.

Under these circumstances Thailand will need to adjust itself as an NIC by moving to higher value added products, increasing its high-technology manufactures and otherwise maintaining and strengthening its international competitiveness. Upgrading human resources is one important way of doing this. In the global trading system, Thailand as an NIC would do well to continue to adhere to the GATT-based trading system. With respect to regional cooperation, greater involvement and reliance on ASEAN and, later on, APEC could promote greater effectiveness in interregional and intraregional trade and investment.

The second and final paper in Part IV (Chapter 16) surveys how Japanese economists and researchers perceive the economic development and industrialization of Thailand. Makoto Sakurai recounts how Japanese research on the development of the Thai economy first started and how it has developed into a model that can be replicated in other economies. The admiration of Japanese economists and researchers for industrialization in Thailand has focused upon a few main areas, namely the success of its macroeconomic policy of structural adjustment and low inflation, the adoption of industrialization and trade policies that stress stronger market mechanisms and less government intervention, and foreign-investment policies that are increasingly liberal and flexible. Thailand's status as the fifth tiger of Asia is assured because it possesses the economic and social ability to respond to international opportunities and challenges, and to transform its economy accordingly.

It is hoped that this book will provide information, appraisal, assessment and analyzes of the industrialization of Thailand and its consequences to wide-ranging groups of people – scholars and general readers alike – wishing to gain a better understanding of the process of economic development in Thailand.

Part I

The Nature and Characteristics of Thai Industrialization

1 Thai Industrialization: An Overview

Malcolm Falkus

Let me begin by drawing attention to three characteristics of Thai industrialization: its recentness, its rapid pace, and its unexpectedness.

Although industrialization had been very evident for some two decades, in 1980 Thailand was still essentially an agricultural country. Agriculture exceeded industry in its contribution to GDP and over 70 per cent of the population was agricultural (mostly small-scale peasant farmers). Just 8 per cent of the labour force worked in the manufacturing sector and the urban population was around 13 per cent of the total (mostly concentrated in Bangkok). The export structure very much reflected Thailand's agricultural economy: 45 per cent of exports were foodstuffs and a further 14 per cent consisted of minerals and other raw materials. The top four export commodities in 1980 were rice, tapioca, rubber and tin (together some 32 per cent of all exports), while only in fifth place came a manufactured commodity – textiles (less than half the value of rice).

Change thereafter was rapid, especially in the closing years of the 1980s. Around 1986 industry exceeded agriculture in its contribution to GDP. For the three years 1988–90 Thailand recorded double-digit GDP growth, reaching 13.2 per cent in 1988. The rates of growth of exports and particular sectors such as construction, banking, transport and other services were higher still. These notable rates were the more striking since they took place at a time when some economies elsewhere were slackening; indeed Thailand probably had the fastest rate of real economic growth in the world in these four years, and although the rates slackened thereafter (8.1 per cent in 1991 and 7.6 per cent in 1992) growth is still very high, especially at a time of general world recession.

It was at the close of the 1980s that the world began to look closely at the 'Thai model' of growth, and talk became common of Thailand reaching NIC status by the end of the 1990s by following the other successful Asian industrializers – Hong Kong, Singapore, South Korea and Taiwan – on a path of export-led industrialization. In April 1990 the prime minister of Baden-Wurttemberg, Dr Spath, on a visit to Thailand, said that 'in the past, everybody thought of only Japan and the four Asian NICs. Now we are saying Thailand will be the fifth tiger'. Among many striking indices of success, we may note that over the years 1982–91 Thailand doubled its share of world export trade, rising from 44th position among the world's nations in 1982 to 34th in 1987 and 28th in 1991. As an importer, Thailand went from 46th to 35th to 22nd place in the same years.

Yet we should remark that in the first half of the 1980s the prospects for sustained industrialization and rapid growth were not at all apparent. Real GDP growth between 1980–85 was only 5.6 per cent a year (lower than in both the 1960s and 1970s), and reached a low point of only 3.5 per cent in 1985. At that time it was a common view that the long period of sustained growth had come to an end; with unfavourable world economic circumstances, high interest rates, a growing budget deficit, a rising service to debt ratio and a weakening balance of payments on current account combining to produce pessimism about the future of Thai economic development.

The rapid and unexpected growth during the period 1987–92 changed the structure of the Thai economy forever. A much more diverse industrial structure, with growing technological sophistication, has been accompanied by huge investments in infrastructure and other projects that will certainly provide an impulse for growth in the coming years. Such projects include the huge eastern seaboard development, new highways, mass transit systems in Bangkok, new dams, industrial estates, hotel and resort complexes, and so on. As far as manufacturing developments are concerned, it is worth noting that in the years 1993–96 new Japanese factories (already planned and approved by the Board of Investment) – many of them joint ventures, producing goods for export and using advanced technology) will open at the rate of one every three days.

With growth has come an upsurge in per capita income, especially in Bangkok, and the emergence of a new relatively wealthy business middle class. In 1980 the majority of passenger cars on the streets were taxis (then small and without air-conditioning). In 1993 the choked Bangkok streets were full of up-market private cars, visibly reflecting the country's growing prosperity.

Of course it would be unsafe to predict that industrialization and economic growth will persist at rapid rates. A theme I will emphasize is the extent to which Thailand has been influenced by external events, and changed external circumstances may well move the Thai economy in unexpected directions. The social, political and environmental consequences of rapid growth have already shown themselves to be momentous. All this means that predicting the future by extrapolating past trends should be undertaken with caution.

That said, let us briefly record some of the salient features of Thai industrialization and economic change. An overview of Thai industrialization should draw attention to a number of basic points.

First, industrialization has been almost entirely a product of the years since 1960. Before then Thailand was overwhelmingly an agricultural country, with some 90 per cent of the population engaged in agriculture and around half the national income deriving from this source. As far as we can tell, real per capita incomes were no higher in 1950 than they had been in 1913.

Second, industrialization has been consistently supported by government policy since the 1950s. In general the government has sought industrial (and economic) growth through a largely liberal, market-oriented approach, within a framework of economic stability and conservative monetary policy. The government has taken concrete steps to promote industrialization, notably through import-substitution policies in the 1960s (protective tariffs and other incentives) and from around 1970 through policies promoting export-led growth (tax concessions, reduced import duties on capital equipment and so on).

Third, not only was Thailand an agricultural country in 1960, but its agricultural structure was remarkably undiversified. Over 80 per cent of cultivated land was used to produce rice, and despite some significant growth in cash crops in the 1950s Thailand was still very much a 'rice economy' characterized by small-scale peasant farming.

Fourth, from the 1950s industrial growth developed at a rapid pace, with a sharp acceleration after 1985.

Fifth, industrialization has been characterized by growth in nearly all sectors of the economy. Agriculture has shown positive growth (and the total agricultural population has continued to rise), while rapid increases have been seen in the construction, trade, transport, financial and service sectors. Thus, while the manufacturing industry has increased its importance in the economy, the overall pattern of growth has been 'balanced' by advance on a broad front.

Six, industrialization has been accompanied by economic growth and rising per capita incomes. At current prices, in 1960 Thailand had a per capita income of US$106; in 1992 it exceeded US$1800.

Seven, economic growth has been rather steady, certainly in comparison with many developing countries. There have been no years of negative growth since 1960.

Eight, the last decades have seen substantial increases in population growth, with enormous implications for the domestic and labour markets. The total population was 18.1 million in 1947, 26.7 million in 1960, 46.5 million in 1980 and around 57 million in 1992.

Ninth, industrialization and economic growth have been, and continue to be, heavily concentrated in Bangkok and the Bangkok region. Bangkok (population around one million in 1953 and eight million today) is overwhelmingly the major urban centre and often regarded as the world's leading 'primate city'. Concentration of growth and industrialization in Bangkok has produced marked regional disparities, and in 1985 around 80 per cent of total industrial output was concentrated in the Bangkok region. Regional differences in 1986 are shown in Table 1.1.

Tenth, a key to Thai economic development over the last thirty years has been diversification. Agriculture has diversified considerably, so that rice has steadily declined in importance while a variety of cash crops, such as maize, cassava, tapioca, sugar and many others, have become significant. Agriculture has 'industrialized', with the rapid development of agribusiness. Canned seafood and canned pineapples have become major export earners. Manufacturing, too, has diversified. In the 1960s the major industries were essentially resource-based food processing, beverages, tobacco. Later, industrialization was increasingly based on labour-intensive manufactures (often still resource-based), such as textiles and garments, agribusiness, petroleum products and so

Table 1.1 Regional differences in population and gross per capita regional product, 1986

	Population (m)	*Gross per capita regional product (baht)*
Bangkok region	5.5	59 885
Eastern	4.1	30 483
Central and West	7.7	19 407
South	6.6	15 542
North	10.5	13 112
North-east	18.6	8321

Source: NESDB.

on. Diversification has continued, with motor cycles, automobiles, electrical appliances, computer parts and a whole range of miscellaneous industries making their appearance and springing into prominence.

Eleventh, diversification of the industrial base has been accompanied by a growing 'outward-looking' economic structure. Thus in 1960 exports and imports combined were 34 per cent of GDP; in 1979 the figure was 48 per cent, and in 1991 72 per cent.

Twelfth, industrialization has been accompanied by the spectacular growth of manufactured exports. In 1960 manufactured goods were less than 2 per cent by value of total exports; in 1980 (after an annual growth rate of around 30 per cent in the 1970s) they were 32.3 per cent; in 1988, 66.1 per cent; and in 1992, 77.8 per cent. Many of these manufactured exports have been produced by foreign firms (or joint ventures) operating on Thai soil. Increasingly they have used more advanced technology and introduced new products.

Thirteenth, fundamental to industrial growth has been capital investment. Most capital investment has come from domestic sources, and key features have been a high domestic savings ratio (around 25 per cent of GDP in the 1980s) and the existence of large industrial and financial 'groups', which have channelled investment into a wide variety of industrial, agricultural, and service ventures. Foreign investment has also played a critical role, concentrated as it has been in the rapidly growing, most technologically advanced sectors, often geared to export markets.

Fourteenth, industrialization has been accompanied by relatively low rates of inflation. In the 1960s average annual price increases were 1.8 per cent, and from 1970–9 there were 9.5 per cent. After rates of 19.7 per cent and 12.7 per cent in 1980 and 1981 (following the second oil shock), official figures showed average price rises for 1982–91 of only 3.7 per cent per year.

We will now go on to put a little more statistical flesh on some of the above summary points. Table 1.2 shows the structure of GDP in 1980 and 1988.

Notable has been the overall growth of GDP and the relative fall in agriculture's share in relation to manufacturing. 'Garments and made-up textile goods' became the leading manufacture in this period, while textiles and garments together rose from 4.7 per cent of GDP in 1980 to 6.2 per cent in 1988. Perhaps the most striking feature in Table 1.2 is

Table 1.2 GDP by industrial origin, at current prices (billion baht)

Industrial origin	*1980* *Value*	*1980* *Share of GDP (%)*	*1988* *Value*	*1988* *Share of GDP (%)*
Agriculture	152.9	23.2	247.7	16.9
Mining and quarrying	22.1	3.4	44.3	3.0
Manufacturing	139.9	21.3	357.9	24.4
Food	17.8	2.7	39.3	2.7
Beverages	10.4	1.6	26.0	1.8
Tobacco and snuff	7.4	1.1	13.5	0.9
Textiles	17.0	2.6	41.4	2.8
Garments and made-up textile goods	14.1	2.1	50.4	3.4
Leather, leather products and footwear	2.8	0.4	16.6	1.1
Wood and wood products	5.8	0.9	9.4	0.6
Furniture and fixtures	2.9	0.4	6.9	0.5
Paper and paper products	2.1	0.3	5.6	0.4
Printing and allied industries	2.2	0.3	4.7	0.3
Chemicals and chemical products	4.8	0.7	11.8	0.8
Petroleum refineries and products	11.5	1.7	22.1	1.5
Rubber and plastic products	4.2	0.6	10.9	0.7
Nonmetallic mineral products	5.2	0.8	13.8	0.9
Basic metal industries	3.7	0.6	4.1	0.3
Metal products (excl. machinery)	3.9	0.6	8.7	0.6
Nonelectrical machinery	3.7	0.6	9.0	0.6
Electrical machinery and supplies	3.4	0.5	9.9	0.7
Transport equipment	11.4	1.7	27.0	1.8
Miscellaneous, n.e.s.	5.6	0.8	26.6	1.8
Construction	34.8	5.3	74.5	5.1
Electricity and water supply	6.3	1.0	37.5	2.6
Transportation and communication	37.9	5.7	106.8	7.3
Trade	110.2	16.7	232.2	15.8
Banking, insurance, and real estate	19.9	3.0	60.0	4.1
Ownership of dwellings	22.8	3.5	52.7	3.6
Public administration and defense	30.7	4.7	56.2	3.8
Other services	81.0	12.3	195.8	13.4
Gross domestic product	658.5	100.0	1465.7	100.0

Source: NESDB, *National Income Accounts of Thailand*, various issues.

the broad spectrum across which Thailand industrialized during the 1980s, with no one sector dominating. Over a longer period, the manufacturing sector's share of GDP, at current prices, rose from 10.5 per cent in 1960 to 15.4 per cent in 1969, 21.3 per cent in 1980 and 25.1 per cent in 1990. Agriculture, meanwhile, declined relatively, from 40.4 per cent of GDP in 1960 to only 14.8 per cent in 1990.

GDP grew substantially, averaging (in real terms) around 7.5 per cent per annum in the period 1960–79. Manufacturing grew at around twice this rate so that, despite positive agricultural growth (about 4.6 per cent per annum in these two decades), agriculture's share of GDP fell, as we have seen. Over the two decades 1960–79 real per capita GDP grew at a rate of 4.6 per cent per annum, so that it more than doubled over the period while total GDP quadrupled. GDP and per capita growth in the 1980s are shown in Table 1.3.

At the core of industrial growth was domestic demand, and here the large domestic market, rising real incomes, the growth of Bangkok, a consumer-oriented and fashion-conscious young population and other factors were all of significance. But for the most rapidly opening sectors, often financed by foreign investment, the export market has played a growing and crucial role. An attempt to measure the sources of industrial growth for the 1960s and 1970s showed clearly the switch from import-substitution to export-led growth (Table 1.4).

A significant element of Thailand's strong industrialization lay in the export drive, with manufactured goods taking a growing share of a rising total. Overall, Thai exports grew from only 14.3 billion baht in 1970, to 60.4 billion baht in 1976, to 150 billion baht in 1981 and 616 billion baht in 1990. Of this total, manufactured exports were a growing share (Table 1.5).

Table 1.3 GDP growth and per capita GDP, 1981–93 (current prices)

	GDP growth (%)	*Per capita GDP (000 baht)*
1981	6.3	15.7
1982	4.1	16.6
1983	7.3	18.2
1984	7.1	19.0
1985	3.5	19.3
1986	4.9	20.4
1987	9.5	23.0
1988	13.2	27.2
1989	12.2	33.2
1990	11.6	38.6
1991	8.1	43.3
1992	7.6	47.7
1993	7.5	52.9

Source: NESDB.

Table 1.4 Sources of industrial growth, 1966–78

	1966–72	*1972–5*	*1975–8*
Domestic demand	64.1	91.0	79.5
Import substitution	29.4	0.5	–7.7
Export-led growth	6.5	8.5	28.2
Total	100.0	100.0	100.0

Source: World Bank, 1986.

Table 1.5 Share of manufactures in total exports, 1960–92 (per cent)

1960	1965	1970	1975	1980	1988	1992
1.2	4.8	15.1	18.6	28.4	63.2	77.8

Source: Bank of Thailand.

Characteristic of industrialization, too, has been the changing composition of exports, which demonstrates clearly the features of growing diversification and sophistication of exports (Table 1.6).

Table 1.6 Leading exports, 1980, 1987 and 1991 (million baht)

1980		*1987*		*1991*	
Rice	19.5	Garments	35.9	Garments	86.7
Tapioca	14.8	Rice	22.7	Computers and parts	46.6
Rubber	12.4	Tapioca	20.7	Gems and jewellery	35.6
Tin	11.3	Rubber	20.4	Rice	30.5
Textiles	9.4	Gems and jewellery	19.7	Frozen prawns	26.6
Integrated circuits	6.1	Integrated circuits	15.2	Integrated circuits	25.8
		Canned seafood	13.7	Canned seafood	25.6

Source: Bank of Thailand.

In 1980 the top ten exports formed 67 per cent of total exports, in 1987 the figure was 56.7 per cent, and in 1991 it was 47.6 per cent, showing clearly the growing diversification of Thailand's export structure.

What explanations can we put forward to account for Thailand's rapid industrialization? Reading the recent economic history of Thailand, one cannot help but be struck by the very large number of favourable factors, some of them fortuitous, that aided Thailand's development. Among significant factors the high rate of investment must be emphasized. Throughout the 1980s the ratio of private investment to GDP stood at around 25–30 per cent, and there was a high inflow of foreign direct investment. The world economic environment has been generally favourable to Thailand, with growing markets for Thai products and the existence of appropriate technology for labour-intensive industries that could be transferred, often with foreign capital investment, from countries such as Japan, Taiwan and South Korea. Thailand has had stable economic policies (despite a number of political upheavals) that have favoured market-oriented industrialization, while many of Thailand's leading industries have been based on the country's own abundant natural resources (for example leather products, canned seafood, frozen prawns and so on). Tourist expenditure has provided a significant boost to particular sectors, and since the mid-1980s net receipts from tourism have been substantially in excess of receipts from the leading commodity export. The number of tourists rose from some two million in 1980 to over five million in 1990, encouraging the construction of hotels and other related developments and indirectly boosting a wide variety of tourist-related industries and services.

At a general level we can find in the literature two broad 'explanations' of Thai development. One places emphasis on internal factors, especially state economic policy. The second looks to external factors, such as American spending during the Vietnam War, the impact of Japanese economic growth and growth of the NICs in providing not only export markets and a source of foreign capital investment but also models of export-led growth, changes in world currency movements, and so on. These 'explanations' are not mutually exclusive, and both groups have been influential; but it will be suggested a little later that neither is convincing without a longer historical perspective that recognizes structural changes in the Thai economy prior to and in the early stages of significant industrialization.

The state-led argument focuses on two themes: (1) the direct impact of the state in promoting industrial projects and investing in infrastructure, and (2) the impact of economic policies that emphasized industrialization through import substitution throughout most of the 1960s and through export-led growth thereafter. State interest was signalled in 1954 by the Act on Promotion of Industries, and in the following years a number of state enterprises were founded, usually under tariff protection, geared to the home market and based on the simple processing of local foodstuffs and primary products. Reasons for this State involvement included 'export pessimism' in the wake of collapse of the Korean-War boom and falling prices of primary commodities, and a fear of over-dependence on a narrow range of primary-product exports (at that time rice, tin, rubber and teak exports still accounted for some 75 per cent of all Thai exports, as they had for the previous half century). Members of the government and army at the time, too, were heavily involved in the promotion of state industrial, commercial and financial concerns.

A change came at the end of the 1950s. Dissatisfaction with such state-led industrial growth, the results of which were unspectacular, coincided with a World Bank report, published in 1959 and based on a mission to Thailand in 1957–8, and with the overthrow of the Phibun regime in 1957 and the emergence of Sarit as the new, strong Thai leader. The World Bank report criticized state-led efforts and advocated the encouragement of private enterprise through government import-substitution policies. Such policies appealed to Sarit, who was himself involved in a number of private ventures, and many of the state projects were dismantled and sold off to private enterprise. The Sarit regime gave an assurance that the state would not create industries to compete with private enterprise, and in 1959 a Board of Investment was established to encourage private-sector investment in desired areas through a variety of incentives, including tariffs and tax concessions. At the same time Thailand's First National Development Plan (1961–6) was formulated, reflecting state policies, emphasizing import substitution and giving priority to a number of infrastructure projects, including road building.

Industrialization in the 1960s bore the hallmark of these government policies, with local manufacture of hitherto imported consumer products, destined for the domestic market and entailing the importation of capital and intermediate goods.

By the late 1960s sentiment had shifted towards export-led growth, and the Third Plan (1972–6) emphasized the promotion of export industries. Much of the policy was channelled through Board of Investment incentives, especially through tax and other concessions to domestic and foreign industries producing for export. The reasons for this shift in policy were several, but in general they incorporated the arguments rather common at the time in a number of developing countries, disappointment with the progress of industries established through import substitution (which were limited by the small home market, were often expensive to run and inefficient, involved the importation of expensive capital goods, and were confined to a narrow range of consumer goods with a low value added), coupled with the examples of Japan and the NICs, who were prospering through export-led growth.

The phase of export-led growth, begun towards the end of the 1960s and pursued increasingly in the 1970s, continued to dominate Thai industrialization throughout the 1980s. Economic policies have fostered industrialization in various ways, especially through generally orthodox and stable financial policies, low levels of taxation and the maintenance of a strong currency, which have all helped to promote both domestic savings and an inflow of foreign funds.

Certainly there can be little argument that state economic policies, through establishing an open, market-oriented economy based on trade and private enterprise, have produced a climate in which industrialization has taken root and flourished. We should, though, be cautious in attributing too much to the state. The experience of the 1960s showed clearly the limits to industrial growth that could be achieved through dependence on the home market and it should be stressed that the state itself was relatively passive in the economy: throughout the 1970s and 1980s budget expenditure as a proportion of GDP was rarely above 17 per cent (much of it involving military and administrative expenditure), while public investment as a proportion of gross domestic fixed capital formation averaged only a little over 6 per cent during the 1960s and 1970s.

The second perspective of Thai industrial development, therefore, emphasizes external, largely exogenous circumstances rather than internal policies. Thailand benefited considerably from American aid and military expenditure throughout much of the 1950s, 1960s and early 1970s. At the same time a generally growing and open world economy, and particularly rapid growth in Japan and other parts of Asia, encouraged Thai trade. Above all, from the 1970s Thailand began to benefit from the sequential spread of industrialization that had already stimulated industrial growth in the Asian NICs. Cheap-labour countries such as Thailand could export labour-intensive, low-technology goods that had become expensive to produce in the industrialized countries. Such goods could also be sold in domestic markets, of course. While some of these products, especially those based on natural resources, could be produced by Thai domestic manufacturers, others were produced by foreign firms (wholly owned or joint venture), usually involving technology transfer. Textile and garment production, and assembly plants for simple electrical goods or vehicles were typical of this phase of industrialization. Further cost rises in the advanced countries and the growing sophistication of enterprises in the new countries has continued the well-established sequential pattern, with industrialization becoming increasingly diversified and technologically advanced.

Thai industrialization certainly fits well with this international perspective of development. In particular, we should focus upon the inflow of foreign capital into Thai industries, with its attendant technology transfer, and also upon the significance in this process of cheap Thai labour and other costs. Tables 1.7 and 1.8, showing projects promoted by the Board of Investment, deserve some reflection.

While direct foreign investment has never been a dominant part of total domestic investment, as mentioned already it has been concentrated in the most dynamic, export-oriented sectors. The tables show that Japan and the United States have played the largest role in this foreign capital inflow, while in recent years Japan and increasingly Taiwan and Hong Kong have been to the fore. Industry has attracted the greatest, and increasing, proportion of investment, with electrical appliances taking first place in 1988, and in this area the leading countries have been Japan, Taiwan, Hong Kong and South Korea.

The jump in foreign investment has been dramatic. In the years 1980–7 net foreign direct investment averaged 6.0 billion baht, with a low of 3.8 billion baht in 1980 and a high of 9.6 billion baht in 1984. In 1988 the figure was 27.6 billion baht and in 1989 39.4 billion baht, with over half going into the industrial sector. Why did foreign capital inflows increase so rapidly in the late 1980s? The major factor was an external one: the sharp revaluation of the Japanese yen in 1986 (along with major revaluations of the Taiwanese and other NIC currencies). For Japan this revaluation, coupled as it was to soaring land prices and labour costs, encouraged firms to locate certain operations abroad. Thailand was well placed to benefit from this investment, with its long

Table 1.7 Registered capital of firms granted Board of Investment promotion certificates (million baht)

Nationality	Accumulated total: 1960–87					Annual total: 1988				
	100%	Joint	Total			100%	Joint	Total		
	owned	venture	Amount	Share	Foreign	owned	venture	Amount	Share	Foreign
Thai	19 514	15 109	34 623	68.5	–	8573	6056	14 629	49.5	–
Foreign	4322	11 583	15 905	31.5	–	4724	10 226	14 950	50.5	–
of which:										
Japan	2971	3340	6311	12.5	39.7	3467	5685	9152	30.9	61.2
Taiwan	32	1290	1322	2.6	8.3	635	1502	2137	7.2	14.3
United States	439	1625	2064	4.1	13.0	14	900	914	3.1	6.1
Hong Kong	40	595	635	1.3	4.0	253	569	822	2.8	5.5
United Kingdom	106	842	948	1.9	6.0	40	286	326	1.1	2.2
Singapore	111	339	450	0.9	2.8	40	462	502	1.7	3.4
Australia	200	152	352	0.7	2.2	0	24	24	0.1	0.2
Switzerland	16	273	289	0.6	1.8	81	4	95	0.3	0.6
Netherlands	185	136	321	0.6	2.0	16	31	47	0.2	0.3
Malaysia	0	233	233	0.5	1.5	0	46	46	0.2	0.3
Panama	25	120	145	0.3	0.9	0	204	204	0.7	1.4
West Germany	20	186	206	0.4	1.3	0	36	36	0.1	0.2
India	8	146	154	0.3	1.0	0	73	73	0.2	0.5
France	0	130	130	0.3	0.8	3	40	43	0.1	0.3
Philippines	0	155	155	0.3	1.0	0	2	2	0.0	0.0
Denmark	0	57	57	0.1	0.4	0	17	17	0.1	0.1
Portugal	0	16	16	0.0	0.1	0	10	10	0.0	0.1
Israel	0	18	18	0.0	0.1	0	0	0	0.0	0.0
Others	169	1930	2099	4.2	13.2	175	325	500	1.7	3.3
Total	23 836	26 692	50 528			13 297	16 282	29 579		

Source: Board of Investment.

Table 1.8 Net foreign direct investment inflows by country and sector, 1970–88 (billion baht)

	1970–87		*1988*	
	Value	*Share (%)*	*Value*	*Share (%)*
By country				
Japan	21.16	132.80	14.59	52.80
Taiwan ROC	1.12	1.70	3.16	11.40
USA	19.19	29.80	3.13	11.30
Hong Kong	4.35	6.70	3.05	11.00
Singapore	2.53	3.90	1.49	5.40
United Kingdom	3.45	5.40	0.88	3.20
West Germany	2.07	3.20	0.62	2.20
Switzerland	1.87	2.90	0.56	2.00
Netherlands	2.45	3.80	0.29	1.00
France	0.79	1.20	0.28	1.00
Malaysia	0.47	0.70	0.04	0.20
Australia	0.57	0.90	0.04	0.20
Italy	0.94	1.50	0.03	0.10
Saudi Arabia	0.24	0.40	0.01	0.00
Others	3.27	5.10	–0.55	–2.00
Total	64.45	100.00	27.63	100.00
By sector				
Financial institutions	–1.39	–2.20	2.18	7.90
Trade and services	20.06	31.10	6.43	23.30
Construction	10.66	16.50	1.94	7.00
Mining and quarrying	10.16	15.80	0.47	1.70
Agriculture	0.93	1.40	0.31	1.10
Industry	24.04	37.30	16.29	59.00
Food	1.95	3.00	1.23	4.50
Textiles	4.01	6.20	1.09	3.90
Metal and non-metallic	1.87	2.90	1.95	7.10
Electric appliances	6.36	9.90	6.31	22.80
Machinery and transport equipment	1.50	2.30	0.73	2.60
Chemicals	3.62	5.60	1.09	3.90
Petroleum products	2.26	3.50	0.83	3.00
Construction materials	0.03	0.10	0.03	0.10
Others	2.43	3.80	3.04	11.00
Total	64.45	100.00	27.63	100.00

Source: Bank of Thailand.

record of steady growth, its long history as recipient of Japanese and other Asian investment, and its large, inexpensive and relatively hard-working and productive labour force.

As a result of the new currency alignments, the Thai baht fell substantially against the Japanese yen – by nearly 100 per cent in the years 1986–9. This raises a more general consideration. Thailand's exports enjoyed undoubted stimulus from relative undervaluation following the 17.3 per cent devaluation of the baht against the US dollar in 1984. Thereafter the baht more or less maintained parity with the dollar, but the dollar itself declined substantially against the yen and major European currencies. Thus over the period 1985–92 the Thai baht was devalued by roughly 100 per cent, not only against the yen but against the Swiss franc and German mark, and by 50 per cent against the British pound. Interestingly, Thai exports over the period 1980–92 expanded more rapidly to the EU (now the major market) and the United States than to Japan; while imports showed the opposite trend. While the trend with Japan and the United States may seem unexpected in terms of exchange-rate movements, the reasons appear to lie in the consequences of Japanese foreign investment. On the one hand such investment has encouraged the importation of Japanese capital goods, parts for assembly and so on. On the other hand the Thai products so produced are often geared to the US export market, supplying products hitherto bought from Japan and the Asian NICs.

Thailand's abundant labour force has been an attraction to foreign investors, and has formed the basis of export-led growth. While skilled labour has been in short supply, cheap unskilled labour has been readily available to industrialists. A wage survey in Bangkok in 1987 (where wages were well in excess, perhaps by 20 per cent or so, of other regions) produced the data shown in Table 1.9. Labour was receiving the equivalent of less than US$100 a month, and real wages for unskilled labour showed little increase over the 1980s as a whole.

It is easy and a little beguiling to put Thailand's industrialization down to a combination of sensible government policies and favourable external circumstances. But a number of nagging questions remain. How, after years of apparent stagnation before 1950, was Thailand able to adapt so successfully to industrial change? Why had significant industrial growth not occurred earlier? What were the domestic sources of entrepreneurship and capital?

In my view we cannot understand Thailand's response to favourable world economic conditions after 1960 without taking into account changes in the Thai economy over a much longer period. Four develop-

Table 1.9 Labour costs in Bangkok, 1987 (baht per month)

	Unskilled workers	*Semi-skilled workers*	*Management*	*Weighted average*
Manufacturing	2282	4834	13 157	4261
Food and beverages	2467	4621	12 280	4352
Textiles and garments	2045	4468	10 614	2879
Furniture and wood products	1970	5577	10 088	4298
Pulp, paper and printing	2621	4950	14 708	6690
Chemicals, petroleum, rubber and plastic	2325	4128	10 088	3711
Non-metallic products	2370	4594	13 199	4724
Iron and basic metals	2337	4969	10 399	4229
Machinery	2298	4566	18 969	4959
Other manufacturing	2027	4251	9601	2764
Construction	2438	4961	10 436	5065
Wholesale trade	2292	4490	15 709	3654
Retail trade	2390	4850	16 078	5562
Hotels and restaurants	2269	5126	9643	5137
Transportation, storage and communications	2426	4561	10 478	5283
Utilities	2434	4347	15 311	3500
Financial institutions	2281	4819	10 162	2971
Other services	2286	4927	13 331	4845
Average (weighted by number of employees)	2360	4867	11 960	4564

Source: Department of Labour.

ments may be briefly noted. First, a combination of the 1932 revolution (which overthrew the absolute monarchy) and the subsequent evolution of the political system produced a state and bureaucratic apparatus that could provide a focus for national economic development. Second, the large numbers of Chinese businessmen and traders provided both small-scale enterprise and the large industrial-financial groups upon which much of later industrialization could be built. Hewison and Suehiro have shown how, in the aftermath of the Second World War, a few large Chinese-dominated concerns, often integrating banking, industrial and agricultural business, joined forces with elements of the bureaucracy and military to consolidate their position in the Thai economy. The Communist victory in China in 1949 was of significance: Chinese remittances from Thailand to China dropped sharply and long-term investment by Thai-Chinese in Thailand was encouraged as links with the former homeland were severed. These large business groupings provided a significant part of domestic corporate investment in modern industry, and have been a principal channel through which joint ventures with overseas firms have developed in Thailand.

A third factor is that despite a long period of apparent stagnation (estimates suggest that per capita GDP in 1950 was no higher than in 1913), Thailand had long been an open, trading economy, having been integrated into the world economy since the second half of the nineteenth century. From the days of King Chulalongkorn before the First World War, conservative monetary and budgetary policies and a reluctance to become burdened with heavy foreign debts were hallmarks of Thai economic policy. Moreover, one should not underestimate the economic infrastructure inherited by Sarit and his followers after 1957: a well-established banking structure (with several domestic banks opened in the 1940s), a developing road system, a nationwide rail network and an extensive canal and river transport system, a new deepwater port in Bangkok (opened in 1954), the extensive resources of Chinese entrepreneurship through immigration, and so on.

Finally, we should note the evolution of cheap labour. Prior to around 1950 Thailand might be characterized as a sparsely populated country with abundant land. The total Thai population was only around 11 million in 1929, 17 million in 1947 and 26 million in 1960. By the 1980s the population had grown to over 50 million. A consequence of sparse population, the existence of a land frontier, and relatively high natural soil fertility was that the Thai peasant had long been able to maintain a relatively high standard of living. Many accounts mention the absence of extreme poverty and starvation in rural Thailand and the comparatively low work intensity of agricultural life. Zimmerman in 1932 spoke of the Thai peasant's 'high average income compared with the rest of Asia'. He also linked underpopulation with low pressure on the peasant to adapt and improve or to work harder, and spoke of 'the harmful effect of under-population on the people. There is nothing like necessity to induce economy and economic improvement. The Siamese peasant lives too easily. Increasing population will make him wish to improve his methods' (Zimmerman, 1931, p. 318). Hubert Freyn made much the same point in 1961: 'What man requires as a rule to change his ingrained customs and ideas is pressure, internal or external. In Thailand this pressure has so far been absent, and only the capital has begun to show the tell-tale signs of the "struggle of existence", whose mental and ethical effects are anything but unequivocally good. It is this struggle which forces men's attention from the hereafter to the here, away from the old religious and toward the worship of Science, Technology and Economics. And what this new Trinity requires of its devotees above all is *dissatisfaction* with man's existence here and now' (Freyn, 1961, p. 53).

Prior to the 1950s, abundant land, high living standards and very inadequate internal communications combined to maintain Thailand as an undiversified rural economy. The opportunity cost to the Thai peasant of an urban occupation was a high one. However, the rapid rise in population led to the 'closing' of the land frontier and pressure on rural incomes. Such pressure, which became increasingly evident in the 1960s and 1970s, manifested itself in various ways: the fragmentation of farms and the growing incidence of tenancy, landlessness and indebtedness in some regions; migration from poorer areas; declining rice output per person; and a growing intensity of labour effort. To picture Thailand as undergoing a 'rural crisis' in these years, as some have done, would be a considerable exaggeration, but it appears that with growing commercialization there were widening differences among peasant families. In 1958, data collected for a United-Nations-sponsored survey showed that in the populous north-eastern provinces of Roi Et, Si Sa Ket and Nakhon Panom the average output of rice was well below that necessary to sustain an acceptable level of subsistence. According to Turton, the average size of farms in the north declined from 16.1 rai in 1963 to 8.8 rai a decade later, while 'in all important food-producing areas, whether commercialized or not, decreases in the size of the average holding were registered between 1950 and 1963' (Turton, 1978, p. 111).

To the varied signs of rural pressure arising directly or indirectly from population growth we should add other factors promoting the growth of 'cheap labour' in the period after 1950. First, there was a growing disparity in income levels between rural and industrial occupations, and especially between Bangkok and provincial regions. Such differentials must have been significant in encouraging migration, which in turn kept down urban wages. The gap, moreover, grew over time. In 1975 the average income in Bangkok was double that of the nation as a whole; in 1986 the figure had increased two-and-a-half-fold. In the former year average incomes in the north-east were 37 per cent of those in Bangkok, in the latter year they were 23 per cent.

Pressure on rural incomes from the consequences of growing population and the closing of the rice frontier led to a widening urban-rural differential. The cessation of large-scale Chinese immigration after 1949 had similar consequences, sharply increasing the demand for Thai unskilled labour (the Thai government also took steps to reserve certain occupations for ethnic Thais). Other factors causing widening income differentials were the operation of the rice premium after 1955 and the high levels of tariff protection to support the import-substitution aims of the first two Development Plans after 1960. Both favoured the urban-industrial sector at the expense of rice producers. The rice premium, by keeping down domestic rice prices and hence urban wage levels, both directly promoted the manufacturing sector and also encouraged the movement of labour from the countryside (the rice premium also fostered agricultural diversification and the expansion of certain 'industrial crops').

In this way, the years around the 1950s marked a watershed in Thai economic history. Prior to this a sparse population with a relatively high rural income was an effective stumbling-block to cheap-labour industrialization. Thereafter the balance changed. The rapidly increasing population and pressure on rural incomes produced circumstances in which Thailand could develop on the basis of labour-intensive, urban-based industrial development.

Finally, and briefly, we should mention some of the adverse effects of industrialization and note some of the factors that may inhibit growth in the future.

The environmental damage brought by industrialization has been well documented: the shrinking forest area (53 per cent of the total area in 1961, now less than 20 per cent), the damaging effects of deforestation and depletion of other natural resources, the building of dams, salination of the soil and so on. All such features have had a savage impact on the lives of those dependent on forests, and have been responsible for floods and other natural disasters. In Bangkok, congestion and pollution have reached levels intolerable even to the easy-going Thais. Some of the nastier consequences of tourism, especially the introduction of AIDS, may have far-reaching consequences (if it is true, as official reports suggest, that some 6–7 million Thais will have contracted AIDS by the end of the 1990s, this is a matter no economic forecast can ignore). To this we should add other adverse social consequences of industrialization, such as the growing number of slum dwellers and the increasing income gap between regions and between rich and poor.

Beyond this, there must be real questions as to whether Thailand can indeed make the transition to tiger status in the foreseeable future. We might note that Thailand still has some way to go to catch up with even the poorest of the tigers as the figures in Table 1.10 show.

Bottlenecks in infrastructure may choke continued expansion, but most serious will probably be the quality of the labour force: a smaller proportion of Thai children go on to secondary school than is the case in Indonesia and Malaysia, and there is already a chronic shortage of skilled labour. This may make the diversification of production up the technological ladder more difficult.

Lastly, we should note that as Thailand has become more dependent on the ebbs and flows of the world economy, so changes to the world economy will influence the Thai economy to an increasing extent. With the world struggling with recession, the future path of the Japanese economy in doubt, and world agreement on measures to liberalize trade still awaited, it would be unwise to predict the future of Thailand's industrialization with too much confidence.

Table 1.10 Levels of per capita GNP, 1991 (US$)

	Per capita GNP
Japan	27 065
Hong Kong	13 800
Singapore	13 600
Taiwan	8685
South Korea	6245
Thailand	1605

Source: World Bank, *World Development Report 1993*.

2 Contributions of Agriculture to Industrialization

Medhi Krongkaew

2.1 INTRODUCTION

After experiencing a GDP growth rate of more than 10 per cent per year, on average, between 1987 and 1991, Thailand is poised to become the fifth member of the so-called newly industrializing countries (NICs) or newly industrializing economies (NIEs) of Asia presently comprising Korea, Taiwan, Hong Kong, and Singapore. Actually Thailand already has several of the economic characteristics required of an NIC, such as the share of manufacturing value added exceeding that of agriculture, and manufactured exports exceeding agricultural exports, but despite this Thailand is still overwhelmingly agricultural in character.

As will be shown in detail later in this chapter, close to two thirds of the population are still engaged in agriculture and Thailand is still the only regular net food-exporting country in Asia. While the industrialization of Thailand is now widely acknowledged, not much attention is being given to the manner and the extent to which agriculture has contributed to industrialization. This relative neglect of the Thai agricultural sector is unwarranted as it still forms an important part of Thai economic development.[1]

The main purpose of this chapter is to trace the development of Thai agriculture over the last three decades, and to discuss its various contributions to economic development in general and industrial development in particular. Section 2.2 describes the patterns of growth and development of Thai agriculture, while Section 2.3 discusses the contributions of agriculture to the industrial sector. Finally, Section 2.4 summarizes the chapter and assesses the role of agriculture in the 1990s and beyond, when Thailand is expected to become the 'fifth tiger' of Asia.

2.2 PATTERNS OF AGRICULTURAL DEVELOPMENT AND TRANSFORMATION

When the first National Development Plan was launched in 1961 Thailand was a typical agricultural economy. Over 80 per cent of the population were engaged in agricultural activities, with rice as a major crop for both domestic consumption and export. Other major crops and primary products for export included rubber, maize, kenaf, teak and tin. The rate of growth of the economy was comfortable, albeit low, at about 2–3 per cent a year. Under the threat of population explosion (the rate of growth of the population was over 3 per cent a year) the government decided to move the economy away from low-level equilibrium and push it into systematic development. The basic development philosophy behind the 1961–6 National Economic Development Plan was that the government would provide the necessary infrastructure for the economy and reorganize government agencies to facilitate orderly economic transformation, but otherwise the private sector would be encouraged to engage in productive investment and transactions.[2]

The transformation from an agricultural to an industrial economy is shown in Table 2.1. From this table it may be seen that, overall, the rate of growth of GDP in Thailand has been quite satisfactory. During the 1960s the economy grew by about 7.9 per cent a year, reducing to 6.9 per cent during the 1970s. Growth slowed somewhat in the early 1980s due to difficulties associated with the energy crisis. But after a few years of structural adjustment and cautious economic management the economy returned to high growth in the latter half of the 1980s. The average growth rate of GDP during the 1980s was 7.8 per cent per annum, but between 1986 and 1990 the economy grew at 11.2 per cent per annum. On a per-capita basis, GNP grew from 1988 baht in 1960 to 36 032 baht in 1990, or an increase of about 10.1 per cent a year, which was higher than the average growth rate of GDP due to the slowdown in population growth during the past three decades.

It is also obvious from Table 2.1 that the relative contribution of agriculture to Thailand's GDP started to decline from the beginning of the period of the First Plan. In 1960 the share of the agricultural sector in GDP stood at 39.8 per cent compared with the 18.2 per cent and 42.0 per cent, respectively, of the industrial and service sectors. Agriculture's share reduced to 28.3 per cent in 1970, 25.4 per cent in 1980 and finally to 12.4 per cent in 1990.[3] The rate of growth of the agricultural sector as a whole was estimated at 5.5 per cent a year on average in the 1960s,

Table 2.1 Sectoral distribution of production and employment, 1960–90 (per cent)

	1960	*1970*	*1980*	*1986*	*1987*	*1988*	*1989*	*1990*
GDP (% share):								
Agriculture	39.8	28.3	25.4	16.3	16.4	16.6	15.0	12.4
Industry	18.2	25.3	28.4	34.4	34.8	35.9	37.5	39.2
(manufacturing)	(12.5)	(16.0)	(19.6)	(23.6)	(23.9)	(24.8)	(25.5)	(26.1)
Services	42.0	46.4	46.4	49.3	48.8	47.5	47.5	48.4
Total	100.0	100.0	100.0	100.0	100.0	100.0	100.0	100.0
GDP (% growth):								
Agriculture	5.5	4.3	4.7	0.3	−0.2	10.2	6.6	1.8
Industry	10.9	9.3	4.4	7.9	12.8	17.4	8.4	−4.4
(manufacturing)	(10.5)	(10.1)	(4.9)	(10.8)	(13.3)	(16.8)	(14.9)	(13.7)
Services	8.4	7.3	6.4	10.0	12.8	17.4	11.1	10.0
GDP	7.9	6.9	5.4	4.9	9.5	13.2	12.0	10.0
Employment (% share):								
Agriculture	82.4	79.3	72.5	63.7	59.8	60.4	61.9	66.5
Industry	4.2	5.8	7.7	12.5	14.3	13.7	13.3	11.2
(manufacturing)	(3.4)	(4.1)	(5.6)	(9.1)	(10.5)	(10.3)	(9.7)	(8.7)
Services	13.4	14.9	19.8	23.8	25.9	25.9	24.8	22.3
Total	100.0	100.0	100.0	100.0	100.0	100.0	100.0	100.0

Notes: The growth rates in 1960, 1970, and 1980 columns are average annual growth rates for the 1960s, 1970s and 1980s, respectively. Percentages may not add to 100 because of rounding errors. Employment shares for 1986–9 were obtained from the Labour Force Surveys, but for 1990 they were obtained from the 1990 Population Census. These two sources were not entirely compatible, although the 1990 employment shares can be compared with those in the 1960, 1970 and 1980 columns which were also obtained from population censuses.
Sources: Medhi, 1992a, p. 25; 1992b, p. 27.

falling to 4.3 per cent a year during the 1970s. Agricultural growth was higher at 4.7 per cent in 1980, but from 1986–90 growth fluctuated more widely. Agriculture had negative growth of −0.2 per cent in 1987; but during 1988 it surged to 10.2 per cent but fell again to −1.8 per cent in 1990. As the agricultural sector has become smaller in relation to other sectors in the economy and more exposed to international conditions, its growth pattern has become prone to wide swings.

In the meantime the industrial sector, which contains the manufacturing, mining, electricity and power, and construction subsectors, increased its GDP share from 18.2 per cent in 1960 to 25.3 per cent in

1970, 28.4 per cent in 1980 and 39.2 per cent in 1990. The growth rate of 4.4 per cent in 1980 was untypical of this sector, and was mainly the result of the second oil shock during 1979–80. As can be seen in Table 2.1, in the latter half of the 1980s the average rate of growth of the industrial sector was continuously high, reaching 17.4 per cent in 1988. Of course the principal growth engine has been the manufacturing subsector, whose performance has been the main reason behind the high growth of the industrial sector. The service sector is also expanding well. As the economy has become more industrialized the service sector – which provides general basic support such as banking, finance and insurance, transportation and trade – has grown in step with it. In fact the fastest growing subsectors in the Thai economy in the last three decades have been banking and insurance.

Although Table 2.1 has shown conclusively the declining economic importance of agriculture as measured by its share of GDP, it does not show the importance of agriculture as a major source of employment and livelihood of the total population. As shown in Table 2.1, 82.4 per cent of the population was engaged in agriculture in 1960. Although this percentage reduced over the following three decades of rapid economic development, a very large proportion of the total population still works in the agricultural sector. For example the proportion of agricultural to overall employment was 79.3 per cent in 1970, 72.5 per cent in 1980 and 66.5 per cent in 1990.[4] In other words, two out of three people in Thailand were still engaged in agricultural employment in 1990, which is one of the highest proportions found among countries at a comparable level of development.

Looking at agricultural development, at the beginning of the 1960s the Thai agricultural sector consisted of four main subsectors, namely crops, livestock, fisheries and forestry. As shown in Table 2.2, crops accounted for about 74 per cent of agricultural GDP, livestock 14 per cent, fisheries 3 per cent and forestry 9 per cent. This subsectoral composition has remained quite stable for the last 30 years. During the 1970s the crop subsector reduced its share to 70 per cent while fisheries increased its share four fold, from 3 per cent to 12 per cent. In the following two decades these relative positions changed very little: crop GDP share remained at around 71–73 per cent, livestock GDP share at around 13–15 per cent and fisheries GDP share at around 8–11 per cent. The only major downward change was in the forestry subsector in the last half of the 1980s as a result of government restrictions on forestry concessions and logging to preserve the remaining forest areas. In terms of growth rates, the crop subsector grew at about 4.7 per cent

Table 2.2 Subsector share in agricultural GDP and its annual growth rates, 1960–90 (per cent)

	Share in agricultural GDP						*Annual growth rate*		
	1960	*1970*	*1975*	*1980*	*1985*	*1990*	*1960–70*	*1970–80*	*1980–90*
Crops	74	70	70	73	71	72	4.7	4.7	3.5
Livestock	14	11	14	13	14	15	3.5	6.6	7.6
Fisheries	3	12	10	9	8	11	20.7	4.6	3.3
Forestry	9	7	6	5	7	2	4.1	1.6	−4.1
Total	100	100	100	100	100	100	5.5	4.7	4.1

Sources: World Bank, 1982; ADB, 1991; Bank of Thailand, 1992.

per year on average during the 1960s and 1970s, and 3.5 per cent during the 1980s. A drastic reduction was also found in the fisheries subsector, which had grown very rapidly during the 1960s. The growth rate of this subsector in the 1980s was 3.3 per cent compared with 20.7 per cent in the 1960s. Over-fishing was partly to blame for this reduction. The livestock subsector, though, has shown slow but significant growth, from 3.5 per cent per annum during the 1960s to 6.6 per cent in the 1970s and 7.6 per cent in the 1980s.

As the crop subsector is still by far the most important component of the agricultural sector, most attention will be given to an analysis of its development. Tables 2.3 to 2.5 summarize the main features of the subsector's growth and development: Table 2.3 presents annual growth rates in area, yield and production of major field crops during the last three decades; Table 2.4 shows the planted area and holding expansion of the crops listed in Table 2.3, and Table 2.5 sums up the relative position of each major crop in terms of its GDP contribution after 30 years of development.

The agricultural development of Thailand from before the beginning of the First Plan to before the end of the Sixth Plan can be divided into four phases. The first phase, which covers the period 1960–70, could be considered one of the most active phases of agricultural development overall as the country was involved in extensive expansion of crop production. The World Bank (1982) called this period the 'capacity acquisition' phase of crop production, and the extended acreage associated with crop expansion involved two categories of crops in addition to rice, the traditional food crop of Thailand. The first category – called 'frontier' or 'extensive' crops as cultivation of them

Table 2.3 Annual rates of growth: area, yield and production of major field crops, 1959–90 (per cent).

	1959–70			*1972–80*			*1980–90*		
	Area planted	*Yield*	*Prod.*	*Area planted*	*Yield*	*Prod.*	*Area planted*	*Yield*	*Prod.*
Paddy	2.3	0.8	3.1	3.1	0.1	3.2	0.5	0.5	1.0
'Frontier' crops									
Rubber	n.a.	n.a.	5.0	n.a.	n.a.	5.6	1.4	7.7	9.1
Maize	13.3	−0.3	12.9	4.2	1.9	6.2	1.7	1.0	2.7
Sorghum	n.a.	n.a.	n.a.	13.7	−6.7	7.0	−4.3	2.0	−2.3
Kenaf	16.0	0.7	16.8	−10.6	1.9	−9.8	−4.0	0.8	−3.2
Cassava	8.1	−1.6	6.4	11.9	−5.3	5.8	2.5	−0.3	2.3
Sugar cane	1.0	0.5	1.5	11.9	−5.3	5.8	3.3	2.1	5.4
'Intensive' crops									
Tobacco	3.4	5.6	9.1	n.a.	n.a.	3.5	−7.8	1.2	−6.5
Cotton	8.4	2.0	10.6	17.1	4.2	22.3	−10.2	1.8	−8.4
Groundnuts	3.3	0.6	3.9	−2.9	−0.9	−3.8	0.6	1.2	1.8
Soybeans	12.7	−2.4	10.0	3.3	−0.2	2.9	20.6	8.2	28.8
Mungbeans	18.6	−2.2	15.9	11.7	−6.4	4.6	0.0	1.6	1.7
'New' crops									
Coffee	–	–	–	–	–	–	12.4	6.1	18.5
Garlic	–	–	–	–	–	–	−1.3	1.0	−0.2
Palm oil	–	–	–	–	–	–	14.8	15.5	30.3
Pineapple	–	–	–	–	–	–	0.0	1.8	1.8

Sources: World Bank, 1985; Office of Agricultural Economics, *Agricultural Statistics*, various issues.

has extended from existing farm holdings into forest reserves or other public lands – includes maize, rubber, kenaf, cassava, upland rice, sugar cane and sorghum. The second category – 'intensive' or 'rotation' crops, grown mainly within the farm holding as supplementary crops – includes tobacco, mung beans, groundnuts, cotton and soybeans.

During this capacity – acquisition phase production of the two groups of crops expanded vigorously. Table 2.3 shows that the average growth rate of planted areas of maize, kenaf, soybeans and mung beans ranged between 12.7 per cent and 18.6 per cent. Cassava was not a widely expanding crop in the 1960s but its growth rate in terms of area planted was a respectable 8.1 per cent. Sugar cane also was not a major upland crop in this first phase, but it was to become one of the fastest-growing upland products in the next decade. As shown in Table 2.4, during this first phase, farm holdings were expanding at a rate of 4.1 per cent per annum compared with the 3.6 per cent per annum expansion of planted areas. This difference means that the expansion of

Table 2.4 Planted areas and holding expansion-average increments, 1960–90 (million rai)*

	1960	*1960–70*		*1970–75*		*1975–80*		*1980–90*		*1990*
	Level	*Area increase*	*Annual growth (%)*	*Area increase*	*Annual growth (%)*	*Area increase*	*Annual growth (%)*	*Area increase*	*Annual growth (%)*	*Level*
Planted area:										
Including rice	46.3	19.5	3.6	15.9	4.4	14.4	4.1	10.6	1.1	106.7
of which rice	37.8	9.3	2.2	5.9	2.4	7.5	3.4	1.8	0.3	62.3
Excluding rice	8.5	10.2	8.2	10.0	9.0	6.6	5.3	8.8	2.3	44.1
of which:										
Frontier crops	7.0	8.2	8.1	10.3	10.9	4.7	4.3	7.6	2.3	37.8
Intensive crops	1.5	2.0	8.8	–0.3	–1.8	1.9	12.4	1.2	2.0	6.3
Farm holding area:	63.1	31.6	4.1	17.2	3.4	6.8	1.2	29.1	2.6	147.8
of which										
Paddy land	38.9	20.0	4.2	11.3	3.6	3.0	1.1	1.0	0.2	74.2
Other crop land[1]	13.0	10.3	6.0	6.9	5.3	6.1	4.3	19.5	4.9	55.5
Idle land and other[2]	11.2	1.3	1.1	–1.4	–2.4	–2.4	–7.0	9.4	8.9	18.1

Notes:
* The relevant year represents three-year average centred on the specified year (e.g. 1960 = 1959–61).
1. Under field crops and tree crops
2. Idle land, waste land, woodland and houselot.
Source: World Bank, 1982, p. 17.

farm holdings was faster than the growth of planted areas, and there existed a considerable excess capacity by 1970, when cropping intensity was estimated at about 69 per cent. Although the terms of trade worked against agriculture during this period, the rapid growth of production enabled the real value of agricultural production to increase at an annual rate of 4.8 per cent, which helped the welfare of farmers in rainfed areas, particularly in the central and lower north regions.

One major reason for the rapid expansion of maize and kenaf production was a large overseas demand for these products, especially from Japan and Taiwan. Towards the latter part of the 1960s large tracts of dense forest land in the lower north and northeastern part of the central plain were gradually cleared and turned into huge maize-producing areas. At the end of the first phase three more major products had joined the list of diversified commodities in Thai agriculture, namely cassava, sugar cane and sorghum. Thus began the second phase of agricultural development, which spanned the first half of the 1970s. This period is often characterized as the 'golden era' of Thai agriculture because of the significant export-price increases brought about by the global commodity boom from 1973–75. As can be seen in Table 2.3, the average annual growth of area planted for cassava and sugar cane from 1972–80 was 11.9 per cent, and for sorghum it was an even higher 13.7 per cent. Table 2.4 shows that the planted areas for the combined frontier crops increased by 10.3 million rai from 1970–75, or a rate of growth of about 10.9 per cent per annum. This was the highest growth rate of planted area of any of the crops under study.

In the third phase (1975–80) expansion of the area planted slowed due to a reduction in the expansion of the frontier crops. This was attributable to the emergence of supply constraints arising from the exhaustion of accessible land. As the possibility of increasing production by expanding total acreage became limited, farmers began to adopt more intensive production techniques on their existing holdings. Cropping intensity, defined as the ratio of total planted area under major crops to total farm holding area, was 69 per cent in the first phase, rising to 72 per cent in the second phase and 81 per cent in the third phase.[5] There was also an increase in upland crops that were more adaptive to marginal land, especially cassava. During this third period falling yields became quite evident, probably due to the effects of soil erosion and deforestation. Furthermore, the generally poorer performance in 1975–80 was exacerbated by a marginal decline in the agricultural terms of trade.

The period 1980–90 could be characterized by retrenchment, adjustment, and change in agricultural production. The fact that all suitable land was being utilized let to increased efforts to improve the existing situation. Agricultural growth at the beginning of the 1980s was dismal owing to persistently poor weather conditions, but production levels improved towards the middle of the decade so that on the whole the declining trend in the agricultural growth rate was arrested. During the 1980s many of the traditional upland crops, such as sorghum, kenaf and to a lesser extent maize, lost their major-upland-crop status, while cassava and sugar cane maintained their positions, with rates of growth of around 2.5 per cent to 3.3 per cent. Of increasing importance were such relatively new crops (as measured by volume of production) as soybeans, coffee and palm oil.[6] For example the growth rate of planted area for soybeans was 20.6 per cent per annum from 1980–90. For coffee it was 12.4 per cent, and for palm oil 14.8 per cent. Land was also turned over to non-crop-production activities such shrimp farming and livestock grazing. Fruit and vegetables joined the ranks of increasingly important agricultural products, both for domestic consumption and for export. These factors together resulted in the agricultural sector as a whole having a higher average annual growth rate than that achieved by the crop subsector (4.1 per cent compared with 3.5 per cent).

Rice was and still is an important crop for domestic consumption, although its current export significance has been challenged by many other crops such as rubber, cassava and sugar for the simple reason that these upland crops fetch a better price on overseas markets. In terms of area planted, rice's growth rate declined from 2.3 per cent per annum in the 1960s to 0.5 per cent during the 1980s after a slight increase during the 1970s (in response to the commodity-price boom in the mid-1970s, as mentioned earlier). As for rubber, its production growth rate increased continuously throughout the three decades, but the rate was exceptional during the 1980s due to an increased world demand for rubber. The latest statistical data on the breakdown of crop GDP over almost three decades of agricultural development (see Table 2.5) has shown that the relative share of rice to crop GDP was 42 per cent in 1989 compared with 53 per cent in 1960.

At least two important implications have arisen from the pattern of agricultural growth and development in the last 30 years in Thailand that may have repercussions on the current and future industrialization of the country. One is that agricultural growth through area expansion, described above, has resulted in an extensive loss of forest areas in

Table 2.5 Breakdown of crop GDP, 1960–90 (per cent)

	1960	*1965*	*1970*	*1975*	*1980*	*1985*	*1989*
Rice	53	49	48	43	39	38	42
Maize	2	3	4	6	5	6	6
Sugar cane	4	3	2	7	5	4	6
Cassava	2	2	2	5	9	6	6
Rubber	3	3	4	3	5	10	12
Other crops	36	40	40	36	37	36	28
Total	100	100	100	100	100	100	100

Source: NESDB, *National Income Account of Thailand*, 1989.

Thailand. As shown in Table 2.6, forest land at the beginning of the modern development period in 1961 constituted 53.3 per cent of the total land area, but it reduced throughout the entire period of agricultural expansion and in 1991 forest land accounted for only 26.5 per cent of the total land area. In the intervening 30 years Thailand lost about 85.6 million rai of forest land, or about 2.9 million rai a year. The rate of deforestation between 1961 and 1973 was estimated at 1.7 per cent per year, increasing to 3.6 per cent between 1973 and 1976 and

Table 2.6 Forest areas of Thailand, 1961–91 (million rai)

	1961	*1973*	*1976*	*1978*	*1982*	*1985*	*1989*	*1991*
North	72.6	71.0	64.0	59.5	54.9	52.6	50.1	48.2
North-east	44.3	31.7	25.9	19.5	16.2	15.1	14.8	13.6
Center	22.3	15.0	13.6	12.8	11.6	10.8	10.7	10.4
East	13.2	9.4	7.9	6.9	5.0	5.0	4.9	4.8
South	18.5	11.5	12.6	11.0	10.3	9.7	9.1	8.4
Total	171.0	138.6	124.0	109.6	97.6	93.2	89.6	85.4
Memo items:								
as % of total land	53.3	43.2	38.7	34.2	30.5	29.1	27.9	26.5
average annual change between periods (%)	–	−1.7	−3.6	−6.0	−2.9	−1.6	−1.0	−2.4

Source: Office of Agricultural Economics, Ministry of Agriculture and Cooperatives.

peaking at 6.0 per cent between 1976 and 1978. It may be observed that the so-called 'golden era' of Thai agriculture during the first half of the 1970s, when the country responded vigorously to the global commodity boom, was also the period of rapid deforestation. At the beginning of the 1980s the felling of trees was reduced as the country began to experience the adverse effects of deforestation, such as soil erosion, flash floods and irregular weather patterns. The government's decision to 'close' the forests to all logging in 1990 was a response to these calamities. However the subsequent attempt to turn the damaged forest areas into agro-industrial areas by allowing commercial tree growing for pulp has run into several difficulties.[7]

The other important implication from past agricultural development is that using land through horizontal expansion without paying much attention to conserving land quality has contributed to stagnant or deteriorating productivity. As shown in Table 2.3, the yield of most crops throughout the three decades of crop production has been quite low or has even declined. For instance the growth of rice yield was estimated at only 0.8 per cent in the 1960s. During the high expansion era of the 1970s, the growth rate of rice yield was only 0.1 per cent a year. This low rate would not have mattered if the initial yield had been high, but this was not the case as Thailand's rice yield in the early 1960s was one of the lowest in the world (despite Thailand being a major rice exporter). Most of the other important upland crops in the 1970s, such as cassava, sugar cane, and sorghum, all had negative rates of growth of crop yield. Not until well into the 1980s did most major crops began to improve their growth rate (cassava being the only crop to retain a negative growth rate of yield). If the future yield of most crops is to increase substantially, the use of necessary inputs such as fertilizers or farm machinery might have to increase substantially also, which could lead to increased industrial production of these necessary agricultural inputs.

2.3 CONTRIBUTIONS OF AGRICULTURE TO INDUSTRIALIZATION

2.3.1 Basic Agricultural Contributions

In a well-known article, Johnston and Mellor (1961) argued that agriculture contributes to the economic development of a country in five ways. First, it increases the supply of food for domestic consumption. Second, it releases labour for industrial employment. Third, it enlarges the size of the market for industrial output. Fourth, it increases the supply of domestic savings. And fifth, it earns foreign exchange. How does Thai agriculture fit in with the above?

Supply of food

Rice is the main staple of the Thai diet, and Thailand has always been a surplus-rice-producing country. Therefore the supply of rice for domestic consumption has always been adequate, except in some years (such as 1974) when high foreign demand and a high external price tended to put pressure on the diversion of the domestic supply for export.[8] The rice premium (or tax on rice for export) and other forms of rice taxation, such as the rice reserve ratio requirement and rice export tax, were instruments used by the government to control the price level and supply of rice in the domestic market. Although the incidence and effects of rice taxation are complex and subject to much debate, it is undeniable that it kept the domestic price of rice low, at least in the early days of Thailand's industrialization in the 1960s and 1970s. The generally low price of rice in the domestic market also had a depressing effect on the prices of other agricultural commodities, effectively reducing the food costs of urban industrial and service workers.

Supply of labour

Industrialization in Thailand has taken place mainly in and around Bangkok because Bangkok has all the facilities for industrial production. The demand for non-agricultural labour in Bangkok and its vicinity has resulted in manpower being drawn from the agricultural sector. The growth in the urban population of greater Bangkok (about 3.4 per cent from 1975–80) has been higher than its natural growth rate (about 2.4 per cent over the same period), the difference obviously being net migration from rural, agricultural areas.

The extent of employment in manufacturing industries in greater Bangkok, as shown in Table 2.7, points to labour being supplied from other areas. As more than three quarters of the total Thai population was engaged in agriculture in the early 1970s (see Table 2.1), the industrial labour supply must have been partly drawn from this reservoir of manpower. In 1986 the National Statistical Office (NSO, 1988, Table D.) conducted a survey on migrants in Bangkok, its vicinity, and other regional growth centres and found that most of the

Table 2.7 Distribution of employment by major sectors and region, 1980–8 (per cent)

	Agriculture			*Manufacturing, utilities and others*			*Services*			*Number employed*		
	1980	*1984*	*1988*	*1980*	*1984*	*1988*	*1980*	*1984*	*1988*	*1980*	*1984*	*1988*
Bangkok	1.9	0.7	0.4	33.6	30.3	28.0	32.4	30.4	28.2	10.5	9.6	9.7
Five Provinces	3.8	2.2	3.3	9.2	12.0	12.8	4.5	5.8	6.2	3.5	3.9	5.0
Centre	23.6	15.1	15.8	20.5	19.1	19.1	19.2	15.0	18.4	16.2	15.5	16.8
North	39.1	25.4	23.4	12.0	15.9	16.0	16.6	17.7	16.8	21.6	22.9	21.1
North-east	72.3	44.8	45.5	12.9	11.2	13.1	16.4	18.2	16.9	36.3	36.1	35.5
South	19.3	11.8	11.6	11.8	11.4	10.9	10.8	12.9	13.5	11.8	12.0	12.0
Total	100.0	100.0	100.0	100.0	100.0	100.0	100.0	100.0	100.0	100.0	100.0	100.0

Source: Jittapatr, 1991, Table 2.1.

migrants in Bangkok came from the north-east. If migrants from the central region are not counted because of the close proximity of this region to Bangkok, workers from the north-east and the north constitute most of the migrants in Bangkok and its vicinity.

It should be pointed out that migration has distinct seasonal characteristics, that is, the number of migrants in the sample was much less in the planting season (from June to December) than in the agriculturally slack season. As explained by Oshima (1987), this is normal and is to be expected in a monsoon economy. Data in Table 2.7 also show that between 1980 and 1988 the proportion of manufacturing employment in regions outside greater Bangkok increased. This could mean that as industrial activities began to spread beyond Bangkok and into the countryside, migration into Bangkok declined. But until rural industrialization becomes successful, the flow of labour from the rural agricultural sector into Bangkok is likely to continue.

Market for industrial output

Again, as the majority of the population are found in the rural agricultural sector, a large part of domestic consumption takes place there. However an inhibiting factor is that since a large proportion of these people are classified as poor (see Medhi *et al.*, 1992), their spending power is quite limited. Nevertheless, income growth in the agricultural sector could provide a promising market for industrial output in the future.

Supply of domestic savings

As a corollary to the low income of farmers, domestic savings in the usual sense are unlikely to be forthcoming from the agricultural sector. However savings from this sector could be, and actually were, extracted in the form of agricultural tax of which the rice premium was the largest and most important tax item. As a unit tax on rice for export, the rice premium dated back to the postwar period and proved to be one of the most controversial elements of Thai economic policy.[9] The majority view seems to be that this tax put a burden on domestic producers – that is, rice farmers – because the foreign demand for Thai rice exports is usually very elastic. The rice premium was therefore a form of agricultural surplus extracted through the tax system. There were also other forms of agricultural taxation such as an *ad valorem* tax on rice for export (in addition to the rice premium, which was a specific tax), the rice reserve requirement, which forced rice exporters to sell rice at a low price to the government in proportion to their export level, rubber cess, sugar and cassava quotas, and so on.

In the 1950s and 1960s, when these agricultural taxes, especially the rice premium, were still very important tools for the government to mobilize domestic resources, the revenues collected were quite substantial. In 1960, for example, the rice premium and the rice export tax together constituted a full 20 per cent of total central government revenue. (Oey Meesook *et al.*, 1988, Table 5.16). As a percentage of the f.o.b. price of rice, these taxes were set as high as 60 per cent in certain years. But such forms of agricultural taxation began to decline, partly because of growing criticism of agricultural extraction of this nature, and partly because of the availability of more efficient or less controversial sources of government revenue. Since the abolition of the rice reserve ratio in 1982, the rice premium being zero rated in 1986, and the lifting of the rice export tax in 1990, rice has been freed from government extraction.

Foreign-exchange earnings

Perhaps the most important contribution of Thai agriculture to the industrialization process of the country has been to help earn the foreign exchange required to purchase industrial inputs and technology. As shown in Table 2.8, for a long time the share of agricultural exports to total exports was higher than the share of agricultural GDP to total GDP, signifying the relatively greater role of agriculture in export earnings. The record in 1960 showed that the share of agricultural exports to total exports was as high as 90.5 per cent. In other words almost all of Thailand's exports, when Thailand embarked on the new age of economic development, consisted of agricultural products. As the country began to industrialize, the proportion of industrial exports increased, and the proportion of agricultural exports declined. In 1970 the agricultural export share was 70.3 per cent, falling to 51.1 per cent in 1980 and finally to 22.6 per cent in 1990. Between the years 1960 and 1990, the annual rate of decline worked out at about 4.7 per cent a year.

It is more instructive to see the change in the incremental value of agricultural exports in a given period of time. The bottom part of Table 2.8 shows that the increment of agricultural exports during the 1960s was about 43.8 per cent of the increment of total exports. This incremental share increased to 56.8 per cent during the 1970s, mainly as a result of the 1973–4 global commodity boom. From 1980 onward,

Table 2.8 The role of agriculture in GDP and exports, 1960–90 (billion baht)

	GDP (current prices)			*Exports (current values)*		
	Agriculture	*Total*	*Share (%)*	*Agriculture*	*Total*	*Share (%)*
Level						
1960	21.5	54.0	39.8	7.6	8.4	90.5
1970	38.5	136.1	28.3	10.4	14.8	70.3
1975	94.1	298.8	31.5	29.5	45.0	65.6
1980	152.9	658.5	23.2	77.6	133.0	58.3
1985	169.9	1014.4	16.7	84.4	193.4	43.6
1990	254.5	2051.2	12.4	133.3	589.8	22.6
Increments						
1960–70	17.0	82.1	20.7	2.8	6.4	43.8
1970–80	137.8	522.4	26.4	67.2	118.2	56.8
1970–75	55.6	162.7	34.2	19.1	30.2	63.2
1975–80	58.8	359.7	16.3	48.1	88.0	54.7
1980–90	101.6	1392.7	7.3	55.7	456.8	12.2
1980–85	17.0	355.9	4.8	6.8	60.4	11.3
1985–90	84.6	1036.8	8.2	48.9	396.4	12.3

Sources: World Bank, 1982; 1985; Bank of Thailand, *Monthly Bulletin*, various issues.

however, the share of agriculture in incremental export value started to fall rapidly, especially between 1985 and 1990. In the 1980s the share of incremental agricultural exports was only 12.3 per cent. Obviously the importance of agricultural exports is much less today than it was 20 to 30 years ago. But the above data show that agriculture has contributed enormously to the foreign-exchange earning capability of the country.

The composition of agricultural exports may be of interest. Table 2.9 shows the rate of growth of agricultural exports by type of crop or commodity. The relative performance of each crop reflected the productive activities or cropping patterns in each particular period. For example, maize and cassava were the two fastest-growing export commodities during the 1960s, along with tobacco. During the next decade (the 1970s) maize lost its export lustre while cassava and sugar surged ahead. Actually, with the exception of maize, most other agricultural commodities also performed very well. In the last 1980s the export picture changed again. This time rubber increased its relative

Table 2.9 Growth rates of major agricultural exports by type, 1962–90

	1962–70	*1970–5*	*1975–80*	***1970–80***	*1980–85*	*1985–90*	***1980–90***
Rice	−5.1	−7.6	15.2	**9.8**	9.0	3.3	**5.6**
Rubber	4.8	4.6	7.8	**5.4**	8.4	11.6	**11.5**
Maize	12.4	6.7	−0.4	**2.5**	0.0	−23.8	**−6.5**
Cassava	12.7	18.3	12.6	**22.4**	3.5	6.8	**4.2**
Sugar	−8.2	46.2	−3.2	**22.5**	13.9	4.5	**8.0**
Tobacco	15.1	6.8	17.1	**15.5**	−2.7	−0.8	**−2.9**
Mungbeans	n.a.	6.7	21.2	**10.0**	3.2	−10.2	**−2.7**
Shrimp	n.a.	20.3	6.4	**11.6**	4.7	37.9	**30.7**

Source: Bank of Thailand, *Monthly Bulletin*, various issues.

importance as an export commodity while sugar and cassava managed to maintain low but significant growth rates. Shrimp exports in the 1980s had an outstanding growth rate of more than 30 per cent per annum.

Table 2.10 depicts the change in the share of agricultural exports by type of agricultural commodity. Rice fell from 40 per cent in 1962 to only 20.8 per cent in 1990. Rice, rubber and cassava together accounted for more than half the total agricultural export value in 1990. Sugar regained its export share slightly, while the share of shrimp exports increased more than three times between 1985 and 1990. Figure 2.1 provides a convenient way of comparing the relative share of each major commodity. In this figure it is easy to see how the rise and fall of each commodity came in a 'wave' at each particular time period.

Table 2.10 Share of agricultural exports by type, 1962–90

	1962	*1970*	*1975*	*1980*	*1985*	*1990*
Rice	40.0	24.0	19.0	26.0	26.7	20.8
Rubber	26.0	21.0	11.0	20.0	16.1	17.7
Maize	6.0	18.0	18.0	9.0	9.1	3.1
Cassava	5.0	11.0	15.0	16.0	17.7	17.4
Sugar	2.0	1.0	18.0	8.0	7.4	13.3
Tobacco	–	2.0	2.0	2.0	1.9	1.4
Mungbeans	–	2.0	1.0	2.0	2.7	1.0
Shrimp	–	2.0	3.0	4.0	4.1	15.3
Others	21.0	19.0	12.0	11.0	14.3	10.0

Source: Bank of Thailand, *Monthly Bulletin*, various issues.

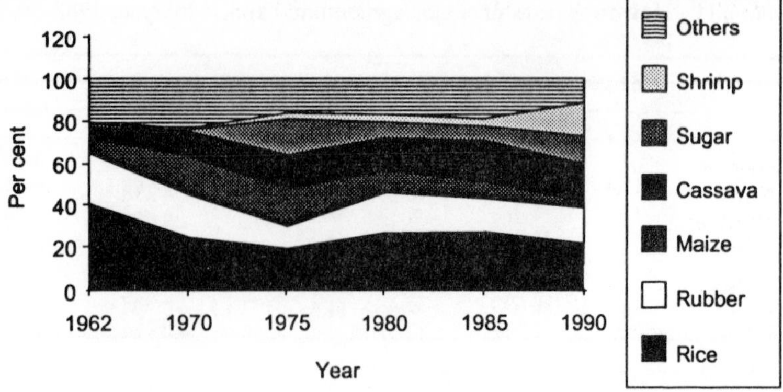

Figure 2.1 Share of agricultural exports, by major commodities, 1962–90

To conclude, agriculture contributed to the industrialization process in Thailand in the ways it was expected to do. It provided cheap food to urban industrial workers and thus helped to keep industrial costs down. Factories and various service subsectors were supplied with labour from the large pool in the agricultural sector. Agriculture also provided the government with revenue through taxation. And finally, agricultural exports as a source of foreign exchange earnings helped the country to acquire the necessary inputs and technology for its industrialization. In more than three decades of agricultural growth and development, agriculture has produced welfare changes both for the agricultural population and for the populations in other sectors, and it is to this subject we now turn.

2.3.2 The Welfare Implications of Agricultural Development

One of the most obvious measures of welfare change in any sector is a change in individual or household income. The results of several household income and expenditure surveys since the early 1960s have shown that the total income of households, that is cash income plus income-in-kind, has grown as the country has developed. This is shown clearly in Table 2.11 – in money terms the average total income of Thai households increased from 8232 baht in 1962–3 to 51 575 baht in 1988, or a more than sixfold increase over 25 years. This does not allow for inflation, so in order to assess the real increase in household income, changes in the overall consumer-price indices were applied to these

Table 2.11 Household total income by region and area, 1962–3 to 1988 (baht per year)

	1962–3	*1968–9*	*1975–6*	*1981*	*1988*
By region					
North	5987	10253	16644	34298	40950
North-east	5915	9481	16572	29606	35196
Centre	9731	15630	24852	43615	50701
South	9411	10893	19920	37381	46259
Bangkok	18690	32432	37848	76702	99186
Whole kingdom	8232	13074	21240	40114	51575
By area					
Urban					
North	10362	15731	28786	49701	84434
North-east	13517	22148	30250	46749	66712
Centre	13613	20099	34253	51680	74978
South	15164	19698	31933	54333	80911
Bangkok	18690	33799	43498	80460	105476
Whole kingdom	14888	26403	36000	63640	95108
Rural					
North	5267	9064	15838	30848	35612
North-east	5259	8069	15541	27465	31524
Centre	8957	13962	24317	40927	45440
South	8233	8957	17872	33405	38420
Bangkok	n.a.	24290	34097	49142	82082
Whole kingdom	6609	9997	18060	32309	37536

Source: NSO, *Socioeconomic Survey Reports*, various years.

incomes to arrive at the real rates of growth for different households from 1962–3 to 1988.

Table 2.12 reveals that during the first decade of systematic development (as shown in the data for 1962–3 to 1968–9), the real income growth of households was positive in all regions except the rural south. In general, income growth in urban areas was higher than that in rural areas, attesting to the hypothesis that the rural agricultural sector supported the urban industrial sector in the early days of development. During the period 1968–9 to 1981, however, Thailand experienced two oil crises, one in 1973–4 and the other in 1979–81, which resulted in high inflation and a great reduction in real household income. Income growth in many regions and locations was either negative or increased very slowly. Nonetheless, because growth in the early 1960s was rather

Table 2.12 Real rate of growth of total household income by region and location, 1962–3 to 1988 (per cent)

	1962/3–1968/9	*1968/9–1975/6*	*1975/6–1981*	*1962/3–1981*	*1981–88*
All Nation					
North	7.3	−0.6	3.6	2.9	−0.3
North-east	6.1	2.0	0.6	2.8	−0.4
Centre	5.9	−0.8	0.0	1.6	−0.7
South	0.2	1.2	0.8	1.0	0.2
Bangkok	7.3	−4.4	1.6	1.2	0.8
Whole kingdom	5.7	0.0	1.3	2.1	0.8
Urban					
North	5.1	0.4	0.3	1.9	5.0
North-east	6.5	−1.7	2.1	0.7	2.3
Centre	4.4	0.3	−2.7	0.7	2.6
South	2.2	−0.7	0.0	0.4	3.0
Bangkok	8.1	−2.9	−0.1	1.5	1.0
Whole kingdom	7.7	−2.7	−0.2	1.3	3.0
Rural					
North	7.4	−0.3	2.6	3.0	−0.8
North-east	5.3	3.5	0.4	3.1	−0.9
Centre	5.4	0.6	−0.7	1.7	−1.4
South	−0.9	2.6	1.7	1.1	−0.9
Bangkok	n.a.	−1.6	−4.6	−0.9	4.7
Whole kingdom	4.8	1.6	0.0	2.1	−0.7

Sources: NSO, *Socioeconomic Survey Reports*, various issues; Bank of Thailand, *Monthly Bulletin*, various issues.

high, average real income growth for the period 1962–3 to 1981 was still positive. For instance, the overall real income increase for the whole country was 2.1 per cent during the years in question. The income of urban households grew more slowly than rural income during these periods, possibly because high inflation during the two oil shocks had a greater impact on urban areas.

From 1981–8, just before Thailand took off on its very high growth path, the urban sector reexerted its greater growth potential. The average real growth rate during this period was 3.0 per cent for urban households but −0.7 per cent for rural households. The income growth of rural households in the 1980s was negative in all regions except for the rural part of Bangkok, or households at the fringe of the Bangkok metropolis. When the households in the two areas are combined, the real income growth rate for the whole kingdom was still positive, largely because of the population size of Bangkok. But for average households in the north, the north-east and the centre the real income growth rate was still negative.[10] How did these patterns of income growth affect poverty and income inequality? Studies by Medhi and Pranee (1985) and Medhi *et al.* (1992) showed that, based on a fixed poverty income level adjusted only by price level, the total poverty incidence for Thailand reduced from about 57 per cent in 1962–3 to 30 per cent in 1975–6, 23 per cent in 1981 and 21 per cent in 1988. Apparently the agriculture-led development in the 1960s and 1970s raised the income of people in all regions and areas, resulting in an overall reduction in the incidence of poverty. However, while absolute poverty declined, relative poverty or income inequality increased during the periods under consideration.[11]

2.3.3 Agricultural Taxation and Other Forms of Intervention

Earlier on it was mentioned that the agricultural sector has been subject to various forms of taxation in the past, and that the taxes on rice were the most important of these. The government may have had many reasons for imposing rice taxes, such as to increase government revenue, to stabilize the domestic price of rice or to keep the price of rice low. Various burdens on rice farmers included the loss of potential income due to the depressed domestic rice price, the lack of incentives to increase productivity through the use of more productive inputs and new technology, and the acceleration of crop substitution and diversification at the expense of rice growers. Of course it could be argued that the success of the diversification of Thai agriculture was partly a result of these taxes on rice, but this was certainly a very punishing way of doing it.

These various taxes not only mobilized agricultural surpluses and savings for use by the government, they also created indirect effects that benefited one group of the population more than the other. Take the case of the various taxes on rice exports imposed since the 1950s, for instance. Oey Meesook *et al.* (1988) believe that these taxes kept the price of rice low, which in turn kept wages low. The macroeconomics of this pricing policy was to lower agricultural incomes and thereby depress aggregate demand. The lower effective demand, in turn, reduced the demand for labour from what it would have been without a tax on the country's staple crop. They concluded that these low wage rates had improved the profitability of industry in Thailand (Oey Meesook *et al.*, 1988, p. 6.30).

But the effects of taxation on rice and other agricultural commodities are quite complex and do not lend themselves to simple conclusions. If the tax burden of agricultural commodities fell on producers, would curtailment of the taxes have benefited the producers or farmers directly? If the rice taxes kept wages low, would lifting the tax have led to increased wages? And who would have benefited? To answer the above questions is not easy. Take, for example, the effect on labour supply. An analysis by the World Bank (1985) showed that if the increase in the price of rice had led to the decrease in the urban real wage for unskilled labour, intersectoral reallocation of labour might have resulted by means of reduced rural-to-urban migration. The induced decrease in addition to the urban labour supply would have tended to drive up nominal urban wages for unskilled labour until equilibrium was reached between the urban and rural markets. According to the above view, the net long-term effect of the price increase on urban real wages was not clear because theoretically it depended on the relative intensity of factor substitution and the extent of resource reallocation in a number of markets.[12]

There is another effect of rice taxes that was briefly referred to earlier. This is the effect that rice taxes had on keeping the domestic price of rice below the world price. In so doing the government (unknowingly, perhaps) helped to reduce the wage costs of non-agricultural employers, which further stimulated import-substitution industrialization, and the overall transfer of agricultural surplus to non-agricultural development. An import tariff would have had the same effect and could have been considered an implicit tax on agriculture.[13]

On the subject of the removal of rice taxes, particularly the rice premium, and its effect on welfare and income distribution among the rural agricultural population and the urban non-agricultural population, the likely theoretical outcome would have been a major redistribution of income away from non-rice producers to rice producers. The real income of urban households would have been reduced and the rural rice-producing households would have gained. A study by Prasarn (1984) showed that if the rice premium had been removed, the largest gains would have accrued to rural households in the highest income brackets, as they were usually the net suppliers of rice. Although rural households in the top income brackets would have gained more than those in the bottom brackets, the study showed that even the bottom 40 per cent would have increased their real income by 27 per cent as a result of the removal of the premium. Oey Meesook *et al.* (1988) also looked at this issue and concluded that 'while the rice premium has served to diminish the fluctuations in domestic prices and has provided a revenue source for the government over the years, its effects on income of the poor have been negative' (Oey Meesook *et al.*, 1988, p. 5.76).

Finally, one of the most important questions is: What effect did government intervention in the form of explicit export taxes, restrictive quotas on agricultural exports, reserve requirements, quota allocations and so on have on the welfare of agricultural households? In other words, what gains and losses were incurred as a result of various interventions by the state in the production, pricing and marketing of various major agricultural commodities? The answer to this question is provided in an influential study by Ammar and Suthad (1989) as a part of a World Bank project on the political economy of agricultural pricing policy using case studies from 18 countries, of which Thailand was one.

In this study Ammar and Suthad followed the common technique of measuring the combined effects of direct pricing policies and those more general economic policies that can have an important but indirect impact on agricultural returns (see Krueger, Schiff and Valdes, 1988). The study ascertained the international prices of the agricultural commodities in question (so-called border prices) and then estimated the above effects from actual prices that deviated from these border prices. Four major crops were selected as the subject of study: rice, maize, sugar and rubber. In the case of rice and rubber, government intervention took the form of explicit export taxes. In the case of maize, it was restrictive quotas on maize exports to countries other than Japan and Taiwan, the principal buyers. As for sugar, the government helped local producers by setting a high domestic price for sugar, restricting its import and setting up a revenue-sharing system between sugar cane growers and sugar millers.

The effects of government intervention were measured on the output, consumption and trade of the four crops in question, as a difference in monetary terms between the simulated situation where all intervention was removed and the actual situation. The results were presented as direct and total effect, that is, both direct and indirect effects together, with three different periods of productive adjustment, that is, instantaneous period, short-run period and long-run period. The total effect was also further presented in two different ways: one total effect assumed that the policies of the Thai government had no effect on the border prices of the commodities (small country assumption), and the other assumed the removal of government policies altogether. With three effects and three adjustment periods, Ammar and Suthad had nine scenarios of the effects of government price intervention. The details may be complicated, but the conclusions were quite simple. For example, intervention in the prices of rice and natural rubber had the effect of penalizing farm producers by reducing their output prices. There was, as a consequence, a shift of resources towards Thailand's industrial sector. As for sugar, the Thai sugar industry would have shrunk to about a quarter of its size during the study period if the government had refrained from intervening.

Another crucial conclusion of the study concerned the net real resource transfers between agriculture and the rest of the economy. As Ammar and Suthad explained, government policies not only influenced the amount that the government extracted from particular sectors but also led to implicit transfers between the consumers and producers of those goods and services by shifting relative prices. The calculation technique called for a reestimation of the nominal income that would have accrued to the sector if the price intervention had been removed. The rural CPI was also reestimated, assuming the removal of all intervention. The authors then took the difference between the real actual income and the real recalculated income – the results indicated a transfer out of agriculture. Again, three adjustment periods were employed in this part of the study. The authors' conclusion was that there was:

> a generally downward trend in the resource flow from agriculture, interrupted by an increased rate of extraction in the mid-1970s, made possible (or politically necessary) by the worldwide commodity boom during that period. The increased extraction of the mid-1970s was accomplished by heavier direct intervention. This slackened sharply in 1982 (Ammar and Suthad, 1989, p. 184).

To illustrate the result of this net real resource transfer between agriculture and the rest of the economy, Figure 2.2 shows total direct and indirect effects using the small country assumption. It will be noticed that in general there were net real resource transfers out of agriculture to the rest of the economy for most of the years after 1960. Only after 1982 were the net real resource flows reversed, that is to say, agriculture began to receive net resources from the rest of the economy.

2.3.4 Reversal of Fortune? Benefits from Industrialization to Agriculture

There is no denying that early on the industrial sector benefited from agricultural contributions and 'sacrifices'. The much higher growth

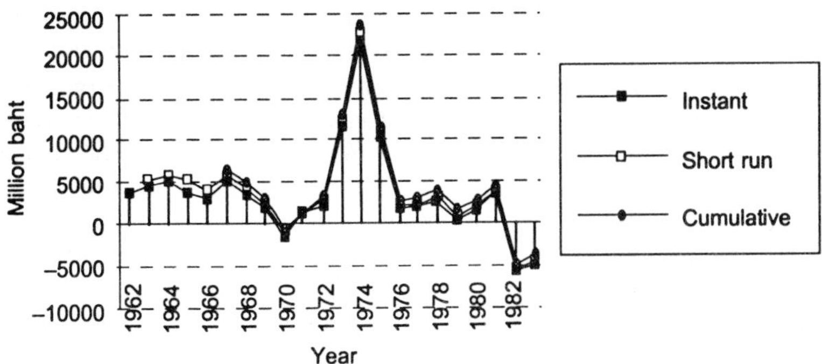

Figure 2.2 Real net resource flows from agriculture to the rest of the economy, 1962–83

rate, much greater productivity and much deeper protection had given the industrial sector a much more favourable position for development. By the early 1980s the share of value added of the manufacturing subsector had already exceeded that of agriculture, and by the middle of the 1980s the majority of export items from Thailand consisted of manufactured products rather than agricultural products. These have been the two most important conditions qualifying the Thai economy as a newly industrializing country, or NIC. And in the process of industrialization benefits from development did trickle down from the industrial (and service) sector to, or had been shared by, the agricultural sector in various guises and forms.

Take, for example, the net resource flows from agriculture to the rest of the economy discussed in the previous section. It was clear from the study by Ammar and Suthad (1989) that net resource flows began to reverse from the rest of the economy to agriculture from 1982 onward, as is evident in Figure 2.2 at the point where the total-effect curves started to dip below the horizontal axis. The reverse flow of net resources to agriculture was made possible by at least two policy measures. One was the removal or abolition of various government regulations, interventions and controls over the agricultural sector, and the other was the continuation of government support to agriculture through its budgetary spending (on rural or agricultural infrastructure, social services and the like). If the situation in 1981–2 is any indication of the trend of such policy measures throughout the rest of 1980s, then there should be no doubt that the net resource flows will continue, and perhaps even accelerate in the 1990s. The government has become much stronger economically and more able to tackle difficult economic issues compared with the early 1980s.

Earlier analysis showed that the agricultural sector achieved little productivity increase in the 1960s and 1970s. In addition land frontier appeared to have closed, so what can explain the increase in the income of the agricultural population during that period? Contributory factors were increased agricultural prices, favourable terms of trade and the opportunities provided by increased industrial and service activities in the form of non-farm work and employment. As shown in Table 2.13, the average, nationwide, non-farm to total cash income of agricultural households in crop year 1980–1 was already 46 per cent. But towards the middle of the 1980s the percentage of non-farm cash income to total cash income of agricultural households was as high as 69 per cent (in the north-east), and the average for the whole kingdom was 59 per cent. This shows that in a bad year, when agricultural production or prices fell, agricultural households were able to supplement their income through non-farm sources. But the trend is also unmistakable that agricultural-household income from non-farm sources is replacing income from farm sources. In 1990, for example, the composition of farm versus non-farm income for the average agricultural household was 47:53 per cent. Only in the north did farm income remain higher than non-farm income (56:44 per cent). Only the increased industrial and service activities associated with increased industrialization of the economy could have made this structural change possible.[14]

There are other indicators to show that general economic development and industrialization brought to agricultural households a greater ability to improve their agricultural techniques and production. On the one hand, the higher household income enabled farmers to invest more in better farm inputs and equipment. On the other hand, the ability to produce or make available these farm inputs and machinery cheaply and in adequate quantity – an expected outcome of the industrial process – also helped the farmers to improve their production.

The benefits from higher income and the availability of new and better farm inputs and equipment is clearly seen in the change in fertilizer use in Thailand, as reported in the agricultural statistics issued by the Ministry of Agriculture and Cooperatives. During the 1970s the growth rate of fertilizer use in Thailand was about 12.9 per cent per year, which was quite high. The high growth rate continued throughout the 1980s, increasing to about 13.9 per cent over the first five years and 18.3 per cent between 1985 and 1990. As a traditionally low fertilizer

Table 2.13 Average farm and non-farm cash income of agricultural households by region (baht per year)

	1980–1	*1982–3*	*1986–7*	*1988–9*	*1990–1*
North					
Farm cash income	14 130	10 607	8652	16 404	21 388
Non-farm cash income	9799	11 451	9945	11 063	16 746
Total cash income	23 929	22 058	18 597	27 467	38 134
% Non-farm to total cash income	41	52	53	40	44
North-east					
Farm cash income	9449	5747	6664	6530	14 255
Non-farm cash income	9618	12 529	11 246	13 318	18 254
Total cash income	19 067	18 276	17 910	19 848	32 509
% Non-farm to total cash income	50	69	63	67	56
Centre					
Farm cash income	18 933	17 194	13 393	30 570	21 724
Non-farm cash income	14 315	15 829	17 605	22 661	31 671
Total cash income	33 248	33 023	30 998	53 231	53 395
% Non-farm to total cash income	43	48	57	43	59
South					
Farm cash income	15 115	11 403	12 263	24 749	24 324
Non-farm cash income	15 352	20 898	21 688	20 637	25 598
Total cash income	30 467	32 301	33 951	45 386	49 922
% Non-farm to total cash income	50	65	64	45	51
Whole kingdom					
Farm cash income	13 354	9821	9010	15 252	18 839
Non-farm cash income	11 330	13 962	13 296	15 014	20,944
Total cash income	24 684	23 783	22 306	30 266	39 783
% Non-farm to total cash income	46	59	60	50	53

Source: Office of Agricultural Economics, Ministry of Agriculture and Cooperatives, *Income and Expenditure of Farmers, Crop Year 1990/91.*

user, Thai agriculture would benefit from a still greater increase in the use of fertilizer in the future.

The results of the 1988 Intercensal Survey of Agriculture conducted by the National Statistical Office (NSO, 1990) confirm the above trends. Thai farmers were shown to have made more use of agricultural equipment and machinery. In 1978, for example, 56.2 per cent of total farm holdings were reported to have used fertilizers of some sort. This increased to 78.4 per cent in 1988. It is also interesting to note that the use of organic fertilizers as the sole fertilizer declined by about 3.2 per cent annually between 1978 and 1988, while the use of manufactured inorganic fertilizers increased at a rate of 6.5 per cent a year. What was more striking was the increased use of such farm equipment as power tillers, seed drillers and fertilizer spreaders. The growth rate of use of these machines was outstanding. Equally impressive was the fact that ownership of them also increased substantially over the years.

All in all, there are reasons to believe that from the early 1980s onwards the economic development and industrialization of the Thai economy began to return the benefits of growth to the agricultural sector, in contrast with what had been taken from the sector in the 1960s and 1970s. This reversal of net benefits is in part attributable to the efforts of the government via various agricultural policies, and in part to the efforts of agricultural households themselves to improve their production and secure employment and additional income outside the farm. Under these circumstances, changes and transformation in the Thai agricultural sector will continue as long as the majority of the labour force is employed or engaged in this sector. If Oshima (1987) is correct, true industrialization will not begin until agricultural labour falls absolutely and the remaining farming practices are highly mechanized.

2.4 SUMMARY AND CONCLUSIONS: THAI AGRICULTURE IN THE 1990s AND BEYOND

It has been widely agreed that as the country is being transformed from an agricultural to industrial economy, agriculture will continue to lose its economic importance and reduce its contribution. But this will not occur until the agricultural sector achieves satisfactory growth in productivity, creating agricultural surpluses as well as releasing labour for the industrial and service sectors.

Thai agriculture seems to have conformed to the standard role played by agriculture in economic development. After the launching of the First National Economic Development Plan in 1961, agriculture was allowed to diversify into many additional cash crops. This involved the expansion of cultivated areas, mainly at the expense of forest reserves. If nothing else, this type of agricultural expansion could be considered successful at least in terms of the increase in production and export of many agricultural commodities in addition to rice. The traditional significance of rice has declined due to various policy measures against it by the government, but it will remain the subsistence crop for many farmers for some time to come. Agricultural productivity did not increase as rapidly as its production, partly because of high fertilizer prices, inefficient farming techniques and a lack of modern farm technology. This situation improved, however, towards the end of the 1980s, when the level of fertilizer use and farm mechanization increased dramatically. However agricultural employment has remained very high in comparison with the contribution of agriculture to the country's GDP, indicating very low labour productivity in the agricultural sector.

Agricultural exports were instrumental in helping the process of industrialization by earning foreign exchange, and domestic costs were kept low by virtue of agricultural taxation. Real income of agricultural households did increase concomitantly with the increase in industrial development, and the incidence of poverty declined as a result, although the disparity in income distribution has increased over the past three decades. On average the non-farm component of agricultural household's cash income now exceeds farm income. Long-term and seasonal migration to seek extra income have become the norm for people in rural areas, especially in the north-east. The government may provide assistance both directly, in terms of budgetary spending on rural and agricultural infrastructure and social services, and indirectly by removing controls and intervention, but the future salvation of the agricultural sector lies in its own structural adjustments and adaptations.

Thai agriculture, therefore, is still changing. The government will have to come to grips with effective policies towards limited land resources, tenancy and ownership issues. There is still much room for improvement with regard to productivity. Higher value-added crops and/or other agricultural activities will be experimented with. In fact, in addition to traditional export crops such as rice, rubber, cassava and sugar, agricultural exports have already expanded to include prawns, frozen fowl, fruit, and flowers. It should be noted that these new exports are not primary products in the strict sense of the word as they require some form of processing, packaging or preservation. The farmers themselves may not remain independent, self-employed, single proprietors, but become contract farmers who enter into arrangements with business companies regarding the type and extent of production, credit, input support, marketing and so on. This new aspect of Thai agriculture will become a part of 'agribusiness', where the private sector starts to replace the public sector as the traditional promoter of Thai agriculture. Indeed this could be what is known as 'the second wave of diversification', where horticulture, aquaculture, tree crops and intensive livestock rearing are all part of the diversification, and substantial research and high technology are required by producers or those who have an interest in and/or control over producers.[15]

But while the 'organized' private sector, in the form of large local or overseas multinational companies, may become more involved in Thai agriculture, it does not mean that the role of the government will diminish. A recent study by a former NESDB official and minister of agriculture (Kosit, 1991) appears to lend some weight to the notion that large agribusinesses can help speed up agricultural commercialization and effectively tackle the above-mentioned second wave of agricultural diversification. According to this view, close collaboration among four groups of players – farmers, private agribusinesses, the government and financial institutions – may be the way forward for Thai agriculture, especially with agribusiness rather than the government playing the role of innovator and lead entrepreneur. But as Christensen (1992b) pointed out, the government's preoccupation with agribusiness as a panacea for the present and future ills of Thai agriculture might distract from deficiencies in the government's own performance. According to him, the promotion of agribusiness alone was 'not enough to correct the policies and bureaucratic weaknesses that presently harness the innovation of incentives. Issues that demand public attention include biotechnology research and the reform of existing institutions, such as property rights laws and credit arrangements' (Christensen, 1992b, p. 2).

Apart from this basic emphasis on the still important role of the government, other current policies could continue. The government should be concerned about the wholesale absorption of agricultural labour into the urban industrial and service sectors. Rural industrialization, despite its current weak status, is still a valid and relevant policy. Rural-to-urban migration, particularly from the poor north-east to Bangkok, in search of additional employment and income is recognized as an important and rational economic decision, but the social and human costs involved in family separation and relocation can be quite large. Rural industries certainly can provide suitable alternatives to disruptive rural-to-urban migration. Perhaps the expanding industries and services associated with a higher level of development could absorb more labour from the agricultural sector in the future, and so could other effective social policies such as the extension of compulsory education from six to nine years, or the provision of an efficient social-security system whereby agricultural workers can engage in occupational change without too much fear of uncertainty and insecurity.

Perhaps it is appropriate to end this chapter by referring to a recent paper by Ammar Siamwalla, an authority on Thai agriculture (Ammar, 1992), which addressed the pertinent issue of the future of Thai agriculture. Ammar was of opinion that Thai agriculture has been subject to several myths that, in many ways, inhibit a true understanding of the problems and their effective solutions. The four myths cited include the myth that Thai agriculture is uniform and homogenous, that Thai farmers are ignorant, that small-scale agriculture is backward and inefficient, and that agriculture is technologically backward and stagnant.[16] By debunking these myths and setting out appropriate policies – such as non-intervention in farmers' decisions on agricultural production, and greater provision of production information, market and credit options, and other resources to the farmers – the farmers themselves can better adjust to the changing conditions and situations. The future of Thai agriculture still lies in traditional commodities such as rice, rubber, sugar and even cassava, with the government playing a more active role in agricultural research and development and keeping the agricultural trade free and open. This policy advice may not give a clear blueprint for the future of Thai agriculture in the wake of rapid industrialization, but it is given in the spirit that, given the right attitude and policies, Thai agriculture will still be able to cope in the changing world of economic transformation.

Notes

1. Although economic development means more than just industrialization, it is undeniable that industrialization is an important manifestation of modern economic development. This chapter, therefore, accepts industrialization as a valid means of economic development. It is recognised, however, that there are many approaches to industrialization, and each approach may lead to a different type of development.
2. The relevant wording in the plan is that the plan was of the view that in Thailand 'increased output will be most readily secured through the spontaneous efforts of individual citizens, fostered and assisted by Government other than through Government itself entering into the field of production', and also 'the key note of the public development is, therefore, the encouragement of economic growth in the private sector and the resources of Government will be mainly directed to projects, both

in the agricultural and non agricultural sectors of the economy, which have this objective in view'.

3. The 1990 relative share figures shown in Table 2.1 are preliminary figures. The agricultural share of 12.4 per cent of GDP is somewhat low; a normal trend adjustment would increase this figure to about 13.8 per cent.
4. As mentioned in the table note, the employment shares in 1960, 1970, 1980 and 1990 were obtained from the population censuses of those respective years. They are different from the employment figures shown for 1986 to 1989, which were obtained from labour-force surveys. The methodologies used in these censuses and surveys are not strictly comparable but at least they show the same uniform declining trend of employment in the agricultural sector. The population census is often criticized as providing figures that overstate the extent of agricultural employment as it does not take into account the change in the pattern of time used of agriculturists or agricultural workers. These target groups could basically identify themselves as farmers or agricultural workers, but actually spend more (or increasingly more) time in off-farm or non-farm activities such as seasonal work in factories or the service sector.
5. However, this cropping intensity dropped to 72 per cent at the end of 1990, the fourth phase of agricultural development. This is a period when Thai agriculture experienced another change. For instance the growth rate of the planted area for rice declined substantially along with other traditional crops. The farm holding area was turned over to other types of activity such as shrimp farming, vegetable and fruit tree growing. Farm holdings have also been turned into housing areas for expanding urban population and into amenities such as parks, golf courses and other recreational areas.
6. In a similar observation, Ammar and Suthad (1989) explained that the emergence of each of these new crops came in waves. The first wave was the maize expansion of the late 1950s and early 1960s. The second wave, quickly aborted, was kenaf in the mid-1960s. The third wave was cassava and sugar cane, which took off at about the end of the 1960s and the early 1970s, the sugar cane wave peaking somewhat earlier. These crops, of minor significance in 1960, are now established as important export commodities and are major sources of livelihood for a large number of farmers.
7. For an analysis of how the agro-industrial reforestation programme in Thailand ran into difficulty, see Apichai *et al.* 1992.
8. An estimate by the World Bank (1985, p. 124) shows that between 1970 and 1980 there was an average rice surplus of about 6.26 million tons (that is, after export, seed, feed and loss) for domestic consumption and industrial use every year. With the total population in 1980 at about 48.4 million, this translates into about 129 kilograms of rice per person. This was actually more than sufficient for the minimum caloric intake of rice of the average Thai, or about 121 kilograms per person per year.
9. For a summary of the debate on the incidence and effects of the rice premium, see, for example, Rangsun, 1987, Ammar and Suthad, 1989, and World Bank, 1985.
10. It should be noted that the rate of real income increase was higher if total income is measured on a per capita basis rather than on a household basis

because the size of households became smaller in 1988 compared with 1981.

11. For details on poverty and income distribution in the last two decades of economic development and industrialization, see Chapter 10 of this book.
12. The World Bank (1985, p. 8) cited the result of a study by NESDB using a multisector macroeconomic model to evaluate the effect of rice-price change on urban real wages. The study showed that the 5 per cent reduction in *ad valorem* export duty reduced the urban real wage of casual labour by only 0.8 per cent. This study also suggested that urban real wages were unaffected by increases in the price of rice, and that the mechanism of adjustment was a reallocation of labour such that nominal wages adjusted upward to hold real wages constant. Also, the increase in nominal wages meant decreased returns to capital for urban employers, which suggested that the real urban beneficiaries of rice export taxation were employers.
13. Again, the World Bank (1985) reported another multisector, macroeconomic study that purported to show the response of the Thai economy to a reduction of import tariffs on non-agricultural commodities from an average of 50 per cent in 1980 to zero in 1989. When compared with a base case experiment in which no policy changes were assumed, the growth rate of GDP remained the same, but the share of agriculture in GDP increased from 18 per cent in the base case to 31 per cent. The Bank then concluded that while the dramatic resource reallocation indicated by these experiments might be exaggerated, they nevertheless implied a significant implicit taxing of agriculture by means of import tariffs. See World Bank, 1985, pp. 10–11.
14. It could also be argued that the situation would have been much better if the farm households could have made this structural change by choice rather than by necessity. It seems that the low returns from agricultural activities, the lack of on-farm employment and the attractiveness of industrial wages had forced the agricultural workers to leave their farms to seek non-farm employment elsewhere.
15. This point was also discussed in Hirsch, 1990b.
16. Although it is true that these myths are worth debunking, in doing so one must not create an opposing set of myths in their place, such as Thai agriculture is unique and area-specific, that Thai farmers are all-knowing, that agricultural officials and bureaucrats are all 'demons', and so on. The real truth always lies between these extreme myths.

3 Export-Led Industrialization

Suphat Suphachalasai

3.1 INTRODUCTION

Thailand has experienced a high rate of growth since 1960, and the country has since become more industrialized. At the early stage of development agriculture played an important role in the country's economic growth with agricultural exports leading the way. Since 1980 the manufacturing sector has become important both in terms of its contribution to GDP and as an earner of foreign exchange. During the past decade there has been a dramatic increase in exports of labour-intensive manufactured products. The objective of this chapter is to investigate industrial performance and policies that have contributed to strong economic performance. The chapter begins with a brief background to industrialization in Thailand, and then it goes on to assess the role of export development and industrialization policy; tariffs, industrial protection and investment promotion; and finally the future prospects for Thai manufactured exports in a global economy.

3.2 INDUSTRIALIZATION IN THAILAND: A BRIEF BACKGROUND

Thailand has passed through various stages of development. The Promotion of Industrial Investment Act of 1960 (and the newly created Board of Investment, or BOI) was the starting point of import-substitution industrialization, with tariff protection and assistance being provided to the manufacturing sector. The promotion policy also favoured large enterprises, which are found generally to be more capital intensive and import dependent. As such, early industrialization policies were said to have caused income inequalities to increase. Import-substituting industries relied heavily on imported materials and capital equipment, causing industries to locate plants near the source of supply: Bangkok (Bautista, 1992). Concentrating manufacturing in the city has militated against small and remote enterprises and in recent years attempts have been made by the BOI to encourage manufacturing enterprises to locate outside Bangkok. The success of that policy is still limited for several reasons, including a lack of infrastructure in non-metropolitan regions.

Although government policy had placed great emphasis on exports since the Third National Economic and Social Development Plan (1972/76), tariff protection remained high – averaging around 30 per cent. This was more or less maintained until 1982, when some changes were made to the structure of tariffs, and in 1991 there was a substantial reduction in tariffs on capital goods.

Agricultural exports throughout the 1960s and 1970s contributed to industrialization. As they were the major source of foreign-exchange earnings and provided the manufacturing sector with the capital needed to obtain imported machinery. In addition, taxing agricultural exports, particularly rice, kept the price of staple food low and hence reduced the domestic terms of trade between agricultural and manufactured products. The price bias against agriculture plus the structure of investment incentives directed resources away from agricultural sector.

Although export incentives have been provided to enhance manufactured exports, these have been partly offset by the negative effects of tariff protection. The tax rebate scheme is one example, where the process of claiming export-tax rebates at first took a long time, although with the introduction of bonded warehouses in the mid-1980s the system improved. The BOI also provided investment promotion for exporting firms, but the firms were required to export around 80–100 per cent of their total production. The promotions allowed exporting firms to acquire imported machinery and intermediate goods at world-market prices by providing exemption from import tariffs.

The rapid expansion of manufactured exports has, to a large extent, been the result of an increase in local competitiveness, and to a lesser extent commodity composition and a growth in demand for Thai exports in overseas markets (Ariff and Hill, 1985). Thailand's rapid export growth of labour-intensive manufactured products began in the mid-1980s. One of the reasons for this was a change in relative costs in the East-Asian NICs, where real wages increased rapidly. This caused a decline in the competitiveness of their low-skill labour-intensive products. Appreciation of the NIE's currencies in the late 1980s also reduced their competitiveness.

A stable domestic economy has been key to Thailand's rapid industrialization and strong economic performance, and its macroeconomic policy has made the country competitive in the world market. The government has implemented conventional monetary and fiscal policies to stabilize the economy (Hughes 1985). The exchange rate of the baht has been kept close to equilibrium for the last twenty years, while inflation rates have been low.

3.3 MANUFACTURED EXPORTS AND INDUSTRIALIZATION POLICY

3.3.1 Export Growth

Manufactured exports have been the most important source of Thailand's foreign-exchange earnings since the mid-1980s. The average export output ratio of the whole sector doubled from 10 per cent in 1972 to 20 per cent in 1980 (Somsak, 1987). From Table 3.1, it can be seen that exports in 1986 amounted to some 233.4 billion baht or US$8.8 billion, representing a 23.9 per cent increase over the previous year. In 1987 exports grew by another 31.7 per cent, reaching 37.2 per cent in 1988, which was the fastest growth rate of exports ever recorded. This happened during a time when world trade was growing at only about 7 per cent a year. Export growth declined to 15.2 per cent in 1990 but recovered to 23.9 per cent in 1991.

In contrast with the situation in the 1960s and 1970s, the largest component of exports is now manufactured products, which in 1991 accounted for more than 76 per cent of total exports. This represents a drastic change in the composition of Thai exports – as recently as 1984 the share of agricultural exports was higher than the share of manufactured exports. Starting from 1985 the share of manufactured exports began to overtake that of agricultural exports. Indeed the export turning point in 1985 further qualified Thailand as an emerging NIC. Today the major manufactured exports are textile products, integrated circuits, jewellery and processed food, especially canned tuna and pineapple.

Most of Thailand's manufactured exports are destined for industrial-country markets. The EU, Japan and the United States are the major markets, accounting for around 50 per cent of total exports (Table 3.2). Since the 1980s the ASEAN and Middle-Eastern countries have also become important export destinations. However Thai exports form a

Table 3.1 Trade by principal commodities, 1985–91 (US$ million)

	1985	*1986*	*1987*	*1988*	*1989*	*1990*	*1991*
Total merchandise exports	7059	8802	11 589	15 781	19 840	22 795	28 257
Agriculture	3106	3607	3975	5063	5749	5209	6034
Rice	829	772	883	1371	1769	1085	1197
Rubber	500	575	798	1075	1028	921	979
Tapioca products	551	726	803	864	933	904	956
Sugar	230	276	333	382	749	692	580
Prawns	127	167	223	383	625	799	1046
Frozen poultry	54	119	156	198	236	303	413
Fresh fish	129	226	259	280	352	356	536
Other	686	746	519	511	57	148	327
Total	3106	3607	3975	5063	5749	5209	6034
% exports	44.0	41.0	34.3	32.1	29.0	22.9	21.4
% annual growth		12.5	7.8	25.3	15.4	–9.8	15.5
Manufactures							
Textile products	868	1189	1888	2318	2880	3302	4295
Integrated circuits	304	487	590	745	717	843	1010
Precious stones	234	310	449	552	639	862	919
Footwear	87	121	230	382	526	790	933
Furniture and parts	48	71	132	262	376	450	534
Plastic products	46	54	86	216	296	356	508
Jewellery	80	191	321	384	466	501	489
Other	1853	2489	3614	5567	7879	10 109	13 005
Total	3521	4912	7310	10 427	13 779	17 213	21 694
% exports	49.9	55.8	63.1	66.1	69.5	75.5	76.8
% annual growth		11.9	13.0	4.7	5.1	8.7	1.7
Mining and other	432	283	304	291	312	373	529
% exports	6.1	3.2	2.6	1.8	1.6	1.6	1.9
% annual growth		–47.5	–18.3	–29.8	–14.7	4.1	14.4
Total merchandise imports (Share of imports, %)	9328	9370	13 283	19 737	25 204	32 543	37 796
Agriculture	9.0	9.5	9.9	9.3	10.0	9.5	10.2
Manufactures	71.0	78.1	79.7	84.9	83.2	83.5	83.6
Mining and other	19.9	12.5	10.4	5.7	6.8	6.9	6.3

Source: Bank of Thailand, *Monthly Bulletin*, various issues.

very small part of total developing countries' exports to industrial countries, and a small part of apparent consumption of manufactures in industrial countries. In the mid-1980s Thai exports constituted only 1 per cent of industrial country imports from developing countries, compared with 3–4 per cent for Malaysia and Singapore, and 14 per cent for Taiwan, the Republic of Korea and China (World Bank, 1986).

Table 3.2 Trade by destination and source, 1985–91 (percentage share)

	1985	*1986*	*1987*	*1988*	*1989*	*1990*	*1991*
Export destination							
United States	19.7	18.1	18.6	20.0	21.7	22.7	21.3
EC	18.0	20.0	20.6	19.3	17.6	19.8	18.8
ASEAN	14.5	14.3	13.6	11.7	11.5	11.4	11.8
NIEs	7.5	8.3	7.0	7.9	7.0	7.8	8.0
Japan	13.4	14.2	14.9	16.0	17.0	17.2	18.1
Australia	1.7	1.8	1.8	1.9	1.9	1.6	1.6
Rest of the world	25.2	23.3	23.5	23.3	23.3	19.5	20.3
Total	100.0	100.0	100.0	100.0	100.0	100.0	100.0
Import source:							
United States	11.3	14.3	12.5	13.6	11.3	10.9	10.6
EC	13.6	13.9	14.7	14.6	13.0	12.7	13.0
ASEAN	18.2	14.2	15.3	12.2	12.4	12.4	12.5
NIEs	6.3	7.5	7.6	8.2	9.2	9.7	11.1
Japan	26.5	26.4	26.0	29.0	30.3	30.7	29.4
Australia	1.7	1.8	1.7	1.7	2.0	1.7	1.8
Rest of the world	22.4	22.0	22.2	20.8	21.7	22.0	21.7
Total	100.0	100.0	100.0	100.0	100.0	100.0	100.0

Source: Bank of Thailand, *Monthly Bulletin*, various issues.

3.3.2 Industrialization and Trade Policy

Industrialization in Thailand entered a new phase around 1936 with a series of public investments in pulp and paper, cigarettes, textiles and food processing (Ingram, 1971). However many of these enterprises went bankrupt due to mismanagement and inefficiency (Mingsarn, 1977). Consequently investment policy underwent a change in the late 1950s. A new era of private-enterprise industrialization began with the First National Economic Development Plan (later changed to the National Economic and Social Development Plan).

The First Plan (1961–6) emphasized public investment in physical and social infrastructure. Industrial policy concentrated on import substitution and favoured private investment. There was to be no expansion of government enterprises. An Investment Promotion Act was introduced in 1960 to implement this policy. The First Plan (Industrial and Mineral Development section) stated that it was intended:

> To encourage domestic and foreign enterprises to undertake more industrial activities in the country. The State will assist and promote industries of various scales to suit the needs of the domestic market. The State will not engage in activities competitive with private enterprise, and will follow the policy set out in the Act of 1962 for promotion of industrial investment. There will be State interference only in regard to quality control.

An import-substitution policy, emphasized in the First Plan, was carried through to the Second Plan (1967–71). In the Second Plan, however, more attention was given to industries that utilized domestic raw materials and to labour-intensive industries. There was an attempt to reduce the importation of intermediate goods. In the Third Plan (1972–6), industrialization and trade strategy had begun to change from import substitution towards promoting exports. Special promotion privileges were provided, particularly for export-oriented firms. Decentralization of investment activities away from Bangkok became an additional feature of industrial policy.

Policies to promote exports continued to be emphasized in the Fourth, Fifth, Sixth and Seventh plans. In the Fourth Plan (1977–81) large-scale exporting firms and trading companies were encouraged, and an export-processing zone was established. The Fifth Plan (1982–6) placed a new emphasis on industrial adjustment and encouraged small-scale industries. In the Sixth Plan (1987–91) the emphasis was on restructuring tax incentives. Attention was also given to agro-based industries and the diversification of manufactured products and export markets. As far as the Seventh plan (1992–6) is concerned, the export-oriented policy has continued, with additional reference to the diversification of export markets as well as industrial location.

3.4 TARIFFS AND INDUSTRIAL PROTECTION

The level of tariff protection in Thailand has fluctuated over time. In the 1960s Thailand had one of the lowest levels of tariff protection in Asia, nominal tariff protection for final consumer goods and intermediate goods averaging around 25–35 per cent, and for capital goods around 15–20 per cent (UNIDO, 1985). In 1969, however, Thailand suffered a large balance-of-payments deficit of over 913 million baht, forcing the government to increase import tariffs as a means of solving this problem. As a result the average nominal tariff rates for consumer imports in 1971 increased to 30–55 per cent while the rates for intermediate and capital imports remained unchanged (World Bank, 1984). But two years later inflation in the aftermath of the first oil shock forced the government to lower import tariffs on raw materials, intermediate products and capital goods in order to reduce the costs of industrial production. Because of this tariff measure the effective rate of protection for finished consumer products became noticeably higher than the nominal rate of protection, as shown in Table 3.3.[1]

In 1975 Thailand again suffered major balance-of-trade and payments deficits, brought on by the abovementioned oil shock. Again the

Table 3.3 Nominal and effective rate of protection, classified by stage of production (per cent)

Industrial group	*1964*	*1969*	*1971*	*1974*	*1978*
Nominal Rate of Protection:					
1. Processed food	17.76	−18.7	50.91	29.9	0–30
2. Beverages and tobacco	220.68	82.8	116.48	52.5	60–100
3. Construction materials	26.00	24.1	21.83	3.75	n.a.
4. Intermediate products I	5.17	−3.7	11.37	4.95	5–100
5. Intermediate products II	26.02	32.7	36.09	33.8	30–44
6. Consumer nondurables	32.86	30.5	44.92	41.63	30–100
7. Consumer durables	27.00	29.8	44.95	59.12	60–80
8. Machinery	21.60	18.7	10.21	5.55	2–30
9. Transport equipment	41.92	29.7	58.79	62.88	30–150
Effictive Rate of Protection (Corden):					
1. Processed food	37.33	−32.6	205.92	−71.19	−2–466
2. Beverages and tobacco	65.47	241.3	439.21	409.83	−25–40
3. Construction materials	21.26	47.4	23.41	−15.93	n.a.
4. Intermediate products I	6.54	2.8	15.28	10.37	−15– −4
5. Intermediate products II	54.55	79.1	50.32	55.74	22–115
6. Consumer nondurables	42.44	32.5	57.44	61.84	72–669
7. Consumer durables	21.96	69.1	93.20	144.75	102.6
8. Machinery	17.74	30.6	7.58	12.89	5–83
9. Transport equipment	121.69	34.9	146.45	181.10	55–392
Average, all items	–	–	87.2	18.6	70.2
Average, all except Items 1 and 2	–	–	44.2	45.9	90.3

Source: Patmawadee, 1993, Table 1.

government resorted to increased import tariffs: the effective rate of protection for all industries (except food, beverages and tobacco) increased from 44.2 per cent in 1971 to 90.3 per cent in 1978, with higher degrees of protection-rate differentials across industries (see Table 3.3).

From the above pattern of policy changes it is quite clear that from 1961 to 1981 import tariffs were used as a means to raise government revenue, to correct balance-of-payments problems and to fight inflation. A major result of this policy was an increase in the intensity of industrial protection. Agricultural products suffered a negative rate of protection because they not only had to pay export taxes, but imports necessary for agricultural production such as fertilizers and farm machinery were also subject to import tariffs. On the other hand, domestic manufacturing industries, whether for import substitution or not, benefited from this industrial protection. Examples of products receiving high effective protection during these two decades were textiles, leather products, cooking oils, bakery and wheat products, cosmetics, rubber products, ceramics and earthenware, household electrical goods, motor vehicles, jewellery and cigarettes.

The Thai government and especially its planning board (the NESDB) had always realized the implicit danger of such industrial protection. Not only did protected industries lack the incentive to increase their production efficiency, there was also a tendency to reallocate resources from efficient export industries to less efficient import-substitution industries. When import-substitution industries reached their useful limits, due mainly to a saturation of demand in domestic markets, the government earnestly began to promote export industries. In July 1981 the government devalued the overvalued baht by 8.7 per cent, effectively reducing its protection of domestic manufacturing industries and at the same time reducing the bias on export industries. On 15 October 1982 the government announced a reduction of the tariff on processed-food imports from 80 per cent to 60 per cent, and an increase of the tariff on several chemical products and machinery items to 30 per cent. This should have had the effect of making the tax system more neutral by providing greater equality in the level of protection amongst various products, that is to say, reducing the protection on finished consumer products and increasing the protection on intermediate products and capital goods. However, two days later the government was forced to reduce the tariff on intermediate products and raw material imports from 30 per cent to 15 per cent, and the tariff on mineral ores from 10 per cent to 5 per cent.

Moreover the government also imposed an additional 10 per cent surcharge on most imports. This surcharge was increased to 20 per cent in 1984 to help the government finance its serious budget deficit.

Another major devaluation of the baht by 14.8 per cent in 1984 resulted in a reduction of effective protection from 28 per cent to 26 per cent (Table 3.4). But persistent budget deficits throughout the early 1980s made it necessary for the government to increase import tariffs again in 1985. This time it was an across-the-board increase of 5 per cent on raw materials and intermediate products, 10 per cent on finished manufactured products, and more than 10 per cent on textile products and automobile accessories. This caused the effective rate of protection to increase from 26 per cent in 1984 to 30 per cent in 1985 (Table 3.4).

Table 3.4 Nominal and effective rates of protection (per cent)

	1981	*1983*	*1984*	*1985*
Nominal rates:				
Overall averages of all products				
Unweighted average	31	33	30	34
Weighted average	14	16	15	18
Weighted sectoral averages*				
Consumer goods	25	22	20	28
Intermediate products	13	16	15	14
Raw materials	2	3	3	5
Capital goods	14	18	17	22
Effective rates:				
Unweighted averages of				
Agriculture	25	26	24	28
Other primary products	5	7	7	10
Agro processing products	115	139	130	135
Manufacturing	77	67	57	66
Weighted averages of*				
Agriculture	11	11	11	13
Other primary products	6	8	8	10
Agro processing products	25	30	29	33
Manufacturing	54	50	49	52
Overall average	28	28	26	30

* weighted by import values.
Source: World Bank, 1986.

It may be concluded, therefore, that the government's efforts to reduce industrial protection in Thailand during the 1980s were not successful due to the recurring problem of fiscal and balance-of-payments deficits. However the beginning of the 1990s saw major changes in the structure of industrial protection in Thailand. In 1990, for example, the government lifted its ban on the importation of motor vehicles with engine size smaller than 2,300 cc, a ban that had been in force since 1978. It also abolished the limit on the number and model of automobiles that could be assembled or produced in the country. The import tariff on machinery, electrical equipment and accessories was reduced from 20 per cent to 5 per cent. In 1991 the import tariffs on computer and computer products were reduced from 10–40 per cent to 1–5 per cent, and on machines, equipment and chemicals for the preservation of energy and protection of the environment from 10–40 per cent to 0–5 per cent.

Under the leadership of Prime Minister Anand Panyarachun in 1992, the government planned to reduce the number of tariff rates from about 60 to just five by 1997. These five rates were 0 per cent for raw materials in short supply within the country, 5 per cent for other raw materials, 10 per cent for intermediate products, 20 per cent for finished manufactured products and over 20 per cent for products whose domestic protection was still needed. Throughout 1992 the government reduced the tariff on more than 1,000 items within 24 major commodity groups. It was expected that with two more major reductions between 1993 and 1997 the target could be reached as planned.

In all, despite the unsuccessful attempt by the government to reduce the level of industrial protection during 1980s, Thailand's average import tariff remained moderate in comparison with those of other developing countries. Table 3.5 suggests that the average nominal import tariff of Thailand was 31 per cent in 1983, which was higher than those of the Asian NICs but lower than those of neighbouring ASEAN countries (except for Malaysia) and the South Asian countries. Moreover quantitative restrictions have been modest. In 1986, for instance, only 65 products required import licenses. Of these, 42 were restricted to protect the producers of such products as automobiles, motorcycles, diesel engines, iron bars and iron rods. Except for drugs and guns, import licenses are granted readily. In addition a tax-rebate system offsets tariff protection for exporters. Imported inputs for manufactured exports are exempt from import duties and taxes such as business and municipal taxes. Firms can either

Table 3.5 Import tariff protection in selected countries (per cent)

	Average Tariff Protection
Bangladesh (1984)	75
India (1979–80)	66
Indonesia (1980)	33
Malaysia (1982)	15
Pakistan (1979–80)	71
Philippines (1982)	44
Republic of Korea (1982–3)	24
Singapore (1983)	6
Sri Lanka (1983–4)	44
Thailand (1983)	31

Source: James, Naya and Meier, 1987.

pay the taxes and be compensated after they have exported the products, or they can use commercial-bank guarantee certificates to avoid paying the charges. Any commercial bank can issue a guarantee statement to the Customs Department, normally charging a commission of about 2 per cent of the amount guaranteed. Most exporting firms requiring imported inputs use this channel if they can. Manufacturers claim that the tax-rebate system has not been efficiently administered in the past; some have alleged that it took exporters from six months to a year to recover the rebates owed to them by the government. Since 1987 there has been an improvement in the tax-rebate process, with rebates being received between one and three months after the products are exported.

3.5 INVESTMENT PROMOTION, CREDIT ASSISTANCE AND DIRECT FOREIGN INVESTMENT

3.5.1 Investment Promotion

The Investment Promotion Act (1960) provided the framework for direct government intervention in manufacturing. A Board of Investment was created to implement the Act. Its main function was to decide which firms would receive promotion privileges. Three categories of industry were defined: Group A included mainly capital-intensive industries such as the chemicals, electrical appliance, automobile and ship-building industries. Group B industries were assembling industries such as transport-equipment assembly, agricultural-machinery assembly, electrical-appliance assembly and the like. Group C industries were mainly labour-intensive and service industries, including food processing, clothing and textiles, hotels and international shipping. Group A industries normally received the highest level of promotion. Industries at all three levels were entitled to (corporate) income-tax holidays of up to five years. Promotion privileges at the three levels were as follows:

- Group A: full exemption from import duties and business and sales tax on raw materials for five years.
- Group B: an exemption of 50 per cent of import duties and business and sales taxes for five years.
- Group C: an exemption of one third of import duties and business and sales tax for five years.

There were no major changes in promotion policies during the 1970s, except for a merger between categories A and B. In the mid-1980s separate categories were abolished but the promotion privileges remained similar to previous ones. Three more types of firm have qualified to apply for promotion assistance since 1986: (1) firms located outside Bangkok; (2) export oriented firms (those exporting at least 80 per cent of their production); and (3) firms located in investment-promotion zones, which now exist in all regions. These changes generally correspond to the Fifth and Sixth Plan objectives to promote exports and encourage firms to locate outside Bangkok.

Tax incentives given to firms have remained similar to those provided in the original Investment Promotion Act. A maximum five-year income-tax exemption still exists. Tax incentives for exporting firms are the same as the promotion privileges given to Group A in the 1960s and 1970s. But for the other types of investment mentioned earlier, import duties and business tax were reduced by a maximum of 90 per cent.

The incentives granted to entrepreneurs are complex and at first sight extensive, requiring a large bureaucratic workforce to implement them. However their impact is not always significant. Most firms intending to invest for the long term do not become profitable for some time, so that five-year tax holidays are not as useful as would seem at first sight. Exemption from import tax is probably more significant, particularly for exporters. The entitlement of promoted firms to request additional protection, in the form of import surcharges, is also important. In 1980 20 product groups were subject to import surcharges that ranged from 10 per cent to 40 per cent of c.i.f. prices for unlimited periods (Narongchai and Juanjai, 1983, p. 85). However import surcharges have been limited since 1987, when the Board of Investment changed the surcharge scheme to a maximum of one year for all products.

3.5.2 Credit Assistance

Two kinds of credit assistance are available to manufacturers. The Bank of Thailand provides manufacturing and export credit assistance. Assistance is given either in the form of concessional interest rates by discounting loans to manufacturers or by export promissory notes. Credit assistance in fact takes the form of short-term loans through discounted promissory notes for 120 days for investment in manufacturing and 180 days for exports. However credit assistance to manufacturers declined sharply from $358 million in 1980 to $26 million in 1990 (Table 3.6).

Export credit assistance has been used on a greater scale than credit assistance for investment in manufacturing. The value of exports under the scheme increased sharply from $1.7 billion in 1980 to $3.5 billion in 1990, accounting for 12 per cent of total exports. Exporters of both agricultural and manufactured products had an equal share of the local credit granted in 1990 (Table 3.6).

3.5.3 Direct Foreign Investment

Foreign direct investment increased steadily from some $45 million in 1970 to $2.5 billion in 1985. From 1970–5, foreign direct investment was important, accounting for around 60 per cent of total capital inflow, but in the latter half of the 1970s foreign direct investment's share of total capital inflow declined to around 30 per cent. Meanwhile external borrowing by public enterprises, classified as private, long-term capital, increased markedly (Paitoon, 1987). Since 1980, however, the volume of foreign direct investment has again increased as a result of a significant increase in private direct foreign investment. Traditionally foreign direct investment had not had a very significant share of gross domestic investment in Thailand. In the last two decades the share of foreign direct investment in gross domestic investment averaged only about 1–5 per cent, but in 1990 it stood at 11 per cent (Table 3.7).

Table 3.6 Amount of manufacturing investment and exports receiving credit assistance

	1980		*1986*		*1991*	
	US$ million	*Share (%)*	*US$ million*	*Share (%)*	*US$ million*	*Share (%)*
Promissory notes for manufacturing	358	100	44	100	26	100
Textiles and clothing	162	41	25	56	2	9
Cement	77	24	25	56	2	9
Steel bars	33	10	neg.	–	–	–
Food products	25	8	13	29	20	80
Others	61	17	7	15	1	neg.
Promissory notes for exports	1719	100	3433	100	3523	100
Agriculture	552	32	1035	30	1573	62
Rice	na	na	446	13	490	14
Maize	na	na	240	7	50	1
Marine products	na	na	172	5	451	13
Others	na	na	172	5	32	1
Manufacturing	1047	61	2398	70	1907	54
Tapioca products	401	23	481	14	321	9
Textiles and clothing	138	8	275	8	344	10
Sugar	133	8	240	7	55	2
Canned and frozen food	114	7	481	14	376	11
Others	120	7	927	27	43	1
Total exports ($ million)	5280	–	9335	–	28 692	
Share of exports receiving credit assistance (%)	–	33	–	37	–	12

Note: neg. = negligible level.
Source: Bank of Thailand, *Monthly Bulletin*, various issues.

Table 3.7 Foreign direct investment (US$ million)

	1980	*1985*	*1986*	*1987*	*1988*	*1989*	*1990*
1. Net foreign direct investment[1]	155	178	276	362	1119	1828	2501
2. Private investment[2]	4248	5935	6203	8755	13 185	18 316	23 893
3. Share of net foreign direct investment in private investment (% of 1/2)	4	3	5	4	9	10	11

Notes:
1. Does not include net capital outflow of Thai investors (equity investment).
2. Does not include depreciation.
Sources: Bank of Thailand, *Monthly Bulletin*, various issues; NESDB, *National Income of Thailand*, various issues; Securities Exchange of Thailand; Bank of Thailand, Research Department.

The manufacturing sector has been the main recipient of foreign direct investment, accounting for around 30 per cent (Table 3.8). Manufactures of electrical appliance, textiles, chemical and petroleum products, and transport-equipment industries have received substantial foreign investment. Paitoon (1987) suggests that such investment has, to some extent, contributed to the diversification of the country's industrial structure.

The United States was the most important source of private direct investment during the 1960s, such investment being channelled especially into mineral resources and manufacturing. There was also some Japanese investment during the 1960s, but the main expansion came in the 1970s, largely in import-substitution manufacturing industries such as textiles, clothing and transport equipment. Since the mid-1980s there has also been a significant inflow of investment from the Asian NICs, notably from Singapore, Hong Kong and Taiwan (Table 3.9). Increasing labour costs in the NICs, appreciation of their domestic currencies and the fragmentation of industrial-country markets by voluntary export restriction (VER) were largely responsible for these investment flows.

In comparison with other South and East Asian countries, however, private direct foreign investment flows to Thailand have been relatively

Table 3.8 Sectoral distribution of net flows of foreign direct investment, 1980–91 (per cent)

Sector	*1980–2*	*1983–6*	*1987–90*	*1991*
Industry	32.6	31.5	49.5	45.4
Electrical appliances	11.9	6.7	18.7	17.4
Chemical	3.4	5.5	7.5	7.5
Metal based and non-metalic	2.2	3.3	5.6	4.3
Food	−0.1	3.4	3.7	3.3
Textiles	2.7	2.1	3.1	2.2
Others	12.5	10.5	10.8	7.1
Trade	13.2	22.1	16.9	14.9
Services	12.5	10.6	16.1	3.5
Construction	19.1	15.8	7.2	6.5
Financial institutions	0.1	1.5	6.7	13.3
Mining and quarrying	20.8	17.1	1.6	4.0
Agriculture	1.6	1.4	1.4	1.2
Others	0.0	0.0	0.7	4.2

Source: Bank of Thailand, *Monthly Bulletin*, various issues.

Table 3.9 Percentage distribution of net flow of foreign direct investment classified by country, 1970–91

Country	*1970–9*	*1980–2*	*1983–6*	*1987–9*	*1990*	*1991*
USA	35.56	27.25	29.71	12.35	9.34	11.52
Canada	0.16	−0.22	0.86	0.29	0.15	0.30
Japan	29.78	22.88	32.87	44.28	44.48	30.34
Hong Kong	9.59	13.88	9.63	11.25	12.00	22.51
Korea, Rep	0.35	0.07	0.09	0.70	0.78	0.58
Taiwan	0.37	0.11	1.29	10.74	11.44	5.36
Singapore	5.11	6.21	3.28	5.87	9.45	12.59
EC	15.4	19.15	11.73	8.47	6.86	7.71

Source: Bank of Thailand, *Monthly Bulletin*, various issues.

low (Paitoon, 1987). Thai policy on foreign investment has been conservative. Two laws – the Alien Business Law and the Alien Occupation Law (1972) – have restricted investment. The Alien Business Law specifies certain business activities that can be undertaken only by firms with a majority Thai ownership. Foreign-owned firms that had been established before the law took effect were required to transfer a major share-holding to Thai partners within a specified period. The Alien Occupation Law reserves certain occupations for Thai citizens, mostly in services, handicrafts and agriculture. In addition the BOI has been conservative in granting promotion privileges to foreign-owned firms and to joint ventures with large foreign shareholdings.

In practice foreign firms that did not apply for promotion privileges were nonetheless able to establish themselves fairly readily, and this accounts for some of the rise in private direct investment in Thailand in recent years. In 1988 Taiwanese investment has overtaken Japanese investment in terms of the number of firms applying for promotion, although Japanese companies still have the highest share in terms of capital as most of the Taiwanese firms are small.

Foreign investment has accounted for only around 5–10 per cent of the country's gross domestic investment, but it has played an important role in manufacturing. Foreign investment has pioneered a number of industrial sectors, covering a large proportion of the country's manufacturing production. A study by Saeng *et al.* (1978) of Thailand's 1000 largest firms found that 51 per cent of sales were either by foreign firms or joint ventures.

Studies of the impact of private direct foreign investment on the Thai economy have found mixed results. Chulacheeb and Somsak (1983) concluded that Japanese investments had had an unsatisfactory impact on economic variables such as balance of payments and on the transfer of technology. The effect of private direct investment on the country's balance of payments was not positive for firms producing import-substitution products because they were dependent on imported intermediate goods and had high remittance rates. They also claimed that the transfer of managerial skills in Japanese firms was slow. Employment growth was relatively low because import-substitution investment was largely capital intensive. Mingsarn (1977), however, suggested that there was technology transfer by Japanese firms investing in import-substitution textiles.

Japanese private direct investment that was home-country oriented was typical in the 1970s (Katano *et al.*, 1978). Japanese firms introduced Japanese styles of management, used Japanese managers as far as possible, and were highly dependent on parent firms. The training and promotion of local staff was limited. The objective of Japanese investment, especially in the early 1970s, was usually to maintain export markets by circumventing tariff protection.

More recently the effects of private direct foreign investment on the textile industry have been found to be positive because they were not only import substituting but also export oriented. Even as early as 1973, Ruchada's (1973) study of the economic contribution of private direct foreign investment to textiles suggested that it had contributed additional savings, foreign-exchange earnings and employment to the economy. These recent investors were largely from other NICs in the Asian region. Lecraw (1977) suggested that investments from regional sources tended to be permanent and largely independent of parent-firms control.

3.6 INTERNATIONAL ECONOMIC OUTLOOK

Without doubt, manufactured exports have played an important role in the industrialization process in Thailand. A question could be raised as to whether Thailand will be able to sustain its export growth, as the global economic environment is less favourable in the 1990s than it was in the 1970s and 1980s. At the time of writing, the GATT Uruguay round negotiations have been concluded but the agreements have yet to be implemented, trade blocs are mushrooming such as the North

America Free Trade Areas (NAFTA), and economic growth in the OECD countries has slowed drastically. All these developments have affected important export markets for Thai manufactures. In addition Thailand has to face stiff competition from labour-intensive products from China, Indonesia and elsewhere. Thailand, as a small player in the world market, has to adjust accordingly. The recent tariff restructuring will enhance competitiveness. Although the so-called 'offsetting policy' is in place, it is not costless in terms of either finance or management. Increased labour productivity is another way to maintain export competitiveness as real wages have increased recently.

Forming a free trade area such as the ASEAN Free Trade Area (AFTA) may help export expansion among member countries and attract foreign investors as they will be able to gain access to the whole ASEAN market. However past experiences of economic cooperation between ASEAN members have not been impressive. A similar ASEAN proposal, the Preferential Tariff Agreements (PTA), has not been implemented effectively.

The exportation of Thai manufactures is expected to increase as investment projects commenced during the investment boom period of 1989–91 come on stream, most of the participants being exporting firms. Although the demand for Thai exports in traditional developed-countries markets could slow down, other market opportunities, particularly in the newly industrializing economies, are still favourable. Such market opportunities include Eastern Europe and Indochina, and a good example is provided by the marked increase in the exportation of garments to Poland since 1991.

3.7 CONCLUSION

Exports have played an important role in Thailand's economic development and industrialization. With agricultural exports leading the way in the earlier decades, manufacturing exports became the most important foreign-exchange earner for the country in the mid-1980s. High growth in the manufacturing sector as well as increased exports has been a result of trade and industrialization policies that have favoured the manufacturing sector. Various forms of protection, and promotion of the manufacturing sector while taxing agricultural exports have contributed to industry's success. Macro policy promoting a stable domestic economy has played an important role in providing the economic environment for economic growth.

The country is now facing a short-term problem stemming from a lack of adequate infrastructure. This is a result of inadequate investment in the early 1980s. However several large infrastructure projects have been undertaken, including highway projects and telecommunications. In the future Thailand could also work towards long-term competitiveness by tariff restructuring and by improving the skills of the labour force.

Note

1. An effective rate of protection shows the percentage by which the value added of a product in a domestic industry can exceed what it would be without protection. If v' is value added per unit of output with protection (in domestic price) and v is value added per unit of output without protection (in world price), the effective rate of protection, g, would be equal to $(v' - v)/v * 100$. For most developing countries the value of g is highly positive, suggesting that their industries are highly protected.

4 Industrializing the Service Sector, with Special Emphasis on Tourism

Somchai Ratanakomut

4.1 INTRODUCTION

Recently Thailand has experienced a growing importance of the service sector in its development process, augmenting traditional development strategies that emphasize import substitution and the promotion of manufactured exports. Under challenge has been strategies emphasizing higher-value production in the agricultural sector as a means to further development. The growth of services in Thailand has been important not only for domestic income generation but also for foreign-exchange earnings and the absorption of a large portion of the rural labour force.[1]

This more or less follows world trends, the expansion of service activities having been encouraged by the pace of technological advancement and the computerization of information. Satellite telecommunications make possible rapid information transmission on a global scale. Such global service activities have also stimulated foreign participation in various service subsectors in Thailand, for example banking, wholesale and retail trade, transportation and construction. Participants range from such familiar names as Citibank, McDonald's, Kentucky Fried Chicken and Seven-Eleven to the more unfamiliar names of Korean and Japanese construction firms.

This chapter touches on various aspects of the service sector in Thailand. Section 4.2 discusses the scope and importance of the service sector, followed by consideration of some general points on service growth. Section 4.3 gives a brief account of tourism as the largest income generator in the service sector. Section 4.4 deals with problems in some important service subsectors, and Section 4.5 discusses the role of government in bringing about necessary changes to the service sector. Finally, Section 4.6 assesses the future prospect of the service sector in Thailand.

4.2 THE ROLE OF THE SERVICE SECTOR IN THE THAI ECONOMY

4.2.1 The Scope of the Service Sector

As we can see from Table 4.1, the service sector has not only increased in size, it has also widened its scope. Technological advancement has enhanced the degree of specialization in service industries by providing more sophisticated computers and improve international communications. The economies of scale generated by this advancement has also supported the activities of small, service-oriented enterprises.

The scope of service sector is certainly very large. Specialized services previously undertaken internally by company departments or family members have become service businesses in their own right. As Dicken (1992) put it,

> The service sector is extremely diverse; far more so, in many respects, than the manufacturing sector. It ranges from highly sophisticated, knowledge and information intensive activities performed in both private and public sector organisations to the very basic services of cleaning and simple maintenance. It includes retail and wholesale distribution and entertainment as well as health care and education services. It encompasses construction activities, transport activities, financial activities, communications activities, professional services. The list is (almost) endless.

4.2.2 The Importance of Service Activities

The service sector is one of the most important and dynamic sectors in the Thai economy. Its share in GDP increased from about 46 per cent in 1970 to about 48 per cent in 1990, while over the same period the share of agriculture fell from 28 per cent to 12 per cent and the share of manufacturing (including mining and quarrying) increased from 25 per cent to 39 per cent. The decline in the importance of the agricultural sector in the Thai economy is, of course, generally recognized.

The service sector has contributed positively to Thailand's overall balance of payments. In 1987, for example, services showed a positive balance of 28.68 billion baht, increasing to 47.34 billion baht in 1991. (Table 4.2). It is also interesting to note that the balance of the merchandise trade deficit from 1987–91 increased at a high rate, from 44.13 billion baht in 1987 to 247.54 billion baht in 1991. This increased

Table 4.1 Classification of international services proposed by the IMF

1. TRANSPORT AND STORAGE
   1.1 Passenger
   1.2 Freight and auxiliary transport services
      1.2.1 Freight
      1.2.2 Rental of transport equipment with crew
      1.2.3 Other transport and storage service
2. TRAVEL
   2.1 Tourism
      2.1.1 Business travellers
      2.1.2 Students and trainees
      2.1.3 Other tourists
   2.2 Other travel
3. GOVERNMENT TRANSACTIONS N.I.E.
4. POSTAL AND TELECOMMUNICATION
   4.1 Postal and courier services
   4.2 Telecommunications services
5. CONSTRUCTION
6. SERVICES INCIDENTAL TO MANUFACTURING
   6.1 Processing (manufacture on a fee or contract basis)
   6.2 Repair services
7. TRADE-RELATED
   7.1 Commission agents' services
   7.2 Merchanting (wholesale trade services)
8. FINANCIAL
   8.1 Services of financial intermediation
   8.2 Services auxiliary to financial intermediation
9. INSURANCE
   9.1 Life insurance, pensions, and annuity services (other than compulsory social security
   9.2 Casualty insurance
   9.3 Services auxiliary to insurance and pension funding
10. BUSINESS
   10.1 Leasing or rental services without operators
   10.2 Computer services
   10.3 R&D, architectural, engineering and other technical services
   10.4 Legal, accounting, auditing and bookkeeping services; taxation services; market research and public opinion polling services
   10.5 Management consulting services
   10.6 Advertising services
   10.7 Information services
   10.8 Other business services
11. MISCELLANEOUS
   11.1 Education services
   11.2 Health and social services
   11.3 Motion picture, radio and television and other entertainment services
   11.4 Other miscellaneous services

Source: GATT, MTN GNS/W/50 13 April 1989, cited in Suthiphand, 1992a.

Table 4.2 Services and the balance of trade, 1987–92 (billions of baht)

	1987	*1988*	*1989*	*1990*	*1991*	*1992*
Merchandise:						
Exports (f.o.b)	298.10	399.17	509.92	583.21	720.54	813.36
Imports (c.i.f)	341.68	449.24	647.80	832.60	963.80	1 015.50
Non-monetary gold import	0.55	1.18	2.30	5.74	4.29	5.09
Merchandise deficit	44.13	101.25	140.18	255.14	247.54	205.22
Services:						
Total services receipts	107.19	150.34	180.97	216.72	243.06	260.07
Freight and insurance on merchandise	10.05	11.60	11.56	11.89	15.21	16.36
Other transportation	8.44	13.58	16.12	22.25	22.97	30.16
Travel	50.02	78.86	96.39	110.57	115.70	123.13
Investment income	6.64	9.36	16.60	27.76	32.42	27.31
Government, n.i.e	3.19	3.28	3.58	3.26	3.57	3.21
Other services	28.84	33.66	36.72	41.00	53.19	59.88
of which: workers' remittance	21.60	23.44	24.24	24.91	25.70	28.60
Total service payments:	78.51	96.06	112.08	153.20	195.72	230.64
Freight and insurance on merchandise	5.13	7.26	9.40	9.33	12.49	16.17
Other transportation	3.78	4.72	6.07	8.21	9.78	12.63
Travel	9.90	15.25	19.20	36.53	48.50	57.32
Investment income	48.09	53.15	57.78	69.19	83.95	85.76
Government, n.i.e	2.69	2.66	3.12	3.21	3.42	2.90
Deficit in goods and services	15.45	46.97	71.28	191.61	200.20	175.79

Source: Bank of Thailand.

the current-account deficits, and the overall balance of payments became more dependent on capital accounts to finance its deficit.

Three of the most important contributors to service receipts are travel and tourism, investment income, and workers' remittances. In the past, travel and workers' remittances have significantly helped to reduce the size of the current-account deficit in Thailand. Investment income has become more important, especially within the last five years. Together they have contributed to the stability of the baht. Smaller important services include freight and insurance on merchandise, income from Thai International Airways and several other items hiding in the 'other services' category.

On the service payments side, investment income, travel and tourism, and 'other services' became increasingly important. Investment income increased from 48.09 billion baht in 1987 to 83.95 billion baht in 1991 (about 30 per cent of the merchandise deficit). Meanwhile travel and tourism and 'all other services' increased from 9.90 and 8.92 billion baht in 1987 to 48.50 and 36.26 billion baht, respectively, in 1991. The growing importance of these services, especially investment income and 'other services', implies a higher degree of foreign participation.

4.2.3 General Trends in Services

The dominant picture in the near future will be the expansion of various service activities by foreign and domestic businesses in a less protectionist environment. With some difficulties both in the world economy and at home, important service items such as travel will also fluctuate around rising trends. Some components of infrastructure, such as transport, insurance, construction and telecommunications will become relatively larger with a higher degree of foreign participation.

In the case of banking, financial liberalization is expected to create competition between foreign and domestic banks. However the Thai banking industry is characterized by heavy government intervention, which has led to limitations being placed on foreign bank branches operating in Thailand. Foreign banks are not allowed to establish more than one office in Thailand; they are not allowed to establish ATMs or join ATM pools; and they are not allowed to access the discount window of the Bank of Thailand. This discrimination has led to a call for free competition in the banking business, to give more benefits to consumers and investors (see Thammanun and Somchai, 1989).

Following the September 1992 election, many economic ministries were controlled by ministers with somewhat conservative backgrounds. This suggests that under the present government any drastic liberalization of the banking sector is unlikely. Government policy has tended to concentrate more on domestic development and overall stability. The next step in Thai banking development will be for domestic banks to try to compete with foreign banks by increasing automation and providing extensive training for bank personnel. Should the banking industry become more liberal, several smaller Thai banks might have to merge in order to gain economies of scale.

4.2.4 Sources of Service Growth

It seems that there are several factors behind the increasing importance of the service sector in Thailand. These factors include the overall economic growth of Thailand, which has led to expansion of domestic and foreign demand for services, and the advancement and internationalization of services. The high growth rate of the economy as a whole has prompted not only domestic but also foreign companies to take a greater part in the service sector, and it has increased demand for infrastructure such as transport, telecommunications, legal services, franchising and insurance, which has in turn led to further investment in various Thai concerns.

Foreign demand for such services as industrial estates, hotels, golf courses and so on has been an important development factor in Bangkok, and in several industrial development zones and tourist sites outside Bangkok. Impetus has come also from the privatization of service activities previously performed by public enterprises, such as the State Railways of Thailand and the Telephone Organization of Thailand.

There has been a need for domestic service businesses to keep pace with foreign competitors. Many service activities, such as banking, airlines, telephone and telecommunications, hotels, television and the retail trade, have gone through significant changes as a result of technological and managerial know-how imported from abroad.

4.3 TOURISM: THE LARGEST SERVICE INDUSTRY

Thailand is said to have an advantage over many other South-East Asian destinations in having attractions of a historical, archaeological, architectural and cultural nature, as well as attractive resorts, a varied nightlife and unique gifts and souvenirs. Tourism is now Thailand's most important source of foreign-exchange earnings. In 1989 income from international tourists accounted for some 96 386 million baht, increasing to 110 572 million baht in 1990. This was more than earnings from traditional exports as textile products, rice, rubber or tapioca (Table 4.3).

Table 4.4 shows that over the last three decades tourism has been growing through an increase in the average length of stay of foreign tourists. The number of tourists fluctuates but the revenue derived is consistently on the rise. It is appropriate to ask whether tourism can continue to grow.

During the past thirty years tourism has expanded through government support, improved access to tourist destinations and the opening

Table 4.3 Comparison of revenue from tourism and other major exports 1989, 1990 and 1992 (millions of baht)

1989		*1990*		*1992*	
Tourism	96 386	Tourism	110 572	Tourism	123 135
Textile products	74 027	Textile products	84 472	Textiles products	111 837
Rice	45 462	Computers and parts	38 671	Computers and parts	55 384
Computers and parts	26 760	Rice	27 770	Precious stones	36 582
Rubber	26 423	Rubber	23 557	Rice	36 214
Tapioca products	23 974	Tapioca products	23 136	Prawns	31 696
Sugar	19 244	Precious stones	22 045	Tapioca products	29 611
Integrated circuits	18 424	Integrated circuits	21 580	Rubber	28 925
Canned fish	16 928	Prawns	20 454	Integrated circuits	28 619
Precious stones	16 419	Footwear	20 213	Footwear	25 582

Source: Bank of Thailand.

of new tourist facilities. Relatively less effort has been made to conserve the existing tourist spots, and action to protect the environment in places such as Patong Beach in Phuket, Khoa Yai National Park in the north-east, and the Similan Islands in the Andaman Sea was belated. Plans for growth are still moving ahead. The Tourism Authority of Thailand is currently implementing a plan to link major provincial tourist destinations – including Chiang Mai, Phuket, Ubon Ratchathani and Udon Thani – to neighbouring countries in order to make Thailand a gateway to these countries.

It should be noted that the impact of tourism has spread to other productive sectors, but the propensity to spend on imports as a result of tourist spending has been kept relatively low as demand can normally be satisfied by domestic production.[2] Also, tourism is a sector that can readily be decentralized, and so creating a demand for labour in the provinces and supporting the general development of provincial areas.

As far as employment is concerned, the Tourism Authority of Thailand showed that direct employment in tourism-related industries accounted for about 458 825 jobs in 1987 (Table 4.5). Restaurants, hotels and entertainment are subsectors that can absorb a relatively large amount of labour. In 1987 the share in total direct employment of restaurants, hotel accommodation, and entertainment and recreation, respectively, was 30.6 per cent, 29.0 per cent and 15.1 per cent.[3]

Table 4.4 Number of tourist arrivals, average length of stay and revenue from tourism 1960–93

	Number of tourist arrivals	*Changes (%)*	*Average length of stay (days)*	*Revenue from tourism (million baht)*
1960	81 340	32.1	3.0	196
1961	107 754	32.5	3.0	250
1962	130 809	21.4	3.0	310
1963	195 076	49.1	5.7	394
1964	211 924	8.6	4.5	430
1965	225 025	6.2	4.8	506
1966	335 845	19.0	4.6	952
1968	377 262	12.3	4.2	1220
1969	469 784	24.5	4.8	1770
1970	628 671	33.8	4.8	2175
1971	638 738	1.6	4.8	2214
1972	820 758	28.5	4.9	2718
1973	1 037 737	26.4	4.7	3457
1974	1 107 392	6.7	4.8	3852
1975	1 180 075	6.6	5.0	21 455
1982	2218 429	10.1	7.4	78 859
1989	4 809 508	13.7	7.6	96 386
1990	5 298 860	10.2	7.1	110 572
1991	5 086 899	–4.0	7.0	100 004
1992	5 136 443	9.7	7.1	123 135
1993	5 800 000	12.2	6.9	127 802

Source: Tourism Authority of Thailand.

4.4 PROBLEMS ARISING FROM CHANGES IN THE SERVICE SECTOR

In order to assess the extent of problems arising from changes in the service sector, the benefits and costs of the increasing importance of service industries need to be analyzed, and we might look at such factors as growth, employment, balance of payments and income distribution. We might ask, too, whether it is appropriate for a country to depend on services as an engine for growth.[4]

For Thailand, it has been argued that a positive impact of the growth of tourism has been the development of infrastructure in provincial towns such as Chiang Mai, Chiang Rai and Phuket. But tourism also brings problems. For example it might create overall economic instab-

Table 4.5 Direct employment in tourism-related business, 1987 and 1992

	1987		*1992*	
Type of business	*Persons*	*%*	*Persons*	*%*
Accommodation	133 226	29.0	354 834	38.0
Travel agent	5 082	1.1	29 116	3.2
Restaurant	140 635	30.6	367 321	39.4
Gift shop	20 041	4.4	84 545	9.1
Domestic transport				
Private	19 007	4.1	52 797	5.7
Public	20 000	4.4	42 298	4.6
Entertainment and recreation	69 129	15.1	n.a.	–
Other related business	51 705	11.3	n.a.	–
Total	458 825	100.0	930 911	100.0

Sources: For 1987, Tourism Authority of Thailand; for 1992, National Institute of Development Administration (NIDA).

ility, increased resource leakages through import demand and environmental problems. An increase in the demand for telecommunications facilities might attract foreign participation to the extent that the future development of the industry might be under the control of transnational corporations or foreign companies.

4.4.1 Economic Instability from Internal Disruptions and External Shocks

Demand for services may vary and produce instability. In Thailand, the number of tourists fell as a result of domestic and international crises. In the past, such fluctuations have created problems between hoteliers and travel agents since hotel room rates also fluctuated accordingly. The instability of the sector also makes it difficult to carry out effective future manpower planning. In this particular regard, the different future projections shown in Table 4.6 would call for different reactions by private business.

4.4.2 The Sustainability of Service Activities

The issue of sustainability is also important since Thailand has experienced environmental deterioration. One possible problem is that

Table 4.6 Projections of international tourists for the Seventh National Development Plan, 1992–6

	Number of tourists (million)		*Tourism income (million baht)*	
	IFCT estimate	*NESDB estimate*	*IFCT estimate*	*NESDB estimate*
1992	5.15	5.60	107 000	141 300
1993	5.79	6.00	120 300	160 500
1994	6.41	6.50	133 200	182 100
1995	7.00	7.00	145 500	206 600
1996	7.50	7.50	155 900	234 300

Source: Dhira 1992.

a large influx of migrants into Bangkok would worsen water pollution and traffic congestion.[5] This would make Bangkok a less attractive place and lead tourists to shorten their stay. The growth of tourism areas such as Pattaya and Phuket is reaching its limits in terms of water supply and waste-water treatment, while the construction of golf courses and tourist resorts in areas such as Khao Yai has created disputes over land use and conflicted with local agricultural activities.

4.4.3 Foreign Participation

Service sectors are able to expand rapidly with participation from foreign capital. The success of Singapore as a financial centre for South-East Asia owes much to foreign capital and business participation. Finance is one of the service areas where Thailand still lags behind Singapore. The role of transnational corporations (TNCs) can be critical in the development of the service sector, especially the tourist industry. But while foreign participation may benefit a country's service sector, it may also mean large sums being remitted overseas, especially in payment of the transfer of technology. Statistics from the Bank of Thailand show that Japan and the United States are two important recipients of technology payments from Thailand. As shown in Table 4.7, remittances to Japan increased from 502.3 million baht in 1981 to about 2819.9 million baht in 1991. The figure for the United States rosed from 349.3 million baht in 1981 to about 1 078.5 million baht in 1991. The figure for the EC was also considerable.

Table 4.7 Outward remittances of technology payments classified by country (technical fees and copyright and patent royalties) (US$million)

	1981	*1982*	*1983*	*1984*	*1985*
Japan	502.3	497.6	640.1	748.3	823.4
USA	349.3	515.9	431.7	512.3	464.5
Switzerland	92.7	71.3	117.8	124.9	146.9
Canada	5.0	3.5	3.4	1.9	5.8
Australia	11.4	2.9	4.5	8.4	11.3
S. Korea	0.0	0.0	3.3	1.9	0.8
Taiwan	0.9	0.8	0.6	2.6	7.8
Hong Kong	39.9	53.7	76.2	95.7	96.7
Singapore	4.9	21.2	31.8	25.8	26.0
Malaysia	2.6	4.2	5.6	3.4	2.7
Philippines	0.0	2.1	2.7	3.9	1.2
UK	186.7	125.4	129.8	107.8	159.6
W. Germany	38.0	34.5	30.5	104.8	133.1
France	15.1	8.9	8.6	12.0	19.0
Netherlands	24.2	19.3	103.0	130.1	86.7
Italy	35.8	36.5	15.3	14.3	10.0
Denmark	10.0	23.0	33.5	16.3	19.2
Belgium	0.6	2.0	3.3	50.7	3.7
Others	11.7	18.9	27.6	28.3	27.7
Total	1331.1	1441.7	1669.3	1993.4	2046.1

	1986	*1987*	*1988*	*1989*	*1990*
Japan	811.1	1040.5	1497.1	2796.0	2819.9
USA	462.5	489.4	758.1	866.7	1078.5
Switzerland	186.7	193.4	213.9	297.9	289.6
Canada	0.5	6.5	10.8	13.7	23.4
Australia	19.2	5.6	26.6	51.5	60.7
S. Korea	2.8	1.3	2.6	25.4	20.7
Taiwan	9.1	10.3	6.2	13.2	9.5
Hong Kong	115.3	103.4	89.8	157.5	225.6
Singapore	25.4	48.1	76.2	129.9	241.7
Malaysia	5.9	3.7	4.3	5.6	7.3
Philippines	0.0	0.0	2.1	1.6	1.1
Indonesia	0.0	0.1	0.1	0.0	2.4
Brunei	0.0	0.0	0.0	0.0	0.1
China	0.0	0.0	0.0	0.0	0.4
UK	136.6	173.9	257.8	201.7	148.2
W. Germany	112.8	154.6	187.8	327.2	326.3
Italy	7.3	14.6	13.5	14.5	19.0
Luxembourg	0.0	7.6	4.1	13.8	109.4
Spain	0.0	0.0	0.0	0.0	0.3
Others	20.2	23.2	92.9	94.8	169.2
Total	2081.8	2382.8	3441.1	5315.1	5834.3

Source: unpublished data, Bank of Thailand.

4.5 GOVERNMENT POLICIES TOWARDS CHANGES IN THE SERVICE SECTOR

As a country develops its service sector tends to expand, and it is reasonable for governments in developing countries to try to support the sector and promote its further development. The expansion of this sector also has positive spillover effects on the agricultural and manufacturing sectors.

There are at least three measures that the government could adopt with regard to the future development of the Thai service sector: liberalization of the sector; protection of the domestic market against foreign competition; and enhancement of the country's infrastructure.[6]

4.5.1 Liberalizing Measures

The present Chuan government proposed to continue the policy of liberalizing financial markets and to improve the competitiveness of local financial services partly by expanding foreign competition. The plan includes the establishment of special-purpose banking facilities such as the Export-Import (EX-IM) Bank and the development of financial services in regional areas. The government foresees Thailand as an international financial centre, and has tried to develop financial linkages with other countries in the South-East Asian region.

4.5.2 Protective Measures

A possible policy is that of protecting domestic investors, but in practice this would be difficult, especially as some service activities, such as telephone and telecommunications networks, depend on advanced technology from abroad.

4.5.3 Investment in Infrastructure

The government has paid constant attention to improving infrastructure, including utilities such as telephones, water and electricity supply, and public enterprises in transport facilities, including air transport, buses and railways.

4.6 CONCLUSION

There is likely to be an expansion of various service activities by foreign and domestic businesses in a less protective environment. It is highly probable that the Thai domestic service sector will face greater foreign competition, whatever the future of multilateral trade systems. Some important service activities such as telecommunications, banking and transportation are expected to become much larger, and with a greater degree of foreign participation.

The service sector may well be constrained both by internal factors (politics, government intervention, and so on) and external ones (for example increasing protectionism). The expansion of the domestic service sector will require proper adjustment to both these internal and external factors.

Recent financial liberalisation and policies proposed by the present Chuan government are unlikely to allow Thailand to overtake Singapore as the financial centre of the region. The Thai financial system still lags several steps behind that of Singapore. Moreover the speedy, large-scale liberalization of many service activities may not be possible. Many services are controlled by governmental agencies such as the Bank of Thailand or are public enterprises (such as the Thai International Airways Corporation, the Telephone Authority of Thailand, the State Railways of Thailand), and they are likely to continue to operate under government control. There may be a higher degree of privatization, but this does not necessarily mean that public services will become more liberalized. Privatization that aims at greater efficiency might create monopolistic practices in the short run. Although the economy may at first experience a positive impact, such practices might not be conducive to continuous growth in the longer run.

Policy recipes for Thailand should be based on diversity, flexibility and adaptability. The government must support service growth by promoting private and public investment in diverse services; by encouraging foreign participation in development; and by giving the private sector incentives to promote technological development. Last but not least, the government should support extensive labour-training programmes and education for the long-term development of various service activities. The success of these programmes will ensure the possibility and sustainability of service-led growth in Thailand.

Notes

1. There is some evidence showing that the service sector is one of the most important sources of employment, raising the question of whether the sector is recession-proof. See Urquhart, 1981, pp. 12–8.

2. For a detailed illustration of the impact of tourism see Somchai, 1990.
3. This figure was only a subset of the whole employment impact. It does not include indirect effects and some informal activities, for example small industries related to entertainment, handicrafts (wood carving, brassware, weaving) and jewellery, which constituted a large part of urban informal employment for the migrant labour force.
4. For example, see Riddle, 1986.
5. Recently, Bangkok lost out to Singapore as the site for APEC head-quarters because of its worsening traffic conditions.
6. Recommendations for trade liberalization, especially services, is discussed extensively in Castle and Findlay, 1988.

5 Public–Private Sector Partnership in Industrialization

Kraiyudht Dhiratayakinant

5.1 INTRODUCTION

The aim of this chapter is neither to analyze the possibility of Thailand becoming the next Asian NIC, nor to analyze the impact of industrialization on the economy and its people and the desirability of continued stress on growth. Instead the focus will be on the nature of the public–private partnership in industrialization over 30 years of development effort. The chapter will also attempt to anticipate public–private relations in future development efforts in the light of economic progress and political democratization in Thailand.

The chapter is divided into five sections. Sections 5.2 to 5.4 analyze three decades of industrial development by focusing on industrial policies and the relative roles of the public and private sectors in the formation of these policies. Section 5.5 looks at the pattern of the public–private partnership in the 1990s. Finally, Section 5.6 offers some observations on the nature of public–private interaction in industrial-policy formulation.

5.2 THE FIRST DECADE OF INDUSTRIAL DEVELOPMENT: THE IMPORTANCE OF THE PUBLIC SECTOR

According to Narongchai (1986, p. 1), Thailand has never been able to formulate a so-called 'industrial plan'. Rather, industrialization in Thailand has come about through policies that formed part of the economic and social-development plan. Though certain strategies have been adopted, there has never been a coordinated and pattern-specific industrial-development approach (Mingsarn and Adis, 1988, p. 157).

The main thrust of industrialization in Thailand has been reliance on the private sector to generate economic growth within the framework of a free-market economy. This approach is the reverse of an industrialization strategy based on formal planning.

The detail of industrial policies has been formulated within this grand strategy. The manner in which these policies were formulated in each five-year development plan reflects the relative role of the public and private sectors in the development process. The development relationship between the public and the private sectors has varied over the past 30 years. For the purpose of the following description the balance of this relationship can be described according to three periods. The 1960s saw the dominance of the public sector; the dynamics of the private sector was preeminent in the 1970s; and in the 1980s the private sector became an equal partner in economic development.

5.2.1 Industrial Policies of the 1960s

The first decade of industrial development in Thailand covered the period guided by the first two national development plans, namely the First Economic Development Plan (1961–6) and the Second Economic Development Plan (1967–71).[1]

After the relatively unstable economy of the 1950s and the unsuccessful attempt with state capitalism in the late 1940s and the 1950s, the first two development plans called for the state to stop expanding its public-enterprise sector (Wirat *et al.*, 1988) and to provide the necessary economic environment in which the private sector could pursue its economic interests.

Specifically, the principal objective in the First Development Plan was to stimulate economic growth via an increase in private investment. To achieve this overall objective the government invested heavily in basic infrastructure, namely electricity-generating stations, highways, inland waterways and air-transport facilities, as well as improving the telephone and postal services. In addition to the provision of physical infrastructure to facilitate private undertakings, the government also reactivated the Investment Promotion Act of 1954, with major improvements in incentive provisions. For example tax concessions (exemption from business tax and import duties) were granted for imported machinery, equipment, raw materials and other imported intermediate inputs used in preferred industries. Five-year income-tax holidays were also given to promoted manufacturers. To be promoted were import-substitution industries. As an added incentive, taxes on consumer imports were raised to protect promoted domestic industries. The Board of Investment (BOI), the administering office of the Investment Promotion Act, became very powerful as it had considerable discretion to grant these incentive benefits.[2]

The revision of the act served as an additional sign that the government was genuinely interested in promoting industrialization. In this sense the incentive measures provided by the revised Investment Promotion Act directly encouraged the expansion of industries producing for import substitution, which was to continue throughout the 1960s. Some economists (for example Mingsarn and Adis, 1988) have suggested that although the inducement effects of these incentive measures were not large, they did serve as an additional positive force in conjunction with other favourable factors (for example increased domestic demand induced by US involvement in Vietnam and the build-up in response to Thailand's internal security problems) to generate increased investment by local entrepreneurs and foreigners in import-substitution industries.

The concept of the public sector as the active provider of basic facilities for the economy was upheld in the Second Development Plan and the government continued to invest heavily in physical infrastructure.[3] Public enterprises were confined to providing utilities.

The Second Development Plan also identified for the first time certain industries with growth potential that would be promoted, namely the paper, chemical-fertilizer, iron and steel, automobile assembly, cement, gunny bag and textile industries. This conveyed to the private sector the message that these industries were officially favoured. The Second Plan also encouraged the private sector to expand its exploitation of mineral resources and explore new mineral deposits, as well as to develop the mining system. Moreover, certain private enterprises invested in other industries that later proved to be the leading industries in Thailand.

The specific measures to promote industries were implemented in conjunction with the overall macro policies adopted to create a stable environment for the economy. Among these were disciplinary fiscal policies that emphasized productive public spending within the constraints imposed by the budget. Funding was met by increases in tax revenue while domestic borrowing was used in such a way as to minimize its impact on price levels. Equally important were the policies of promoting a free-market economy and restricting the role of public enterprises in direct competition with private undertakings.

5.2.2 The Formation of Industrial Policies

The first two national economic development plans were the product of Thai bureaucrats at the Office of the National Economic Development Board which later became the Office of the National Economic and Social Development Board (NESDB) with the assistance of Western experts.[4] The objectives and the policies adopted were, of course, influenced by Western economic-development theories of the time.

Thus the industrialization strategy was formulated within the bureaucracy and without the participation of the private sector. The import-substitution strategy adopted was a product of the then orthodox understanding of economic development. It was also a reasonable response to the economic situation of the time. The exportation of agricultural products was increasing slowly, while the importation of consumer products was rising, creating increased trade deficits. More than just the saving of foreign exchange, the import-substitution strategy was also viewed as an effective way of reducing Thailand's dependence on imports of foreign consumer goods.

The 1960s saw the public sector as the leading sector, both as the formulator of industrial strategy and as an active investor in areas essential to industrialization. This predominant role of the public sector is understandable for two reasons. One has to do with the prevalent understanding of the economic development process in the Western world, and the other the perception of the private sector in the development process within Thailand.

The economic-development literature of the time noted the failure of the market system to generate and accelerate the expansion of an economy, given the rigidities of the economic subsystems. With the predominance of Keynesian economics, the extension of the role of the state in the development process of a developing economy was reasonable. When the formal development process was initiated with the launching of the First National Development Plan, the Thai private sector, which had shown enterprise since the opening of the country to the world, was already thriving in commercial ventures (Suehiro, 1989; Ingram, 1971). It was only natural to place greater emphasis on the public sector to initiate important investment projects of certain size in the expectation that the new economic environment would prompt private entrepreneurs to seize the opportunities thus opened to them. Fortunately for Thailand this expectation was realized in the next decade and beyond, despite the existing obstacles.

5.3 THE SECOND DECADE OF INDUSTRIAL DEVELOPMENT: THE DYNAMISM OF THE PRIVATE SECTOR

5.3.1 Economic Environment of the Thai Economy

The 1970s saw instability in both the economic and the political sphere. In the first year of the decade the Thai economy experienced reductions in exported agricultural products and increases in imported capital and consumer goods. The trade balance was in the red and Thailand's international reserves decreased steadily.

The first oil shock in 1973 rocked the world economy. The developed countries had to adjust their policies in the face of rising oil prices and cope with economic fluctuations and recession. Thailand was more fortunate in this instance. Although rising oil prices caused the import bill to increase considerably, Thai agricultural exports also commanded higher prices, reducing the size of trade deficits. Rising prices of agricultural exports also raised the income of the agricultural sector and sustained the expansion of import-substitution industries in the face of the economic instability generated by the world market.

However, because of worldwide economic fluctuations, domestic investment also decreased. Political instability in the period created an atmosphere of economic uncertainty, making the domestic economy more unstable and more unpredictable. Political changes in neighbouring countries increased the weight of the internal security issue and encouraged public measures to mitigate political discontent. Equally important was instability within the political sphere. There were several changes in the government and several coup attempts during the decade.

5.3.2 Industrial Policies in the 1970s

Facing potential decline in domestic demand due to the phasing out of US involvement in the Vietnam War in the early 1970s, the formulators of industrial-development policies made certain changes of emphasis in the Third and Fourth Development Plans. The period covered by the Third Plan (1972–6) was a period of export-promotion strategies. Stronger measures were enacted to generate export manufacturing industries. Among these measures the most significant were the revision of the Investment Act in 1972 and the improvement of public and bureaucratic services. The Investment Promotion Act was revised to increase tax incentives to promoted investments. For example, import tax was removed from imported inputs used in export activities, and business tax was lifted from exported products. The Bank of Thailand was empowered to offer discount facilities on short-term loans for export activities.

The industrial policies of the Third Plan also set priorities for the types of exports to be promoted, namely industries using domestic raw materials and labour-intensive industries located in regions outside the Bangkok Metropolitan Region (BMR). Tourism, as an important part of the export sector, began to receive due attention in the period of the Third Plan. Policies to develop and encourage the expansion of domestic facilities for tourism were pursued more systematically during this period. In order to facilitate the investment process changes in laws and regulations were made to facilitate business transactions and speed up government permits and privileges.

While the export-promotion policy created a new sense of direction, the promotion of import-substitution industries was continued as a matter of routine when existing privileges did not conflict with the new export-promotion policy. In fact there was a reduction in import tariffs on raw materials, intermediate products and capital machinery during the middle of the Third Plan, which obviously benefited import-substitution industries relative to export industries. The requirement of local content was introduced for car assembly. Small and medium-scale industries in provincial and rural areas also received some attention during this period, although effective measures were not implemented (Somsak, 1990).

The emphasis on the export sector and support for import-substitution industries were continued under the Fourth Development Plan. The approach was to encourage both sectors, but with variations of emphasis between the two. Detailed policy measures were almost wholly confined to these principal sectors.

The period of the Fourth Plan, identified by the experts as 'the big-push period' (Mingsarn and Adis, 1988), or as 'the second import-substitution period' (Paitoon, 1987), saw marked changes in the Thai industrialization policy. A large-scale industrial development programme, the so-called Eastern Seaboard (ESB) Development Programme was formulated. The programme represented a strategy of regional industrialization and large-scale planned investment that covered three provinces along the eastern coast of Thailand. In Chon Buri Province, the Laem Chabang area was the designated location for light and export-oriented industries. The Rayong area was to house heavy industries, mainly the petrochemical complex at Mab Ta Put. Further inland is the Chachoengsao area, which was to site various agro-based industries.

The ESB programme was prompted by the discovery of natural gas in the Gulf of Thailand and the intention of utilizing it to speed up the industrialization process. The Eastern Seaboard was to serve as an alternative industrial location to the BMR, where most industrial undertakings were to be found, and as a gateway to the development of the lower north-eastern region of Thailand. The investment programme to be implemented was very ambitious. A deepsea port, and export-processing zone, a piped-water reservoir and a railway line, among other things, were planned for the Laem Chabang area; and a major industrial estate was to be built at Mab Ta Put, where the existing deepsea port and airport were to be expanded. Electricity supply, road links and telecommunications were also to be improved.

The full potential of this industrial complex has yet to be realized due to an inability to generate the capital required for such an ambitious undertaking, although the amount needed was later scaled down. Slow implementation was also due to the hesitancy of certain leading public policy makers in the face of the financial constraints and continued fluctuations of the world economy. Nonetheless necessary investments were made, and government support was given to all succeeding industrial policies, although the soundness of the programme has been questioned.[5]

Another new aspect of the industrial policy in this period was the increased protection given to heavy industries producing intermediate and capital goods, which have increasingly become the major users of foreign exchange. This new policy prompted some economists, as noted earlier, to view this period as the second import-substitution period. The promotion of intermediate and capital-good industries was made in conjunction with the development of the Eastern Seaboard.

5.3.3 The Dynamism of the Private Sector

The industrial policies expressed in the Third and Fourth Development Plans were again the product of the public sector, the principal actor being the NESDB. The economic, political and social problems of the period were identified by the bureaucrats and the measures to alleviate or eliminate them were those considered by these bureaucrats to be the most effective. The analyses and conclusions were still coloured by the economic-development theories of the West, which played an important role in all stages of plan formulation.

Prior to the 1980s the private sector had never been prominent in Thai public decision making. Private entrepreneurs, even very successful ones, were looked upon by bureaucrats with suspicion and were considered rather to be selfish profit seekers who lacked proper regard for the public interest. Attempts by politicians from the private sector to involve business organizations and leading private entrepreneurs in economic policy formulation within the existing bureaucratic setting also failed. This was so in spite of the fact that as early as the Third Plan organized businesses were encouraged to participate formally in the formation of economic policies.[6] In the context just noted, reasonable complaints and economic advice from the private sector were regarded as self-serving and of benefit to private interests alone at the expense of the public interest.

In spite of the good intention of the development plans and the government that adopted them, the economic environment was not always favourable to the private sector. Moreover, tax privileges and other investment incentives were added over the period without effective coordination, resulting in confusion and lower effectiveness (Mingsarn and Adis, 1988, p. 192). It has also been noted that this 'ad hoc and complex system of investment incentive almost certainly has many unintended and counterproductive consequences that are contrary to the policies' stated goals' (Dapice and Flatters, 1989, p. 7). Certainly the private sector tried to make use of these tax privileges and investment incentives despite administrative inconvenience and economic drawbacks, though a number of expanding manufacturing industries that had not even been on the promoted-industries list became producers for export.

Despite these constraints the Thai economy did move ahead at a satisfactory pace. This suggests that the prime mover of the economy was the private sector. It was noted, albeit with some exaggeration, by former Prime Minister Kukrit Pramoj that 'economic growth thus far has been the result of the exclusive efforts and initiatives of businessmen, while the government has been indifferent and passive throughout. [Only] when problems arise does the government step in, mostly to control or to regulate selling prices' (quoted in Anek, 1992, p. 130).

In other words, the private sector took the economic environment, both favourable and unfavourable, as given and seized the economic opportunities that had opened in the domestic and international markets. Private entrepreneurs secured information on trade and drew their own conclusions. They were sufficiently dynamic to react profitably to economic implications and the prevailing situation. Their actions were rewarded by larger profits, greater wealth, and increasing confidence and expertise. The economy grew at a respectable rate over the decade as a result of the private sector's initiatives within the policy framework set by the public sector.

5.4 THE THIRD DECADE OF INDUSTRIAL DEVELOPMENT: THE INCREASING ROLE OF THE PRIVATE SECTOR IN POLICY FORMULATION

5.4.1 The Economy in the 1980s

The early 1980s was a period of slow growth for the Thai economy. Because the world economy again was experiencing instability as the result of the second oil shock, more trade protection was observed in leading industrial economies. Thailand's exports were not growing as rapidly as had been expected and agricultural exports actually experienced a decline in value. The situation created greater uncertainty in the export market for Thai manufactured and agricultural products, and there was an increase in the trade deficit. The domestic budget moved into the red with rising external debt, resulting in high inflation. This negative aspect of the economy was reinforced by natural resources such as land, forest and fishery being depleted at an alarming rate. Moreover, in spite of the growth experienced by the Thai economy, income inequality in terms of people and regions increased and certain areas of the country were still in extreme poverty.

Industrial activities were still concentrated in the BMR, despite efforts by the government to regionalize industrial location. As a consequence traffic congestion was, and still is, a major problem in Bangkok, which has become a bottleneck in the movement of goods and people.

The latter half of the 1980s saw an improvement in the Thai economy. From 1986 the growth rate was high, generating a widespread feeling that the economy had finally reached a take-off stage and that Thailand was about to join the ranks of the Asian NICs. Towards the end of the decade the economy registered double-digit growth for three consecutive years (1988–90). Continued growth created a shortage of skilled manpower, causing wage rates to creep upward. Undersupply of infrastructure facilities became increasingly obvious in the late 1980s, pushing up costs of production.

5.4.2 The Industrial Policies of the Period

The general direction of industrialization policies were similar to those adopted in the 1970s. The export sector received the greatest attention, while tourism, as a principal component of the export sector, received greater support from the government along with other export manufacturing sectors, via monetary and fiscal measures.

As earlier, promotion of the export sector was not carried out at the expense of domestic manufacturing industries. The latter were continuously promoted, and the establishment of industries in regions away from the BMR was encouraged. More attention was given to rural industries. Private investment was encouraged in progressive agricultural areas to provide employment for rural people. In short, regionalization of industries producing for the domestic market and/or for export received greater emphasis in the 1980s. Promotion criteria expressed in the Investment Promotion Act were revised in 1989. The attractiveness of promotion privileges varied with location, which were classified into three zones for the purpose of investment promotion.

The 1980s also marked a new approach to Thai industrialization. The role of the private sector was appreciated and development policies of this decade called for greater participation of the private sector in the development effort, particularly in spreading economic benefits to other parts of the country via location decisions. The adoption of a 'privatization' philosophy was more energetic, as expressed in the Sixth Development Plan (1987–91).

Although Thailand has always adopted a 'free-market' philosophy it was not until the 1980s that the private sector was expected to participate in the expansion of activities (such as the telephone service, expressways, or research and development in science and technology) that were formerly considered to be in the public domain. The private sector, considered broadly to include non-profit private organization and other informally organized private groups (NGOs), was encouraged to participate in the prevention of economic and social problems and the identification of their solutions.

5.4.3 The Process of Private Participation

Private-sector participation entered a new phase in the 1980s and in light of the triumph of free-market ideology worldwide this will probably endure. The private sector actually began to participate in the policy-formulation process,[7] especially with regard to short-term measures to alleviate economic problems facing the private sector. Because of its historical importance the development of the private sector as an actor is described below.

At the outset it should be noted that interactions among leading figures in the public and private sectors predated the formalization of an active partnership between the two sectors. Interactions were based on personal friendship and an informal network of social acquaintances. When the economic order was not very complex, the scope of economic activities was not wide-ranging and the number of businessmen in all fields was within a manageable size, informal interactions to channel desired actions and remedy problems was easily undertaken and the results sometimes significantly changed the course of economic events. However, when the economy became increasing complex, the scope of economic activities broadened, the number of businessmen increased and the number of commodity groups became extensive, informal or personal interactions could no longer act to steer the economy in the desired direction. The multidimensional facets of problems could not be addressed by the limited access to information and narrow perspectives that characterize personal interaction. The necessity for a formal channel of communication was increasingly drawn to the attention of government leaders.

The private sector, too, realized that the complexity of economic problems faced by businessmen called for a consultation mechanism to settle differences and come up with effective solutions. The leading trade associations (the Thai Chamber of Commerce, the Association of Thai Industries and the Thai Bankers Association) formed the so-called the Private Consultative Committee (PCC) with membership from all these associations and a rotating chairmanship. This active cooperation among different private-sector economic groups anticipated and indeed set the example for the realization of the formalized cooperation between the public and the private sectors.

In 1981, under the leadership of the then prime minister General Prem Tinsulanond, the Joint Public–Private Consultative Committee (the JPPCC or the Joint Committee for short) was established to solve economic problems, with secretarial assistance being provided by the

National Economic and Social Development Board (NESDB). It should be noted, however, that prior to 1981 there had been many attempts to formalize an active public–private partnership, though without much success. The failure to bring about such a partnership was due mainly to a lack of mutual trust and confidence and an underdeveloped capacity for joint effort.

The establishment of the Joint Committee ushered in a new philosophy of development in Thailand: development that was carried out jointly by the public and private sectors. It indicated the government's determination both to seek advice and cooperation from the private sector in solving national economic problems and to assist the development of the private sector as an institution working responsibly for the development of society.[8]

The Joint Committee proved able to iron out certain problems and obstacles faced by Bangkok businessmen, so the idea of setting up provincial public–private consultative committees was enthusiastically received. Provincial JPPCCs have been set up throughout Thailand under the supervision of the Ministry of Interior. The chairman of each provincial JPPCC is the provincial governor and its members are heads of government agencies and leading businessmen in the province. The task of provincial JPPCCs is to help solve local problems and promote the local economy. This may require the assistance of central government, and the provincial governor, as head of the local administration, can request help from central government directly or through the National JPPCC machinery (see Sawaeng, 1986).

5.4.4 Policy Contributions by the Private Sector

Since its inception the National Joint Committee has focused mainly on the following areas: (1) reviewing and improving laws and regulations that obstruct private entrepreneurial activities, (2) policy formulation, (3) information collection and dissemination, (4) developing agriculture and the agro-industry, and (5) developing a provincial partnership. This is not the place for a critical evaluation of the impact of the JPPCC, but a few points might be made.[9]

The most important achievement in the area of laws and regulations was the revisions of customs duties and procedures. The speedy introduction of value added tax in 1992 may be attributed to its acceptance by the JPPCC. In the area of policy formulation, two important areas of emphasis by the JPPCC were export promotion and tourism. Representatives from the JPPCC were invited to join several government trade missions to the United States, Europe and Asia during the prime ministership of General Prem to highlight export policy action and encourage privately led trade and investment policies. Trade expansion with Soviet Russia and countries in the Eastern Bloc was also the result of the JPPCC initiative.

In many instances the influence of the JPPCC was indirect, through representation on the executive BOI committee and subcommittees, on the national committees on industrial policy, and on other policy committees.

5.5 THE NATURE OF THE PUBLIC–PRIVATE PARTNERSHIP IN THE 1990s

5.5.1 Economy and Polity of Thailand in the 1990s

There is no turning back for the Thai economy. Its march towards NIC status seems unstoppable, although it may take longer than anticipated due to the recent internal political instability and the increasing call for more redistributive measures. At the same time the Thai economy faces a greater degree of competition in its traditional export markets. The grouping of countries into trading areas represents a greater potential for as well as a threat to the growth of Thailand's exports. However, given the enterprising nature of the private sector, the principal determinant of the continued growth of the Thai economy will be public policies that assist private enterprises and enhance Thailand's international competitiveness.

New policies along these lines are now taking shape in a new political structure.[10] The latter part of the 1980s saw the continued process of democratization in Thailand. The government of General Chartichai Choonhavan, and members of the cabinet were involved in business both at the local level and nationwide. This reflected the increasing involvement of business in Thai politics.

This setting has led to active private participation in the political process and in the formation of public policy, and policies favourable to the private sector in the context of public interest have been advanced.[11] It has been noted that political openness and the informal interaction between businessmen and politicians were important ingredients of the so-called 'buffet cabinet' of the Chartichai government. Corruption charges emanating from these close political–business relations were cited among the reasons for the coup d'état of February 1991.

The new government of Anand Panyarachun, under the tutelage of the so-called the National Peace-Keeping Council, was private-sector oriented by profession and inclination. Prime Minister Anand was head of the Federation of Thai Industries (FTI) before becoming the head of the new government, and a number of his cabinet members were leading executives of big corporations. There were accusations that policies adopted by the Anand government promoted the private interests of certain groups at the expense of the public interest.

Anand Panyarachun was reappointed prime minister after the May uprising of 1992, but after a short interlude the present democratic government took over. Democratization in Thailand will, at least for the time being, continue. With many businessmen as cabinet members, the active role of the private sector is expected to continue.

5.5.2 Policy Formulation in the Early 1990s

The end of the 1980s and the beginning of 1990s was a period in which a new national plan was formulated and endorsed by the government. The private sector had greater involvement in the formulation of the Seventh Development Plan (1992–6). Amnuay Virawan, Chairman of the NESDB executive board, has been a leading banker in Thailand and in early 1994 became deputy prime minister in the current Chuan government.[12] Other Board members also come from the private sector. Input for the Seventh Development Plan came not only from leading bureaucrats and academicians, but also from elected politicians and non-elected cabinet members directly involved in the policy-formulation process. Moreover, various private groups, business associations and NGOs also put forward their views.

We should also emphasize that the existence of a formal public–private partnership (via for example the JPPCC) can counteract the possible negative impact on the economy generated by informal, personal partnerships. Similarly, informal channels in the public–private partnership may actually enhance the effectiveness of a formal partnership such as the JPPCC. This would happen when policies advocated by the JPPCC coincide with the interests of businessmen who also have personal political contacts. In view of the fact that informal public–private partnerships have been made more effective by political democratization, it is necessary to stress the importance of strengthening the effectiveness of the formal mechanism of public–private partnership.

The fact that meetings of the national JPPCC are infrequent does not by itself suggest that the private contribution to policy formation is small, but the involvement of the private sector in public policy must increase in line with the private sector's growing stake in the economy. The private sector's wealth and economic significance will inevitably force it to play a more active role in order to protect its interests.

5.5.3 Anticipated Improvements in the Quality of the Public–Private Partnership

The Thai economy in the 1990s is increasingly dependent on the export sector and is thus significantly affected by the world economy. Economic fluctuations in developed countries have an impact on Thailand's exports. The economic grouping of countries will also create greater competition for Thai exports. To prosper in the face of such trends the Thai economy must be quick to identify potential problems and possible solutions, flexible in its adjustment and effective in implementing policies.

Rapidly identifying problems and solutions requires speedy access to information and well-documented past issues and solutions. Flexibility of adjustment implies a public bureaucracy that is ready to adopt required changes in policy. Effective implementation of policies suggests provision of adequate resources and an effective accountability system.

The private sector can be very effective in generating information on problems and possible solutions. Industrialists facing similar problems to those of government are in the best position to analyze them, and an effective channel should be set up between the public and private sectors to expedite the flow of information and reduce its cost. Since it is in the private interest to effect such channels, public–private cooperation may be expected to be strengthened in the 1990s.

The Thai bureaucracy has adjusted well to the new circumstances, which include adopting development policies. Until the late 1980s changes and adjustments were more or less effected from within. The clear emergence of a vociferous private sector in the early 1990s, speeded up by the recognition of its importance in the industrialization process and nurtured by political democratization, represents an external pressure that could force the changes necessary to maintain the continued prosperity of the private sector. In this circumstance public–private cooperation in the 1990s will be one in which the private sector will begin to be more assertive. The multitude of demands for corrective measures to sustain the economy and the quick response of the bureaucracy after the recent uprising are evidence of this development.

The demand for results by the private sector, NGOs included, will lead to greater accountability of the public sector. With an ever bigger stake in the well-being of the economy it is in the interests of the private sector to push for the effective implementation of relevant policies. Channels of communication may become more informal as the private sector assumes a more active stance in the political process. Accommodation of private demands might not take place through the formal apparatus of cooperation, which remain as set up in the early 1980s, but because of the fuller development of the mass media, business associations and other private interest groups will figure significantly in the decision-making process in the public sector.

5.6 CONCLUDING REMARKS

The industrialization strategy of Thailand would not have been as effective over such a long period had the economic environment for private enterprise been less stable and favourable. In any public arena, the economic environment is governed by fiscal, monetary, trade and industrial policies. The private arena is influenced by economic and non-economic events generated from within and outside the economy. When favourable economic policies coincide with a favourable general environment, private enterprise will flourish. This scenario has actually happened in Thailand over the past 30 years. The success story of Thailand has to do with favourable exogenous economic circumstances (or one might say 'luck') that reduced the severity of economic instability caused by economic fluctuations in developed countries, and stimulated Thai exports. But these favourable economic circumstances would not have born fruit if energetic private entrepreneurs had not existed in Thailand. Similarly, a sizeable private sector would not have been present if the industrial policies pursued by the government had been unfavourable or unstable.

The upsurge of the private sector has placed a greater demand on the government to handle economic and environmental policies with competence. In the light of democratization presently taking place in Thailand, it remains to be seen whether or not the government will be able to provide a stable political environment in which the private sector can confidently carry out its development tasks.

Notes

1. The First Development Plan consisted of two phases, each covering a period of three years. The First Development Plan was thus a six-year plan while the succeeding plans covered five years each.
2. For early development of the BOI and the incentives offered, see Silcock, 1967, ch. 11.
3. Due to the political situation in the country induced by fear of the communist ideology, special emphasis was placed on the rapid expansion of the road system throughout the country and the expansion of telecommunications in the north-eastern and the southern regions.
4. For a history of the development plans, interested readers are referred to, for example, Wirat *et al.*, 1988.
5. For more detail of the ESB development programme, see Savit, 1990.
6. For a detailed historical account of business associations and their emerging role in policy formulation, see Anek, 1992.
7. For a description of the process from the perspective of a policy scientist, see Somboon, 1990.
8. For a detailed description of formal mechanism for cooperation, see Kraiyudht, 1990.
9. For a detailed evaluation of the policy contribution of the national JPPCC, see Kraiyudht, 1990. For specific actions, see NESDB, 1986b, 1987a and 1988. Sawaeng (1986) offers an early evaluation of the JPPCC apparatus. For an evaluation of provincial JPPCC, see Ministry of Interior, 1992.
10. A recent attempt to interpret the nature of Thai polity is Anek, 1992.
11. We do not intend to pass judgment here on whether or not private interest will truly coincide with public interest. We merely intend to show that private entrepreneurs try to promote their interests by emphasizing that the economy as a whole will prosper if their suggestions are heeded.
12. In July 1994, however, Amnuay resigned from the government to set up his own political party expected to contest in the next general election.

6 Rural Industrialization: Problems and Prospects

Nipon Poapongsakorn

6.1 INTRODUCTION

Thailand has been widely regarded as one of the economies with the most successful industrialization based upon an export-oriented policy. Although this belief should be questioned, Thailand's success can be largely explained by highly disciplined macroeconomic management policies, despite the fact that all Thai governments have lacked sound microeconomic policies (Christensen *et al.*, 1992). Industrialization, however, is highly concentrated in and around Bangkok. Industrial decentralization has just started but the extent of rural industry is still very limited, largely because of rural poverty, small market size in the rural area, inadequate and poor infrastructure facilities and negative government policies against rural and small-scale industries.

The objective of this chapter is to explain the slow growth of rural industry.[1] Section 6.2 describes the changes in the pattern of regional industry. The limited nature of rural industry is discussed in Section 6.3 and Section 6.4 provides an analysis of the factors that prohibit the growth of rural industry. Finally, Section 6.5 presents the conclusions.

6.2 CHANGES IN THE REGIONAL INDUSTRIAL PATTERN

6.2.1 Trends in Industrial Decentralization

Most available records show that since the late 1980s most manufacturing activities have been heavily concentrated in and around Bangkok. For example the Registries of Factories from the Department of Industrial Works show that in 1987 the number of manufacturing establishments in Bangkok and its surrounding provinces (so-called inner-ring and outer-ring provinces) accounted for some 60 per cent of total manufacturing establishments in the whole kingdom (Table 6.1). More importantly, the value added from these manufacturing activities in Bangkok and its vicinities often constituted more than three-quarters of the total value added from manufacturing activities for the whole country. However, it appears that there was some attempt to decentralize these manufacturing activities during the late 1980s. As shown in Table 6.1, since 1987 manufacturing establishments have not only dispersed towards the inner ring, but also towards the outer ring and outer regions, especially the north-east and the north. As a result of very high growth rates during the 1987–91 period, the combined share of manufacturing establishments in these three regions now exceeds that of Bangkok. In fact the share of establishments in Bangkok started to decline in the early 1980s, and by 1991 it had already declined by almost 10 percent-age points, reflecting the higher cost of locating plants in Bangkok.

Within the inner ring, Samut Prakarn has the largest number of factories, but the birth rate of new establishments was the highest in the provinces of Nakhon Pathom, Samut Sakhon and Pathum Thani (Tables 6.2 and 6.3). Other provinces with large numbers of factories

Table 6.1 Regional distribution and change of manufacturing establishments, 1981–91

	1981	*1985*	*1987*	*1991*		*Growth rate (%)*	
				(%)	*(no.)*	*1981–7*	*1987–91*
Bangkok	45.01	45.06	41.68	36.50	20 248	−0.4	4.5
Inner Ring	9.70	10.90	12.25	13.68	7801	4.8	11.3
Outer Ring	10.74	9.79	9.82	10.68	6089	−1.1	10.6
Centre	6.29	6.53	6.59	6.88	3927	2.6	9.6
North	7.75	8.66	9.35	10.60	6046	4.1	11.6
North-east	13.19	11.80	12.90	15.05	8581	0.5	12.3
South	7.32	7.21	7.41	7.61	4341	1.1	9.2
Total %	100.00	100.00	100.00	100.00	–	–	–
Total no.	38 476	37 776	40 591	–	57 033	0.9	8.5
Rice Mills (no.)	41 741	47 245	46 638	–	45 690	1.9	−0.5

Note: inner ring = Samut Prakan, Samut Sakhon, Pathum Thani, Nonthaburi and Nakhon Pathom; outer ring = Ayutthaya, Angthong, Saraburi, Nakhon Nayok, Chachoengsao, Chon Buri, Suphan Buri, Ratchaburi, Kanchanaburi and Samut Songkhram.
Source: Division of Factory Control, Department of Industrial Works.

Table 6.2 Number of manufacturing establishments in selected provinces, 1981–91

				Annual growth rate (%)	
Province	*1981*	*1987*	*1991*	*1981–7*	*1987–91*
Bangkok	17319	16920	20248	−0.39	4.59
Centre	2290	2673	3927	2.61	10.09
Inner Ring	3733	4974	7801	4.90	11.91
Samut Prakan	1950	2526	3716	4.41	10.13
Samut Sakhon	446	767	1317	9.46	14.47
Pathum Thani	364	462	800	4.05	14.71
Nonthaburi	473	609	871	4.30	9.36
Nakhon Pathom	500	610	1097	3.37	15.80
Outer Ring	4259	3986	6089	−1.10	11.17
Ayutthaya	267	300	411	1.96	8.19
Angthong	137	76	208	−9.35	28.62
Saraburi	328	326	490	−0.10	10.72
Nakhon Nayok	45	48	97	1.08	19.23
Chachoengsao	347	331	529	−0.78	12.44
Chon Buri	1237	1030	1344	−3.01	6.88
Suphan Buri	367	584	786	8.05	7.71
Ratchaburi	883	624	922	−5.62	10.25
Khanchanaburi	522	574	1134	1.60	18.56
Samut Songkhram	126	93	168	−4.94	15.93
North	2982	3795	6046	4.10	12.35
Lampang	452	503	626	1.80	5.62
Chiang Mai	465	577	676	3.66	4.04
Phitsanulok	201	662	709	21.98	1.73
Nakhon Sawan	486	643	666	4.78	0.88
North-east	5074	5236	8581	0.53	13.14
Udon Thani	696	1044	1105	6.99	1.43
Khon Kaen	624	962	1016	7.48	1.37
Nakhon Ratchasima	1424	1955	2148	5.42	2.38
Ubon Ratchathani	424	472	558	1.80	4.27
South	2816	3007	4341	1.10	9.61
Surat Thani	283	523	554	10.78	1.45
Nakhon Si Thammarat	401	525	590	4.59	2.96
Songkhla	668	668	721	0.00	1.93
Whole Kingdom	38476	53039	57033	5.50	1.83

Source: Factory Registration Files, Department of Industrial Works.

Table 6.3 Distribution of manufacturing establishments in Bangkok and the inner ring, 1984–91

	All establishments 1984		*New establishments*				*Birth rate (%)*	
			1987		*1991*		*1984–7*	*1987–91*
	(No.)	*(%)*	*(No.)*	*(%)*	*(No.)*	*(%)*		
Bangkok	16 920	77.28	1256	67.00	1695	62.90	7.42	9.33
Samut Prakan	2526	11.54	306	16.30	396	14.70	12.11	13.98
Samut Sakhon	767	3.50	114	6.10	216	8.00	24.52	n.a.
Pathum Thani	462	2.11	78	4.10	111	4.10	16.88	20.56
Nonthaburi	609	2.78	54	2.90	71	2.60	8.87	10.71
Nakhon Pathom	610	2.79	67	3.60	202	7.50	10.98	29.84
Total	21 844	100.00	1875	100.00	2691	100.00	8.56	11.32

Note: Birth rate in 1984–87 = number of new factories in 1987 divided by all factories in 1984; Birth rate in 1987–91 = number of new factories in 1991 divided by all factories in 1987.
Sources: World Bank, 1989, p. 103; original data obtained from Factory Registration Files, Department of Industrial Works; 1991 data are from Factory Registration Files, Department of Industrial Works.

and a high growth rate of manufacturing enterprises include Nakhon Ratchasima and Khon Kaen in the north-east; Chiang Mai, Phitsanulok and Nakhon Sawan in the north; Songkhla and Surat Thani in the south.

The data on the distribution of new projects receiving investment privileges from the Board of Investment (Table 6.4) are even more revealing. Since 1988 increasing numbers of new large projects have chosen to locate their plants in the outer ring and other regions rather than in Bangkok. Until 1987 more than half of the industries under the 21 standard TSIC categories (16 in 1977 and 12 in 1987) had more than 50 per cent of factories registered in Bangkok (Table 6.5, p. 122).[2] However in 1991 only five industries had more than 50 per cent of factories located in Bangkok. This clearly shows that more and more industries have found it more profitable to locate outside Bangkok. Yet there are still some that have to take advantage of agglomeration economies by remaining in Bangkok. Examples of these are the garment, printing and plastic industries. Except in the inner ring area, manufacturing activities are generally concentrated into a few resource-based industries. The food, beverage and machinery industries are the three most important industries in all regions outside Bangkok. Wood products and non-metallic mineral products are the next most

Table 6.4 Regional distribution of BOI-approved projects, 1986–91 (%)

	1986	*1987*	*1988*	*1989*	*1990*	*1991*
Bangkok and Samut Prakan	34.8	44.9	29.1	29.0	26.0	21.6
Four surrounding provinces[1]	15.2	26.0	15.9	16.9	16.9	10.2
10 provinces in the centre[2]	20.5	12.1	23.3	27.4	26.9	25.4
Centre[3]	7.3	5.8	9.8	8.0	8.4	12.0
North	2.7	2.7	3.2	6.3	7.5	9.1
North-east	2.0	1.9	2.3	4.7	5.7	10.6
South	16.2	6.0	16.3	7.6	8.5	11.1
Not specified	1.3	0.6	0.1	0.1	0.1	0.0
Total	100.0	100.0	100.0	100.0	100.0	100.0
Memo item: number	302	635	1482	1179	933	606

Notes:
1. Pathum Thani, Nonthaburi, Nakhon Pathom and Samut Sakhon.
2. Samut Songkhram, Ratchburi, Kanchanaburi, Suphanburi, Angthong, Ayutthaya, Saraburi, Nakhon Nayok, Chachoengsao and Chon Buri.
3. The rest of the provinces in the central region.

Sources: Board of Investment, Annual Reports, 1986–91.

important industries in the south, the north and the central region. In all areas, however, there has been a trend towards a wider distribution of industry types, with the three-sector and five-sector concentration ratios falling over the 1981–91 period.

When the regional distribution of different sizes of manufacturing enterprises is examined, three main characteristics can be observed. First, despite the fact that establishments employing not more than seven workers or two-horsepower machinery do not have to register, small-scale firms, employing up to 20 persons accounted for at least 82.9 per cent of total industries in all but one region (Table 6.6). The inner ring has the smallest share of firms with 1–20 workers. Moreover the dominant position of small firms has shown no sign of diminishing.

Second, as the size of the enterprises has increased, the combined percentage of those located in Bangkok and the inner ring increased in relation to the remaining regions (Somluckrat, 1989, p. 2). The inner ring also appears to be the most preferred location for larger firms. Almost 7 per cent of enterprises in the inner ring employ 200 or more workers, compared with 1.1 per cent in Bangkok. Therefore the average firm size in the inner ring (62 persons in 1987) was the highest (Biggs *et al.*, 1990, p. 20).

Third, within Bangkok the proportion of smallest firms declines from 82 per cent in the city core to 46 per cent in the outer areas. But moving towards the surrounding provinces (or the inner ring) the proportion of medium-sized firms (50–199 workers) is higher than that in Bangkok and other provinces. In 1987, among the inner-ring provinces, Samut Prakan and Samut Sakhon had the highest share of newly established medium-sized and large (over 200 workers) firms (Table 6.7). But in 1991 this position went to Pathum Thani because of new roads connecting Pathum Thani with Bangkok and other provinces in the outer ring. It is also interesting to observe that the share of small firms (1–19 workers) in three provinces in the inner ring increased significantly during the 1987–91 period. This may be explained by three factors, namely improved infrastructure, externalities that arise when provinces reach a certain threshold number of industrial establishments, and higher land prices in Bangkok.

6.2.2 Industrial Concentration and the Decentralization Trend

The above discussion only describes changes in the regional distribution of manufacturing establishments. The pertinent question is: what factors determine the distributional pattern and the changes in regional distribution? Specifically, four questions may be asked. Why is industrial activity so heavily concentrated in Bangkok? Why do small firms tend to locate in the inner city and larger firms tend to move to the suburban area and the surrounding provinces? What factors explain the industrial decentralization trend in the late 1980s? Why do rural industries concentrate on a few resource-based activities? This section will answer the first three questions, while the last question will be analyzed later.

Bangkok has more than 35 per cent of the country's 57 000 manufacturing enterprises. Almost every type of industry including agro-processing activities, can be found in Bangkok. Several studies have argued that the high degree of industrial concentration can be explained by the powerful economies of urban agglomeration which are the effects of the primacy of Bangkok (World Bank, 1983, pp. 11–12, 1989, p. 95; Biggs *et al.*, 1990, p. 28)[3] Such economies are likely to be economies of scope in both the input-supply side (production services, credit services and skills), and on the output side (the multiplicity of transport, marketing and communication services that can be used to reach consumers and markets elsewhere). Such positive externalities greatly reduce the costs of all firms and the cost savings

Table 6.5 Distribution of registered factories classified by TSIC, 1987*

TSIC	*Industry*	*Greater Bangkok*	*Centre*	*North*	*North-east*	*South*	*Whole kingdom*	*Memo: whole kingdom 1993*
311	Food	6.82	36.27	19.89	47.76	18.47	17.25	15.70
313	Beverages	0.32	0.46	0.85	0.31	0.54	0.40	0.48
314	Tobacco	0.03	0.01	6.51	0.00	0.00	0.58	n.a.
321	Textiles	5.15	1.03	0.44	1.15	0.34	3.41	3.76
322	Clothing	5.84	0.03	0.67	0.07	0.00	3.56	3.58
323	Leather	1.23	0.01	0.00	0.02	0.00	0.74	n.a
324	Footwear	0.98	0.04	0.00	0.00	0.00	0.59	0.74
331	Wood products	5.65	9.83	9.40	4.12	13.04	6.94	n.a.
332	Furniture	2.94	1.43	2.71	2.93	3.82	2.75	9.73
341	Paper products	1.49	0.19	0.28	0.04	0.14	0.96	1.32
342	Printing and publishing	5.76	1.51	1.89	1.74	2.40	4.16	2.80
351	Industrial chemicals	0.53	0.25	0.15	0.00	0.07	0.37	n.a.
352	Other chemical products	2.81	0.42	1.24	0.31	0.41	1.90	1.14
353	Petroleum refineries	0.00	0.03	0.03	0.00	0.00	0.01	n.a.
354	Petroleum and coal products	0.08	0.04	0.03	0.00	0.03	0.06	n.a.
355	Rubber products	1.56	2.25	2.48	1.89	5.47	2.03	1.42
356	Plastic products	5.95	0.13	0.15	0.26	0.51	3.65	3.55
361	Pottery	0.24	1.34	1.96	0.22	0.41	0.56	n.a.
362	Glass products	0.18	0.01	0.00	0.00	0.00	0.11	3.95

369	Other non-metallic mineral products	1.33	6.70	6.87	6.90	8.44	3.64	n.a.
371	Iron and steel basic industries	0.63	0.06	0.05	0.11	0.27	0.42	n.a.
372	Non-ferrous metal basic industries	1.21	0.10	0.28	0.04	0.07	0.77	1.17
381	Fabricated metal products	20.91	3.18	4.65	4.12	4.29	14.07	10.94
382	Machinery	9.54	15.10	20.04	10.55	19.49	12.03	n.a.
383	Electrical and electronic products	3.18	0.93	1.29	0.57	0.57	2.25	13.31
384	Transport equipment	5.74	5.70	5.14	5.09	4.29	5.52	n.a.
385	Professional and scientific equipment	0.43	0.04	0.03	0.00	0.00	0.27	12.93
390	Others	9.44	12.86	12.96	11.78	16.96	10.99	13.47
	Total	100.00	100.00	100.00	100.00	100.00	100.00	100.00

*Excluding rice mills.
Source: Provincial Factory Directories, Ministry of Industry.

Table 6.6 Distribution of registered factories by number of employees and region, 1974–91 (per cent)

Employment	*Greater Bangkok*	*Centre*		*North*	*North-east*	*South*	*Whole kingdom*
1974							
1–9	67.8	58.9		56.7	52.6	61.8	63.3
10–49	28.0	30.3		35.2	40.5	31.9	30.3
50–99	2.6	5.9		5.9	4.7	3.5	3.8
100–199	1.1	3.0		1.2	1.8	1.6	1.7
200 or more	0.5	1.8		0.9	0.4	1.2	0.9
Total %	100.0	100.0		100.0	100.0	100.0	100.0
Total no.	10 042	4778		1269	1374	1196	18 659
1984							
1–9	63.7	61.9		61.4	68.5	66.4	63.8
10–49	31.1	26.5		31.2	27	27.7	29.2
50–99	3.0	5.0		4.2	2.5	3.2	3.6
100–199	1.1	3.3		1.6	1.3	1.8	1.8
200 or more	1.0	3.3		1.6	0.7	0.9	1.6
Total %	100.0	100.0		100.0	100.0	100.0	100.0
Total no.	19 355	10 470		3328	5024	2607	40 784
1987		*In*	*Out*				
1–9	63.8	43.2	71.2	67.9	71.1	66.6	64.3
10–19	19.1	17.2	14.6	15.8	18.3	16.2	17.7
20–49	11.7	17.6	8.3	9.9	6.7	10.8	10.9
50–199	4.9	15.1	4.2	5.1	3.2	5.1	5.4
200–499	0.7	4.6	1.0	1.1	0.5	1.3	1.2
500 or more	0.4	2.2	0.6	0.2	0.3	0.1	0.5
Total %	100.0	100.0	100.0	100.0	100.0	100.0	100.0
1991							
1–9	57.8	41.0	n.a.	77.7	n.a.	n.a.	n.a.
10–19	19.6	16.5	n.a.	9.8	n.a.	n.a.	n.a.
20–49	14.2	18.4	n.a.	4.2	n.a.	n.a.	n.a.
50–199	6.8	16.7	n.a.	4.2	n.a.	n.a.	n.a.
200–499	1.1	5.4	n.a.	0.4	n.a.	n.a.	n.a.
500 or more	0.5	1.9	n.a.	0.2	n.a.	n.a.	n.a.
Total %	100.0	100.0	n.a.	100.0	n.a.	n.a.	n.a.
Total no.	21 472	6680	n.a.	3142	n.a.	n.a.	n.a.

Notes: Excluding rice mills. In = inner-ring provinces (see Table 6.2); out = outer-ring provinces (see Table 6.2).
Source: Department of Industrial Works.

must be large enough to offset the high wage, rent and congestion costs in Bangkok. Moreover Bangkok is also the largest single market for manufacturing products because of the size of the population, economic activities and purchasing power.

The size distribution of firms in Bangkok is highly skewed towards small enterprises, since 95 per cent of Bangkok's 20 000 firms employ

Table 6.7 Distribution of newly registered factories in Bangkok and the inner ring, 1987 and 1991

Province	*Year*	*Employment Sizes* *1–19*	*20–49*	*50–199*	*200–299*	*300 or more*	*Memo: Total Number*
Bangkok	1987	69.35	20.06	8.52	0.96	1.11	1256
	1991	n.a.	n.a.	n.a.	n.a.	n.a.	1006
Samut Prakan	1987	43.70	22.88	25.82	4.25	3.27	306
	1991	53.26	21.58	18.90	2.94	3.32	783
Samut Sakhon	1987	43.86	21.93	26.32	6.14	1.75	114
	1991	53.69	23.77	19.26	0.82	2.46	244
Pathum Thani	1987	61.54	14.10	17.95	1.28	5.13	78
	1991	46.12	20.63	25.11	3.59	4.48	223
Nonthaburi	1987	79.63	7.41	7.41	1.85	3.70	54
	1991	69.14	17.14	9.71	1.71	2.29	175
Nakhon Pathom	1987	56.72	16.42	22.39	1.49	2.99	67
	1991	57.95	20.51	17.95	1.02	2.54	195
Total	1987	63.15	19.89	13.28	1.87	1.81	1875
	1991	n.a.	n.a.	n.a.	n.a.	n.a.	2626

Source: Department of Industrial Works.

less than 50 workers. Obviously small firms find it profitable to operate in the densely populated city where, despite the high rent, they benefit from agglomeration economies and efficient and well-integrated input markets. The externalities include a large supply of skilled labour, easy access to various infrastructure, government and business services, input supply, availability of repair and delivery services, as well as proximity to larger firms which often have a subcontractual relationship with small firms. Moreover the size of the market and the diversified market niches can also provide small firms with numerous business opportunities. The lack of land-use control enables small firms to choose any location in the city because electricity, road access and telecommunications are readily available. As a consequence of these external benefits the central areas of Bangkok serve as an 'incubator' in the birth of small firms that are vital to the economy (World Bank 1989, p. 99; Biggs *et al.* 1990, p. 31). Other main cities in Thailand are also breeding grounds for small firms. For example small firms account for 98 per cent of all firms in Nakhon Ratchasima in the north-east, 95 per cent in Chiang Mai in the north, and 93 per cent in Songkhla in the south.

Unfortunately most government planners and decision-makers do not understand this incubator function of the cities. In order to reduce congestion in Bangkok and mitigate regional disparities in industrial development, the government has pursued explicit spatial policies aimed at dispersing manufacturing industries from Bangkok without paying heed to the locational needs of small firms.[4] From 1987 the BOI ceased to grant investment privileges to projects locating in Bangkok and Samut Prakan, but it has made exceptions for large export-oriented firms with at least 200 employees. Such a policy change is obviously biased against small firms. Two other policy measures are retarding the development of small industries in Bangkok and the surrounding provinces. First, in the Bangkok General Plan the planners seem to have favoured an industrial development to the east of Samut Prakan by establishing a greenbelt buffer zone between Samut Prakan and the new industrial area (World Bank, 1989). But Samut Prakan is already the second largest industrial province in Thailand. As the eastern seaboard industrial development proceeds, the industrial expansion in Samut Prakan will increase and extend towards the eastern seaboard because small firms that are growing tend to follow their parent industries. Second, the Bangkok General Plan does not allow industries in Bangkok to locate outside industrial estates or along major roads. But land prices in industrial estates in the Bangkok metropolitan area are 100–300 per cent higher than in comparable sites nearby.

As small firms grow and expand to medium size they need more space and infrastructure. Moreover, firms whose activities are highly polluting are subject to frequent complaints from nearby residents. They are not able to obtain a factory permit to locate their enlarged plants in residential areas, but the choice of new locations is limited. They cannot locate on underdeveloped private land far from the main road and infrastructure facilities because the initial capital-investment costs are too high. They also find that the price of land in the industrial estates is too high. Two decades ago medium-sized firms could find cheap land on main roads in suburban areas to the west and east of Bangkok. This is why a large number of factories have clustered along the roads in Pra Pradaeng and Pu Chao Samingpry in Samut Prakan. Unfortunately the land areas behind such rows of factories are unused because there is no access to them. Since the late 1980s the concentration of industries in Samut Prakan has become so high that the roads are heavily congested and frequently flooded. Land prices in suburban areas and Samut Prakan also increased by more than 200 per cent during the rapid economic expansion in the 1987–90 period. As a consequence medium-sized factories now have to find new locations in other inner-ring provinces. Other site alternatives for medium-sized firms are small industrial estates in the suburbs of Bangkok and Pathum Thani. Most of these estates were developed by private land developers before the explosion of land prices in 1987. The land and building prices in these estates were not as high as in large industrial estates because the developers did not have to build all the infrastructure required by the Industrial Estate Act. Such development was made possible by another law, the Land Development Act, which allows developers to develop land according to less stringent conditions than those required by the Industrial Estate Law.

In 1987 there was an important shift in industrial policy towards dispersing industries to other regions. The question is whether or not this policy has affected the decentralization trend. A regression analysis by Nuttapong and Bunluesak (1992) found strong evidence to substantiate the hypothesis that industrial decentralization has already occurred in the central region and the north-east. But when a policy variable is added into the time-trend regression of the proportion of investment projects that receive BOI privileges, it is not statistically significant. Moreover, a detailed statistical analysis by the same authors also found that decentralization had actually begun a few years prior to 1987. The results implied that industrial decentralization is affected by market forces rather than by policy measures. Among the factors affecting decentralization, the congestion cost of doing business in Bangkok is perhaps the most important variable since Bangkok has been losing its comparative advantage over time.[5] Since 1985 new factories, especially large ones, have tended to locate in the inner-ring provinces rather than Bangkok because of the cheaper land prices there.

Industrial decentralization is also affected by market size and agglomeration economies. A simple regression of the proportion of factories in province *i* to all factories on the percentage share of provincial value added to GDP found a statistically significant positive relationship. Moreover a covariance analysis of the change in the pattern of industrial decentralization shows that between 1981 and 1985 there was no trend towards decentralization. Since then industrial dispersion has taken place. One study shows that it was rapid economic growth from 1987 that brought about the decentralization process (Nuttapong and Bunluesak, 1992).

6.3 THE LIMITED NATURE OF RURAL INDUSTRY

This and the following section will address two related questions. The first is, why is rural industry is concentrated in a few manufacturing activities? To answer this question the characteristics of rural industry will be analyzed. The second question is, what are the factors limiting rural industry growth?.

As discussed above, there are few kinds of rural industries and most of them are closely related to the agricultural sector. This is because 61 per cent of the Thai labour force still work in the agricultural sector. Although most rural workers spend some of their time earning supplementary income in the non-agricultural sector, agricultural income still accounts for at least half of their annual earnings. The influence of the agricultural sector on rural industry is through agricultural linkages and seasonality. Other important characteristics of rural industry include its service-type character, high transportation costs, low investment and low labour costs.

6.3.1 Linkages with the Agricultural Sector

Agricultural expansion leads to powerful consumer demand, and forward and backward linkages to both agricultural and non-agricultural activities. However the linkage effect occurs in rural areas only if the products generated by the linkages are non-tradeable or the rural areas have a comparative advantage in their production (World Bank, 1983; Biggs *et al.*, 1990). Most of the linkage effects on the rural economy are via non-tradeable goods because the rural economy has a well-developed road network linking rural villages with towns and major cities.

Consumer-demand linkages include trade, services, construction and the manufacturing of certain consumer goods. Several studies have argued that consumer-demand linkages exert a most powerful effect on rural non-agricultural activities (World Bank, 1983, p. 6; Somluckrat, 1989, ch. 3; Biggs *et al.*, 1990, pp. 49–50). They reasoned that the marginal budget shares and income elasticities of non-agricultural activities are higher than those of agricultural products. Therefore agricultural income is spent increasingly on non-farm goods and services. Although the argument is correct, this chapter will argue that the effects of the manufacturing activities in rural areas are relatively small.

A detailed analysis of household expenditure over the 1975–86 period by Somluckrat (1989) found strong evidence that households in all areas – municipal, sanitary district and village – have been buying more manufactured products in terms of variety as well as in terms of the total amount spent on these items. The most noticeable increase has been the in household items and home improvement, and transport and communications. Despite an increase in absolute value, the share of expenditure on food, beverages, tobacco and clothing showed a declining trend. The relative share of other items remained constant over time, that is reading, recreation, education, medical and personal care. As income increased over time, provincial households not only purchased more manufactured products, their purchases outweighed the increase in their income. In fact for many items village households' elasticity of demand is greater than that of the municipal area.

However Somluckrat (1989) also found that most of the products demanded by provincial and rural households were produced in the greater Bangkok area despite the fact that more than 60 per cent of the provincial industries were selling over 80 per cent of their products in the province where the factories were located.

There is strong evidence to suggest that although the increase in rural households' income will have a large effect on non-agricultural activities, most of the impact will fall on the service sector. The linkage effect on rural manufacturing activities may be quite small and most of the effects will be via non-tradeable goods.

At the macro level there is a clear correlation between agricultural and mining income and manufacturing output. But the size of the regression coefficient is somewhat small–roughly, a 10 per cent increase in agricultural and mining income induces an increase in manufacturing output of about 2.5–3.3 per cent. The fact that agricultural processing is about 10–15 per cent of manufacturing value-added may account for a substantial part of this parameter (Ammar, 1990, p. 14).

When the size of demand linkages is estimated from household-expenditure surveys, it is found that a relatively small share (about a fifth) of increased income is spent by rural households on manufactured goods. The manufactured goods with the highest marginal budget share are clothing and footwear, medicine and medical services. The service sector has the largest marginal budget share (54–76 per cent), arising largely from marginal expenditure on housing and transportation.[6] The high shares of housing and transportation have two implications. First, a proportion of housing expenditure is spent on construction materials and furniture produced in the area. The high marginal budget share is also confirmed by the fact that almost every village in Thailand has a gang of four to five construction workers who hire themselves out to build houses during the dry season. Second, part of the marginal budget share on transport is spent on transport services in rural areas, but a large proportion accrues to producers of vehicles manufactured in the city and to producers of motorised carts produced in rural areas.

In effect, the demand linkage effect on manufacturing activities is not so large as the effect on the service sector. Moreover, most of the increase in household expenditure as a result of income growth will be spent on products produced in Bangkok.

The second source of demand for non-agricultural goods and services is the forward linkage effects on agricultural processing activities and transportation services generated by major crops. These include cassava flour and pelleting factories, rice mills, sugar factories, fruit and vegetable canning factories, canned-fish and frozen-seafood factories, cereal silos and vegetable oil factories, and animal-feed factories. However these factories are not necessarily located near their sources of raw materials.

The decision to locate factories in rural areas is governed by (1) the weight-losing nature of particular processes and (2) the perishability of the raw materials used. Examples of weight-losing processes are cassava chipping and rice milling. Industries that use perishable raw materials include those involved in fruit canning, rice-bran oil extraction, fish products, frozen seafood and so on. Some industries involve both weight-loss and perishability, such as cane-sugar factories and the production of rubber sheets. Most of these industries are in small-scale units, but where economies of scale exist the factories can be very large, such as sugar factories, pineapple-canning factories and corn silos. Transportation and loading–unloading costs are also critical in the choice of location. Corn is grown in the north-east and the north and most is loaded from lighters onto ships. This is why most corn silos are located along the river in Ayutthaya, because the location minimizes the cost of trucking as well as the cost of water transport. Processing activities that do not involve perishability or weight loss are frequently found in urban areas, which are also the major market: flour and rice milling, food processing and vegetable-oil extraction.

The third source of agricultural demand for non-agricultural activities is backward linkages such as metal workshops, agricultural machinery, animal feed, fertilizers and pesticides. The latter two types of good are tradeable and thus are produced in urban areas or imported from abroad. However their sale does generate some employment in rural areas.

Mechanization has played an essential role in stimulating the production of agricultural machinery. Larger farm size due to expansion requires mechanization. Moreover tractors encourage farmers to farm larger tracts than would be possible using just animal power. Most machinery production has arisen from the innovation and adaptation of small repair workshops in response to customer demand and complaints about imported machines. The most popular home-grown machines produced by these firms include small tractors and rice-threshing machines. Successful small firms either quickly expand or are displaced by larger, better-managed firms .

As a result of rising urban income over the last two decades, the demand for poultry products and pork has increased rapidly in the major cities of all regions. The expansion of the poultry industry has been accompanied by the growth of the animal-feed industry, which tends to locate near poultry farms, but it should be noted that since Bangkok is the largest market for poultry products, poultry farms and animal-feed industries are concentrated in a few provinces surrounding Bangkok.

6.3.2 The Seasonality of Agriculture

Agricultural production is seasonal and heavily dependent upon the monsoon rain – which is concentrated in only four months – because only 15 per cent of the cultivated area is irrigated. In the peak agricultural season the demand for agricultural labour is so high that every hand in the family must be used. When the demand for labour declines in the dry season, a few million workers become idle. About a million of these seek temporary jobs in non-agricultural activities. These non-agricultural activities must, therefore, have two characteristics. First, they must have low capital–labour ratios because capital is scarce and will be idle in the rainy season. Second, they must be counter-seasonal. Most of the non-agricultural activities in rural areas tend to have such characteristics. They are small shops, transport services, handicraft production, silk production, fishing nets, carpets, mats, baskets, cloth and so on. The products are made in households or small factories. Besides being of low capital intensity, they often use female or child labour on a seasonal basis.

6.3.3 Service-Type Manufacturing

Many manufacturing activities are located in rural areas because they have a service-type character that gives them a cost advantage over competing firms from other areas, for example there are 45 000 rice mills or one in almost every village. Others include small factories producing highly perishable goods such as soft noodles, soy-bean curds, pickles and ice.

6.3.4 High Transport Costs

Furniture and construction materials such as bricks, cement blocks, windows and door frames are usually produced in rural areas because of the high cost of transporting both the inputs to these products and the products themselves.

6.3.5 Other Characteristics

A few other manufactured and processed products are produced in rural areas. Examples are artificial flowers for export, cut gems, pottery and earthenware. Artificial-flower production is a subcontracting activity, while gem cutting is an independent business of villagers who buy uncut gems, cut and polish them, and then sell them to merchants in nearby towns. These activities exist in villages for the following reasons. First, because they employ cheap female and teenage labour at home, these workers can also engage in agricultural production. Second, the skills required to perform the tasks can be acquired within a few months. Third, the activities require only a small financial investment. For example, the capital cost of gem-cutting is less then 7500 baht, while the working capital required is only 2500–6500 baht per month (Ngaosilp, 1991). Fourth, because gem-cutting machines are powered by electricity, rural electrification has opened up job opportunities in some villages. Fifth, the cost of shipping stones to the villages and transporting the cut gems to Bangkok is very small relative to the value of the gems. Finally, the availability of clay and possession of the skills allow some people to produce pottery and earthenware in their own villages.

6.4 FACTORS PROHIBITING THE GROWTH OF RURAL INDUSTRY

There are several factors, on both the demand and the supply sides, that are not conducive to the growth of rural industry. The demand factors include low population density, low purchasing power and the slow growth of the agricultural sector. On the supply side, lack of physical and social infrastructure are important barriers. There are also some policies that are biased against rural industry, especially small firms.

6.4.1 Extensive Agriculture

Up until the mid-1980s the average area cultivated per household was still rising because of land abundance. This explains why Thailand has a very large agricultural labour force. The availability of forest land, which needs no fertilizer in the first few years, enabled farmers to extend their holdings and adopt extensive farming method, which was not conducive to the growth of towns (Ammar, 1990). Moreover rural people did not want to settle permanently in towns while there was new forest land to be taken (since the forest lands were occupied illegally the farmers had to live on them in order to claim ownership). One other reason why the need for large-scale emigration from rural areas to towns has not occurred until recently is because the seasonal labour market functions rather well (Bertrand and Squire, 1980). Seasonal migrants do not need to acquire industrial skills because after a few months of working in cities they return to their rural homes. Provincial towns and cities have only small populations which makes it difficult for manufacturing activities to expand.

6.4.2 Rural Poverty and Purchasing Power

Prior to 1986 the agricultural sector was heavily taxed in various ways such as export taxes, export quotas, over-valued exchange rates, and tariffs on manufactured products. It is estimated that from 1963–84 there was a net transfer of 30 000 million baht from the agricultural sector (Ammar and Suthad, 1989), resulting in rural poverty and income disparities and negatively affecting the growth of rural industry. The poorest rural people, who represent the largest portion of the population, are found to spend a smaller proportion of their income on manufactured products (Ammar, 1990).

The low price of agricultural products in the early 1980s and the exhaustion of the land frontier in the late 1980s also served to slow the growth of the agricultural sector, which in turn affected the purchasing power of rural households.

Lack of demand not only directly impedes industrial growth, it also prevents industry from enjoying the economies of scale and scope. Demand factors, therefore, are the most critical factors in explaining the growth of rural industry. In the coming decades Thai farmers will have to adopt intensive farming methods as the land frontier has already been reached. This means that towns will be more densely populated as large-scale emigration from rural areas occurs. But if the government can find appropriate measures to reduce rural poverty, there will be more demand for manufactured products, many of which could be produced in rural or provincial areas as the rural market may be large enough for the industry to exploit the scale economies.

6.4.3 Lack of Input Supplies

Previous studies (Saeng *et al.*, 1977; Somsak and Chesada, 1985) found that the major constraints limiting the growth of small and medium-sized enterprises are (1) market constraints, (2) lack of credit or access to formal sector credit, and (3) a shortage of raw materials. Shortage of skilled labour or lack of entrepreneurial skills were not found to be the problem. Most of the skills required are acquired by workers either from their parents as a part of the learning process in their daily life, such as weaving skills, or are acquired from a short period of on-the-job training in factories farm trailers, ploughs or furniture, in sugar mills. According to the World Bank, 'Thai labourers, despite their rather limited education, have proven themselves to be quick learning, adaptable and skilful at the level of skill being demanded of them' (World Bank, 1983, p. 123). The only serious problems are a lack of marketing know-how and, for example, the inability of small firms producing two-wheel tractors to produce four-wheel tractors. A study by Nanthana (1991) of entrepreneurs in the north-east found that marketing know-how is the most important factor explaining the success of some small entrepreneurs.

Studies by Narongchai *et al.* (1983) and Sarote (1989) found that credit is not the most serious problem facing rural entrepreneurs. But the studies revealed that the bank transaction costs of making loans to small rural industry are high relative to the controlled interest rate, partly because of high risk and high average lending costs. Most entrepreneurs have to rely upon their own savings as a source of finance. However this does not necessarily mean that there is a failure in the financial market that requires government intervention. In fact the market is already too regulated. Not only is the interest rate controlled, but the market is also protected by not allowing new competitors. Financial liberalization will enable small entrepreneurs to have more access to scarce financial resources.

Lack of raw materials is cited as the fourth most serious problem behind the problems of too much regulation and high taxes. This problem is most acute in regions where industry is dependent upon local raw materials (Somsak, 1989; Wattana, 1989).

6.4.4 Infrastructure

It is very common for government officers and national planners to blame the lack of infrastructure and input shortages as the main causes of industrial underdevelopment in rural areas. However infrastructure is not necessarily the engine of growth. In many provinces where the central government has invested large sums on infrastructure, industrialization has never taken off. In the last decade there has been investment in ports and industrial estates in many provinces. And yet the facilities remain idle. There is also evidence to show that lower transportation costs following infrastructural development can have a negative impact on some local activities, which have increasingly to compete with products from larger, urban-based factories. Infrastructural investment becomes a critical factor only when provinces or areas show potential as industrial sites. In Chiang Mai in the north and Nakhon Ratchasima in the north-east), previous infrastructural investment has opened up opportunities for firms in the export market and in direct sales to factories in Bangkok. These two provinces have experienced rapid industrial growth in the last few years, as evidenced by the factory data from the Ministry of Industry. Moreover, as these cities (or secondary growth centres) expand their industrial activities, opportunities for off-farm employment will grow too because villagers will be able to work in the city while maintaining residence in their villages (Cochrane and Manchnes, 1982).

Rural areas not only lack physical infrastructure such as telephones, reliable electricity and water supplies, roads and port facilities, but most public schools and hospitals in rural areas are of low quality because they receive a lower budget allocation than those in Bangkok and employ personnel with lower educational qualifications (NEC, 1989). It is extremely difficult for rural public schools to offer any extra activities because they depend heavily on small subsidies from central government.

6.4.5 Centralized Government

Fiscal decisions and public administration in Thailand have traditionally been highly centralized. Local governments have almost no autonomy in self-governing and fiscal decisions. As a consequence most resources are transferred from every corner of the country to Bangkok. The total budget of local governments accounted for only 5 per cent of the central-government budget in 1990. In Samut Prakan, a province to the south-east of Bangkok, central government collected sales-tax revenue worth 5424 million baht in 1988, but only 9 per cent of is was returned to the province.

Rural development therefore has been retarded. Rural areas are not only provided with little physical and social investment, but they are also not allowed to provide important public services required by investors. Factory-permit issuance, passport applications, license applications, customs clearance and other services must be done in Bangkok. Such practices make it more costly to do business in places other than Bangkok. For example the new international port in the eastern seaboard does not provide a customs service during the weekends.

In effect it can be hypothesized that centralized government may be the most important factor prohibiting rural industrialization. Not only are huge resources transferred to Bangkok, but the subsidies and investments rural areas receive from central government may not correspond to the needs and demands of rural people.

6.4.6 Policy Bias against Rural Industry

Beside the problem of unequal government services, some policies militate against the growth of rural industry. In the past, most, if not all, investment privileges were granted to large-scale firms, most of which were concerned with import substitution. The investment-promotion policy has been gradually changed. Target industries are now export industries, except in some specific activities; the minimum firm size to be eligible for the privilege has been reduced drastically and an industrial spatial policy has also been adopted in order to disperse industry away from Bangkok. The new policy prevents privileges or tax holidays being offered to industries in Bangkok, except to exporting industries in industrial estates. Firms located in the inner ring of Bangkok will receive some privileges, but these are fewer than those offered to firms in other provinces. However the measures are still biased against small firms. Firstly, firms investing less than 5 million baht are not eligible for promotional status. Secondly, since the cost of applying for the privileges is fixed and not insignificant, it is comparatively cheaper for large firms to apply. Thirdly, the BOI tends to favour firms that locate in industrial estates because they will receive more privileges, and the promotional status is easily obtained. Since the price of land in the estates is usually two to three times the price elsewhere, the policy measures clearly discriminate against small firms.

Before early 1992 the interest rates on loans were controlled. In 1991 the ceiling was 16.5 per cent per year. Given the ceiling, there was excess demand for loans and so banks tended to discriminate in favour of large borrowers. Moreover, the Bank of Thailand adopted some measures that favoured large companies. Packing credit for agricultural exports at subsidized interest rates has been mainly obtained by large exporters. Credit growth control in 1983 also inflicted heavy losses on small businessmen who were not able to obtain credit from banks.

The minimum-wage policy also tends to increase the labour cost in rural areas. Because of the nature of the political process of minimum-wage determination, committee members from both unions and employer associations, whose interests are in Bangkok, tend to favour larger increases of the minimum wage in rural areas than in Bangkok (Nipon, 1993).

Finally, the local development tax, which is a tax levied annually on land owners, is slightly progressive for lower-valued property but regressive with respect to total value for high-price land.

6.4.7 Statistical Analysis

The qualitative arguments about the factors affecting the growth of rural industry in this chapter are merely a set of hypotheses. In order to assess the relative significance of those factors, the results from several empirical studies will be utilized (Table 6.8). It should be noted that only limited comparison is possible since these studies used different variables. Moreover they provided neither coefficient estimates in terms of elasticity nor other information to estimate the relative size of the coefficients. However one study did report the relative influence of each variable (Nuttapong and Bunluesak, 1992). The most important variables in the growth of provincial industry are market size, as measured by per capita gross provincial product (GPP), and population. These two variables are significant in all studies.

It should be noted that per capita GPP and population are also proxies of agglomeration economies. The interesting result is that these variables significantly affected the growth of resource-based industries (Nuttapong and Bunluesak, 1992).

Table 6.8 Regressions explaining provincial industry

Variables	*Nuttapong and Bunluesak*[1] *(1991)*	*Somsak*[2] *(1989)*	*Rachain*[2] *(1989)*
Intercept	−846.51*	−0.69	7.99
Per capita GPP	0.02*	0.35*	0.53*
Population	0.74*	0.24*	–
Population density	–	–	4.06*
Electricity[3]	−33.98	–	–
Per capita telephone	−702.95	–	–
Roads (km)	2692.03*	–	–
Secondary education[4]	−16.26*	–	–
Per capita hospital beds	463 456.72*	–	–
Credits/deposit	252.38	–	–
Distance from Bangkok (km)	0.05	−0.13*	–
Log of distance from Bangkok	–	–	−2.42*
% Agricultural value added	–	−0.69	–
% Public utilities value added	–	0.59*	–
R-squared	0.98	0.64	0.71
F-statistics	500.73	23.93	n.a.
DW	n.a.	1.89	n.a.

Notes:
* Statistically significant at 95% level of confidence.
** Opposite expected sign.
1. Dependent variable is the number of factories in each province
2. Dependent variable is the share of manufacturing GPP of the i province
3. Percentage of villages with electricity in province *i*.
4. Percentage of primary education graduates in the secondary level.
Sources: Nuttapong and Bunluesak, 1992; Somsak, 1989; Rachain, 1989.

The second most important group of variables is infrastructure, including access to roads and electricity. Another study also found that water supply and the credit–deposit ratio significantly affected the percentage share of manufacturing value-added to GPP (Chesada, 1989). It also found that roads do not significantly affect the number of resource-based factories, and other infrastructure variables have less influence on resource-based industries than on the market-oriented and footloose industries.[7]

Finally, the statistical analysis also confirms the hypothesis that quality of life and amenities (or social infrastructure) can significantly affect the choice of location because workers bring along their families when they move. But only per capita hospital beds is significant. Further research needs to be done on other aspects of quality of life and amenities.

Yet these empirical studies, which are based upon a simple regression analysis and a few more sophisticated techniques, failed to incorporate into their analysis the important policy variables that are postulated to affect the growth of provincial industry. Data limitation also resulted in some important variables being left out of the regression, such as variables to test the hypothesis of large cities playing an incubator role for small enterprises.

6.5 CONCLUSION

There has been a clear pattern of industrial decentralization since 1985. The decentralization process was not caused by spatial policy, but rather by market forces, especially rapid economic growth since 1987, market size and agglomeration economies. The location of rural industries is determined largely by transportation costs, the perishability of both inputs and goods, the weight-losing process and a few other factors. Rural industry is closely related to the agricultural sector, but this chapter has argued that the effects of an increase in rural income on rural industry are smaller than those on the service sector.

The growth of rural industry is found to be affected mainly by final demand as measured by per capita GPP and population, agglomeration economies, and the availability of infrastructural facilities and amenities. But this chapter has also strongly argued that many policy measures have had a directly or indirectly negative effect on rural industrialization. As long as they remain, particularly the highly centralized fiscal policy, which results in a net transfer of resources from rural areas to Bangkok, rural industrialization may never be realized. Unfortunately the impact of the policy measures has never been subject to quantitative assessment.

Future research should therefore attempt to include more policy variables in the analysis. Two types of policy variable should be distinguished. The first type are variables that directly affect the growth of rural industry. They are, for example, industrial spatial policy, minimum-wage rates and so on. The second group consists of variables that negatively affect rural income and local-government revenue and expenditure, which in turn influence the growth of rural industry. This means that a more complex and realistic model must be built. Data and information not now available will have to be collected for future research. More serious work on the behaviour of rural industry is needed since it will not only provide a better understanding of the rural economy, but will also enable the government to devise a more appropriate rural industrialization policy. Previous policy measures, which were not based upon an understanding of market forces, tended to be very costly and largely ineffective.

Notes

1. In this chapter rural industry is the same as provincial industry .
2. When the factories were grouped into 58 major categories, 40 categories had more than 50 per cent of factories in each category located in Bangkok in 1977. The number declined to 29 categories in 1987.
3. About 69 per cent of Thailand's urban population reside in Bangkok. Important determinants of the primacy of Bangkok include central government, a major port, a conduit for interregional traffic, a low level of urbanization in the countryside and so on.
4. See the discussion of government policies in Section 6.4.
5. Comparative advantage is measured by a location quotient index, which is the ratio of the density of factories in the region to the density for the whole kingdom. Bangkok has the largest index, which declined from 288 in 1978 to 242 in 1989. The indices for the inner- and outer-ring provinces show an increasing trend (Nuttapong *et al.*, 1991).
6. The importance of rural housing and transportation is in striking contrast to the finding in Malaysia, where the marginal budget shares of the items of the rich is below that of the poor in Thailand (Ammar, 1990, p. 23). The heavy expenditure on shelter reflects the determination of most rural households to stay put, despite the rapid industrialization of the economy.
7. Resource-based industries are raw-material intensive and weight-losing industries. Market-oriented industry involves perishability of products and high transportation costs. Footloose industries do not necessarily have to locate near raw materials or market sources.

Part II

Economic Impacts of the Industrialization Process

7 Impact of Industrialization on Government Finance

Direk Patmasiriwat

7.1 INTRODUCTION

The speculation that Thailand will soon join the class of newly industrialising countries to become 'the fifth tiger of Asia' is well documented (for example Teerana, 1990; Thammasat University, 1989), and the economic boom of 1988–91 has heightened this belief. Asset and land prices rose sharply, stimulating a further increase in aggregate demand through wealth and expectation effects. Higher economic growth induced by an inflow of direct foreign investment strengthened the momentum towards export activity and further industrialization, and convinced the government of the importance of export-led growth. Land speculation and the boom in tourism hastened the decline of farmland as many farmers gave up their land in exchange for unexpectedly high land prices. Sudden increases in aggregate demand led to supply shortages, notably in construction materials, manpower (especially engineers and skilled technicians) and, most seriously, public infrastructure.

The unexpected upturn in the economy enabled the government to collect much larger tax and non-tax revenues and to accumulate sizeable fiscal surpluses. After some delay the government began to respond to the boom in three ways. Firstly, it increased the wages and salaries of public employees. Secondly, it began to expand capital-investment expenditure which had been on the decline due to the tight fiscal policy of the early 1980s. Thirdly, it allowed more private-sector participation in transport and communications sectors. The Gulf War and the coup d'etat early in 1991, and the events in Thailand in May 1992 undoubtedly caused an economic setback and slowed growth. However in the midst of these events there was progress in institutional development in at least two directions: the democratization process and government policy towards deregulation and privatization.

The main objective of this chapter is to assess the impact of industrialization on government finance, and to project future scenarios of government finance. The chapter takes into consideration institutional changes, especially recent political events that are likely to shape the future of policy making in Thailand. The chapter anticipates that government revenue and expenditure will be affected by three changes. First, political parties will play an increasing role in the determination of national economic policy while the influence of bureaucrats will decline which should turn fiscal policy in the direction of higher expenditure and budget deficits. Secondly, as more workers are drawn from agriculture and self-employment to work in industry and services, an increasing share of wage and salary earners will gradually increase the share of direct taxes and broaden the tax base. Thirdly, concern about international competitiveness and the tax reforms undertaken in other countries will turn the Thai tax structure in the direction of lower and more uniform tax rates. On the whole, total government revenue may not deviate very far from its historic growth rate, but it is possible that its composition may change considerably.

Section 7.2 briefly describes the development of fiscal policy in Thailand, taking into account the changing political settings and government policy determination over the past decades. Section 7.3 summarizes the characteristics of government finance and addresses the impact of industrialization. Section 7.4 considers the future outlook of government finance, and Section 7.5 provides an overall summary.

7.2 BACKGROUND ON FISCAL-POLICY DEVELOPMENT

Although the Thai government is actively involved in shaping the economic direction of Thailand via development planning, large capital investments, development spending and regulations, government expenditure as percentage of GNP was only about 20 per cent in 1991, which is not large by the standards of developed countries.[1] There are at least two explanations for this. First, since the beginning of the First Economic Development Plan in 1961, the policy of the government has been not to interfere with business decision making but to allow for private participation in most economic activities. Second, unlike those of many Western countries, state-run public-welfare programmes in Thailand are still relatively undeveloped.

Fifty years ago the role of the government in the economy was much smaller than it is today. Fiscal policy in those days could be described as 'conservative', with a balanced budget being the norm (see Ingram, 1971; Ammar, 1975). Over time the ideas and concepts of government finance have changed. Since the announcement of the First Plan in 1961 the role of government in the economy has increased, initially because of the creation of new public development projects, and later due to the expansion of social services (notably education and health). Due to limited domestic savings, foreign borrowing by both the public and the private sectors was brought in to fill the gap. Trade deficits and government budget deficits were common phenomena.

Because of the boom in commodity prices in the early 1970s the impact of the first oil shock was not very severe. But the commodity price increases led to a sudden increase in the rate of inflation, hitherto usually less than 5 per cent per year but nearly 20 per cent per year between 1973 and 1974. Fortunately this turbulence was only temporary. In fact the government's macroeconomic performance during the first oil shock was satisfactory, and the government was able to increase tax collection from both imports and exports.

The period 1976–82 saw a significant increase in both government expenditure and the number of public employees. This was due to a combination of factors. First, the windfall gain from rising commodity prices stimulated government spending, higher expectations and higher aggregate demand. Second, the government that came into power after the student-led uprising in 1973 adopted several socially oriented policies such as rural public-works programmes, and free bus and hospital care for the needy, which are fiscally expansive. In 1976 the student movements were crushed by the military, and the new military-supported government voted for a large military budget in order to fight communist insurgency, which had gained strength from the student movements. It was during this period that government debt, both domestic and foreign, rose sharply. Thirdly, higher oil prices following the second oil shock in 1979 and the government's refusal to adjust prices for public utilities resulted in financial losses in many state enterprises, which then demanded government subsidies. By 1981 the fiscal position of the government (then under General Prem Tinsulanond) was in dire shape, with inadequate public revenues.

Between 1982 and 1986 the Thai economy experienced a recession. A series of measures were undertaken to manage aggregate demand and restore confidence in the baht. These government measures included two devaluations (in 1981 and 1984); a freeze on the rate of increase of public employment to not more than 2 per cent per year; borrowing from the IMF; upward adjustment of the ceilings on domestic interest rates; restraining commercial banks' credit expansion to not more than 18 per cent per year; controls on the price of selected commodities, such as cement, milled rice, sugar and so on; and controls on wages and salaries of public employees.

The period 1987–91 was in marked contrast to the period 1982–6: there was a much larger inflow of direct foreign investment, leading to significant and positive changes in the economy; oil prices fell; crop prices increased; and export performance was very favourable. The government sector gained in terms of tax revenue from the upturn of the economy, and the government budget went from deficit to surplus, which was unusual. As shown in Table 7.1, the increase in tax revenues during these periods was very clear. After some time-lag the government began to increase spending by (1) allowing for wage and salary increases, (2) embarking upon public investment projects and (3) retiring public debt (see Table 7.2). Table 7.2 also shows the rapid increase in treasury reserves. Another important change was in the style of economic management under the new Chartichai government, which came into power in August 1988 after the resignation of General Prem. Under Chartichai several large-scale investment projects were approved in quick succession, despite criticisms that they were not well-studied, and that public benefits would be less than private benefits. At any rate, it is worth emphasizing that the change of government had a significant impact on fiscal policy.

Table 7.1 Government revenue and its sources, 1984–92 (million baht)

	Income tax		*Import*	*Export*	*Business*	*Excise*	*Others*	*Total*
	Personal	*Corporate*	*duties*	*taxes*	*tax*			
1984	17 194	14 616	29 692	1862	30 191	34 209	20 478	148 242
1985	19 841	15 390	30 742	1079	29 515	37 642	26 443	160 652
1986	19 218	15 549	31 106	806	28 150	46 332	28 764	169 925
1987	19 194	17 623	40 002	1301	34 726	57 154	32 021	202 021
1988	24 545	27 351	58 664	870	51 796	61 054	33 889	258 169
1989	28 958	38 755	71 173	412	67 244	72 822	47 785	327 149
1990	41 524	58 658	93 218	69	90 157	72 210	55 816	411 652
1991	49 200	74 934	82 809	9	101 789	89 413	64 454	462 608
1992	50 109	85 586	89 769	13	93 087	106 135	86 756	511 545

Source: Bank of Thailand, *Monthly Bulletin*, various issues.

Table 7.2 Central government finance, 1984-91 (million baht)

	Actual revenue	*Actual expenditure*	*Cash balance*	*Net borrowing Domestic*	*Foreign*	*Use of treasury reserve*
1984	148 079	181 262	−33 183	−33 869	−715	381
1985	160 570	199 548	−38 978	31 588	14 190	−693
1986	169 834	203 984	−34 150	50 249	−6451	−1678
1987	202 364	211 225	−8861	10 638	−3271	1828
1988	258 231	222 133	36 098	−28 824	−4537	−3211
1989	328 248	262 913	65 335	−11 150	−6197	−43 383
1990	411 746	304 700	107 046	−11 864	−39 218	−54 424
1991	462 540	362 115	100 425	−46 872	−3780	−57 055

Source: Bank of Thailand, *Monthly Bulletin*, various issues.

7.3 INDUSTRIALIZATION AND GOVERNMENT FINANCE

7.3.1 The Influence of Direct Foreign Investment (DFI)

It is difficult to deny the importance of DFI in the Thai economy. At the end of the 1980s an enormous amount of DFI was already flowing into the ASEAN region. Explanations of this have been offered by various authors. Pasuk (1990), for instance, stressed the impact of the yen appreciation:

> The yen appreciation which began in September 1985 had led to an increase in foreign investment in Asia-Pacific region, not only flowing from Japan but also from the Asian NICs, from the US., from Europe, and from other Asian countries. The yen appreciation has changed the competitive map of the Asia-Pacific region and indeed the world . . . Japan responded to yen appreciation by relocating more of her production processes overseas in order to reduce production costs. This in turn caused other countries to follow suit, for the same reason, to remain competitive (p. 92).

Yoshida (1990) added that oil prices and interest rates were favourable for economic growth:

> The Thai economy began to show signs of recovery in the latter half of 1986, due to an increase in manufactured exports, the falling price

> of crude oil and the lowering of interest rate. Moreover, due to high appreciation of the Japanese yen after the Plaza Accord of September 1985 as well as the appreciation of Asian NICs currencies such as those of Taiwan and South Korea, many firms in these countries have started to relocate their production and export base into Thailand. The large inflow of foreign investment also contributed to the country's economic recovery, leading in turn to the current investment boom and further progress in the field of industrialization. Foreign direct investment has had various impacts upon the Thai economy. Its impact was first seen in the structural change in exports in the form of the sizeable increase in manufactured goods. Furthermore, a structural change in production can be exported in the near future, whereby the industrial sector will move into a more advanced stage and become well diversified (p. 23).

The ASEAN region also received a sizeable amount of DFI from Taiwan and Korea. A study by Lee Tsao Yuan (1990) indicated that among ASEAN countries, Thailand and Malaysia had become more important to Taiwanese investors, whereas Indonesia was still the most important to Korean multinationals. She further observed that while there was a greater concentration of Korean investment in manufacturing in Indonesia, Taiwanese investment in Thailand had been in construction as well as manufacturing, and in electronics in Malaysia (p. 132).

One of the much debated policy issues in Thailand concerns the granting of investment privileges. Should the Thai government continue to grant tax privileges to investors as in the past decades? Is the benefit from tax privileges worth the cost in terms of tax expenditure? And, at one extreme, should the BOI be abolished? Yoshida (1990) referred to the proposal made at the end of 1989 to abolish the BOI or to reorganize it as the Board of Export. The argument at the time was that Thailand had reached a stage of development where it was able to attract foreign investment without having to offer tax and duty concessions. In other words, foreigners invested in Thailand not because of tax and duty concessions, but because they enjoyed the economic stability and all the prerequisites for production (including infrastructure) that Thailand had to offer. The BOI, however, counterargued that it was necessary to have a system of investment promotion because Thailand still possessed the ability to attract foreign investment from neighbouring countries. However high-ranking officials of the BOI admitted the need to change the role of their organization and concentrate more on promoting large-scale projects or Thai investment abroad (p. 61).

The author of the present chapter foresees no drastic change in government policy on investment promotion; only a gradual change is likely. In fact the introduction in 1992 of the value-added tax in place of the business tax has somewhat reduced the advantages of promoted firms over unpromoted ones. This may convince the government to take no further action on the BOI. From the viewpoint of the BOI, granting tax privileges should be continued to promote regional industry. Yoshida (1990) again commented that:

> The business tax will be nullified by the introduction of the value-added tax . . . Nullification of the business tax is good for the development of industry in that it has often been singled out as an obstacle to fostering a social division of labour. On the other hand, it means the loss of one of the tax and duty concessions that the BOI currently provides. This tax privilege is one of the measures aimed at spreading investment in the direction of the provinces. As for the reduction of import duty on raw materials, according to the most recent reports, this will be changed to a system of tax refunds, which means an increase in the burden shouldered by the firm receiving promotional privileges. The BOI, therefore, needs to work out another system of promotional privileges for the firms located in the provinces and to find a way to lessen the burden of firms promoted by a reduction in the import duty on raw materials (p. 62).

7.3.2 Government Finance in Transition

The following summarizes the salient features of the government finance in Thailand.

First, government revenue in Thailand, as in many other countries, moves procyclically with general economic activity. This is confirmed by studies of tax buoyancy conducted or cited by various authors (see for instance Bhanupongse, 1992; Medhi *et al.*, 1988). During an expansionary period the demand for imports tends to increase sharply, as does the aggregate demand for goods and services. As a result, tax collections from import duties and business and excise taxes increase. In Thailand the boom in the land market over the past few years has also led to substantial tax increases through adjusted property values. Inflationary tax, through the income-tax-bracket creep, has provided an additional source of revenue.

Second, government expenditure usually lags two years behind the business cycle. Institutional factors are important in this regard, and budget preparation has to be carried out about 15 months in advance. Using the budget year 1994 as an example, the Thai budget cycle required that all government agencies submit their 1994 budget proposals (in full detail) to the Bureau of the Budget (BOB) by December 1992. And by February 1993 the 'Big Four', that is the Bank of Thailand (BOT), the National Economic and Social Development Board (NESDB), the Ministry of Finance (MOF) and the Bureau of the Budget (BOB) had to determine the total expenditure (the budget ceiling) and submit this figure to the cabinet for approval. Following this, budget allocation by ministries and line agencies had to be prepared by the BOB by June 1993 and submitted to the cabinet. After approval, the government presented the draft of this 1994 budget bill to the National Assembly for scrutiny and approval, and this process had to be completed by September 1993 in order to start the 1994 fiscal year on 1 October 1993.

Third, the demand for increased government spending on education and health has continued to strengthen, as indicated by health and education's share of overall government expenditure (Table 7.3) and their high growth rates (9.93 per cent per annum between 1970 and 1990 compared with the 7 per cent growth rate of GNP for the same period). Policies to expand public services (health, education and family planning) since implementation of the Third Plan can be seen in the increased number of public schools and health clinics in rural areas. While it is fair to say that these public-service targets have been

Table 7.3 Composition of government consumption expenditures

	1970	*1980*	*1990*
National income (NI) (billion baht)	121.3	533.5	1574.6
Government expenditure (% of NI)	14	15.6	9.6
General administration*	29.9	23.7	19.6
Defence*	30.3	32.2	28.4
Justice and police*	8.3	7.7	7.8
Education and research*	18.8	25.5	31.2
Health*	3.8	5.6	7.7
Special welfare*	0.8	0.5	0.8
Transport and communications*	7.2	3.4	2.4

*Percentage of government consumption expenditure.
Source: NESDB, *National Income Accounts*, various years.

reasonably well achieved, it cannot be claimed that equal opportunities exist between urban and rural dwellers, or between rich and poor. The opportunities for intermediate and higher education for the poor are still too low by any standards. Current expenditure on social welfare, research and development, and environmental rehabilitation constitutes only a small portion of the budget. However there are signs that spending on these could increase sharply in the future, especially spending on environmental preservation and rehabilitation.

Fourth, reforms of the tax structure cannot be neglected, and indeed a series of reform measures have been undertaken since the Fifth Plan. There are several objectives that the government would like to accomplish through these tax reforms, for example a reduction in industrial protection, the adoption of uniform tariff rates, the cutting of tax burdens on export industries, the tightening of tax loopholes, a broadening of the tax base and so on. In 1982 the government committed itself to implementing several tax measures using a structural adjustment loan (SAL) from the World Bank. These politically unpopular measures were even harder to implement when the country was experiencing economic difficulties. The measures, including the introduction of the VAT were postponed on several occasions. VAT had been planned for about ten years before it was finally put into effect in January 1992. A major argument against the introduction of this tax was that business enterprises in Thailand generally do not keep adequate business records and accounts. As implemented, VAT has many systemic loopholes as various exemptions and zero rates are granted without good reason. Table 7.4 shows a projection for the tax structure before and after the adoption of VAT, predicting that income tax and VAT combined would provide more than half of total tax revenue in the post-VAT period.

Fifth, government investment expenditure (GIE) has been moving on a downward trend, that is the share of GIE in terms of GDP or in comparison with private investment has fallen over time. This was due to both planned and unanticipated circumstances. In response to economic recession and the high budget deficit in the early 1980s, the government had little choice but to cut its capital-investment spending simply because it was more difficult to trim recurrent and consumption expenditures. Our regression estimate has confirmed that GIE was primarily affected by the lagged government revenue, that is, whenever the revenue position was favourable, GIE would increase significantly in the following years. With respect to large-scale investment projects, we have witnessed greater private participation in recent years, espec-

Table 7.4 Projection of the tax structure before and after tax reform, 1991 (percentage of total revenue)

	Before tax reform	*After tax reform*
Income tax	24.2	27.8
Individual	–9.6	–5.3
Corporate	–14.6	–22.4
Business tax or VAT	21.8	28.7
Excise tax	18.1	16.0
Customs duties	22.5	18.6
Other taxes	1.5	0.5
Other revenues	11.8	8.4

Source: Panas and Somchai, 1991, p. 47.

ially in highway construction and telephone and telecommunications networks. Private franchises have become more acceptable than in the past. The government of Anand Panyarachun greatly encouraged private participation. His government has also succeeded in undermining various monopolistic forces and rent-seeking activities, for example by lifting the import ban on fully-assembled cars, by lowering car tax, and by increasing the number of taxi licences.

Sixth, local governments play a limited role in providing public goods and services in Thailand. Under the present system there are three forms of local government: (1) municipality administrations (Bangkok Metropolitan Administration and Pattaya City are special cases but could be included in this category), (2) sanitary district administrations, and (3) provincial administrative organizations.[2] The roles of these local governments are limited by law as well as by the revenues they collect. Available statistics show that the proportion of local government expenditure to national income is less than 10 per cent. Some of these local governments have unsuccessfully requested greater autonomy from the Ministry of Interior, their controlling organization.

The chance for a major change in this area in the future is, however, quite high because under democratic government the power of the bureaucracy in economic management has weakened. In fact, when the Chartichai government came to power, there was a modification of the revenue-sharing rule. Formerly, the Ministry of Interior's revenue from the business-tax surcharge was shared between the Bangkok Metropolitan Administration and the provincial municipalities at a ratio of

70:30. Since October 1991, however, this has changed to 60:40. Moreover, two policy issues are hotly debated today. The first concerns the election of provincial governors, and the second concerns the structure and administration of local taxes. Should the provincial governor be elected by local voters in each province in place of the present system whereby governors are appointed by the MOI in Bangkok? How many provinces are ready to have elected governors and engage in full self-governments? Can local tax structure and revenue-sharing between central and local government be adjusted in ways that are economically feasible and politically acceptable?

7.4 FUTURE EXPECTATIONS

This section analyzes future scenarios for government finance in Thailand, taking into account recent developments in the political situation and the political economy with regard to policy making in Thailand. In the past, the patron-client model has been popularly used to analyze the political economy and public policy making in Thailand. In this model, the bureaucrats or policy makers were perceived as patrons and businessmen as clients. It could be argued that this model is not an appropriate tool to analyze the present situation in Thailand. This chapter adopts a new position and argues that there are many players in the game of public policy making, and each player competes to reap the highest benefits, either alone or in cooperation with others.[3]

First of all, the bureaucrats are not a unified body. There are many government agencies, and these agencies have different opinions. But it is difficult to deny that there are inherent incentives for government agencies to propose or support new public-spending projects because these projects enhance their economic power and increase the size of their departments. Second, there are no incentives for other government agencies to object to proposals made by other agencies, despite the fact that they may disagree or see the projects as not worth the cost. Each government agency has its own specific objectives and responsibilities; their power depends on the work outcome and this requires resources and manpower. To enhance their power there is an incentive to create new projects or to support the projects of others (for example private projects) that are subject to their control. Government agencies directly responsible for macro-stability are few – possibly only four could be clearly identified: the BOB, the BOT, the MOF and the

NESDB. There are, however, many government agencies whose objectives are to provide services for the general public and are thus inclined to seek higher budgets. Broadly, the big four have played an influential role in macro-policy determination in the past. But their influence was not constant. There were times (such as when General Prem was prime minister) when they were quite effective at killing off unsound public projects proposed by some ministries, but at other times (during the Chartichai government, for instance) the role of these organizations was less effective.

As for the government, there are inherent incentives for the government to initiate or approve new projects since it can claim to have stimulated economic progress, and the governmental sector will gain from increased government revenues in the short run as revenues tend to move procyclically with business activity. Whether those projects or schemes are successful or not cannot be easily ascertained in the short run. In essence, the above analysis assumes some myopic behaviour, that is, decision makers and agencies do not have a clear vision about the future, and they tend to weigh short-term benefits more highly than long-term consequences. (In other words, the discount rate applied to the long-term benefits and costs is quite high.)

It is not always easy to describe the policy stance of government. The political business-cycles model distinguishes two types of government, namely the strategic government and the responsive government (Alt and Chrystal, 1983). The strategic government adopts policies that will attract the greatest number of votes or support. The responsive government adopts policies in accordance with the preferences of supporters. Applying these concepts to our study, it may be asserted that the Chartichai and Anand governments took a strategic-policy approach that aimed to support the advancement of trade and industry and the increasing role of the private sector. The Prem government was more enigmatic and less clear-cut, but could claim to be more balanced.

The followings are some propositions that follow on from the above speculations.

(1) Assuming no major change in the Thai political system, it is most likely that the government will adopt an expansive fiscal policy.

Explanation: For a long time policies on budgetary and financial matters have been largely determined by bureaucrats–politicians have played little part in setting macro-policy. Each year budget has been prepared by the four major agencies, as mentioned above. In the past three decades most government policies have been shaped by technocrats who adhered to the conservative macro-policies suggested by these agencies. With the arrival of democratic government the situation changed. Political parties and politicians now want to be more active in policy making and implementation to show voters that they are doing their jobs well. Under the democratic government the rate of growth of government expenditure has tended to be larger than under bureaucratic governments – Kukrit and Chartichai governments may be cited as examples.

(2) There will be political pressure to amend the law governing the budgeting system in Thailand, and the amended act(s) will allow politicians to play a more important role in shaping the government budget.

Explanation: The current budgeting system is to a large extent based on the principles and guidelines set out in the Budget Procedure Act B.E. 2502 (1959). Under this law, the annual budget plan is prepared entirely by the top bureaucrats in the four agencies referred to above. In the past the cabinet has usually approved the budget proposals prepared by these four agencies because it lacked the factual and technical information needed to question the proposals. Members of parliament (MPs) play a minor role in budget debates in parliament; they have the power to cut the budget but not to increase spending. One of the limiting factors is that MPs by and large have insufficient knowledge or information to counter the bureaucrats' proposals. There is a clear need for the legislative side to strengthen its research and information capability on fiscal policy and public project analysis. To do this, the Budget Procedure Act B.E. 2502 and other related laws need to be amended.

(3) The demand for increased public spending is likely to be pronounced in the following areas: public education, social welfare, agricultural subsidies, especially price-support programmes similar to those practised in high-income countries, research and development activities, and measures to correct environmental degradation.

Explanation: In the past the income elasticity of social expenditure (in the case of Thailand, on education and health) greater than one has been confirmed by many authors. This trend will continue in the future. And judging from the policies announced by many political parties in Thailand in mid-1992, public expenditure for this purpose may rise above its past trend. With respect to environmental issues, past governments' policies have been passive, but this cannot continue in the future because the current situation demands the implementation of strong measures. It should also be noted that the Anand government set, for the first time, separate budgets for environmental protection and rehabilitation.

(4) It is possible that government finance will switch from today's surplus to a permanent deficit.

Explanation: A deficit budget is not uncommon in the Thailand. The budget surplus in the fiscal years 1988–92 may be considered an exception rather than the rule. The 1993 budget, which marked the beginning of the Chuan government, was already in deficit, although the size of this deficit (25 000 million baht) was in comparison with the size of the overall government budget and GNP. But this is only the beginning of the story. As in the past, the 1993 budget was prepared by bureaucrats and was approved by three governments (Suchinda, Anand and Chuan). Chuan, therefore, could claim that the 1993 budget was not really his own. The budget for 1994 will be the real test as to whether the budget under a democratic-government will deviate significantly from those of bureaucratic governments.

(5) Future government revenue, as a percentage of GNP, will increase gradually. The chance of drastic change, despite the tax reform is very limited, but it is possible that revenue composition in the future may differ markedly from that pertaining at present.

Explanation: The government has tended to follow the tax reforms adopted by high-income and neighbouring countries. Based on this premise, the future policy direction is rather clear, that is, the lowering of tax rates, simplification of the tax-collection process, and the adjustment of existing tax rates to more uniform rates. The tax base, particularly direct tax, will be enhanced by policies and by the modernization process as formal employment increases. Tax rates in general will, however, be reduced to promote or support industrialization and international competitiveness. It should be noted that in February 1992 at the ASEAN summit meeting in Singapore, Thailand proposed a scheme for an ASEAN Free Trade Area (AFTA), which will have implications for taxation. First of all, the government agreed to bring down tariff rates to about 20–30 per cent within the next 7–8 years. Second, tariff rates will be reduced further to 10 per cent by the year 2007. Third, 15 products or commodities, including such items as palm oil, plastic products, cement and so on, will be targeted for 'fast-track' tariff reductions. Hence the importance of tax revenue from international trade will decline further.

(6) Given the social environment of today, the demand for local government and public services will expand rapidly and there will be strong political pressure to revise local taxation and the revenue-sharing formula between central and local governments.

Explanation: Today, the mood for local self-government is very strong. Over the past decades local governments have been passive and their role in providing public goods has been confined by limited authority and resources. This is confirmed by the low percentage share of local-government expenditures relative to that of central government in the consolidated public-sector account. In the general election of September 1992 all political parties announced policies to support stronger local government. Current contentious issues include the election of provincial governors, the selection of provinces to go first, the raising of fiscal resources for local governments, and so on. On this last crucial issue, many alternatives are possible. Central government could provide more grants; local governments could be given the authority to collect new taxes; or central government could redesign the revenue-sharing formula between central and local government.

7.5 SUMMARY

Industrialization has progressed strongly in Thailand in the past decades, and has accelerated rapidly since the end of the 1980s, when there was a huge inflow of DFI from Japan and the Asian NICs. This had a substantial impact on the Thai economy and government finance. The governmental sector gained from this economic transition in terms of increased tax collection without having to increase tax rates. This was possible because of (a) the nature of taxation which moved procyclically with economic activity, and (b) the broadening of the tax base as seen by the increase in the share of formal-sector employment in total employment. Encouraged by the Treasury's sizeable surplus, the government began to increase expenditure by adjusting the wages and salaries of public employees which for years had lagged behind those of private sector, and by easing in public-investment projects, which had been frozen in the recessionary period of the early 1980s.

Regarding the future, the author of this chapter envisages changes in government finance in three main directions. First, the past fiscal stance may be changed substantially due to institutional factors, the most important being the increasing influence of the political parties in macro policy making, which in the past has been almost entirely in the hands of bureaucrats. The government budget will return to deficit, after running a surplus for the past several years. It is possible that the Budget Procedure Act B.E. 2502, which for a long time has served as the principal guideline for government budgeting, will be amended in the near future and will pave the way for the greater influence of MPs. This is not necessarily to imply that future fiscal policy will be reckless and irresponsible.

Second, under democratic government and the decline of the bureaucrats, the tools used to analyze public policy making in the future will need to be more sophisticated. The simple patron-client model may become inappropriate. Using concepts from game theory and the competition-for-political-influence model, it is speculated that the Thai government will adopt economic policies that in general, will be favourable and conducive to industrial growth. With respect to social issues, the government may adopt a responsive stance.

Third, government involvement, measured in terms of the size of public expenditure in relation to GDP, may increase only gradually; likewise the size of government revenue as a percentage of GDP. But the composition of revenue may change markedly.

It is very likely that tax collections from international trade will decline further as Thailand strives to maintain its international competitiveness. A series of tax reforms, in addition to VAT, are underway. The tax measures that will follow the formation of the ASEAN Free Trade Area are likely to strengthen the bargaining power of Thailand and will have a significant impact on government finance. Raising property taxes, by continuously adjusting the assessed value of property, is a plausible undertaking, and this should help the growth of local government. Revising the revenue-sharing formula between central and local government is another policy issue for the future.

Notes

1. Government expenditure, consumption and investment averaged 14.89 per cent of GNP for the period 1970–90, with GCE on a rising trend but GIE on a declining trend. It should be recalled that there are other forms of government expenditure such as transfer, interest and debt payments.
2. Municipality administrations are the most advanced form of local government in Thailand where municipal administrators are directly elected by the local people. Areas to be designated municipal areas must be large and developed enough in terms of local revenue generated. A local area not developed or urbanized enough to be promoted to a municipality may be given the status of sanitary district and is governed by sanitary district administration whose executive officers are partly elected by the local people and partly *ex officio* members of the local Ministry of Interior officials. The remaining area in a province which is not a municipal area or a sanitary district will fall under the jurisdiction of the provincial admin-

istrative organisation which is also run by officials from the Ministry of Interior in coordination with locally elected officials.

3. This approach is suggested by Becker (1983). According to Becker, political equilibrium depends on the efficiency of each group in producing pressure and the deadweight costs of taxes and subsidies. He proposes the following propositions:
   – A group that becomes more efficient at producing political pressure would be able to reduce its taxes or raise its subsidy.
   – An increase in deadweight cost reduces the equilibrium subsidy.
   – Politically successful groups tend to be small relative to the size of the groups taxed to pay their subsidies.
   – Competition among pressure groups favours efficient methods of taxation.

8 Industrialization, Financial Reform and Monetary Policy

Naris Chaiyasoot[1]

8.1 INTRODUCTION

This chapter aims to provide an overview of Thailand's financial sector and an analysis of the many reforms and deregulation efforts that have been undertaken. Thailand's financial reforms have been prompted primarily by the desire to mobilize domestic savings and compete for increasingly scarce foreign capital inflows. These funds are needed to finance sustained industrialization efforts and infrastructure building, which are seen as prerequisites for Thailand's ability to maintain high economic growth in the future.

Section 8.2 provides a summary of Thailand's economic development from the 1950s to the present with a special emphasis on its financial development. Section 8.3 takes a more detailed look at Thailand's financial sector and monetary policy. Finally, Section 8.4 looks at the trouble-free implementation of Thailand's financial-reform package in the context of the rich literature that exists with regard to the financial-reform experiences of other countries.

8.2 THAILAND'S ECONOMIC DEVELOPMENT IN PERSPECTIVE

8.2.1 Postwar Economic Development

Thailand's postwar development can be roughly divided into three phases. The first phase (1950–70) can be characterized as one based on rapid infrastructure building and subsequent industrialization through an import-substitution strategy. The building of infrastructure – particularly transportation networks, electricity supply and irrigation – was assisted partly by foreign aid and loans and was motivated, apart from economic-development objectives, by national-security considerations. Agriculture in particular benefited from this infrastructure, especially with regard to the production of rice and several other crops that were major foreign-exchange earners.

Import-substitution industrialization succeeded in maintaining industrial growth at double-digit levels during its initial phase. However by the late 1960s it had become clear to Thai policy makers that avenues for continued industrialization through import substitution would be severely constrained by the small domestic market. As a result, policy makers began to turn to an export-oriented approach as an alternative means of sustaining industrialization efforts.

Throughout the period fiscal and monetary policy remained conservative. Government deficits during the period averaged below 2 per cent of GDP while monetary growth ranged from 10–15 per cent per annum. As a result, annual inflation averaged only about 5 per cent during these two decades. The period also saw the Thai baht pegged to the US dollar from 1963 onwards, and the exchange rate between the baht and the US dollar remained unchanged until the 1980s.

The second phase of Thailand's economic development (1970–85) not only saw a shift towards a more outward-oriented development strategy but also the need for economic adjustments in the face of severe external shocks in the form of two energy crises. The period 1973–85 saw Thailand's terms of trade deteriorate by about 36 per cent. Yet the export-oriented strategy and other favourable external factors resulted in the ratio of exports to GDP rising from a low of 10 per cent in 1970 to a high of 20 per cent in 1982. Nevertheless average GDP growth for 1973–85 fell to about 5 per cent per annum, well below those attained during the previous period. The average inflation rate increased sharply, with peaks of 25 per cent and 20 per cent, respectively, in 1973 and 1980. A substantial and persistent current-account deficit emerged, averaging about 6 per cent of GDP. This in turn led to a significant increase in Thailand's external debt and debt service.

Thailand's policy reactions to the first and second oil shocks were very different. After the first oil shock there was an attempt to cushion the impact of energy-price increases and restore past growth rates. Energy subsidies were introduced, which kept the domestic cost of energy well below world prices. At the same time public expenditure increased sharply and a substantial fiscal deficit emerged, which was increasingly financed by external borrowing. The second oil shock saw Thailand's trade balance deteriorate sharply as the baht continued to appreciate. Thailand was in a much weaker position then and was less able to cushion the impact of this external shock. While the level of foreign debt and debt services remained manageable, the rapid rate of debt accumulation was an increasing concern. At the same time the domestic economy was becoming increasingly strained by the distortions created by unrealistic energy pricing, price controls and tariff increases.

In 1980 the government decided to undertake a comprehensive economic-adjustment programme. Loans from the IMF and the World Bank assisted the government in its efforts to reduce the twin fiscal and current-account deficits, to eliminate price distortions, to undertake interest-rate-ceiling adjustments and to dismantle tariff barriers. The baht was devalued by almost 15 per cent in November 1984. It was also delinked from the US dollar. The system of fixed exchange rate, which was the hallmark of Thailand's foreign-exchange policy, was replaced by a system of managed float based on a basket of key foreign currencies. Although the authorities refused to disclose the weights of the foreign currencies used to determine the value of the baht, it was obvious that the US dollar dominated the basket.

Policy-reform successes began with the easing of ceilings on interest rates and inflation, thereby helping to restore positive real interest rates after 1982. Domestic energy prices were raised to world-market levels, eliminating distortions and disincentives to energy conservation. The range of tariff rates was narrowed and quantitative restrictions on some imports were lifted. Tariff rates were not significantly reduced, however, as improvements in the government's fiscal position proved more elusive. It was found that the problem was a chronic tendency to overestimate revenue and a lack of responsiveness of the tax system, due mainly to numerous tax exemptions. To deal with the problem the government adopted a conservative revenue estimate mechanism, which now consistently underestimates revenue, on average, by about 2 per cent of GDP. Expenditure was also significantly reduced by adopting policies that allowed only moderate increases in the salaries of government employees, by reducing capital expenditure to about 1 per cent of GDP, and by increasing the prices of public enterprises' services and reducing their capital investments.

8.2.2 The Boom Years, 1986–90

Economic reforms undertaken during the first half of the 1980s helped place Thailand in a strong position to take full advantage of the US-led world economic recovery, which began in earnest in the latter part of the decade. Inflation was brought down to about 4 per cent in 1986. Government fiscal deficit, which reached a peak of 5 per cent of GDP in 1984–5, turned into surplus in 1986–7, peaking at 5 per cent of GDP in 1990.

Thailand's economic performance from 1987–90 was impressive even when judged in terms of its past commendable standards. Real GDP growth was 9.5 per cent, 13.2 per cent, 12.2 per cent and 11.6 per cent, respectively, in the four years from 1987 to 1990. This growth resulted primarily from a boom in manufactured exports, which averaged about 30 per cent annually, and the massive inflow of private foreign investment particularly into the export-oriented manufacturing sector. By late 1989, however, it had become clear that bottlenecks were fast emerging and the economy was in danger of overheating. Lack of adequate transportation, port capacity, and electricity and water supply were becoming more and more apparent. Shortages of skilled personnel, especially engineers, was another emerging problem. More importantly, the capital inflows and balance-of-payments surpluses resulting from direct foreign investment was accelerating monetary growth, a trend that the Bank of Thailand increasingly found difficult to sterilize in view of the growing openness of the capital account. Accelerating import growth in order to implement investment projects was a major factor contributing to large current-account deficits, which were estimated at a worrying 8.5 per cent of GDP in 1991. The effectiveness of monetary policy will be discussed in more detail below. At this point it is sufficient to add that the massive inflow of foreign funds and intensified economic activity pushed up the rate of inflation up to beyond 6 per cent in 1990. The economic expansion also led to a frenzy of speculation in the real-estate and stock markets causing the value of these assets to more than double from 1986–90.

In response the Bank of Thailand asked commercial banks to put voluntary lending limits on 'non-productive' activities (such as golf-course investments). It also reintroduced the 10 per cent withholding tax on interest payments on foreign loans. The ceiling on deposit interest rates was abolished, while at the same time the ceiling on lending rates was increased from 15 per cent to 16.5 per cent. Finally, Bank of Thailand bonds worth 13.5 billion baht were sold in open market operations.

These measures, combined with effects of the Persian Gulf crisis, slowed down the Thai economy in 1990. The military coup in February 1991 further eroded economic confidence and depressed the economy to a growth rate of about 8 per cent in 1991. Expectations of economic recovery in 1992 were somewhat dashed by the violent clash between civilians and the military in May, in which scores of people were killed. However the economy recovered remarkably quickly from the May incident, and attained a rate of growth of 8 per cent in 1992. With the return to democracy following the general election in September 1992, coupled with continued world economic recovery, it was believed that Thailand's economic expansion to the end of the Seventh Plan in 1996 should satisfy the planned annual growth rate of 8.2 per cent.

8.2.3 Current Policy Issues

There is a realization among Thailand's policy makers and top technocrats that Thailand's future prosperity lies in its ability to cope successfully with an increasingly competitive world economy. The means by which Thailand's economic prowess could be enhanced is through continued commitment to liberalization and deregulation, in effect exposing the Thai economy to greater internal and global competition.

There is also a need to address the problem of insufficient infrastructure. This needs to be financed in part by increased domestic (private) savings, although the government's fiscal position remains strong. The major policy goal is, of course, to maintain the pace of economic expansion primarily through continued rapid industrialization. Moreover, Thailand's future industries need to be more capital and technology intensive, in line with the growing scarcity of labour in Thailand and the loss of comparative advantage in labour-intensive industries to places such as China, Indonesia and the South Asian countries.

Financing industrialization and infrastructure building would require the Thai government to try as far as possible, to increase the availability and reduce the cost of capital. Liberalization and promotion of the financial sector is considered the best way of doing this. A more open and efficient financial sector would, it is believed, contribute significantly to the mobilization of domestic savings and attract increasingly scarce foreign capital. Apart from developing the financial sector to support these key objectives, it was also advocated by Thai policy makers that the financial sector should be developed for its own sake because Thailand can fill a niche as a subregional financial centre, particularly as a provider of financial services for the reconstruction of Indochina. The government has been particularly keen to establish off-shore banking units (OBUs). The government has shown a readiness to give 15–20 licences for the establishment of OBUs, and responses from both Thai and foreign banks have been enthusiastic. In broad terms, regulations laid down by the government are aimed particularly at the promotion of 'out–out' transactions, especially the channelling of funds from various sources to Indochina. Some incentives exist for 'out–in' transactions – that is inflows of funds from foreign sources into Thailand – but these incentives have been tempered by a concern that domestic banks should not face competition that is too intense, a concern that is in keeping with past protective policies of the government.

Other development objectives include the need to improve human resources, to close the urban–rural income gap and to deal with the growing problem of environmental degradation. While these are important national issues, they are not a primary concern of this chapter. Instead, we will concentrate on the development and reform of Thailand's financial sector, particularly its role in supporting a continued rapid pace of industrialization. Monetary policy and policy mechanisms will also be discussed in this regard, particularly the way in which financial reform and deregulation as well as Thailand's increasing openness will make the conducting of monetary policy more challenging and complex.

8.3 THAILAND'S FINANCIAL SECTOR AND MONETARY POLICY

During the 1980s the size of Thailand's financial sector nearly doubled as a percentage of GDP. In particular, the ratio of financial assets to GDP increased from 69.2 per cent to 121.2 per cent. At the same time the ratio of M2 to GDP increased from 34.2 per cent to 67.4 per cent (Robinson, Byeon and Teja, 1991; Tseng and Corker, 1991).

While the financial system has broadened considerably the capital market has remained quite small with the exception of the fast-expanding stock market. This can be seen in the growing role of the stock market in savings mobilization at the expense of the financial institutions. For instance, the share of total savings mobilized by financial institutions and the stock market were 70.7 and 8.6 per cent, respectively, in 1986. These shares changed markedly in 1991 as financial institutions managed to account for only 50.7 per cent of total savings whereas the share of the stock market rose to 28.8 per cent (Patira, 1992).

Nevertheless the variety of financial instruments available to both users and providers of funds is limited at present. To remedy the situation, the Thai authorities have laid out a wide-ranging programme of financial reforms aimed at boosting domestic savings, enhancing the competitiveness of the Thai financial sector and establishing Thailand as a subregional financial centre, primarily to serve the needs of reconstruction in Indochina.

8.3.1 Financial Institutions

The Bank of Thailand – the country's central bank – forms the core of the Thai financial system. As of early 1992 there were 29 commercial banks and three specialized banks owned by the government: the Government Savings Bank, set up to mobilize household savings through an extensive branch network; the Bank for Agriculture and Agricultural Cooperatives, which makes mostly concessional loans to the agricultural sector; and the Government Housing Bank, which finances home purchases by those with moderate incomes. These specialized government banks accounted for nearly 9 per cent of financial assets in 1990.

The 29 commercial banks, which accounted for 71 per cent of total financial assets in 1990, dominate the Thai financial sector. Most domestic banks were originally established by business groups and trading houses to help finance their operations, and they maintain close links today. The banking sector is highly concentrated, with the five largest domestic banks accounting for some two thirds of total bank assets. The sector is also mainly closed to foreign competition as the 16 local commercial banks, with their extensive branch networks (2112 domestic and 22 foreign branches), account for 95 per cent of bank assets. The 14 foreign banks, which account for 5 per cent of bank assets, are disadvantaged with respect to domestic banks in three respects: (1) they are unable to offer retail banking services since they are allowed only one branch in Thailand; (2) they are not juristic entities, so they cannot be quoted on the stock exchange and are thus not allowed certain tax breaks; and (3) they pay a withholding tax on dividends transferred overseas.

The 94 finance and securities companies are the second largest group of financial institutions, accounting for about 15 per cent of total financial assets. They are relatively new institutions, having emerged in the early 1960s as affiliates of commercial banks. They were set up primarily to undertake higher margin but higher risk consumer finance as well as to provide services that the parent bank could not undertake directly. Their activities subsequently expanded into certain types of corporate finance. The finance and securities companies expanded rapidly during the 1970s but were stalled in the early 1980s following financial crises in 1979 and, particularly, in 1983. The 1983 financial crisis, triggered initially by large losses in a finance company and its affiliates, subsequently affected one third of all financial companies accounting for one fourth of financial assets. Important factors leading to this financial crisis included the slowdown in growth and tight monetary policy, the weak management practices of the finance companies (particularly with regard to extending credit and guarantees to projects in which the institution's directors and shareholders had vested interests), and the weak supervisory and regulatory framework of the central authorities.

One of the authorities' responses was the setting up of the Financial Institutions Development Fund to rehabilitate ailing financial institutions. Among the various schemes to revive the ailing institutions, the 'lifeboat scheme' was the principal means by which liquidity was provided in exchange for control by the Ministry of Finance who will try to strengthen the institution's management, credit-collection procedures and financial plan with an aim to return those institutions to health.

Supervision and regulation were strengthened also. The Bank of Thailand revoked the licences of some 24 financial institutions and intervened in 30 more from 1983–6. The Bank of Thailand's legal, regulatory and supervisory powers were strengthened. It was empowered to enforce compliance by direct intervention, and when necessary it can order an increase in bank capital and remove bank directors and officers.

Finally, other specialized financial institutions that make up the Thai financial sector include the Industrial Finance Corporation of Thailand (IFCT, a privately owned development bank financed primarily through foreign borrowing with government guarantees); over 2000 savings and agricultural cooperatives; 18 credit foncier companies (financing and leasing of immovable assets); life insurance companies and numerous pawnshops. These are estimated to account for a little more than 5 per cent of total financial assets.

8.3.2 Monetary Policy

Thailand's monetary authorities have declared that monetary policy serves several policy objectives, namely growth, stability and economic development (Bank of Thailand, 1990). A primary objective is, however, to maintain domestic price stability. This was accomplished in all but two short periods in which domestic inflation rate rose to double-digit levels: 25 per cent in 1974 and 20 per cent in 1982. Thai monetary authorities have consistently kept monetary-base growth in line with real economic growth. For example, monetary-base growth from 1960–71, 1972–9, and 1980–90 were 11 per cent, 14.5 per cent, and 19 per cent, respectively. Compared with real economic growth during the same period, the excess of monetary growth over real economic growth averaged 6.3 per cent, 7.2 per cent and 11 per cent, respectively. As a result, the inflation rate in Thailand over the past 30 years has been very similar to that which prevailed in industrialized countries, particularly the United States (Virabongsa and Pakorn, 1988).

The comparability of Thailand's inflation rate with the United States did not occur by chance. Thailand pegged the baht to the US dollar for over 20 years – from 1963 to 1984. The pegging of the baht to a basket of currencies since then has turned out, in practice, to be an implicit continuation of past policy to keep the baht closely aligned with the US dollar. Arising from this is the fact that Thailand's monetary policy has been used to defend the exchange rate, in particular to redress external-balance problems when they arise. For example the authorities kept the rate of growth of M1 at 4.0 per cent and 2.4 per cent below nominal GDP growth from 1972–9 and 1980–6, respectively, as a means of both curbing inflation and restraining widening external deficits. In short, monetary policy in Thailand has traditionally been assigned the task of maintaining both domestic price stability and external balance under a regime of fixed exchange rates and subsequently a 'dirty float', which kept the baht in close parity with the US dollar.

The main monetary policy instruments in Thailand are open-market operations in the repurchase markets and, to a lesser extent, lending by the Bank of Thailand. Changes to interest-rate ceilings were also resorted to, especially in the 1980s, but ceilings on both deposit and lending rates have been completely abolished as of June 1992. The Bank of Thailand also intervenes in the foreign-exchange market. Changes to reserve ratio requirements have rarely been used as an instrument of monetary policy. As such, the basic reserve requirement of 7 per cent of deposit liabilities (2 per cent deposit with the Bank of

Thailand, 2.5 vault cash and the rest in government securities) has remained unchanged for the past 20 years.

The primary instrument of monetary policy is open-market operations in the repurchase market. As the sole seller in the market, the Bank of Thailand can readily inject or absorb liquidity as the situation warrants. Securities traded in this market are government bonds. However, following a substantial improvement in Thailand's external position and growing liquidity in the banking system in 1986, the Bank of Thailand actively drained liquidity through consistent government-bond purchases. The need to continue draining liquidity and the growing importance of open-market operations led to the introduction and sale of the Bank of Thailand's own bonds from 1987.

The other monetary instrument, central-bank lending, is carried out via a general loan window and a refinancing facility. These instruments have not really played a significant role as tools for economic stabilization. The former facility essentially provides short-term liquidity for financial institutions but requires government securities as collateral. Banks must also show that they have no alternative sources of funds. Lending under this window amounted to only 2.4 billion baht or 0.15 per cent of total bank deposits, underscoring the 'last-resort' nature of this window. Changes in loan-window interest rates have been more frequent, especially in recent times. These changes have been used to signal shifts in the Bank of Thailand's monetary policy.

Interest-rate ceilings cannot initially be considered instruments of monetary policy since they were set by legislation to 'prevent excessive competition' and ensure 'stability' of the financial system. Lending rates were set at 15 per cent, which kept domestic interest rates significantly positive during periods of low inflation prior to the 1970s. Moreover, foreign interest rates were stable at 5–6 per cent, thereby keeping a margin that was sufficient to uphold the level of capital inflow necessary to maintain the external balance. However, periods of high interest rates and inflation during the 1970s led to periods of significantly negative real interest rates, threatening to dry up capital inflows and bringing about severe credit tightening in Thailand. Credit rationing was particularly severe in 1979, causing a great deal of commercial hardship, and was a prelude to the subsequent crises in the financial sector that were mentioned above.

As a result the authorities amended the law to enable the Bank of Thailand to announce changes in interest-rate ceilings in 1980. The Bank of Thailand increased bank deposit and lending rates by 3 per cent that year followed by another upward adjustment in bank and financial-company lending rates to reach 19 per cent and 21 per cent, respectively, in 1984. Variations in interest-rate ceilings were used as instruments to affect money and credit until ceilings on all interest rates for bank deposits were abolished in March 1990. This was followed by a removal of ceilings on lending rates for commercial banks and other financial institutions in June 1992. In short, the Thai authorities have been very mindful of ensuring that domestic interest rates closely track foreign interest rates. In particular, domestic interest rates have been significantly positive in most years. The systematic liberalization of interest rates, beginning in 1989, signalled a comprehensive approach to reform that was consistent with Thailand's level of economic maturity and rapid industrialization.

The Bank of Thailand's refinancing facility is designed to allocate more financial resources to priority sectors at preferential interest rates by providing credits to commercial banks against their promissory notes. Commercial banks lend to these priority sectors at rates not exceeding 10 per cent while refinancing interest rates are 3–5 per cent depending on the sector in question. Some 90 per cent of the loans go to exports, with the rest allocated to manufacturing and agricultural activities, and rural development. The amount of refinancing outstanding was 22 billion baht in 1990.

8.3.3 Financial Reforms

Apart from the abolition of interest-rate ceilings discussed above, Thailand also undertook financial liberalization in the following areas.

Relaxation of foreign exchange control

On 22 May 1990 Thailand officially accepted Article VIII of the International Monetary Fund Agreement, which obliges it to allow unrestricted international payments with respect to current-account transactions. This was, in effect, the first stage of foreign-exchange control liberalization aimed at boosting confidence among investors and entrepreneurs as well as improving Thailand's credit worthiness in international markets. Measures to relax foreign-exchange controls include allowing commercial banks to grant all foreign-exchange transactions relating to international trade and to approve repayments of foreign loans and remittances of securities sales for up to US$500 000; increasing the maximum limits on foreign-exchange transactions relating to services accounts; and increasing the limit on travel allowances, education and other remittances.

On 1 April 1991 the Bank of Thailand announced the second stage of foreign exchange control liberalization which included, among other things, allowing repatriation of investment funds, dividends and profits as well as loan repayments and interest payment without requiring prior authorisation; allowing unrestricted direct foreign investment by residents to their affiliated companies abroad to an amount not exceeding US$5 million, although the purchase of immovable assets and securities abroad still require Bank of Thailand approval; and allowing Thai individuals and juristic persons in Thailand to maintain foreign-currency accounts under certain conditions.

Liberalization of commercial banks and other financial institutions

The Thai authorities embarked on a strategy to promote and widen the scope of activities of commercial banks and other financial institutions not only as a means of improving the mobilization of domestic savings and foreign-capital inflows, but also to strengthen the competitiveness of Thai commercial banks and other financial institutions. In this regard the authorities anticipate that successful completion of the Uruguay Round of GATT negotiations will inevitably require Thailand to open up its financial sector to foreign competition in the near future. Thus, ongoing liberalization is partly in anticipation of, and in preparation for increased competition in the Thai financial market. In particular, from 3 November 1987 commercial banks were permitted to undertake the following activities: preparation of feasibility studies for investment projects; loan syndication; provision of consulting services on acquisitions, mergers or consolidation; and management of trust funds.

The implementation of the Securities and Exchange Act (SEA), passed on 16 May 1992, is expected greatly to expand the scope of activities of commercial banks. Banks can now manage as well as act as a trustee of a mutual fund. Several major banks have already obtained licences and are setting up mutual funds. SEA also allows banks to act as selling agents of government and state enterprise agencies (bonds, debentures and notes). The scope of commercial bank services were further broadened, allowing them to act as sales agents for debt instruments of government and state enterprises, to provide information services for clients, and to act as financial advisers. Finally, banks can now issue negotiable certificates of deposits.

The maximum limit of net open foreign asset position with respect to the capital funds of commercial banks was increased from 20 per cent to 25 per cent on 9 April 1990. On 13 November the same year, the ratio of securities holdings to total deposits required for new branch opening was reduced from 16 per cent to 9.5 per cent. Since 5 June 1991 bond issues by state enterprises, which were not guaranteed by the Ministry of Finance, can be counted as required reserves for branch opening. Moreover, the ratio of securities holdings was further reduced to 8 per cent and 7 per cent, respectively, on 13 September 1991 and 14 February 1992.

On 23 June 1991 the type of reserves required to maintain a 7 per cent reserve ratio was relaxed to include liquid assets such as Bank of Thailand bonds, debentures, bonds or other debt instruments issued by state organizations and state enterprises. Foreign currencies held by commercial banks are also counted as cash on hand.

In line with government policy to promote Thailand as a regional financial centre, the government plans to issue as many as 20 licences to foreign banks to set up offshore banking institutions under the Bangkok International Banking Facility, or BIBF. This plan was initiated in 1990 by the Bank of Thailand, which, in view of the successful financial liberalization carried out so far, felt that Thailand was ready and the timing and opportunity were right. Banks under the BIBF will be authorized to undertake the following activities:

- In the form of foreign currencies: take in deposits and loans from abroad and extend loans to both overseas (out–out) and local (out–in) markets.
- In baht: take in deposit and loans from banks (both Thai and foreign) abroad and make loans to banks abroad (out–out in baht). Note that BIBF will not be allowed to lend in baht to local markets.
- Engage in cross-currency foreign-exchange trading.
- Provide aval and guarantee facilities for foreign-currency loans extended to overseas borrowers.
- Handle trade finance for overseas customers.
- Engage in loan syndication by acquiring foreign-currency loans extended to overseas borrowers.

Many key foreign banks have expressed keen interest in BIBF and viewed it as a first step towards being granted a full commercial bank operating licence in Thailand. Major Thai banks have shown some concern that offshore banking institutions will intensify competition in acquiring foreign loans for the domestic market (out–in), an area they have dominated in the past. The package of incentives subsequently granted by the government in this regard, such as retention of the 10 per cent withholding tax for such BIBF loans, will however temper the competitiveness of BIBF vis-à-vis local banks. It is also an indication that the Thai central-bank authorities are well aware of the competition and are determined to ensure that this competition against local banks will not be excessive.

Concerning the effects of BIBF on local banking, it is probable that BIBF will slow down corporate lending by local banks. Large corporations will seek to obtain more funds through BIBF. Local banks will therefore have to place greater emphasis on retail banking and fee-based income, where there will be greater competition with finance companies (Thanisr, 1992a). Another implication is that the expected inflows of out–in transactions by BIBF will certainly increase the domestic money supply. Again, the withholding tax will help slow down such inflows. The BIBF will also enable Thai businesses to acquire foreign loans at lower cost. Moreover, the greater integration of the Thai financial market with the global market will help narrow the spread between domestic and foreign interest rates, thereby benefiting investors and savers. In addition the BIBF is expected to promote a significant increase in out–out transactions, in particular loans from overseas into Indochinese countries. It is here that BIBF and Thai banks are expected to complement rather than compete with each other. The opening of Thai bank branches in Indochina will create an important financial network that will help facilitate BIBF activities in Indochina (Thanisr, 1992a).

With respect to finance companies, the Bank of Thailand has advocated that they be allowed to expand into areas previously reserved for commercial banks. Established and reputable financial companies will, for example, be allowed to deal in foreign exchange business. As a result, top-tier finance companies will be almost indistinguishable from banks.

Concerning the capital market, the principal aim of the Securities and Exchange Act of 1992 was to create and develop the primary-securities market. Previously a company wanting to mobilize funds directly from the public had to meet very stringent conditions to become a public company. Subsequently companies that were listed and authorized by the Stock Exchange of Thailand (SET) were allowed to issue new shares for public subscription and to float debentures. But this did not meet the primary objective of developing the primary market, for it was tantamount to making use of the secondary market to determine the role of the primary market. The new SEA allows both public and ordinary limited companies to issue debt instruments for fund-mobilization purposes (Patira, 1992). The success in this regard could provide yet another important source of direct finance for Thailand's industries in line with the government's industrial-promotion policy. It would, at the same time, further erode the corporate-finance activities of local commercial banks, which may have to adjust by providing consultancy and fee-based services to companies wishing to obtain finance from the primary market.

As regards the equity market, the passage of the Securities Exchange Act has streamlined the supervision of the SET by a separate and independent institution modelled along the lines of the US Securities and Exchange Commission. The SEC also promises to expedite the time needed to evaluate and authorize company listing in the SET. Delays and strict evaluation procedures have led some firms to gain 'back door' entry by taking over firms that are already listed in the stock market. Other firms have explored the over-the-counter (OTC) market as an alternative means of raising capital, and this is attracting some interest at present.

All in all, however, it must still be concluded that the Thai financial market is not yet well developed. The main financial instruments available to individuals are still essentially limited to bank deposits, promissory notes issued by finance and securities companies, and shares. The primary sources of finance are loans from banks or finance companies, share issues and, for larger companies, foreign borrowing. While other financial instruments exist – such as commercial paper, transferable certificates of deposit, short-term notes and debentures – they have in practice played a limited role. Nevertheless recent reforms, as noted above, suggest that the Thai financial sector could continue to be a dynamic and fast-growing sector of the economy.

8.4 INDUSTRIALIZATION, FINANCIAL REFORM AND MONETARY POLICY

8.4.1 Assessment and Evaluation of Thailand's Financial Reforms

Widespread acceptance of the effectiveness of market forces as the most effective means of promoting economic development has led many countries to comprehensively liberalize and deregulate their economies. Many such liberalization efforts have succeeded in spurring growth, yet a significant number have produced adverse repercussions that are serious enough to undermine the policy reforms. A brief survey of the literature below revealed that the financial reforms in Thailand have been undertaken in the correct sequence, as prescribed by empirical evidence.

Because of the importance of the sequencing of reforms, a body of literature on this subject has been developed. For example Edwards (1987) argued that the domestic economy should be reformed before the external sector is liberalized. In particular, on the domestic side fiscal deficit must be controlled before inflation is dealt with. Once this has been done domestic financial reforms can be undertaken, leading to the raising of domestic interest rates. Within the external sector, the current and capital accounts should not be liberalized at the same time. Liberalizing the capital account first would most likely lead to rapid inflows of capital, generating real appreciation of the domestic currency, making it more difficult for the tradeable goods sector to adjust to world competition. Instead the current account should be liberalized first, and only after the new productive structure has been established should the capital account be slowly set free.

The *1991 World Development Report* concluded that macroeconomic stability formed the basis upon which successful reforms, particularly those concerning the financial sector, could be carried out. Empirical evidence also revealed that the goods sector should be reformed first because the financial sector adjusts itself more quickly than the product sector. This is particularly so with respect to the liberalization of the trade and capital accounts.

According to McKinnon (1988), who carried out several studies on the interest-rate policies of some Asian and Latin American countries, financial liberalization and significantly positive real interest rates are, on average, associated with higher economic growth. He also found that full liberalization of the banks during high and variable inflation is not warranted because unduly high real interest rates are likely to prevail in such circumstances. There are limits to which interests rates can be raised without incurring the danger of adverse risk selection among borrowers. High real interest rates not only allow the riskiest borrowing to remain, but actually encourages the practice. And this could create a moral-hazard problem for the banks themselves, especially when bank supervision is weak and ineffective.

Villanueva and Mirakhor (1990) further expanded on McKinnon's work and concluded that macroeconomic stabilization and stringent bank supervision must occur before complete interest-rate liberalization can take place. Where the economy is unstable and bank supervision is weak, interest-rate liberalization should be gradual and accompanied by both strong macroeconomic policy to stabilize the economy and strict supervision of the banking system. Where supervision is already effective but macroeconomic instability exists, the economy should be stabilized before introducing gradual interest-rate liberalization. Where macroeconomic stability has been attained but supervision is inadequate, supervision should be boosted while interest rates are regulated. Macro stability and effective supervision help the reforming country avoid the adverse consequences of financial liberalization, namely sharp increases in interest rates, bankruptcies of financial institutions and loss of monetary control.

Thailand's situation exhibits many of the characteristics necessary for successful financial reforms. First, domestic stability has always been maintained as inflation has been kept low. Second, real domestic interest rates have been kept at levels that are consistently higher than world rates. Third, Thailand successfully dealt with its fiscal problems and strengthened supervision of the financial sector prior to embarking on comprehensive financial liberalization in the latter part of the 1980s. Fourth, the tradeable-goods sector has been relatively free of distortions. Protection of the domestic market has been confined to moderate tariff rates and quantitative restrictions existed only in exceptional cases. It is therefore not surprising that liberalization of Thailand's financial sector and capital account were carried out smoothly without any subsequent instabilities or adverse impacts (Bank of Thailand, 1992). The prospects are also good that implementation of further liberalization policies such as the BIBF, undertaken with the Thai financial authorities' usual care and caution, will bring about no serious repercussions.

8.4.2 Implications for Monetary Policy and Economic Stability

As mentioned earlier, the task that Thai policy planners have set for themselves is the maintenance of economic growth rates comparable to past performance while at the same time addressing the problem of growing inequality and environmental degradation. Concentrating on economic growth, the Seventh Plan has set a target growth rate of 8.2 per cent per year between 1992 and 1996. In this regard, industry and exports are expected to be the primary means by which this growth rate is to be achieved, that is, these two sectors are expected to expand at an annual rate of 9.5 per cent and 14.7 per cent, respectively. Meanwhile, inflation is to be kept to below 5.6 per cent per annum while the current-account deficit as a percentage of GDP is predicted to fall from a high of 8.5 per cent in 1991 to an average of 5.2 per cent during the Seventh Plan period.

The Seventh Plan also set ambitious goals, particularly in relation to growth in the industrial sector and exports. Financial reform and liberalization, it is hoped, will help significantly to mobilize domestic savings, which have been estimated to fall short of investment demands over the next five years. Further maturity and expansion of the stock-exchange market, growth of mutual funds and insurance companies, and expanded activities of commercial banks, particularly the setting up of offshore banking units, are all expected to play an important role in mobilizing domestic savings.

In addition, reforms in the financial and real sectors are expected to attract additional capital inflows, preferably of the direct-investment variety. Yet, with the economic slowdown of Japan and other countries that are major investors in Thailand, and the additional time needed fully to restore foreign-investor confidence in the Thai economy, it is increasingly clear that direct-investment inflows cannot be relied upon to play a dominant role in boosting domestic investment. Indeed, the inflow of direct investment fell 20 per cent, from a peak of 58 700 million baht in 1990 to 46 700 million baht in 1991. Direct foreign investment fell further at the rate of 33 per cent in the first quarter of 1992. The continued postponement of economic recovery among the major industrialized countries is bound to have adverse effects on direct foreign investment.

Instead, investment financing will be more dependent on portfolio investment and short- and long-term capital inflows. Indeed Thailand's liberalization of the foreign-exchange market and capital account will undoubtedly encourage greater flows of such capital. Yet the greater openness and capital mobility has important implications. Domestic interest rates will be increasingly determined exogenously, corresponding more or less to world interest rates. While the authorities may wish to keep the Thai baht fixed to the US dollar in keeping with the past practice, they will find the supply of money increasingly difficult to control. For example, attempts to tighten the domestic money supply, leading to increases in domestic interest rates, will only induce greater capital inflows, which will eventually restore the differential between domestic and foreign interest rates. In the extreme case, monetary policy will not be able to influence domestic money supply and price levels if interest rates are exogenously determined and the exchange rate is fixed (Mundell, 1962).

Even prior to liberalization of the financial and external sectors, evidence of the openness of the Thai capital account was recognized. Robinson, Byeon and Teja (1991), utilizing quarterly interest-rate data from 1978–90, concluded that the Thai capital account was quite open. With subsequent liberalization, they expressed the view that maintaining a relatively fixed exchange rate is increasingly likely to constrain the conducting of monetary policy in Thailand.

Evidence of greater capital mobility has already emerged. The inflow of portfolio and short- and long-term capital increased by more than 130 per cent from 107 185 million baht in 1989 to 247 011 million baht in 1991. The inflows were induced by the wide disparity between domestic and world interest rates, the stability of the baht and, more importantly, liberalization of Thailand's foreign-exchange sector. It is noteworthy that increased volumes were very evident for short- and long-term private capital inflows. As recently as 1987, for example, it was central-government borrowing and direct investment that dominated Thailand's capital account. In 1991 short- and long-term private borrowing accounted for over 80 per cent of capital inflow into Thailand. From only 4.1 billion baht in 1987, short-term private borrowing accelerated to 157.66 billion baht in 1991, notwithstanding the fact that 1991 saw considerable turmoil in the form of a coup d'etat in Thailand and fighting in the Gulf. Continuing financial liberalization particularly the advent of the BIBF, will most certainly further boost such short-term inflows. As it now stands, private short-term inflow accounts for more than half of total capital inflow into Thailand.

The increase in the inflow of such a mobile source of funds can indeed prove to be a destabilizing influence. In fact the inflow helped increased the rate of growth of M1 in 1991 from 1.1 per cent in the third quarter to 13.8 per cent in the fourth quarter. Shielding the domestic economy from external instability and restoring the effectiveness of monetary policy can be attained only by greater willingness on the part of the Thai authorities to accept increased fluctuations in the exchange rate. For example, attempts to curb the domestic money supply will put pressure on interest rates. This will lead to capital inflows, which will in turn cause the domestic currency to appreciate. This appreciation will reduce the competitiveness of the tradeable-goods sector, thereby further reinforcing the deflationary impact of restrictive monetary policy.

Such fluctuations in the exchange rate may not be readily acceptable to Thai authorities and traders since over the decades they have grown accustomed to the exchange rate being more or less fixed. The argument that greater exchange-rate fluctuations create uncertainties need not apply in the case of Thailand, however. While greater fluctuations in exchange rates are likely to occur, the Thai financial system should be mature and dynamic enough to develop the means by which traders can hedge risks in foreign-exchange fluctuations. However, excessive fluctuations in the exchange rates that cannot be hedged must indeed be undesirable as they could have an adverse destabilizing impact on Thailand's industrial and tradeable-goods sectors.

The other implication has to do with the impact of financial reforms on the demand for money. A stable and predictable relationship between monetary aggregates on the one hand, and income and wealth, prices and interest rates on the other is a crucial element in the formulation and effectiveness of monetary policy. Financial liberalization creates potential for change and, more importantly, instability in money demand. In the case of Thailand, it can be surmised that freeing interest rates so as better to reflect economic returns could prompt portfolio shifts. The shift could be accounted for by money-demand functions that contain appropriate interest terms. Yet the estimated coefficient based on past events when interest rates were not really allowed to vary may not have reflected the true relationship between money demand and interest rates. As interest rates become more flexible, previously dormant influences of interest rate on money demand could become transparent.

Measures to improve the functioning and depth of financial markets could result in both portfolio shifts and affect the sensitivity of money demand to changes in income and interest rates. For example, Thailand's intention to increase competition between various financial institutions (for example banks and finance companies) could lower transaction costs in financial markets, thereby allowing money demand to respond more rapidly than before to interest changes. Moreover, better regulation of and information about financial institutions (such as the setting up of a credit-rating agency) may alter the relative risk of different financial assets, leading to both discrete portfolio adjustments and a change in the interest elasticity of money demand.

The introduction of new, attractive assets could lead to a gradual portfolio shift away from monetary assets, independently of income and interest-rate changes. The gradual, perhaps disjointed shift away from money assets will make more difficult the task of arriving at a stable estimate of the demand for money. At the same time, to the extent that the policy of financial-market development encourages reintermediation – that is, attracting domestic savings away from informal 'curb' money markets – the direction of the effects on broad monetary aggregates may be to increase the demand for all financial assets, including money.

In short, as summed up by Tseng and Corker (1991), financial liberalization could lead to one-off or more gradual shifts in the level of money holdings, as well as to changes in the measured income and interest elasticity of money demand. The practical difficulty, as mentioned above, lies with gradual changes in income and interest-rate elasticity of demand, which would take longer to detect. This would render money demand relationships unstable over a longer period.

Tseng and Corker (1991) looked at nine Asian countries, including Thailand, and attempted to estimate their money demand in light of the financial reforms being carried out in those countries in the 1980s. They found that the estimated long-run elasticities of narrow money demand varied substantially among countries: the elasticities exceeded unity for four countries and were less than unity for five, of which Thailand was one. This suggested monetization in the former cases and attempts to economize on cash balances in the latter cases. Interest rates had significant negative coefficients in the M1 equations for all countries.

On the other hand, the long run elasticities of broad money demand (M2) exceeded unity in all countries except Korea. This reaffirms the decline in the velocity of broad money that was found in Asia in the 1970s. The large income elasticities do not necessarily reflect monetization; instead the growth in money demand may have resulted from the rapid growth in wealth.

For several countries, including Thailand, broad money demand was found to be negatively related to an opportunity-cost variable defined as the return on alternative assets minus the average interest rate paid on broad money balances. This suggests that broad money demand is affected by relative asset returns as opposed to the general level of interest rates.

Significant for Thailand was the fact that stable long-term relationships could not be found for either narrow or broad money demand. Narrow money does not appear to have a stable long-term relationship with income and interest or inflation rates. Income and interest-rate elasticities of demand for narrow and broad money were, however, all statistically significant and large. Income elasticities for narrow and broad money were 0.85 and 1.72, respectively. Interest-rate elasticities were strongly negative at −1.53 for narrow money and −2.46 for broad money, reinforcing the belief that financial liberalization will increase the sensitivity of money demand to interest rates.

8.5 CONCLUSIONS

Financial reforms in Thailand are being carried out both to mobilize savings to finance industrialization efforts and to enhance the ability of domestic financial institutions to cope with global competition. These goals are indeed laudable and can contribute significantly to the sustained growth of the Thai economy envisaged by Thai economic policy makers. Moreover, Thailand appears to have placed itself in a position to maximize the chance of successful financial reform and liberalization. Its reform package is comprehensive, if perhaps a little too cautious with respect to opening up domestic banks to greater foreign competition. More importantly, Thailand possesses the ingredients that have made financial reforms successful, namely a stable macroeconomic environment and competent financial-institution supervision. Moreover, liberalization of the real sector is well under way and Thailand's traded-goods sector is in a strong competitive position.

Financial reforms and liberalization have important implications. As the prospect of increased direct foreign investment is diminishing because of the slow pace of world recovery (especially in Japan), and because of the increased competition for such investment in Europe, the former states of the Soviet Union and even the North American Free Trade Area (NAFTA), capital mobility will be increasingly relied upon to finance domestic investment. The greater openness has increased this capital mobility. Greater capital mobility also means that interest rates will be increasingly determined exogenously. However capital mobility when the exchange rate is more or less fixed, as is the case in Thailand at present, would make sterilization of capital flows difficult. The implication is that the ability of the Bank of Thailand to control the money supply will be reduced. Since fiscal policy tends to be a cumbersome tool for macroeconomic stabilization, especially in developing countries such as Thailand, it is likely that the Thai authorities will choose to restore the efficacy of monetary policy as a primary means of macroeconomic stabilization.

Increasing the effectiveness of monetary policy will, however, require greater fluctuations in the exchange rates. This may not be in keeping with the past policy of the Bank of Thailand in trying to maintain a stable exchange rate in order to facilitate trade and other external transactions, but it looks as though greater variations in the exchange rate will be difficult to avoid in the future. This need not have a destabilizing impact on the tradeable-goods sector, so long as hedging mechanisms are developed to eliminate risks arising from fluctuations in exchange rates. It is in this regard that the development of exchange-rate hedges will play a central role in Thailand's financial-reform efforts. At the same time the central authorities will have to take care to coordinate monetary policy with foreign-exchange rate policy.

Financial reforms will also significantly affect the relationship between money demand, income and interest rates. The increasing variety of monetary instruments will make monetary policy more difficult to conduct. Moreover, the impact of financial reforms on money demand can be both immediate and gradual, making the relationship difficult to quantify. Available evidence has shown that, in the case of Thailand, money-demand relationships could be unstable over a longer period of time. The inability to establish a stable demand for money function could in turn jeopardize the ability of the central bank to conduct effective monetary policy. In other words, with liberalization and openness comes the inevitable prospect of increased uncertainty and instability.

Note

1. I would like to express my appreciation to Assistant Professor Bhanupongse Nidhiprabha of the Faculty of Economics, Thammasat University and Dr Thanisr Chaturongkul of the Bangkok Bank. Both were kind enough to read this chapter and provided valuable comments and suggestions. Any errors and omissions are, of course, mine alone.

9 Urbanization Problems in Thailand's Rapidly Industrializing Economy

Peter J. Rimmer

9.1 INTRODUCTION

The Thai economy since the late 1980s has provided a unique opportunity to explore the interrelationship between rapid industrialization and accelerated urbanization (i.e., the increased share of the population living in urban areas).[1] In 1988 and 1989 the real GDP growth rates were 13.2 per cent and 12.0 per cent respectively (Medhi, 1992a, 1992b). Some of the newly industrialising economies (NIEs), notably Korea, Taiwan and Singapore, have achieved similar two-digit levels of growth, but Thailand still offers distinctive physical, social and political features worth exploring. Although Thailand is approaching NIE status, more than two thirds of its population is still engaged in the agricultural sector, the level of urbanization is low compared with countries at similar levels of development, and its capital city, the Bangkok Metropolitan Region (BMR), is characterized by extreme primacy (Figure 9.1).[2] As the capital region propels the national economy, the economic growth of Bangkok is indistinguishable from Thailand as a whole. Following modernization, restructuring and the end of the Cold War in South-East Asia a new, international, urban hierarchy is emerging in which Bangkok occupies a pivotal position to rival Singapore as a major hub for mainland South-East Asia.

Before Bangkok's status as an international hub is confirmed, several complex issues relating to industrialization and urbanization, privatization and decentralization need to be resolved. How has Bangkok's development been influenced by the extraordinary economic growth of the 1980s? More specifically, how has the attraction of export-led manufacturing to the expanding BMR affected its spatial structure and environment during this period? How have the different rates of growth and prosperity between the BMR and the rest of the country been accommodated? In particular, how should the economic

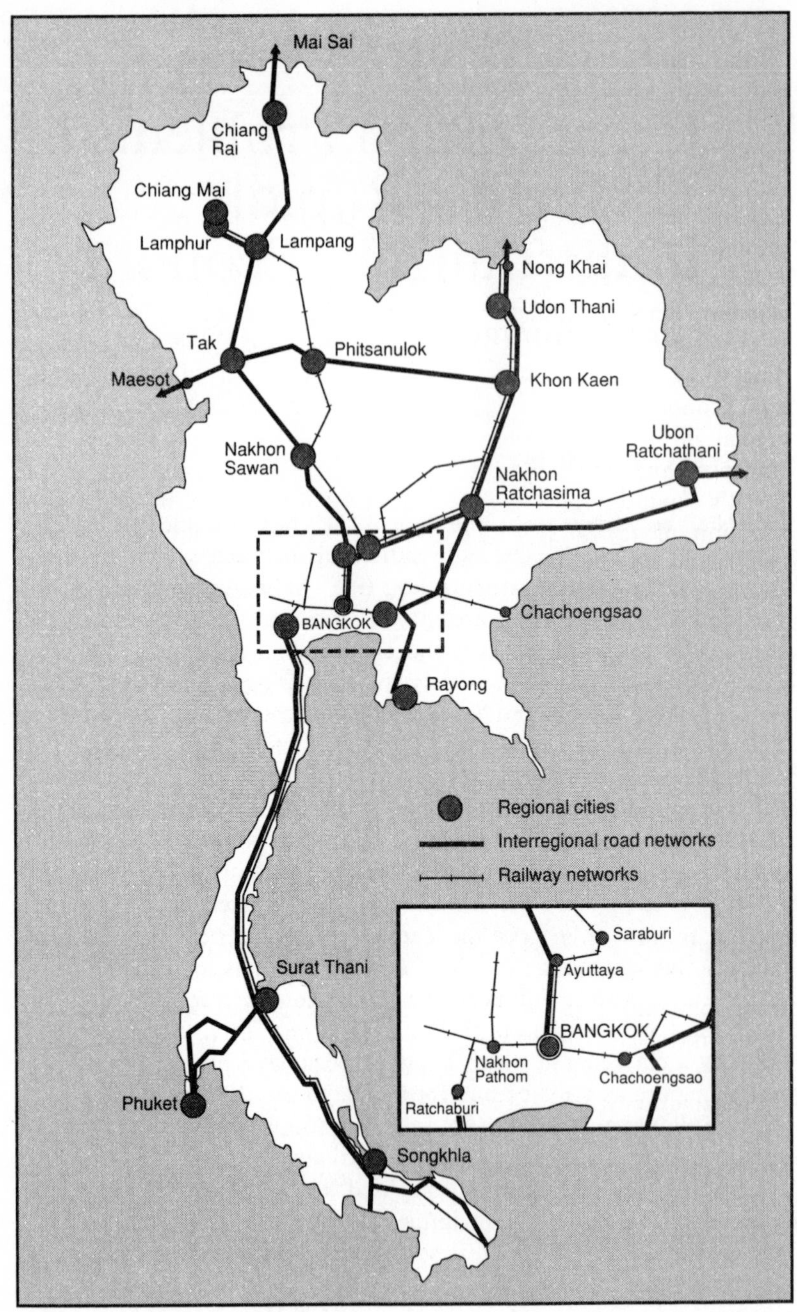

Figure 9.1 Interregional road and rail networks showing the main regional cities

opportunities provided by Bangkok's growth be further used or exploited; and how should regional cities be promoted? Looking ahead, how do planners seek to facilitate and manage these changes in the urban system to accommodate the continued and rapid economic growth that is anticipated between 1991 and 2020?

Underlying these questions is the transformation of the Thai economy between 1961 and 1990, when there was a shift from a rural to an urban-based society centred on Bangkok. The extranational dimensions of industrialization and urbanization during the period of high economic growth – foreign trade, investment and tourism – were crucial in the development of Bangkok's role as an international transport and communications hub. The benefits and costs of the BMR's expansion need to be balanced, as exemplified by the corporatization of transport services. Resulting inequalities of economic conditions between the BMR and the outer regions have led to attempts to decentralize by designing a 'regional network strategy' and proposing a new urban hierarchy. Planning must also transcend Thailand's borders and consider linking the Extended Bangkok Metropolitan Region (EBMR) into a South-East Asian Development Corridor stretching from Chiang Mai to Bali. This chapter considers each of these issues and concludes by highlighting the importance of regional integration on an international scale.

9.2 ANTECEDENTS, 1961–90

Thailand's First National Economic Development Plan in 1961 initiated the modern era of development. The government shifted from dominating the economy through public investment to becoming a facilitator of private enterprise by supplying the necessary infrastructure and guidelines (Table 9.1). Although the economic transformation from agriculture and industry had occurred before the First Plan the process was accelerated after its promulgation. Orchestrated by subsequent five-year plans the country moved progressively from an agrarian economy through a semi-industrialized state towards an industrialized economy. This economic transformation has had marked effects upon Thailand's rural–urban configuration. It was not until the Fourth Plan (1977–81), however, that an explicit urban policy was specified and the importance of channelling development away from Bangkok was highlighted. The key features of changes in the interconnected industrialization and urbanization

Table 9.1 National strategies for urban development

Plan	*Main provisions*
First Plan (1961–1966)	The strategy of import substitution – urban-based industrialization – was fashioned from both traditional policies (the transfer of rural surplus for metropolitan development) and new policies (promoting and protecting import-substituting infant industries).
Second Plan (1967–1971)	The initial strategy was maintained and full duty exemption on capital goods and raw material imports was given for protected industries which almost without exception chose to locate in Bangkok.
Third Plan (1972–1976)	Economic growth was still paramount in development planning but there was increasing concern for social justice.
Fourth Plan (1977–1981)	It emphasized for the first time the importance of channelling economic and urban growth away from Bangkok. The Plan proposed a strategy aimed at decentralizing urbanization to achieve a more balanced system by promoting regional growth centres or 'secondary city' projects at Khon Kaen, Nakhon Ratchasima, Ubon Ratchathani, Udon Thani, Chon Buri, Phitsanulok, Chiang Mai, Phuket and Songkhla-Hat Yai. A polycentric settlement pattern was suggested for decelerating and the controlling Bangkok's spatial pattern together with the decentralization of international port facilities.
Fifth Plan (1982–1986)	Retained the commitment to 'balanced regional development' through its intervention activities on a limited number of provincial cities. But it focused more attention on continued implementation of the 'new economic zone' at the Eastern Seaboard in order to encourage the development of new industrial sites for basic industry. A major improvement programme for transport within the Bangkok Metropolitan was commenced (including expressways) together with major flood control and water-supply programmes.
Sixth Plan (1987–1991)	Recommended a new 'urban management policy' for the more orderly and efficient growth of the Bangkok Metropolitan Region through better integration of physical planning and infrastructure investments. It incorporated a new urban financial strategy that featured four key elements – cost sharing, cost-recovery, revenue enhancement and privatization. The need for improved institutional

Plan	*Main provisions*
	arrangements for the effective implementation of the new urban-management plan led to the creation of the Bangkok Metropolitan Development Committee. Also there was still an emphasis on strengthening secondary-city programmes.
Seventh Plan (1992–1996)	Constructing more and better transport and communications between urban centres within the Bangkok Metropolitan Region and emphasizing a variety of different roles for urban centres in all regions (that is, regional-network cluster strategy).

Source: NESDB.

processes are described below. This analysis draws heavily upon the two-volume, Final Report of the National Urban Development Policy Framework prepared jointly for the Seventh Plan (1992–6) by the National Economic and Social Development Board, United Nations Development Programme and the Thailand Development Research Institute (NESDB/UNDP/TDRI, 1991). Its visions provide an important counterpoint to the harsh realities of urbanization in Thailand's rapidly industrializing economy.

9.2.1 Industrialization and Urbanization

The process of industrialization in Thailand is discussed in more detail elsewhere in this book. Suffice it to say that increased industrialization has brought about increased urbanization. The overall level of urbanization during the 1970s was considered to be relatively low but the rate of urban population growth was quite high. Between 1975 and 1980 the average annual rate of growth of the urban population was 4.1 per cent while the rural population grew by only 1.4 per cent per year (Medhi,, 1992a). In 1975 almost 43 per cent of the urban population lived in Bangkok, which is forty-three times larger than Chiang Mai, the second-ranked city (Table 9.2).

Between 1980 and 1988 Thailand's urban population increased from 12.5 million in 508 urban areas to 15.8 million in 660 urban areas (Table 9.2). The level of urbanization defined as proportion of total population living in urban areas, increased from 26.5 per cent to 28.7

Table 9.2 Number and percentage of urban population, number of urban places, level of urbanization by region, 1975–88

	1975	*1980*	*1985*	*1988*
Urban places (number)				
Bangkok	1	1	1	1
Bangkok vicinity	30	36	39	41
Sub-central	45	47	48	49
East	37	46	55	62
West	44	55	59	60
North-east	117	147	187	215
North	105	125	148	167
South	45	51	59	65
Whole kingdom	424	508	596	660
Urban population (million)				
Bangkok	4.4	5.2	5.4	5.7
Bangkok vicinity	0.6	0.7	0.9	1.3
Sub-central	0.5	0.6	0.6	0.7
East	0.5	0.7	0.9	0.9
West	0.5	0.7	0.8	0.8
North-east	1.5	2.0	2.6	3.0
North	1.4	1.7	2.1	2.3
South	0.8	0.9	1.0	1.1
Whole kingdom	10.2	12.5	14.3	15.8
(BMR)	n.a.	6.9	n.a.	9.0
Urban population (%)				
Bangkok	42.8	41.4	37.6	36.2
Bangkok vicinity	5.6	5.8	6.3	8.0
Sub-central	5.1	4.6	4.3	4.2
East	5.2	5.5	6.0	5.9
West	5.4	5.6	5.5	5.2
North-east	14.8	15.8	18.4	18.7
North	13.6	13.8	14.4	14.3
South	7.5	7.6	7.7	7.5
Whole kingdom	100.0	100.0	100.0	100.0
Urbanization level (max 100%)				
Bangkok	100.0	100.0	100.0	100.0
Bangkok vicinity	31.5	34.6	36.3	45.1
Sub-central	21.4	22.5	23.4	23.8
East	20.9	23.8	25.9	26.0
West	21.1	24.7	25.5	25.5
North-east	10.3	12.2	14.6	15.3
North	15.4	17.9	19.8	21.0
South	14.6	16.2	17.2	17.4
Whole kingdom	24.0	26.5	27.7	28.7

Note: Urban places refer to municipal areas and sanitary districts with populations in excess of 5,000.
Source: NESDB/UNDP/TDRI, 1991, vol. I, pp. 2.32–3.

per cent. Bangkok's share of total population declined from 41.4 per cent to 36.2 per cent but the concentration of urban population in Bangkok remained high. The index of primacy fell from 17.1 to 10.7 between 1980 and 1988.[3] Since these figures refer to the BMA and exclude the surrounding cities that now form part of the BMR, the primacy index could be higher and counter any suggestions of polarization reversal. The fastest-growing areas in terms of urban population were Bangkok vicinity and the surrounding sub-central region – a trend manifested in the construction boom. Although Thailand's average annual urban growth rate between 1980 and 1985 slowed to 2.8 per cent, during the recession it was still higher than the rural rate for the same period (Medhi, 1992a, p. 5). Between 1985 and 1988 the urban-population growth rate recovered while that of the rural population fell. These trends support the conclusion that the Bangkok vicinity and the sub-central region will be the dynamic areas of future urban development – a reflection of the centralization of government power, spatial biases in government policy, agglomeration economies and the strength of linkages with the world economy (NESDB/UNDP/TDRI, 1991, vol. I, p. 3.2).

9.3 EXTRA-NATIONAL DIMENSIONS

Bangkok is not solely a product of Thai culture. It is profoundly entangled in the world system with all sectors (from banking to labour migration) affected by economic and social forces that are increasingly transnational in scale – a reflection of the fact that modern technology has transformed our concepts of space, territory and nation. During the 1980s Bangkok entered an era in which it has been increasingly shaped by these factors. Although not matching London, New York and Tokyo as a global control centre of the world economy supported by corporate hierarchies and international capital, Bangkok's economic base has become more closely tied to extra-national economic, social and political forces. Bangkok is the prime focus through which the Thai Government projects its influence in the Asia-Pacific region and reflects the changing conditions of global labour supply and demand associated with the new international division of labour. Already it is tied into transnational linkages through foreign trade, foreign direct investment (and portfolio investments), tourism and international labour migration as well as real-estate speculation in 1990 and 1991. These external linkages put a great deal of pressure on Bangkok, but in the process it has become an important international transport and communications hub for goods, passengers and information flows.

9.3.1 International Hub

Severe competition for supremacy within Pacific Asia's urban hierarchy is occurring among major metropolitan areas – Bangkok, Jakarta, Kuala Lumpur, Hong Kong, Manila, Osaka, Seoul, Singapore and Tokyo. Assisted by strong flows of direct foreign investment, the availability of overseas aid for infrastructure improvements, and privatization and deregulation, Thai administrators are using new international seaports and airports, research parks and urban amenities to heighten their capital city's attractiveness to suppliers of financial and other services. In particular, there is a battle between Bangkok and Singapore for the premier position within South-East Asia. An analysis of container shipping, air freight, air passenger and telecommunications traffic shows the conflict is still unresolved.

A major obstacle to comparing Bangkok's position as a gateway port to that of Singapore, is the lack of appropriate origin and destination data – aggregate container statistics measured in twenty-foot equivalent units (TEUs) are used as surrogate data. Both load centres are heavily dependent upon complementary feeder ports and short-distance container shipping services because land-bridge services by rail and the basic infrastructure in South-East Asia (for example container-freight stations and inland container depots) are still undeveloped. As the world's busiest container port, Singapore is a highly competitive load centre handling five times more units than Bangkok (Figure 9.2). Draft and length restrictions on vessels navigating the Chao Phraya River have resulted in Bangkok remaining a feeder port to the Singapore, Hong Kong and Kaohsiung mainline hubs. Singapore is growing at a faster rate than Bangkok because it attracts larger ships and is the base for major carriers and consortia (for example the American President Line, Sea-Land and Nippon Yusen Kaisha).[4] Nevertheless Bangkok outstripped the growth of other major South-East Asian regional ports between 1973 and 1989 and is now the second ranked port – a remarkable achievement for a river port reliant on feeder services. These services are likely to be decentralized from Bangkok following the opening of the new mainline port at Laem

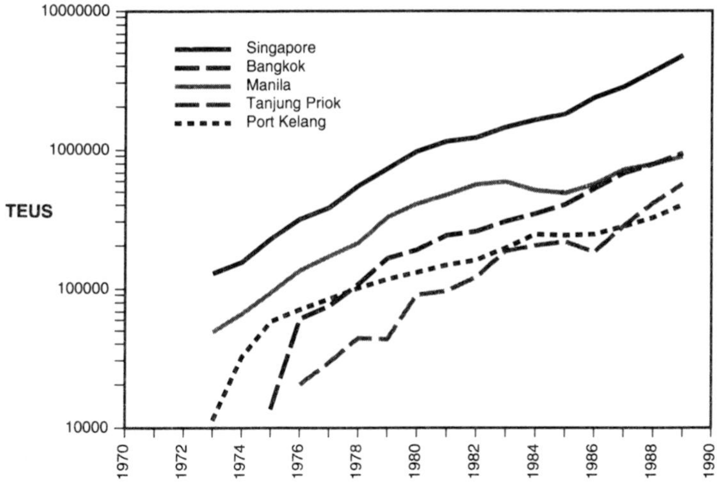

Figure 9.2 Total container movements through South-East Asian ports, 1973–1989

Chabang on the Eastern Seaboard in 1990. This may alleviate port congestion, which has prompted some Thai shippers to use air freight.

During the 1980s both Bangkok and Singapore became important air-freight centres following the establishment of offshore manufacturing bases and the need to transport high-value electronic parts. Although the annual growth of Bangkok's air freight was 26 per cent between 1983 and 1990 it has been surpassed by Singapore's 33 per cent. South Asia and the Middle East are the only markets in which it has an edge over its rival (Table 9.3). Singapore has widened the gap markedly in South-East Asia, Europe and North America. Most significantly, it has reversed Bangkok's earlier pre-eminence in East Asia, which has become the dominant market for both centres. Air freight's importance is a recent phenomenon that came with the accelerated industrialization of South-East Asia. Previously it was subordinate to air-passenger considerations.

Bangkok and Singapore were ranked among the top twenty-five airports in terms of international passengers embarked and disembarked during the 1980s. Although Bangkok ranked twenty-first in

Table 9.3 Absolute and relative changes in Bangkok's and Singapore's airfreight market, 1983 and 1990

	1983			*1990*		
	Bangkok	*Singapore*	*Difference*	*Bangkok*	*Singapore*	*Difference*
Tonnes:						
Europe	15033	19654	−4621	35968	54510	−18542
Australasia	2030	10836	−8806	7551	30347	−22796
North America	30	1803	−1773	775	7861	−7086
East Asia	29538	23020	6518	101103	109099	−7996
South-East Asia	15194	23293	−8099	35704	63310	−27606
South Asia	7824	4655	3169	14685	13254	1431
Middle East	2041	1498	543	10498	2516	7982
Total	71690	84759	−13069	206284	280897	−74613
Percentage share:						
South-East Asia	21.2	27.4	−6.2	17.3	22.6	−5.3
East Asia	41.2	27.2	14.0	49.0	38.8	10.2
South Asia	10.9	5.5	5.4	7.1	4.7	2.4
Middle East	2.9	1.8	1.1	5.1	0.9	4.2
Europe	21.0	23.2	−2.2	17.4	19.4	−2.0
North America	0.0	2.1	−2.1	0.4	2.8	−2.4
Australasia	2.8	12.8	−10.0	3.7	10.8	−7.1
Total	100.0	100.0		100.0	100.0	

Source: derived from ICAO, 1984, 1991.

1983, it had moved to eleventh ranking by 1990 whereas Singapore had shifted from tenth to ninth position over the same period (ICAO, 1984, 1991). While Bangkok handled fewer passengers than Singapore, its annual growth rate of 16 per cent was 6 per cent greater. A market analysis of passengers embarked shows that much of Singapore's importance stemmed from short-distance traffic within South-East Asia whereas Bangkok was much stronger in East Asia and South Asia (Table 9.4). Over longer distances, Singapore was foremost in Australasia and North America while Bangkok was foremost in the Middle East. In 1990 Bangkok handled more European passengers than Singapore – a reflection of its function as a fuelling base on the one-stop Australia–Europe flights. Telecommunications is another area where Bangkok is developing as a hub.

It is difficult to assess the success of Bangkok's challenge in this field as time series data on cities and their major telecommunications correspondents is not readily available. There is, however, information for 1990 on international public voice circulation, measured in Minutes

Table 9.4 Absolute and relative changes in Bangkok' and Singapore's passenger market, 1983 and 1990 (thousands)

	1983			*1990*		
	Bangkok	*Singapore*	*Difference*	*Bangkok*	*Singapore*	*Difference*
Number:						
South-East Asia	520	1503	−983	973	2440	−1467
East Asia	714	581	133	1744	1269	475
South Asia	207	160	37	364	305	59
Middle East	56	28	28	175	24	151
Europe	283	313	−30	646	587	59
North America	3	29	−26	38	101	−63
Australia/ New Zealand	42	322	−280	197	726	−529
Pacific Islands	–	–	–	–	5	−5
Africa	–	–	–	–	35	−35
Total	1825	2936	−1121	4137	5492	−1355
Percentage share:						
South-East Asia	28.5	51.2	−22.7	23.5	44.4	−20.9
East Asia	39.1	19.8	19.3	42.2	23.1	19.1
South Asia	11.3	5.4	5.9	8.8	5.5	3.3
Middle East	3.1	1.0	2.1	4.2	0.5	3.7
Europe	15.5	10.6	4.9	15.6	10.7	4.9
North America	0.2	1.0	−0.8	0.9	1.9	−1.0
Australia/ New Zealand	2.3	11.0	−8.7	4.8	13.2	−8.4
Pacific Islands	–	–	–	–	0.1	−0.1
Africa	–	–	–	–	0.6	−0.6
Total	100.0	100.0		100.0	100.0	

Source: derived from ICAO, 1984, 1991.

of Telecommunications Traffic (MiTT) (Table 9.5). The number of Singapore's outgoing calls was more than three and a half times greater than that of Bangkok. Besides links with adjacent centres, both hubs have strong connections with Hong Kong, Japan and the United States. Strict comparability is difficult, however, as the Singapore data omits Malaysia and the Bangkok data excludes traffic to Cambodia, Laos and Vietnam. Following the end of the Cold War these countries are the targets for increased Thai commercial penetration.

Thailand's boundary zones have remained sparsely populated. Originally they were seen as fortified marginal spaces in a world built around a centrist state. This notion has been rendered obsolete by the shift from land-based to air- and sea-based military strategies using

Table 9.5 Bangkok and Singapore and their major telecommunication correspondents, 1990

	Bangkok (Thailand)		*Singapore*	
Destination	*Outgoing MiTT mill.*	*Market share per cent*	*Outgoing MiTT mill*	*Market share per cent*
Indonesia	n.a.	n.a.	20.5	13.5
Malaysia	4.9	11.5	n.a.	n.a.
Philippines	n.a.	n.a.	4.1	2.7
Singapore	6.0	14.1	–	–
Thailand	–	–	7.1	4.7
Hong Kong	5.6	13.2	19.4	12.8
Japan	6.4	15.0	19.7	13.0
Taiwan	2.6	6.1	10.6	7.0
India	–	–	6.9	4.5
United States	5.7	13.4	19.7	13.0
Italy	1.1	2.5	–	–
United Kingdom	2.4	5.6	10.3	6.8
West Germany	1.3	3.0	–	–
Australia	1.1	2.5	10.2	6.7
Sub-total	37.1	86.9	128.5	84.7
Others	5.4	13.1	23.3	15.3
Total	42.5	100.0	151.8	100.0

Note: MiTT = Minutes of Telecommunication Traffic. Data are for international public voice circulation only. The Bangkok data excludes traffic to Cambodia, Laos and Vietnam and Singapore data excludes Malaysia; n.a. = not available.
Source: derived from Staple, 1990.

developments in satellite communications, air and rapid transport technology, transnational banking, and trade and international labour migration. With assembly-line production and commuting, the full potential of transborder areas as important centres of production and urban life can be realized. By attracting both international capital and migrant workers they can take advantage of the different levels of economic development that are evident in different land and labour costs. While developments involving Thailand with Indonesia and Malaysia in the 'Northern Triangle', and other permutations linking it to Cambodia, China, Laos and Myanmar are unlikely to attain the dimensions of Western European or even United States–Mexico developments, there is need for cooperative transborder arrangements to manage transport infrastructure and other policy matters.

The external pressures brought about by the globalization of economic growth have had a profound impact on Thailand's economy and the way in which its people live and work. The industrialization and associated urbanization processes have created new problems affecting settlement and the environment. Thailand's urban infrastructure – roads, telecommunications, water and sewerage and transport – is strained to breaking point. Apart from the economic boom of the late 1980s, the increased exposure of the Thai economy to international economic forces has also compounded the unequal distribution of income, though the overall urban poverty level has improved.[5] The benefits accrued to the foreign-related economic sectors have not been shared by the population at large because of the government's non-interventionist approach towards business and weak fiscal redistributive policies. As the trickle-down effects were slow, urban areas (notably the BMR) rather than the rural areas were the beneficiaries of internationalization. The incidence of urban poverty has been highest in the north-east (34.6 per cent) and lowest in the greater Bangkok Metropolitan Region (3.5 per cent). Yet the largest absolute numbers of poor live in the 1000 slums located within the latter's inner areas – a feature reflecting the high concentration of investment projects and job opportunities in both its formal and informal sectors (NESDB/UNDP/TDRI, 1991, vol. II, pp. 6.6–7).

A mixture of fiscal incentives and the availability of industrial finance has compounded Bangkok's advantages for overseas firms because the efficiency of its urban structure has enhanced Thailand's international competitive position to attract industry and services. Even within Bangkok, however, the benefits of economic growth and urbanization and the costs in terms of quality of life and the impact on the environment are uneven. This is borne out by an examination of the costs and benefits involved in its urban restructuring, which was brought about by the need to change land-use patterns to create space for its domestic needs and newly-acquired international functions.

9.4 THE BANGKOK METROPOLITAN REGION

The BMR plays a crucial role in Thailand's economic development and structural transformation by state and public enterprises, multinational manufacturing and trading corporations, and domestic capitalist groups (Suehiro, 1989). It provides economies of scale and agglomeration advantages for manufacturing and service activities unrivalled by other cities. The BMR has access to ports, markets, government services and superior, though inadequate, infrastructure. Over half of the country's factories (27 000) are within the BMR – the main export-oriented activities include textiles, garments, leather goods, rubber and plastic products, chemicals and electrical machinery (NESDB/UNDP/TDRI, 1991, vol. I, pp. 1.1–30). Indeed this area accounted for almost 75 per cent of value added in manufacturing between 1981 and 1988. Twelve of the country's 23 industrial estates, managed by the Industrial Estate Authority of Thailand, are located within its confines and Board of Investment application data showed that the BMR's five inner provinces attracted the bulk of approved projects. Not only are income and employment opportunities available for a large number of people but it is the biggest consumer market (nine million people) for durable and non-durable products, the major transport hub and enjoys the best social infrastructure (for example piped water, telephones, hospitals and leisure facilities). Of Thailand's three million motor vehicles, 1.8 million are in the BMR. Under the Sixth Plan (1987–91) the BMR attracted almost 92 per cent of total investment in infrastructure – 96 per cent in transport (Department of Land Transportation, 1990). The sudden economic boom of the late 1980s, however, aggravated the problems associated with inadequate infrastructure.

Contrary to conventional planning wisdom, the desire to decentralize industrial activities may be economically inefficient as a large metropolitan area may be desirable, at least during the initial phase of industrialization. Indeed there has been a shift in emphasis among planners towards managing the BMR's spatial structure more efficiently and equitably rather than trying to stop its growth (Phisit, 1988, pp. 80–97). While it is important to accommodate growth, the development process should not become a burden or inequitable to large sections of the urban population, particularly the poor who need improved security of tenure, upgraded physical environments (for example walkways) and increased access to health care and education in slum areas and on construction sites. Invariably the new management objective lays stress upon the integration of physical planning and infrastructure investment programmes, financial policies (for example improved expenditure, utility pricing efficiency and correct resource allocation) and institutional management – no less than 50 national and local-government agencies are involved in urban development within the BMR. While the benefits of Bangkok's economic progress, dynamism and wealth are evident, they have to be contrasted with the diseconomies of scale arising from environmental problems and increasing congestion in the inner core (that is, indicators of underinvestment and mispricing of urban infrastructure).

One environmental problem is land subsidence caused by extensive public and private use of underground water. A sample survey of factories in Samut Prakan, for example, revealed that less than 0.5 per cent of water used was purchased from the Metropolitan Waterworks Authority as it is cheaper to use subterranean supplies (NESDB/UNDP/TDRI, 1991, vol. II, p. 8.20). These factories compete with other heavy users of water, notably agriculture, aquaculture and golf courses. Bangkok is sinking at 10 cm per year, and if this groundwater extraction rate continues much of the BMR will be below sea-level and subject to flooding when heavy rain is generated by future tropical depressions. As typified in Samut Prakan, there is no history of land-use zoning and the explosive growth of industry has generated ribbon development along major highways without reference to any overall plan. These problems have been aggravated by the absence of effective control over the interaction between land use and transport.

9.4.1 Transport Land Use

Since the 1960s Bangkok has spread horizontally and haphazardly. In this uncontrolled expansion residential dwellings, factories and shops have become intermixed. On the periphery, areas reserved for agriculture have been invaded. Rice paddies, orchards, fish ponds and poultry farms have given way to houses, factories and golf courses. New roads (and new bridges) from the core area have supplanted the past focus on the canals and have quickly become the centre of ribbon developments housing commercial and retail activities, often without the benefit of water and sewage systems. High-rise condominiums, shopping complexes and business offices have sprung up in place of the traditional row houses in inner-city districts, with little or no thought being given to frontage access and environmental impact. Paradoxically, plots of unused land have been left vacant by speculators – a reflection of the inadequacy of property or land taxes.

Accessibility to work and social activities is perceived as Bangkok's most critical problem. With its car population outstripping the growth of its human population, Bangkok's road systems are unable to cope with demand. Between 1972 and 1990 the number of cars increased from 243 000 to one million whereas the length of primary roads increased by only 82 kilometres (that is, the rate of motor traffic per road space is higher than the European or North American cities). By 1990, peak-hour traffic on most of the roads within the middle ring road was under 10 kilometres per hour (PADECO, 1991). These problems were aggravated by the lack of efficient traffic control, poor road discipline and incomplete road networks, badly designed frontage development and inadequate access routes.

The reaction to these capacity constraints has been the dispersal of central business district functions. Between 1980 and 1987, 32 per cent of the permits issued by the BMA for buildings over six storeys were in the inner city area (within 2.5 km of the city centre). The adjacent ring (2.5–5 km from the city centre) accounted for 56 per cent of the approvals granted. If attention is confined to offices, commercial buildings and multiple-use buildings the comparable figures are 44 per cent and 49 per cent. This dispersal of traditional central business district activities is confirmed by studies of shifts in the location of other activities – a pattern that will contribute to the spread and intensification of Bangkok's traffic problems.

In 1978, 57 of the headquarters of Thailand's top 100 private companies were in the central area (Kidikoro, 1992). By 1987 their number had been reduced to 49 as eight companies had moved their main offices outside the city centre – another four had moved to its fringe. Seven of the ten new companies in the 'top 100' list in 1987 were based 5–10 km from the city centre. This predilection for outer-area location was even more marked among major shopping plazas. In 1978 seven out of ten were in the city centre but by 1987 this had dropped to less than one third of the 27 plazas. Dispersal has been also been encouraged by the inadequacy of the BMR's transport system, despite it receiving the highest priority status during the Sixth Plan (1987–91) (NESDB, 1986a, 1986d).[6]

9.4.2 Corporatization, Deregulation and Privatization

During the Sixth Plan measures involving corporatization, deregulation or privatization were adopted in transport and other public-sector urban services concentrated in the BMR (Phisit, 1988; Rimmer, 1988a, 1988b; Rimmer *et al.*, 1989). Privatization proposals designed to improve the performance of public enterprises – or cut their continued financial losses – have included private provision of the construction and operation of an urban mass transit railway, a second expressway, an elevated expressway and railway, interprovincial bus and truck terminals, car-parking facilities, and the interprovincial tollway extending beyond the region. Apart from new expressway construction, however, implementation has not been impressive due to conflicting interests between politicians and relevant groups hindering the mobilization of resources and 'the cultural habit of lax decision-making and enforcement' (NESDB/UNDP/TDRI, 1991, vol. I, p. 4.75). Yet there is still support for privatizing and deregulating the large, state-owned Bangkok Mass Transit Authority, which is reputed to be the fourth-largest bus company in the world.

In 1990 the Bangkok Mass Transit Authority owned 4865 buses and controlled the activities of 3200 private operators with both conventional stage buses and minibuses. Services have suffered from poor maintenance, the abandonment of bus lanes and marked increases in private-vehicle use. Less than 10 per cent of the vehicles are air-conditioned. The remainder are dilapidated – most over ten years old – and overcrowded in the peak period. Given the existing traffic conditions they are slow, unreliable and major contributors to air pollution. Further, there are diseconomies of scale, a narrow range of price-quality options and externalities which are unlikely to be priced in such a monopoly situation. It is also doubtful whether transit subsidies are the best way of helping the urban poor as they apply to all passengers (Wilson, 1986). Rather than extending privatization and deregulation to Bangkok services, the initial emphasis has been on the introduction of corporatization.

The 'in-house' approach used by the royal Thai government for improving the efficiency of the Bangkok Mass Transit Authority is focused on new planning and accountability mechanisms embodied in the corporate plan (Rimmer, 1991).[7] As shown in Table 9.6, the Authority's corporate plan anticipates a remarkable turnaround in its fortunes – an annual loss of 1000 million baht will be transformed into a surplus from 1989, with a concomitant reduction in accumulated losses. The keys to the anticipated boost in revenue stem from a progressive increase in the flat-fare rate for ordinary buses and the production plan being realized (that is, having 90 per cent of buses in operation on any one day). Although the Authority has plans for a string of new depots and an articulated bus fleet, the government has encouraged it to contract out services as part of its general policy of increasing private involvement in both investment and operations.

Clearly the crux of the corporate-planning exercise hinges on the Authority being given primary responsibility for pricing. The government has taken steps in that direction, but cabinet approval of prices is

Table 9.6 Revenue and expenditure in the Bangkok Mass Transit Authority's corporate plan, FY 1987–91 (million baht)

Item	*Actual*	*Projected*				
	1986	*1987*	*1988*	*1989*	*1990*	*1991*
Fares	3017	3045	4350	4570	4794	5509
Other	127	137	218	223	225	251
Revenue	3144	3182	4568	4793	5019	5760
Operations	2112	2126	2370	2626	2691	2804
Maintenance	1003	1099	1166	1113	1216	1298
Administration	175	206	200	219	243	272
Central office	292	257	284	303	331	350
Loan interest	598	611	593	522	427	229
Expenditure	4180	4299	4614	4783	4908	4953
Profit/loss	–1037	–1166	–45	10	111	807
Accumulated	–8132	–9278	–9323	–9313	–9202	–8395

Note: Rounding-off errors.
Source: BMTA, 1987.

still required. Until now prices have been kept artificially low for political and social reasons. Simultaneously, it has failed to reimburse the Authority for the cost of social services. As fickle decision makers have been unwilling to introduce the cost-based pricing and peak/off-peak pricing necessary to overcome congestion, there is little chance of the corporate plan being realized. This situation leads to over-investment in public transport and roads that are key features of transport-land-use strategies for overcoming congestion and pollution.

9.4.3 Transport Land-Use Strategies

A four-pronged strategy has been proposed by the Bangkok Metropolitan Region Development Committee to overcome the BMR's transport problems (Table 9.7). Initially the emphasis, as derived from the Seventh Plan Urban and Regional Transport Study (SPURT), is on increasing the road surface by constructing the Second Stage Expressway and the Ekamai-Ram Inthra-road project and completing the missing sections of the middle ring road.[8] As this option alone will not relieve congestion the second strategy is to develop mass transit systems. Apart from the token reference to making better use of water

Table 9.7 Transport strategies proposed for the Bangkok Metropolitan Region

Strategy	*Key features*
Control traffic volumes	Recommendations include: – staggered office hours; – streamlined administrative procedures in public offices to reduce unnecessary visits; – exclusion of heavy trucks from the inner city; – collecting fees for entry into the central business districts; – prohibition of curb-side parking; – promotion and expansion of parking facilities.
Improve traffic control system	Control of traffic lights should be fully computerized and coordinated with expressway control. Enforcement of traffic laws and regulations should be strengthened. The public should be educated about traffic laws and regulations, and the rules of good driving.
Increase the road surface	Construction of new roads and highways including: – the second-stage expressway linking the northern and southern gateways; – the remaining sections of the ring road and other missing links; – the construction of peripheral truck terminals to exclude heavy trucks from the inner city.
Develop and improve public mass-transit systems	– streamlining of BMTA administration and removal of controls over its operations and pricing (including new depots and increase in air-conditioned buses). – encouraging construction of a new 'Skytrain' mass transit system. – water transport should be encouraged.

Source: NESDB/UNDP/TDRI, 1991, vol. II, pp. 8.53–4.

transport the main emphasis is on freeing the Bangkok Mass Transit Authority from fare and operational constraints and on building the Skytrain. Assuming funds are forthcoming from private sources for the latter, there will still be a time lag before it can be constructed due to delays in land acquisition, overbidding and a lack of qualified staff and finance. Hence the attendant emphasis on improved traffic-control systems. While this measure, coupled with the enforcement of traffic laws, could be effective it would have to be complemented by a series of 'software options' such as staggering working hours, controlling access by heavy trucks and a cordon-pricing system in the central business district (an option that has proved difficult to implement). The main shortcomings of the transport sector, however, are financial and institutional. The government is unwilling to accept the financial implications of private-sector involvement (for example rational user charges) in contracting out service provision or 'build, operate and transfer' projects while different public agencies promote competing schemes.[9]

Unless institutional arrangements are reformed there is little likelihood of the planned projects being implemented. If the six megaprojects are completed there will be conflict at 54 different intersections and elevations.[10] Additional expressways are planned without more collector and distributor roads. These situations stem from multiple bodies being involved in road construction (four agencies), transport regulation (five agencies) and transport management (three agencies) (Table 9.8). Inevitably their individual objectives result in conflicts. Yet there is no coordinating body to resolve such conflicts – the Bangkok Metropolitan Administration has no control over roads and railways, buses and traffic management. The study of urban coalitions would be a fruitful research topic, as indicated by the involvement of technocrats from different agencies in projects associated with politicians and private organizations (Machimura, 1992). This is evident in the long-running saga over the development of mass transit systems – it is still unresolved after twenty years.

Three alternative, privately sponsored schemes comprising separate technologies, more than 100 kilometres of track and capable of moving over three million passengers daily have been mooted (Figure 9.3). Each is being promoted by a different arm of government on a thirty-year build, operate and transfer basis (Handley, 1992):

1. In 1988 the 36-km 'Skytrain' network, connecting the expanding eastern and northern suburbs and using light-rail, linear motor technology, was originally awarded to SNC-Lavalin of Canada by the Expressway and Rapid Transit Authority, which comes under the aegis of the Interior Ministry (cost 60 billion baht).

Table 9.8 Responsibilities of agencies and committees involved in transport decision making

Agency	*Responsibilities*
BMA	City Planning Division (CPD) prepares land use plans including transport networks for BMA area. Department of Public Works (DPW) plans, designs, builds and maintains roads in BMA area. Traffic Engineering Division (TED) designs and implements traffic engineering schemes and minor road improvements in BMA area. Other city and provincial governments carry out similar functions outside Bangkok.
BMTA	State enterprise operating buses in Greater Bangkok, which includes Nonthaburi, Samut Prakan and Pathum Thani.
DOH	Planning, design, construction and maintenance of major highways in Thailand.
DLT	Regulation of truck and bus operators.
PWD	Planning, design, construction and maintenance of river bridges across the Chao Phraya river.
DTCP	Preparation of land-use plans, including transport networks for all cities in Thailand.
ETA	State enterprise responsible for planning, constructing and operating expressways (as toll roads) and rail mass transport in Thailand.
HD	Planning and regulation of inland waterways and coastal transport including ferry services.
OCMRT	Prepares traffic analyses, traffic policies, and traffic-management schemes for cities in Thailand.
SRT	State enterprise responsible for planning, building and operating national railway.
TPD	Enforcement of traffic laws and regulations.
BMRCD	Powerful advisory committee on issues affecting the development of the BMR.
CCCERC	Establishment of transport policies to promote safe and efficient movement of vehicles and pedestrians; preparation of transport plan for the operation and coordination of projects approved by related government agencies; initiation of traffic-improvement measures
LTCP	Formulation of land-transport policies.
LTCB	Control of number of public-transport operators and vehicles in BMA area and between provinces; fixing of bus routes; fixing of transport charges; regulation of transport stations; vehicle regulations.

Source: NESDB/UNDP/TDRI, 1991, vol. II, pp. 8.117.

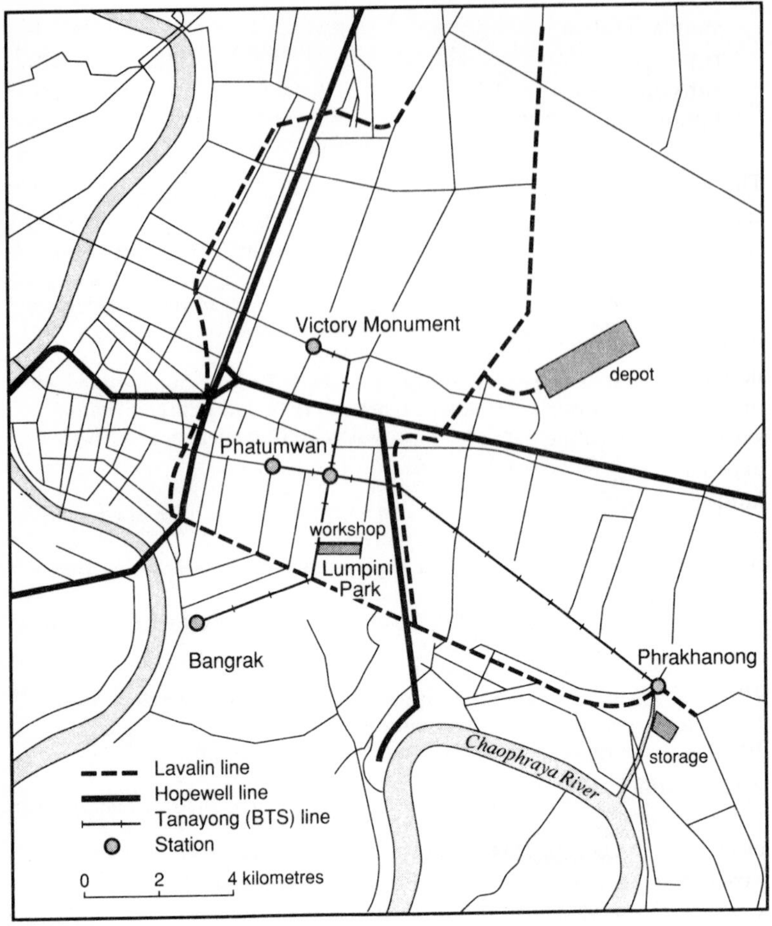

Figure 9.3 Bangkok mass transit routes

2. In 1990 the 60-km Hopewell network, using the State Railway of Thailand's rights-of-way and combining commuter and main rail lines with new highways and retail space in a multi-deck design, was proposed by Gordon Wu, managing director of Hong Kong's Hopewell Holdings, contracted by the Chartichai Choonhavan government and backed by the Transport and Communications Ministry (cost 80 billion baht).[11]
3. In 1992, the 14-km Tanayong network, comprising two routes running down Sukhumvit and Silom Roads respectively and using

simple light-rail technology, was awarded by the Bangkok Metropolitan Administration to the Bangkok Transit System, a subsidiary of the Thai property developer Tanayong (cost 18 billion baht).

There are 30 locations where these networks intersect and conflict with each other and with existing expressway systems, thereby necessitating cantilevered construction arrangements. In 1992 SNC-Lavalin withdrew from the Skytrain project and it has been reopened to new bids (after the government initially considered undertaking the project itself). On 7 August 1992 ground-breaking occurred on the Hopewell network – the first stage Rangsit–Yommarat (25 km), is scheduled to open in 1995. Joint talks have been held with Tanayong to make their systems compatible. Should these systems prove to be no more than expensive coping mechanisms – a doubtful proposition without strong land-use control, a quality bus system and the absence of private-vehicle constraint – it will not be long before foreign consultants propose similar projects for Thailand's regional cities, which are now experiencing some of the problems afflicting the BMR.

This last point about the problems of regional cities deserves a concluding remark. Before 1986 regional cities had small populations and areas, but since then they have expanded, boosted by industry and tourism. Consequently a similar litany of problems to those of the BMR are being experienced – environmental degradation, inadequate water supply and sewage treatment, and increased urban poverty, made evident by regional-city slums without water supply and electricity. Although smaller in magnitude than in the BMR, concerns are already being expressed about traffic congestion, in particular in Chiang Mai, Nakhon Ratchasima, Phuket and Hat Yai (including Songkhla), following increases in motor-vehicle ownership and traffic volumes and the emergence of major bottlenecks. So far they have gone unchecked but they need to be countered to prevent eventual crises and urban deterioration. Without further detailed analysis there is always a danger that capital-city problems will be passed on to regional cities (Rimmer, 1986).

9.5 NEW STRATEGY

A National Urban Development Policy has been mooted for Thailand in the Seventh Plan (1992–6) which envisages growth in real GDP will be more than 8 per cent (in manufacturing, 9.5 per cent). Key elements of the Seventh Plan involve changes in regional development strategy, administrative and organizational structures of urban government, and the financing of urban activities.

9.5.1 Forecasts, 1990–2010

Forecasts of Thailand's population, undertaken as part of the National Urban Development Policy in the Seventh Plan anticipate that it will increase from 56.1 million in 1990 to 71.1 million in 2010 – an increase of 15 million or 26 per cent (Table 9.9). These are based on an average growth rate of 1.4 per cent between 1990 and 1995 and 1.2 per cent between 1995 and 2010. Within the BMA, population densities in the core area will decline slightly and growth will occur on the urban fringe. The most striking developments, however, will not occur in the BMA but in the BMR which also incorporates the five adjacent provinces.

The population of the BMR is expected to increase from 8.9 million in 1990 to 12.6 million in 2010 – an increase of 16.3 per cent (NESDB/UNDP/TDRI, 1991, vol. I, p. 1.11). This projection is based on a 1.5 per cent growth rate between 1990 and 2000 and 1.1 per cent between 2000 and 2010. The latter is much lower than that of the five adjacent provinces, which are expected grow at 3.6 per cent during the first decade of the twenty-first century. Between 1990 and 2010 their population will more than double from 1.5 million to 3.5 million. At the same time the level of urbanization will increase from 54.1 per cent to 75.8 per cent. Urbanization rates throughout the country, however, will change less dramatically than in the BMR as only the eastern

Table 9.9 Thailand's projected population, 1990–2010

	Population (million)			*Urban (per cent)*	*Annual growth rate*		
	Total	*Urban*	*Rural*		*Total*	*Urban*	*Rural*
1990	56.1	18.1	38.0	32.3	–	–	–
1995	60.2	21.4	38.8	35.5	1.4	3.3	0.5
2000	64.1	25.0	39.2	38.9	1.3	3.1	0.2
2005	67.8	28.8	39.0	42.5	1.1	2.9	−0.1
2010	71.1	32.9	38.3	46.2	1.0	2.6	−0.4

Source: NESDB/UNDP/TDRI, 1991, vol. I, pp. 3.70.

region is projected to have more than half of its population living in urbanized areas by 2010 – the north will have 37.5 per cent, the west 34.7 per cent, the north-east 32.9 per cent and the south 32.1 per cent. With its high natural-population growth rate, the south is the only other region expected to increase its share of the national total.

Between 1990 and 2010 the BMR will receive net immigration from other regions of the country – the only other region with the same status will be the Eastern Seaboard. Between 2005 and 2010 the BMR will receive 316,900 immigrants and the eastern region 116 000 (Table 9.10). By then attention should be focused on projected increases in the Extended Bangkok Metropolitan Region (EBMR)–BMR, Ayutthaya, Saraburi, Chachoengsao and the Eastern Seaboard areas – which will grow from 12 million to 17 million and increase its share of total population from 21.5 per cent in 1990 to 24.3 per cent in 2010 (NESDB/UNDP/TDRI, 1991, vol. I, pp. 1.11–12). Clearly any changes in regional-development strategies must acknowledge the importance of the expansion of the BMR's urban fringe and the economic waste created by traffic congestion, pollution and unplanned growth (Figure 9.4). Without land-use control; a repetition of ribbon development along major transport routes will occur not unlike that existing along the Bangna–Trat Highway in Samut Prakan.

9.5.2 Changes in Regional Development Strategy

The EBMR has been incorporated into the new National Urban Development Policy Framework, together with a new urban hierarchy, as part of a revised regional network strategy (NESDB/UNDP/TDRI, 1991). This supplements the growth-pole or growth-centre policy that

Table 9.10 Projected net immigration to the Bangkok Metropolitan Region and the eastern region, 1990–2010

	Bangkok Metropolitan Region			*Eastern Region*
	Bangkok	*Five Provinces*	*Total*	
1990–1995	124.3	181.9	306.2	94.5
1995–2000	115.0	194.9	310.0	105.2
2000–2005	108.1	206.2	314.3	111.3
2005–2010	103.5	213.4	316.9	116.0

Source: Medhi, 1992a.

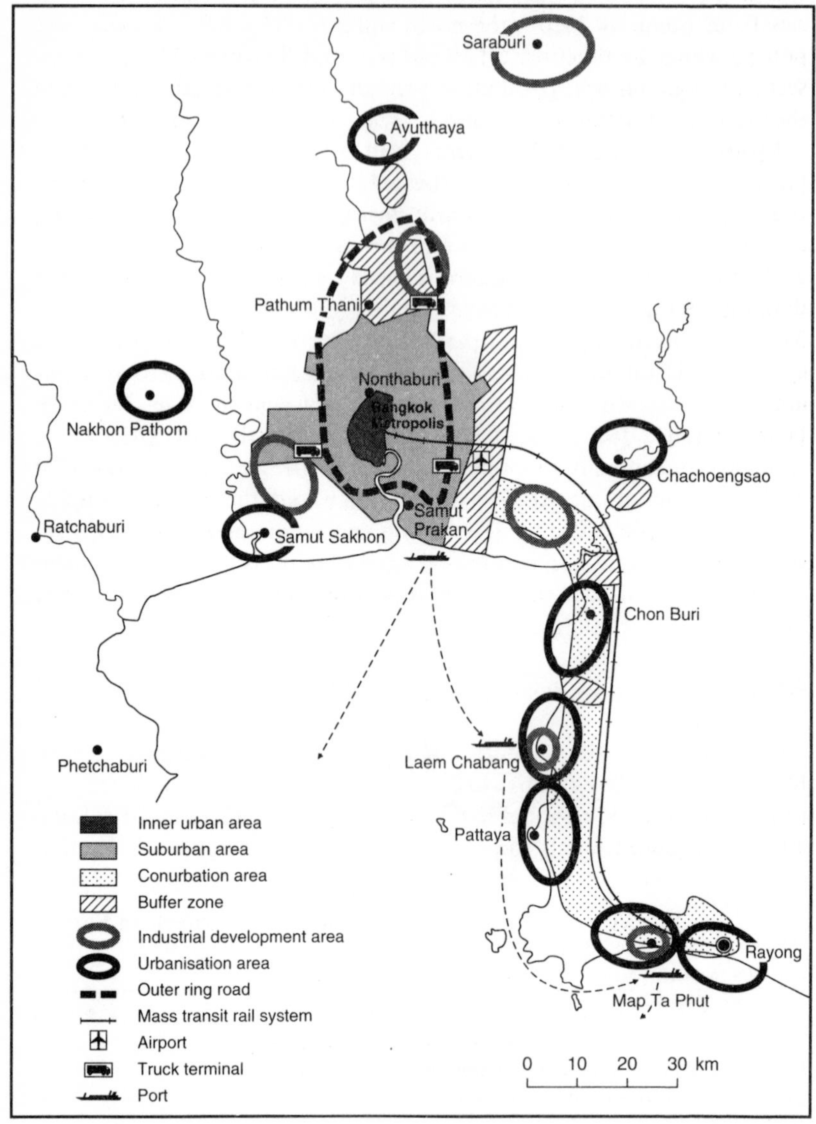

Figure 9.4 The Extended Bangkok Metropolitan Region

was originally adopted in Thailand's Fifth Plan to decentralize industries from Bangkok to other urban centres.[12] Unlike the growth-pole policy, which focused on urban-based manufacturing as the leading sector in regional development, the regional-network policy recognized the multisectoral nature of local development in rural areas (Figure 9.5).

Moreover, most growth-pole policies adopted an implicit central-place system based on the importance of city size, whereas the proposed regional-network policy found this yardstick to be an inadequate indicator of either growth potential or local linkages and believed that cities of the same class should have very different functions and development profiles (NESDB/UNDP/TDRI, 1991, vol. I, pp. 3.21–34). An omnibus centre for a region, the clustering of many settlements, each with its own specializations and localized hinterland relationships, are preferred to a single, large city. Thus small towns in one area could be made marketing centres for a particular crop, whereas others could specialize in regional administration or become cultural centres. The artificiality of central-place theory and rural–urban dichotomies (that is, rather than linkages) could be overcome by integrating these centres through transport links and institutional development.

The regional-network approach could ameliorate the spatial inequalities generated by urban-based industrialization by inducing regional economic expansion through accelerated rural development. Although Thai agriculture has made significant progress in diversification over the past decade, improvements could still be made in the intensification of land use and production of higher-value added crops for domestic consumption and export. The increase in agricultural productivity would make this rural-led development policy successful, and the advancement of rural hinterlands would become as important as town-centred or urban investments. Under the new arrangement: (1) the EBMR concept would be recognized to cover the Eastern Seaboard Areas, Ayutthaya and Saraburi; and (2) six different types of regional centres would be identified as nodes (Table 9.11).

In the EBMR, this new strategy will enable the Government to target corridors between major urban centres. These corridors will offer sites for industrial parks and higher-order services, such as hospitals, universities and recreation parks. They will attract skilled labour from the nearby towns (for example the high-technology industrial park in Ayutthaya, which is close to Don Muang, Bangkok's international airport).

Within the regions, the network approach was designed to move from focusing on a single municipality to the coordinated exchange of

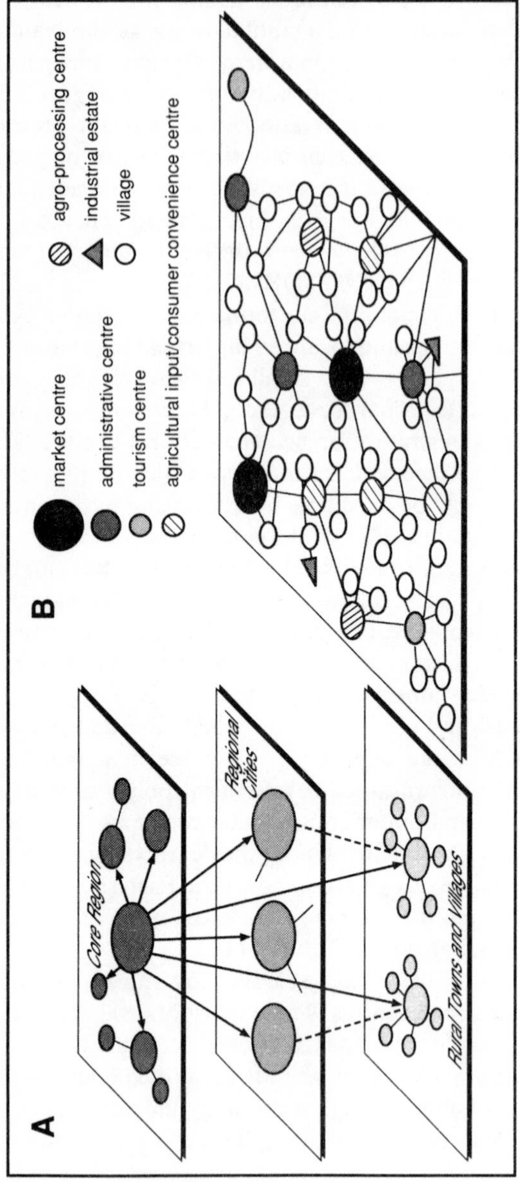

Figure 9.5 Different images of regional development: growth pole versus regional network model

Table 9.11 The proposed new urban hierarchy

City level	*Characteristics*	*Examples*
Level 1	The most developed urban growth centres in a region	Every city in the Bangkok Metropolitan Region, Chiang Mai, Khon Kaen, Nakhon Ratchasima, Phuket, Songkhla-Hat Yai
Level 2	High, rather than extraordinary, economic potential	Ayutthaya, Chachoengsao, Nakhon Sawan, Phitsanulok, Rayong, Ratchaburi, Saraburi
Level 3	Community urban growth centres with average growth potential	Kanchanaburi, Lamphun, Surat Thani, Ubon Ratchathani, Udon Thani
Level 4	Community urban growth centres with slightly below-average growth potential	Chiang Rai, Lampang, Lopburi, Nong Khai, Nakhon Si Thammarat, Yala
Level 5	Below-average potential	Nakhon Nayok, Maha Sarakham, Sakhon Nakhon, Roi Et, Uttaradit
Level 6	Cities with lowest regional growth potential	Chainat, Chumphon, Sukhothai.

Source: NESDB/UNDP/TDRI, 1991, vol. II, pp. 40–1.

goods, people and information between regional clusters of cities. As illustrated for the northern region of Thailand, first-ranking Chiang Mai is the dominant regional centre, though it is 364 km from the tourist centre of Mae Hong Son. Other pivotal roles are played by second-ranking Nakhon Sawan and Phitsanulok and fourth ranking Tak (Figure. 9.6). Lamphun's potential is limited by its proximity to Chiang Mai, and Nan, Phrae and Phrayao are left to develop into larger centres to create better ties with their agricultural hinterlands. This proposed system, however, could not operate under existing institutional arrangements. Thus changes to administrative and organizational arrangements have to be instituted.

9.5.3 Institutional Changes

A new national-level committee has been recommended for establishing policy and managing the EBMR – an upgraded Bangkok Metropolitan Region Development Committee, which at present coordinates urban

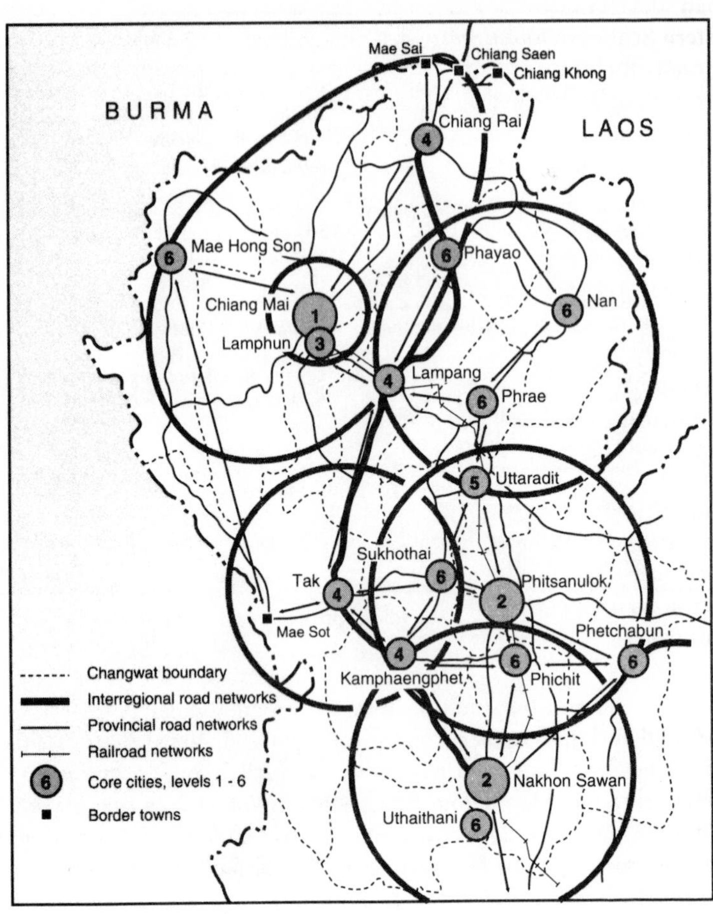

Figure 9.6 The new urban hierarchy within the northern region

policy. The committee would be headed by the prime minister and comprise high-level officials from various government agencies so that its responsibilities will be effectively discharged. It would be supported by a strong secretariat to plan the BMR's integrated development, coordinate agencies and, most importantly, evaluate major infrastructure projects and manage the degree of private-sector involvement.

These new arrangements for the EBMR will have to matched by new urban development corporations for special projects (for example Eastern Seaboard and new towns) and changes in the administration of regional-city governments to lessen regional inequality and income distribution. As greater administrative and fiscal autonomy for elected city councils hinges on the Ministry of the Interior relinquishing control of local government, rapid progress is not anticipated. Unless this change occurs the management of regional cities will continue to be slow and indecisive, and the eventual transition of Thailand into an urbanized economy retarded.

Besides these needed rearrangements, a new administrative and organizational structure has been recommended at the national level. A new body – the Urban Development Bureau, Ministry of Urban Development or Office of National Urban Development – has been proposed to frame urban policy and oversee its implementation. This change will be more difficult to engineer than the decentralization of power to regional cities. The availability of the financial resources required to fund the new infrastructure envisaged in Thailand's new urban-development policy, however, will have a decisive effect – the government, for example, spends less than 0.24 per cent of GNP on environmental protection (the comparable OECD rate is between 1 and 2 per cent).

9.5.4 Financial Changes

Between 1990 and 1995 over 525 billion baht will be required for the infrastructure components. As shown in Table 9.12, a number of financial strategies have been identified that draw on central-government, local-government, public-utility and private-sector sources. Both local government and the private sector have been given a higher profile than in previous plans. Most strategies rely on boosting the resources available to local authorities by increasing the power to tax, reducing dependence on the central authority, increasing the powers to collect users' charges, fees and fines and increasing the power to borrow, and identifying opportunities for privatization (for example contracting out service provision and 'build, operate and transfer' projects). Targeted projects for private involvement include intercity bus terminals for the BMTA, freight terminals, parking facilities and road networks.

Table 9.12 Strategies for financing urban activities

Strategy	*Details*
Improving the efficiency of tax collection and widening of the tax base	Improve administration and the structure of the building and land and local development taxes. Replacing these taxes in the longer term with a new property tax is revenue adequate, income elastic, incentive oriented and structurally simple. Share the revenue generated from land-registration (ownership transfer) fee between central and local government.
Service fee improvements	Establish central-government guidelines for fee imposition to be observed by local officials, allowing the exact fee to be levied for any specific service to the discretion of local government. Fees should be related to the cost of the service and should be imposed whenever beneficiaries can be identified and the benefit clearly identified.
Restructuring the present municipal lending organizations	Create a new organization, perhaps called the Local Grant Development Corporation, to facilitate funding of local-government development and expand local investment opportunities. The sources of funding for this organization will be from (i) local governments, (ii) central government, (iii) private financial organizations, and (iv) foreign sources.
Establish a regional development grant	Establish a regional development grant for allocation to local governments in high-priority, target areas. The minimum area for a grant will be the province because an urban centre cannot be developed in isolation without concurrent and supportive development occurring in surrounding rural areas.
Modernize the grant allocation mechanism	Revise the so-called general grant based on per-capita allocation basis to take into account local tax-collection efforts (that is, incentives for local governments to improve their tax-collection efficiency).
Other financial strategies	Impose special assessment levies to mobilize resources from developers for the use of existing and planned infrastructure services (for example, for Bangkok's flood protection).

Source: NESDB/UNDP/TDRI, 1991, vol. I, pp. xlvi-xlvii, plan.

9.6 CONCLUSION

By 2010 almost half of Thailand's population will be urban. At that stage the EMBR will be linked into complex networks with regional cities. As admitted by contemporary planners, even the EMBR concept will probably be inadequate by then (NESDB/UNDP/TDRI, 1991, vol. II, p. 8.86). Thus, it will be tempting to overhaul laws and regulations and develop a national urban management committee to provide the required infrastructure (for example the Ministry for Urban Development or an Office of National Urban Development) to serve 'complex and compound regional systems consisting of central cities, exurbs, satellite towns, and extensive intervening areas of dense population and intensive traditional agricultural land uses in which wet-paddy cultivation tends to dominate' (Ginsburg, Koppel and McGee, 1991, p. xiii). At best, this is a temporary solution as urbanization problems will have become international rather than national.

The longer-term prospect is the development of a higher level of linkage within an emerging development corridor stretching across international boundaries from Chiang Mai to Bali – the counterpart to an emerging East Asian development corridor running from Pusan to Hong Kong. Within this new South-East Asian zone of interaction brought about in response to economic penetration from East Asia, notably by Japan and Taiwan, there will be a further blurring of the outmoded distinction between urban and rural. Also, there will be an emphasis on linking the network hubs, such as the extended metropolitan regions of Bangkok, the Klang Valley and greater Singapore (that is, the growth triangle), and Jabotabek and Surabaya, with improved land-based transport and communications connections befitting their status as national and international production, financial and service centres. Stretching along these trunk connections there will be a mixture of non-agricultural and agricultural activities supporting a dense population – the lightly populated areas of plantation agriculture in Malaysia being an exception (McGee, 1991, p. 7).

A higher proportion of the budget will be spent on nodes (for example seaports and airports) rather than on links. Already plans are being made to deconcentrate these hubs within extended metropolitan regions. For example, Bangkok's international airport will be relocated. There will also be stress on a total logistics system based on container movements and electronic data interchange. Heavy expenditure for inland transport modes will be focused on expressways and high-speed passenger rail, superimposed on networks dominated by 'low-tech' transport.

This vision will be anathema to environmentalists. The concentration of construction activities on load-centre ports, superhub airports and their supporting connections within this emerging development corridor will be perceived as wasteful in investment, prodigal in energy use and peripheralizing people and places beyond their bounds. Inevitably this will lead to a demand for an overall land-use-transport and communications plan that is international in context and canvasses alternative transport and communications networks that will generate sustainable settlement forms.

Notes

1. Two definitions of 'urban' are employed. The first defines urban as comprising municipal areas and large sanitary districts with populations in excess of 5000. Whereas the administrative areas are 'underbounded', with densely built-up areas traversing their boundaries, a second definition of 'urban' is used. It comprises residential and/or industrial areas with over 5000 persons and a minimum average density of 1000 persons per square kilometre. The initial administrative definition is used here for determining the number of urban places whereas the geographical definition is used in forecasting (NESDB/UNDP/TDRI, 1991, vol. I, pp. 2.9–10).
2. Bangkok Metropolitan Region (BMR) or Greater Bangkok comprises the Bangkok Metropolitan Administration (BMA) and five provinces – Samut Prakan, Pathum Thani, Nakhon Pathom, Samut Sakhon and Nonthaburi. The Extended Bangkok Metropolitan Region (EBMR) comprises the Bangkok Metropolitan Region and five neighbouring provinces – Ayutthaya, Chachoengsao, Saraburi, Chon Buri and Rayong.
3. The 'index of primacy' is defined as the ratio between the population of the largest city and the population of the next three cities combined (Medhi, 1992a, pp. 3–4).
4. Singapore's purpose-built container terminals were first operational in 1972 whereas Bangkok's facilities were not operational until 1978. Even then they were used by feeder vessels from Singapore and Hong Kong.
5. In 1976 the difference in average per capita household income between Bangkok and north-east Thailand was 2.2. times. By 1988 the figure was 3.4 times – 29 880 baht compared with 6,868 baht. Bangkok's urban growth, therefore, had brought about greater inequality in Thailand (Medhi, 1992a, p. 11).
6. The Sixth Plan sought: (1) to improve public transport as an alternative to the private car by increasing the number and quality of Bangkok's buses, constructing a network of bus ways, improved bus lanes and bus priorities, encouraging competition in the bus industry, adjusting fare

policy and diversifying service offerings; and (2) introducing expressway tolls to the rest of the central area road network and improvement of the road network through the construction of missing links, distributor roads and highways (NESDB, 1986d, p. 1 12).

7. In March 1984 corporate planning became mandatory for all 15 state transport enterprises, including the Bangkok Metropolitan Transit Authority.
8. SPURT was conducted for the National Economic and Social Development Board (NESDB) by Halcrow Fox and Associates, Pak-Poy and Kneebone Pty Ltd. and Asian Engineering Consultants Corp. Ltd.
9. A survey of urban transport costs and fares in Metropolitan Bangkok by PADECO Co. Ltd (1991) highlighted the way the current modal split is biased in favour of low-occupancy vehicles (for example taxis and private cars). To overcome this problem it recommended an increase in fuel taxes and annual licensing fees; the maintenance of high purchase-related taxes and those on tyres and spare parts at current levels; the charging of tolls where practicable; the implementation of differential parking charges; the introduction of a graduated, distance-based bus-fare structure; and the exemption of school buses from customs duties to encourage the use of high-occupancy vehicles.
10. The six mega-projects are Skytrain, the Hopewell scheme. the Second Stage Expressway, the Ekamai-Ram Inthra expressway, the Don Muang tollway and the Klong San Saeb tollway (Joint NESDB/UNDP/TDRI, 1991, vol. II, p. 8.19).
11. The Hopewell Group was granted concessions to derive income from mass-transit rail tickets, urban-freeway vehicle tolls and commercial developments.
12. Even before the First National Economic Development Plan (1961–6), the royal Thai government chose Chiang Mai and Khon Kaen as centres to attract growth from Bangkok. Apart from the establishment of universities, little further transpired until the Third Plan (1972–6) when five provincial centres adjacent to Bangkok were nominated for accelerated growth – Nakhon Pathom, Nonthaburi, Pathum Thani, Samut Prakan and Samut Sakhon. In the Fourth Plan (1977–81) a further seven provincial cities were nominated as 'first-generation centres'. During the Fifth Plan (1982–6) a growth-pole strategy was adopted but areas rather than specific centres were named as alternatives to migration to Bangkok – the eastern seaboard, the lower north-east, the upper northern, western and southern border. As the eastern seaboard exhibited no signs of being successful, the Sixth Plan (1986-91) returned to the emphasis on specific regional growth centres – the five 'first-generation' centres were augmented by six 'second-generation' centres and thirteen 'third-generation centres'. Before the small and medium-scale enterprises pivotal to this strategy could get started, the government switched its attention to large-scale, capital-intensive industrialization evident in the eastern seaboard project (Medhi, 1992a).

10 Industrialization and Welfare: How Poverty and Income Distribution are Affected

Pranee Tinakorn

10.1 INTRODUCTION

Since 1960 Thailand has had a remarkable record of high growth. During the 1960s the average growth rate of GDP was around 8 per cent per annum. In the following decade it slowed to about 6.7 per cent. During the early 1980s, despite the international recession experienced by many countries, Thailand registered growth rates of around 3–7 per cent, with even higher rates towards the end of the decade. On average the growth rate during 1980–1990 was around 7.8 per cent per annum.

Such a rapid increase in GDP has had many consequences for the Thai economy. Among other things, it has resulted in higher income per capita and higher standards of living. The structure of production has also been altered as the growth rates of the industrial and service sectors have been higher than that of the agricultural sector. Although high growth is a desirable macroeconomic objective, it does not necessarily lead to a higher standard of welfare for everyone. It is quite well known that GDP and its affiliates (such as GNP and per capita income) do not measure environmental damage, change in the quality of products, underground and unrecorded activities and so on, all of which affect the welfare of the people in a society. Most importantly from the focal point of this chapter, GDP, from which we measure growth, does not measure the distribution of income. This is not to say that GDP is not a good measure; simply that it is not designed or intended to account for the distribution of income.

Perhaps, we cannot agree on what constitutes a 'just' or 'fair' distribution of income. However there is probably a consensus that a distribution with fewer households in poverty would be better than a distribution with more households in poverty. There may be even a consensus that, given an increase in total income, less inequality in its distribution would be an improvement.

It is the purpose of this chapter to look into the trends in growth, distribution and poverty reduction in Thailand since 1960, when the country started the First National Development Plan. (The significance of the First Plan lies in its emphasis on changing the government's active role in expanding state enterprises in the previous decade to a more supportive role of encouraging private investment and private enterprise.) Section 10.2 discusses the trend in income distribution and poverty incidence. Section 10.3 discusses the evolution of industrial policies since the 1960s and addresses some aspects of industrial policy that may accentuate the inequality in distribution. Section 10.4 provides a conclusion.

10.2 TREND IN INCOME DISTRIBUTION AND POVERTY

There are two types of distribution that we may consider: the functional distribution of income and the size distribution of income. The functional distribution of income refers to the income received by different factors of production, such as return to labour, land, capital and entrepreneurship. The size distribution of income refers to the income received by different households or individuals. While it would be desirable to analyzse both types of distribution, the available data permits limited analysis on the functional distribution of income.

10.2.1 Functional Distribution of Income

An investigation into the distribution of personal income (Table 10.1) shows that there is an increasing trend in the proportion of personal income coming from employment. This proportion was 27.9 per cent in 1960 and 38.8 per cent in 1990. The proportion of income from property and entrepreneurship also increased, from 9.7 per cent in 1960 to 12.3 per cent in 1990. While the share of these two factor income categories increased, the share of income from unincorporated enterprises decreased from 62 per cent in 1960 to 48.3 per cent in 1990. This may be a result of the movement of the economy towards a more organized and more formal production process. Nevertheless, despite its decreasing trend, the share of income from unincorporated enterprises was still dominant in 1990.

Table 10.1 Distribution of personal income (percent)

	1960	*1970*	*1980*	*1990*
Income from employment	27.9	23.4	32.9	38.8
Income from unincorporated enterprises*	62.0	64.6	55.3	48.3
Income from property and entrepreneurship	9.7	11.7	11.1	12.3
Corporate transfer payments	–	0.1	0.1	0.1
Current transfer from general government	0.2	0.1	0.2	0.2
Current transfer from the rest of the world	0.2	0.2	0.4	0.2
Total personal income	100.0	100.0	100.0	100.0

*Income from farms, professions, and other unincorporated enterprises received by households
Source: NESDB, *National Income of Thailand,* various issues.

When we distribute the remuneration of employees by industry, as shown in Table 10.2, it is clear that the proportion going to the agricultural sector has reduced in favour of the non-agricultural sector. In 1960 the share of agriculture was 16.2 per cent, but it declined to only 6.5 per cent in 1990. Among the non-agricultural sectors, manufacturing seems to have gained the most as its share increased from 8.2 per cent in 1960 to 27.3 per cent in 1990. Coupled with the fact that a large proportion of labour employment remains in agriculture while a

Table 10.2 Compensation of employees by sector (per cent)

	1960	*1970*	*1980*	*1990*
Domestic				
Agriculture	16.2	10.3	10.7	6.5
Mining and quarrying	1.2	2.2	1.8	0.7
Manufacturing	8.2	14.3	20.6	27.3
Construction	13.8	8.1	7.1	9.6
Electricity and water supply	0.6	1.5	1.7	2.1
Transportation and communications	8.7	8.3	7.0	6.8
Wholesale and retail trade	8.3	8.7	6.1	7.0
Banking, insurance and real estate	2.0	4.1	4.8	6.0
Public administration and defence	19.3	23.3	17.2	12.7
Services	21.7	19.4	18.8	17.8
The rest of the world	–	−0.3	4.1	3.6
Total	100.0	100.0	100.0	100.0

Source: NESDB, *National Income Accounts*.

relatively small portion shifted to manufacturing, it is no wonder that the agricultural sector engulfs a majority of poor households, not to speak of the income inequality generated through such shifts in income and employment.

In order to make a more meaningful analysis of the functional distribution of income, perhaps one should look at the trend in the productivity of different factor inputs. However this would require an extensive analysis of factor input data. In addition, the aggregate statistics on national income do not allow measurement of the contribution of individual factors. For example, income from unincorporated enterprises, which dominated 48.3 per cent of personal income in 1990, is a mixture of the remuneration for the owners' labour, land and other property, which cannot be clearly separated out.

Besides, the functional distribution of income does not offer an indication of how income is distributed among different households. If we believe that the welfare of a household is related to its income, no matter from what factors of production, then we should move on to an analysis of the size distribution of income.

10.2.2 Size Distribution of Income[1]

The study of size distribution of income and poverty incidence in Thailand became possible with statistical surveys of household income and expenditure. The National Statistical Office (NSO) of Thailand began collecting such data in 1962–3. Similar surveys continue up to the present time at about 3 to 5 year interval. The available surveys are 1962–3, 1968–9, 1971–3, 1975–6, 1981, 1986 and 1988.[2]

A number of empirical studies employing various surveys support the general belief that the distribution of income in Thailand since the early 1960s has deteriorated. This worsening trend is illustrated by the income shares and Gini coefficients presented in Tables 10.3 and 10.4.[3]

Although one would like to connect the information in Table 10.3 with that in Table 10.4 to see a longer-run trend between 1962–3 and 1988, one has to be mindful of the fact that the concepts of income used in different studies are not exactly the same. The income shares provided in Table 10.3 are based on money income while those in Table 10.4 are based on total current income, which includes money income, income-in-kind and imputed rent. Even though Medhi (1979) and Somluckrat (1978) provided Gini coefficients based on adjusted income, the concept used was different in their studies.[4] Therefore the

Table 10.3 Income share by quintile groups, 1962–3 to 1971–3

Quintile	*1962–3*		*1968–9*		*1971–3*	
1 (Lowest income group)	2.9		3.4	(4.5)	2.4	(2.5)
2	6.2		6.1	(5.5)	5.1	(6.4)
3	10.5		10.4	(12.5)	9.7	(10.4)
4	20.9		19.2	(20.5)	18.4	(19.0)
5 (Top income group)	59.5		60.9	(57.0)	64.4	(61.0)
Gini coefficient (money income)	0.5627		0.5550	(0.545)	0.6051	(0.576)
Gini coefficient (adjusted income)	0.4559	(0.414)	0.4822	(0.466)	0.5348	(0.499)

Sources: Figures in parentheses are from Somluckrat, 1978; figures not in parentheses are from Medhi, 1979.

Table 10.4 Income shares by quintile group, 1975–6 to 1988

Quintile	*1975–6*	*1981*	*1986*	*1988*
1st (Lowest income group)	6.05	5.41	4.55	4.50
2nd	9.73	9.10	7.87	8.09
3rd	14.00	13.38	12.09	12.27
4th	20.96	20.64	19.86	20.26
5th (Top income group)	49.26	51.47	55.63	54.88
Gini coefficient	0.426	0.453	0.500	0.479

Sources: The 1975–6, 1981 and 1986 data are from Suganya and Somchai, 1988, the 1988 data are from Medhi, Pranee and Suphat, 1991, 1992.

author preferred to look separately at the trends between 1962–3 to 1971–3 and 1975–6 to 1988.

The calculation of income shares by region, as shown in Table 10.5 reveals that there is a regional disparity in the distribution of income. The proportion of the population living in Bangkok and its vicinities in 1988 was 14.6 per cent but its income share was about 32 per cent, the highest among all regions. In contrast, the north-east which had the highest population share (34.3 per cent) had only 20.4 per cent of total income. The north-east has been known as the poorest region in the country and it has remained so. The separate Gini coefficients for each region indicate varying degrees of income inequality within each region. The 1988 data show that income inequality was highest in the north, followed by the south, the north-east, the centre and Bangkok. The inequality within regions and between regions renders a higher inequality index for the whole country.

Table 10.5 Income share and Gini coefficients by region, 1988

Region	*Distribution of:* *Household*	*Population*	*Income*	*Gini coefficient*
Bangkok and vicinity	16.20	14.58	31.99	0.385
North	21.69	19.73	17.79	0.453
North-east	30.68	34.27	20.43	0.410
Centre	18.80	18.53	18.36	0.408
South	12.63	12.89	11.43	0.439
Whole kingdom	100.00	100.00	100.00	0.479

Note: Bangkok and vicinity includes Pathum Thani, Nonthaburi and Samut Prakan.
Source: Table 2.6 in Medhi, Pranee and Suphat, 1991.

10.2.3 Poverty Incidence

The first to attempt to estimate poverty incidence in Thailand were Medhi and Chintana (1975). They estimated poverty incidence to be 46.75 per cent in 1968–9. However they did not use the basic-needs approach but instead employed the break-even levels of estimated Keynesian consumption functions to arrive at poverty bands, from which they estimated poverty incidence. There were also studies by Oey Meesook (1975, 1976) and World Bank (1978), which estimated poverty incidence from arbitrarily cut-off income levels.

Poverty studies based on the basic-needs approach began with the work of Oey Meesook (1979) and World Bank (1980a). The poverty lines were derived from elaborate calculations based on the nutritional-adequacy method. However, due to inconsistent definitions of urban and rural areas in the 1962–3 and 1968–9 socioeconomic surveys (SES), Oey came up with different sets of poverty incidence to compare with the 1975–6 SES. [5] It was found that the reduction of poverty was more gradual than had been supposed in the 1978 World Bank report.

Employing the same concept of nutritional adequacy as Oey (1979), Medhi and Pranee (1985) found a significant reduction in poverty incidence between the 1975–6 and 1981 socioeconomic surveys, that is, from 31.7 per cent to 23.9 per cent. A later work by Suganya and Somchai (1988) extended the lines used by Medhi and Pranee to 1986 and estimated a decline in poverty incidence from 30 per cent in 1975–6 to 23 per cent in 1981, and then an increase to 29.5 per cent in 1986. Medhi, Pranee and Suphat (1991) found a reduction of poverty to 21.2

per cent in the 1988 SES. The details about poverty lines and poverty incidence during 1975–6 to 1988 are summarized in Table 10.6.

The rate of poverty incidence in 1988 would translate into about 11.7 million poor in Thailand. Of this number about 10.4 million, or about 89 per cent of all poor, lived in rural villages and about 1.3 million or 11 per cent of all poor, lived in municipal areas and sanitary districts. The rate of poverty incidence also varies among regions and community types. The north-east has the highest rate of poverty incidence while Bangkok has the lowest.

Both Suganya and Somchai (1988) and Medhi, Pranee and Suphat (1991) found that the highest incidence of poverty was among agriculturalists when compared with other occupations. It is no surprise, then, to find a worsening of poverty in 1986 when there was a sharp decline in both farm prices and the value of agricultural products which greatly affected agriculturists' income.

We may summarize the findings of the above-cited studies as follows. There appears to have been a general decline in poverty in Thailand over the past two decades. Most of the poor (about 89 per cent in 1988)[6] live in rural areas and they are mainly farmers and farm

Table 10.6 Poverty lines and poverty incidence, 1975–6 to 1988

	1975–6	*1981*	*1986*	*1988*
Poverty lines (baht per person per year):				
Urban	2961	5151	5834	6203
Rural	1981	3454	3823	4076
Poverty incidence (%)				
By community type				
All municipal areas	12.5	7.5	5.9	6.1
All sanitary district areas	14.8	13.5	18.6	12.2
All villages	36.2	27.3	35.8	26.3
By region:				
North	33.2	21.5	25.5	19.9
North-east	44.9	35.9	48.2	34.6
Centre	13.0	13.6	15.6	12.9
South	30.7	20.4	27.2	19.4
Bangkok and vicinity	7.8	3.9	3.5	3.5
Whole kingdom	30.0	23.0	29.5	21.2

Note: In both of the studies cited below, poverty incidence was calculated by applying the rural poverty lines to sanitary district areas.
Sources: The data for 1975–6, 1981 and 1986 are from Suganya and Somchai, 1988, and those for 1988 are from Medhi, Pranee and Suphat, 1991.

labourers who depend very much on income-in-kind as a major source of household income. The rural poor tend to have larger families and fewer income earners compared with the non-poor, and their household heads have low educational attainment.[7] A majority of them also lack such basic amenities as toilet facilities, piped water and electricity.

It should be mentioned here that, Medhi, Pranee and Suphat (1991) also reported another way of measuring of poverty incidence that is based on 'adjusted' poverty lines. The adjusted poverty lines were calculated to allow for the changes in the population structure, nutritional requirements and consumption patterns that occurred during the twelve years between 1976 and 1988. The 'unadjusted' poverty lines reported in Table 10.6 were based on the 1976 calculation of basic needs with the adjustment only on price changes. Based on the adjusted poverty lines, the rates of poverty incidence in all regions were either double or more than double those based on the unadjusted lines. The poverty incidence for the whole kingdom rose to about 48.8 per cent – it is more than a little shocking to think that almost half the population of Thailand lived in poverty in 1988.

The picture from the unadjusted poverty lines shows that, despite the remarkable record of growth over the past three decades, about 11.7 million people are still living in poverty. Taken with the fact discussed in Section 10.2.2 that the growth of income has been unevenly distributed, one cannot help wonder whether the 'trickle down' mechanism suggested by classical economists has worked well.

10.3 INDUSTRIAL POLICES AND WELFARE

It is quite difficult, if not impossible, to trace and quantify the effect of industrial policies on income distribution and welfare. That task is beyond the scope of this chapter. What has been shown in the previous sections is the long-term picture of growth, income distribution and poverty in Thailand during the time in which the country became more industrialized. The pace of growth and industrialization in Thailand has been such that many people expect it to become the 'fifth tiger' of Asia in the near future.

In this section we will briefly discuss the path of industrial development in Thailand since the 1960s and make some qualitative judgement about its contribution to income distribution and poverty.

10.3.1 Industrial Policies in the Past Three Decades[8]

We may consider the Promotion of Industrial Investment Act (B.E. 2503) in 1960 to be the starting point of the modern period of industrialization in Thailand. Prior to this there was an Industrial Promotion Act (B.E. 2497) of 1954, which proved largely ineffective due to the ambiguity of statements in the Act and excessive delays in handling applications.

The importance of the 1960 investment law lay in the fact that it created a Board of Investment (BOI), which was empowered to encourage domestic and foreign investment in industrial activities. This law, with its amendments in later years, provided many incentives for private domestic and foreign investors to venture into industrial activities. Among the many incentives provided were a guarantee against nationalization and competition from the state, exemptions of import tariff on capital goods and raw materials, income tax holidays and permission to export manufactured products, repatriate profits and so on.

Perhaps the most important aspect of industrial policy during the 1950s and early 1960s was the switch of government policy from its active role of expanding state capitalism to a supportive role of encouraging private investment and private enterprise. Previously, or since the 1932 revolution which changed Thailand from a regime of absolute monarchy to one of constitutional monarchy, governments had concentrated on expanding economic activities by expanding state enterprises under the doctrine of 'economic nationalism'. While a few state enterprises had been established before 1932, in 1957 there were as many as 141 engaged in various activities under the control of nine ministries and other public organizations (Riggs, 1966, p. 305). These state enterprises were evaluated by the World Bank mission in 1959 to be inefficient and without profits, except for monopolistic activities (World Bank, 1959, pp. 90–4). The World Bank mission also suggested (pp. 20–1):

> Further government ventures into industrial operation are considered inadvisable, and a review of existing government industries is proposed to distinguish between those for which continued operation may be justified and those which should be discontinued. . . . It is also noted that most promising way to develop industry is to encourage private domestic and foreign enterprise, first by leaving the field clear for private initiative and second by special tax and other inducements, creation of institutional credit arrangements

> and provision of such physical facilities as sites, buildings, power and water services, roads, housing, etc.

The Thai government followed the above lines of suggestions and industrial activities have expanded successfully since then. From 1960–72 the manufacturing sector registered an average annual growth rate of 10.8 per cent compared with only 5.3 per cent from 1950–59. The period 1960–72 was evaluated by many scholars as a period of import-substitution industrialization for many reasons, but particularly because of the high effective rate of protection given to consumer products and the negative rate of effective protection for export products. Briefly, other reasons were explicit legal protection from import competition, high tariff walls, the high percentage of investment promotion given to the consumer-goods industry and so on.

By the early 1970s it had become evident that this import-substitution industrialization policy, though successful in terms of growth, has caused some problems that need to be corrected. For example, import-substitution industrialization was able to reduce the quantity of imported consumer products, but it increased the import value of capital goods and raw materials due to the fiscal incentives provided by the investment law. This resulted in the trade deficit increasing from around one billion baht in 1960 to around ten billion baht in the early 1970s. The consistently huge trade deficits caused the balance of payments to be in deficit for three consecutive years – 1969, 1970 and 1971. Another problem with industrialization by import substitution was the size of the domestic market, which limited industrial expansion after some point. In addition, international organisations such as the Asian Development Bank (1971, pp. 19–20) and the World Bank (1972, pp. 52–3) urged the Thai government to turn towards export-promotion industrialization.

Therefore in 1972, which was the starting year of the Third National Development Plan, it was declared that industrial policy would turn towards export promotion. The old investment law was abolished and a new one was promulgated in 1972. The new law provided many incentives for export-oriented industrial investment. In addition there were other measures not administered through BOI to help promote exports, such as export credit facilities, administered by the Bank of Thailand and import-tax rebates and production-tax rebates for exporters, administered by the Ministry of Finance. In April 1975 an exports service centre was established within the Ministry of Commerce to help exporters with information on products and foreign markets.

Although there remain several measures in the investment law, including import tariffs, that still provide protection to the import substitution industry, the period from 1972 to the present is usually regarded as a period of export-promotion industrialization in Thailand. Pranee (1988, p. 206) provided data to show that the average growth rate of exports of industrial products was around 33 per cent from 1970–80 while the average growth rate of total exports was about 24 per cent. As a result the ratio of all industrial exports to total exports increased from 25 per cent in 1970 to 48 per cent in 1980. This ratio increased to 55 per cent in 1984.[9] During the 1980s the growth rates slowed down, due partly to the worldwide recession in the early 1980s. But, overall, this industrial policy seems to have worked out for the country.

10.3.2 Industrialization and Distribution

Along with industrial policies, other policies such as fiscal and monetary policies, labour policies, educational policies and so on have been implemented. Although the present situation with regard to poverty and income distribution is not the result of industrial policies alone, there may be some aspects of industrialization that tend to accentuate it. In this section we will briefly discuss some of these aspects.

First, investment promotion in the past has tended to favour large-scale, capital-intensive firms. In addition to the fiscal incentives given to imported capital, there has been a minimum-wage law that has made the relative price of capital cheaper than it ought to have been. This resulted in low employment in the industrial sector. Thus, while the agricultural sector produced about one seventh of real GDP in 1990 it still absorbed about two thirds of the labour force. This may be one explanation why poverty incidence is high among those engaged in agricultural activities.

Second, although an Industrial Estate Authority of Thailand (IEAT) was established in 1972 to plan for industrial and export zones, its task in distributing factories appeared unsuccessful. There is a concentration of factories and industrial activities in Bangkok and the central region. The vital factor behind this is probably basic infrastructure (communications systems, electricity, water supply and so on), which has been inadequate in the other regions. This has led to a wider regional disparity of income, as shown by the data in Table 10.7.

Table 10.7 Regional distribution of GDP and regional per capita GDP in current prices

	1960	*1970*	*1980*	*1989*
Distribution of GDP (%):				
Bangkok and vicinity	22.6	29.0	31.1	48.1
Centre*	28.8	27.7	29.0	18.5
North	15.4	15.1	13.9	11.4
North-east	17.4	15.7	14.4	12.9
South	15.7	12.4	11.5	9.1
Whole kingdom	100.0	100.0	100.0	100.0
(Value in million baht)	53 984	136 060	684 930	1 775 978
Regional per capita GDP (baht):				
Bangkok and vicinity	5715	12 838	45 300	96 239
Centre*	2537	5005	20 447	30 587
North	1454	2739	10 511	18 833
North-east	1046	1782	6294	11 981
South	2594	3958	14 052	21 955
Whole kingdom	2056	3956	15 280	32 028

*Excluding Bangkok and vicinity (Bangkok, Nonthaburi, Pathum Thani and Samut Prakan).
Source: Calculated from NESDB data.

Third, the strategy of unbalanced growth by giving special privileges, protective measures and various incentives to large investors in the industrial sector has resulted in a high business concentration. A study by Krirkkiat shows that in many industries just a few big firms controlled the whole market. In some industries just three or four firms took 50–80 per cent of the market share (Krirkkiat, 1981). Such a concentration can lead to monopolistic and/or oligopolistic power, which penalizes small consumers. In addition, small investors and entrepreneurs not receiving such BOI benefits are also penalized by import tariffs and export taxes. Such phenomena tend to reduce income equality.

Last, but not least, we need to study the environmental impact of such rapid industrialization. For the sake of growth, the impact of industrialization on the environment may have been neglected. This is an issue that appears to affect everyone's welfare, but in reality it is probably the poor in the rural areas who bear most of the burden. For example, in an effort to provide sufficient electricity to support rapid industrialization, the government increased its construction of large dams. This has not only depleted forest areas but also meant the relocation of a significant number of rural families, most of whom were poor.

10.4 CONCLUSION

From the above account on growth, one probably has to admit that the successful expansion of industrial activities in Thailand has been helpful in raising total and per capita income. If the 'trickle down' mechanism works, then we should expect everyone to be better off. At the least poverty should be reduced, if not eradicated. Indeed we have found that to be the case for Thailand, but we have also found that income inequality has become worse. Of course growth, distribution and poverty are determined by many interrelated factors and policies, and it is difficult to point to any specific factor or policy as the major cause of the present situation. For example, pricing and exchange-rate policies, which have been adverse to the agricultural terms of trade vis-à-vis other sectors, must have also contributed to the worsening trend in income distribution but we have not investigated the role of these other factors. In this chapter we have only investigated some aspects of industrialization that may have contributed to growing inequality.

The reduction of poverty incidence from something above 40 per cent in the 1960s to about 21 per cent in 1988 may look good. But the translation of it into a number of about 12 million poor people with about 89 per cent of them in rural areas can take the gloss from the picture of successful growth. That fact, combined with the worsening trend in income inequality, reveals a very unbalanced strategy of past development policies, of which industrialization has played a part.

Not that no attention has been given to the rural or the agricultural sector. We can find ample evidence of policy statements and public programmes that concerned rural development. For example the Accelerated Rural Development Agency was established in 1966 with the assistance of USAID. The Public Works Programme was initiated in 1975 and later evolved into its present form of the Rural Job Creation Programme. The Fourth National Economic and Social Development Plan (1977–81) mentioned support and provision of incentives for small-scale industries in provincial areas. This so called 'rural industry' policy seemed to fade away from policy makers' interest as the large-scale industrial development of the Eastern Seaboard (ESB) Project consumed their interest in the Sixth Plan

(1987–91). It is quite ironic to observe that the 1980s were declared the 'Decade of Rural Development' by Prime Minister Prem Tinsulanond in 1981, and five years later the government pledged to promote large-scale industrial development without any specific programmes to promote rural industry.

These examples and the present situation of growing inequality leads one to believe that there must have been bias in policy implementation that favoured industrial over agricultural activities, large over small business, and urban over rural people. Perhaps this was done for the sake of growth and belief in the 'trickle down' process. But one may wonder whether we have put too much belief in this process for too long.

Notes

1. This part is drawn primarily from the author's own work in Medhi Krongkaew, Pranee Tinakorn and Suphat Suphachalasai, 'Priority Issues and Policy Measures to Alleviate Rural Poverty: The Case of Thailand,' a research report submitted to the Economics and Development Resources Center, the Asian Development Bank, May 1991.
2. The years attached to each survey follow those of the NSO publications, which may not necessarily reflect the precise time (in terms of months) at which the surveys were conducted. The most recent survey is that of 1990, which had not been released for public use at the time of writing.
3. For more details see Pirom, 1976, Medhi, 1979, Somluckrat, 1978, Oey Meesook, 1979, Medhi and Pranee, 1985 and Suganya and Somchai, 1988.
4. Medhi (1979) adjusted income to approximate the national income while Somluckrat (1978) adjusted for income-in-kind and imputed rent from data provided in the survey. For more details please see the cited studies.
5. In the 1975–6 SES, communities were separated into municipal, sanitary and villages whereas in the 1962–3 SES sanitary areas were included with municipal as urban areas and in the 1968–9 SES sanitary areas were included with villages as rural areas. The author prefers not to discuss their figures of different sets.
6. If we count sanitary districts as rural then the percentage of the poor living in rural areas would be 95 per cent of the total.
7. Medhi, Pranee and Suphat (1991) found that about 97 per cent of poor household heads in 1988 had at most elementary or no formal education.
8. This section is drawn primarily from Pranee, 1988.
9. The calculation of these statistics by Pranee (1988) was based on a comparison of BTN (Brussels Tariff Nomenclature) codes with Input–Output and TSIC (Thailand Standard Industrial Classification) codes. Such complications plus data-publication lags, provide a reason why the author has not attempted to update such statistics.

Part III

Impact on Political Structure, Governance, Environment and Social Values

11 Economic Development and Democracy

Chai-Anan Samudavanija

11.1 INTRODUCTION

If we look back, we will realize that economic development in Thailand is not a new phenomenon. The Thai economy has grown continuously for over half a century with more rapid and higher sustained rates of growth in the past decade, especially during the last three years of the 1980s. But why have the new amalgam of social and political forces not been able to consolidate themselves and reshape the character of the state?

This question leads on to others. Are capitalism and democracy in Thailand related? Is democracy the only alternative political framework to support and promote capitalism? In other words, does capitalism and its basic trait – industrialization – need democracy in order to sustain and expand itself? The most relevant question is whether economic and political inequality caused by rapid economic development is temporary and self-correcting.

Before we answer these questions, we should look at some peculiar traits of economic development in Thailand. I would like to highlight only a few characteristics that are unique in the Thai case. As Medhi pointed out:

- Economic changes took place in a situation where the labour force was still predominantly in the agricultural sector (close to 60 per cent); where the secondary school attainment level was one of the lowest in Asia (about 30 per cent of the age-group); where the primacy of its capital city, Bangkok, increased even more with development, effectively dominating all other cities in the kingdom.
- Unlike most other developing countries, the average size of landholdings had not become smaller as the country developed. This strange phenomenon could be explained partly by the fact that the rate of deforestation was very extensive, but also partly by the fact that the population growth pressure was substantially reduced

> by a very successful family-planning policy within the period of only less than two decades (Medhi, 1991, p. 2).

According to the above view there has been a persistence of the agricultural sector in Thailand over a long period of time, and it is quite clear that industrialization had not to any significant extent been able to absorb the agricultural sector. Because of this, we can safely state that Thai society is largely bifurcated into the private–corporate sector and the people's agricultural sector, composed mainly of small farmers. Development in Thailand does not concern only the leading private–corporate sector, it is inextricably linked with the less-developed agricultural sector. It is also important to point out that economic growth in Thailand has been achieved not only through industrialization but also through diversification in the agricultural sector.

The attitude of the state towards the industrial and agricultural sectors, especially its final decisions concerning conflicting claims over natural resources under state control, should be the focal point of our analysis of the link between industrialization and the development of political democracy in Thailand. There have been a number of studies about the role of business associations as well as relationships between certain industrial sectors and the state which conclude that, while politics in Thailand is highly unstable, the relationship between state and private actors has been very stable and institutionalized (see especially Anek, 1992, and Doner, 1991, p. 264).

Both Anek and Doner were interested in the upper level of civil society – the private corporate sector – and it is not surprising to discover that this part of civil society has been gaining acceptance from the state and is becoming a partner in progress. Such cooperation has led to a different political model–authoritarian pluralism instead of democratic pluralism (Christensen, 1992a, p. 35), which is the same point as one made earlier about technocratic pluralism (Chai-Anan, 1990a). It is quite clear that state – private-sector cooperation and authoritarian pluralism are complementary to each other. They formed an alliance that is coming into conflict with the poor agrarian sector in its drive towards industrialization. If we want to analyze the relationship between industrialization and democracy in Thailand we should test it from the state's policies and actions towards the access and utilization of natural resources, for this is the area in which industrial and agricultural interests are sharply in conflict. It will be argued that industrialization inhibits the development of democracy, especially in a country that depends heavily on its natural resources as the main basis for economic development. Industrialization through the utilization of natural resources creates an urban–rural conflict of a zero-sum game or negative sum-game nature since the gain of one sector is the loss of the other sector. While the state has adjusted its strategic alliance with the private corporate sector by coopting it into the high-level decision-making process, the state has been reluctant to use the same inclusionary measure with the rural agricultural sector, and has been less responsive to its demand for participation beyond periodic electoral channels. Not only powerless small farmers but also organized agricultural interest groups suffered from this drive towards industrialization, which links closely with international competitiveness. For example, proposals for a regional free trade area in South-East Asia require Thailand to strip protection from two of the three major agro industries currently enjoying state subsidies: palm oil and soybean (Christensen, 1992a, p. 34).

In the capitalist developmental state, 'while state bureaucrats rule, politicians reign'. The role of state bureaucrats or technocrats in national development is more dominant in the so-called high-productivity investment areas such as key industries, and in traditional economic-management areas such as planning, budgeting, and fiscal and monetary policy making. Wade's governed market theory (1990), for example, discussed the role of the state in directing or governing the advanced section of civil society, that is, capitalist market forces with major industrial bases. It seems that authoritarian states have had a better record on industrial development than on agricultural development. When authoritarian states have had to deal with pressures from the agrarian sector simultaneously with those of the urban industrial sector, they have not been able effectively to solve this dual crisis and have usually had to resort to non-democratic means such as coup-staging or declaring national emergency to solve the problem. Hence, it is fair to say that the military and its technocratic alliance are able to manage the business sector when it comes to decisions concerning technical economic policies and measures, while politicians may not be able to rule. But the political brokerage of politicians cannot be replaced when it comes to more substantive conflict in the agricultural sector or between the industrial and agricultural sectors.

In this sense state elites may retain significant independence from business in the formulation of macroeconomic policy involving the more developed part of the economy, that is, major industries and the market, but they cannot possibly maintain the same degree of autonomy from the mobilized agrarian sector. This is due to the fact that the state has a primary function in maintaining political stability and security. Its top-down policy tends to create conflict and confrontation with the rural population in the long run, especially with underprivileged landless farmers. The state does not own capital but it owns reserved forests. It is at this level that the state finds it most difficult to retain its independence, which it does retain when dealing with the more affluent sector. The politics of joint, cooperative interests is inherently the politics of concrete gains and losses, and it is extremely difficult to manage a non-antagonistic coalition between urban industrial interests and rural agrarian interests.

Perhaps it is irrelevant to ask whether certain political systems are better than others at promoting growth or whether there is an inevitable trade-off between democracy and development. It is pertinent to ask: growth of which subsystem of civil society, or growth for whom? If we look carefully into the process of economic development in Thailand we will find that growth has been beneficial only to the urban industrial sector, and that the gap between rich and poor has widened in recent years.

11.2 INDUSTRIALIZATION AS A SOURCE OF INTERSECTORAL CONFLICT

I will use the case study of the reforestation of a reserved forest to analyze the relationship between industrialization and the development of political democracy in Thailand. I would like to show that when it comes to substantive politics of resource utilization, bureaucrats, the military and businessmen are becoming increasingly antagonistic to the masses. This is the area where democratic development faces a real challenge, not in the area of upper-level economic management. The future of democracy and sustainable development depends not on the state – business coalition, but on how effectively such a coalition is able to deal with challenges from below in order to maintain its hegemony in an export-led capitalist economy. If it fails to come to terms with the demand for popular participation, or misperceives or miscalculates its long-term interests, the unresolved conflict between industrialization and democratisation could lead Thailand in the direction of the reversed development of Argentina.

I am proposing that it is more important carefully to analyze the non-economic impact of industrialization on Thai society than to find out how democracy supports industrialization. Industrialization as a development policy implies a significant change in the state's development priorities. Industrialization that occurs prior to democratic development may create rapid economic growth in aggregate terms, but it could also lead to greater underdevelopment of the rural sector, especially when that rural sector lacks meaningful political participation. In an activist bureaucratic state industrialization may occur without much government intervention or promotion, but the development of political democracy in such a state is state-imposed rather than a natural process concomitant with socioeconomic development. If the development of political democracy in Thailand poses a direct challenge to the state, the state will limit popular participation rather than promote it. If so, what institutional mechanisms and processes could manage conflicts arising out of the non-economic impacts of industrialization? Could industrialization occurring under authoritarian pluralism lead to sustainable development?

We should not confuse more participation by the private sector in the decision-making process as a positive trend towards democratisation. There is no evidence of political trickle-down effects where elite-level participation automatically leads to mass-level participation. Far from it. Elite-level participation leads to consolidation of technocratization and entrenchment of the top-down development syndrome. In the West the bourgeois state developed into a democratic state, resulting in greater participation by the underprivileged classes. In developing countries it is doubtful whether the same pattern will repeat itself because the bourgeoisie is politically weak, especially when it is an ethnic minority. That is why we cannot expect the political trickle-down effects of gradual democratization.

It has been pointed out that in Thailand economic growth took place when the labour force was still predominantly in the agricultural sector, and the average size of landholdings did not become smaller as the country developed. This means that economic growth was possible through the expansion of agricultural land which resulted in rapid deforestation. No matter what kind of regime was in power when economic growth occurred, it was essentially based on diversification of the agricultural sector. In this sense past economic development had less conflict of interests between the industrial and the agricultural sectors. The agricultural sector, to a large extent, benefited from the growing manufacturing industries as they provided alternative or additional sources of cash income. Industrialization that emphasized import substitution and the diversification of agricultural production complemented one another. When there was a shift from import-substitution to export-led development, which coincided with the exhaustion of natural resources, industrialization became detrimental to the interests of the agricultural sector, particularly those of poor landless farmers. It is at this transition point that the discontinuous nature of the developmental process began to show its negative effects. The shift of development strategy, which was an inevitable consequence of a successful import substitution strategy, brought industrialization and democratization into greater conflict. The ban on worker unions after the February 1991 coup was welcomed by technocrats and businessmen, who saw trade-union activism as the major obstacle to industrialization But, as the National Peace Keeping Council found out, it was difficult to control farmers' demonstrations and the activism of non-governmental organisations at the grassroots level. The growing activism of farmers in the post-Communist Party of Thailand (CPT) period in Thailand seems to have been a direct response to the shift of development strategy, which also changed the pattern of land utilization. It is not surprising, therefore, to see that major protests occurred in the north-east, the poorest part of the country, and that all the protests centred around land-use problems ranging from the proposed construction of a dam to the use of land for rock-salt mining, which caused pollution of major rivers in the rice-growing areas.

Farmer activism in the 1980s was different from that of the 1970s. In the 1970s the main problem was land rent rather than land use, but in the 1980s land use became the central issue involving not landowners or tenants, but the government in its attempts to turn occupied deforested land, which was still classified legally and technically as forest reserves, into large-scale commercial plantations. The demise of the CPT in the early 1980s made it possible for the state and the business sector to a new look at prospective investment on frontiers that were once under the control of the CPT. Political stability gained after the post-CPT period not only institutionalized the semi-democratic regime, but also gave the state much more latitude for policy options. Once the country was free from the threat of internal insurgency the elites could be more imaginative in their development strategies. The Eastern Seaboard Project was conceived during this period (1980 onwards), and the export-led growth strategy gained credibility in the eyes of both government and foreign investors. Due to the peaceful situation in the countryside, technocrats began to shift their attention to correcting the sectoral imbalances between urban and rural areas. This means that 'many of the countryside's natural and social features that in the past were more or less left alone as long as they provided some surplus to the bureaucracy and commercial sectors are being retooled for more direct use by the world market' (Lohrmann, 1991, p. 11).

With the shift to export-oriented development, which coincided with the international market's demand for wood chips and the establishment of the paper-pulp industry, formerly marginal areas are increasingly earmarked for takeover by commercial eucalyptus plantations. The Master Plan for Reforestation in Thailand calls for private plantation firms to plant eucalyptus and other fast-growing trees on 43,000 square kilometres of national-reserve forests. Seven to ten million people are generally estimated to be living in national-reserve forest areas, a sizeable proportion of whom inhabit zones designated for commercial plantation (Lohrmann, 1991, pp. 7–8).

11.3 POLITICAL BEHAVIOUR OF THE STATE IN ECONOMIC DECISION-MAKING

The behaviour of the Thai state was heavily influenced by the challenge of the Communist Party of Thailand, which enabled the security apparatus to have a dominant role in the decision-making process at both national and local level. During the 1960s and 1970s, when CPT activities were at their height, although the security imperative had a diverse effect on democracy, the military somehow learned from its experiences that it had to consider seriously the plight, grievances and demands of poor farmers in order to win the people's war. During this period governments often changed their stand on forestry and land policies. In the north-east, the stronghold of the CPT, the government was always very lenient to farmers occupying forest reserves. In many cases the regional army encouraged farmers to occupy frontier lands and guaranteed their right to utilize them in exchange for their loyalty, support and cooperation.

In those years the major political, administrative and military decision-making structures and processes were unified into a single command from cabinet level down to field operations. Security and development dimensions were fused and decisions were usually made with political considerations. The nature of the communist challenge was fundamentally political and it forced the military, technocrats and businessmen to be flexible and more careful in dealing with the masses.

The CPT challenge created political consciousness among certain sections of the military, especially in the field command (Chai-Anan, 1982). This contributed to the soft authoritarian nature of military governments in the 1970s and led to their reluctant compromises with emergent socioeconomic forces in the 1980s. Such continuity of the internal security threat had enabled the military and the technocrats to learn to work together in various areas of security-related development. This close and continuous socialization process was responsible for the recognition on the part of the military of its limitations in technical economic matters. Hence the instability and the common perception of a possible communist victory (which had already occurred in Indo-china) on the part of the military, the technocrats, the businessmen and the liberal academics cemented an enduring tie among the so-called 1960s generation that has been responsible for Thailand's economic development over the past three decades.

This is the strength of what I termed the semi-democratic system in Thailand. The democratic interlude under Chartichai disrupted the stability of this entrenched alliance. The behaviour of the coup group of February 1991, which showed tremendous restraint in not intervening in the management of the economy, reflected this deep concern by leaving the task of economic development to the technocrats.

The semi-democratic period (1980–88) enabled the technocrats to consolidate their power. But without the challenge that had been afforded by the CPT the decision-making structure and process began to disperse among a number of technical agencies, such as the National Social and Economic Development Board (NESDB), the Ministry of Finance and the Prime Minister's Advisory Group, which, in recent years, has become more or less an institution. Such dispersal or deconcentration of economic decision making has led to conflicting policy formulations and implementation, especially in the area of resource management, which is under the jurisdiction of more than 20 departments in different ministries.

The political dimension of the bureaucratic decision-making process has become less threatening after the demise of the CPT. During the semidemocratic period under Prem's leadership (1980–88), the technocrats were able to exert their influence over all major policies and they depoliticized the economic decision-making process through controlling the economic ministers meetings. The depoliticization process excluded elected politicians from major decision making but it politicized the technocrats, who became the new power brokers. Due to this development the technocrats of various departments in different ministries became increasingly overzealous in planning and implementing their policies. The NESDB, which is essentially a planning body, became heavily involved in initiating new projects and also in managing them.

The political dimension of the economic decision-making process was regarded as undesirable, parochial and unproductive. Gradually the elected politicians and parties were pushed to the periphery of the power centre. The Chartichai civilian regime, which prided itself on being an elected representative government, reacted in an extreme fashion by dismantling previously entrenched technocratic machinery. The government and its regime thus threatened the apparatus of the state, which suffered a great psychological crisis due to the sudden change in power relations. This group of technocrats quietly sabotaged the nascent regime through various means, and worked closely with the military to overthrow what they called parliamentary dictatorship in February 1991.

Due to the long period of technocratization and deconcentration of decision-making power among staff and operating agencies, the political aspect of development was lost. The NESDB drew up its National Social and Economic Development Plan with little regard for the feelings of the rural masses. At the elite-level the NESDB created the Joint Public and Private Consultative Committee (JPPCC), composed of government representatives and representatives from the Board of Trade, the Association of Thai Industries and the Thai Bankers Association. The government also promoted the establishment of provincial chambers of commerce, but when it came to setting up the Agricultural Council it downplayed the equal representation of farmer groups.

The prevalent view of the technocrats on political development is that it is one of the important factors of sustainable development. However, to the technocrats, political development implies the involvement of a rational-decision making process in economic and other development issues. It is argued that sustainable long-term development will be possible only under the circumstances of a rational decision-making process. This is of particular importance in the case of Thailand, as the development of the country has reached the level where the rational decision-making process will become the most important determinant of the sustainability of the future development of the country (see Kosit, 1990).

Although participation in development is regarded by technocrats as a crucial factor, there is always a concern that the developmental process will be under the control of a few vested interest groups where decisions are made for the benefit of small ruling or privileged groups. The technocrats see themselves as guardians of national interests and are more willing to cooperate with the military than with the politicians. The development imperative is the reason of the state, and developmentalism, not democracy, is their ideology. The developmental process has been a continuous process resulting in the creation of like-minded developmentalist technocrats, while the democratic process has suffered discontinuity, factionalism and political fragmentation. That is why a pluralist democracy is unlikely to develop from an entrenched bureaucratic polity, especially where the bureaucratic polity is not a static entity, but an entity that utilizes the ideology of development to redefine its role (Chai-Anan, 1990b, p. 337).

The technocrats became very confident of their success in leading Thailand towards being a more industrialized nation with spectacular rates of growth. Their attitude and their misconception of democracy isolated them from the masses. They became arrogant, overconfident and antidemocratic. They equated democracy with corruption, inefficiency and parochialism. However there was a lack of legitimacy in the government, as evidenced by the May 1992 mass uprising against the assumption of power by a non-elected prime minister, who had been the mastermind behind the overthrow of the civilian regime in 1991.

The Thai political structure has not changed much after 60 years of democracy. The legislature is still bicameral with an appointed senate composed mainly of the military, technocrats and their business and intellectual allies. The administrative structure is not much different from that of the 1980s, although it has greater penetrative capability into the periphery. The cabinet system and its decision-making structure is still highly bureaucratic and bogged down with routine matters.

If we closely examine the relationship between state and society in Thailand we will quickly recognise the difference between the state's behaviour towards the corporate private sector and towards the poor and powerless agricultural sector. Economic development in Thailand has not only resulted in the economic expansion of the private sector, it has also led to a closer alliance among bureaucratic, military, political and economic elites. This alliance became firmly entrenched, and in the post-CPT period these groups are much more convinced of their right to act without political constraints from below. Thailand, like Brazil, is a case of a late-developing dualistic economy where the needs trade off, the equality trade off and the liberty trade off seem to be a sustained process rather than a temporary and self-correcting one (Donnelly, 1984).

11.4 UNGOVERNABILITY AND 'INSTITUTIONALIZED ANARCHY'

It is not surprising that Thailand in the 1990s is becoming ungovernable. The coup-makers fully recognized this problem but were not willing to allow politics to evolve unobstructed. Thus political democracy has no chance of becoming institutionalized because it will have no time or opportunity to prove its positive aspects in the long run. In other East-Asian countries, export-led development was made possible under effective political authority, although the nature of that political authority was undemocratic. In Thailand we are standing at a crossroads. On the one hand the system is not yet democratized, on the other hand institutions of political authority are suffering a legitimacy crisis and cannot be effective as long as the disadvantaged extra-bureaucratic groups do not accept the dominant role of the military.

The transition from a primary-producing economy to an import-substitution economy was not such a big test for Thailand. The transition from an import-substitution economy to an industrial nation will be much more difficult and challenging. Unlike Korea, Thailand has no heavy industry. Compared with Taiwan, the rural sector is uncommercialized and unproductive. Unlike Hong Kong and Singapore, Thailand is neither a city-state nor an international financial centre and still has a very large rural sector. Industrialization in Thailand is bound to result in the extraction and utilization of natural resources located in the rural area. If no democratic framework for peaceful bargaining, adjustment and participation exists, industrialization will lead to intense conflicts of an inter- and intrasectoral nature.

I have argued that authoritarian regimes tend to be more successful in managing the technical aspects of the economy and coopting the private corporate sector than in managing intersectoral conflicts involving industrial interests and the masses. The security dimension is the most important factor for authoritarian regimes when legitimizing their rule and maintaining a growing economy. In South Korea and Taiwan there has been concern over the possibility of invasion by neighbouring communist countries. Because to this, even though the military penetrates more deeply into civil society in Korea and Taiwan than in Latin American countries, the sociopolitical role of the military may hold greater legitimacy in these two countries than in Latin American NICs because of the prevalent view that economic development and social mobilization are critical for national survival (Cheng, 1990, p. 385).

The effectiveness of the Kuomintang regime is its ability to develop state institutions responsible for the management of the three dimensions of state – society relations (Winckler, 1981, p. 485). The fact that there are three sets of power-creating institutions in the state – one for development, one for legitimation and one for security – has enabled the KMT to surround society. Good coordination among these three sets of institutions, especially the development set and the legitimation sector, could preempt political opposition by sponsoring a broad distributional coalition. In Taiwan the sponsorship and maintenance of a distributional coalition from above went hand in hand with political liberalization (Cheng, 1990, p. 169).

In the Thai case the security imperative remained strong only during the import-substitution period. By the time Thailand had shifted its development strategy to industrialization with an export-led orientation, the Cold War had ended. The Communist Party of Thailand was defeated, the Indochinese states were beginning to be more liberal in their economic development, and there was a strong global trend of internationalization of capital. Without the security imperative the legitimacy of an authoritarian military regime is bound to dwindle quickly. In the past three decades of development, democracy has not been a legitimating factor in capitalist development – economic growth has. But socioeconomic development has also created a larger middle class and strong provincial interest groups that seek to protect and expand their interests through the democratic process. Provincial interests are concentrated in the urban parts of rural areas and have become more and more antagonistic to Bangkok-based interests, as is evident in the conflict between provincial chambers of commerce and the Bangkok-based Thai Chamber of Commerce (Anek, 1992). The development of capitalism in Thailand has been Bangkok-centric, and in sectoral terms most of its industries have been concentrated in the Bangkok metropolitan region (Christensen, 1992a, p. 14). Industrialization in Thailand will, therefore, lead not only to intersectoral conflict, but also to growing urban–rural antagonism.

Socioeconomic development in Thailand has another peculiar characteristic, namely a shortage of commercialization in the countryside. As Christensen pointed out, electoral politics failed to create a coalition of alliances between the capital and the towns to cut across the urban–rural cleavage. Parties were financed primarily by urban bourgeoisie who were themselves not united. Multiple parties competed for the allegiance of a rather small tier of middle- and upper-income agriculturalists, traders and town dwellers (Christensen, 1992a, pp. 17–18).

In this context, Thailand has no strong social and economic bases for democratic development. The agricultural sector is not largely commercialized. The middle class, which is mainly ethnic Chinese, is not an independent bourgeoisie. Political parties are disorganized and have not yet consolidated their rural base. The military, the technocrats and the intellectuals are critical of 'kleptocracy'. In the East-Asian situations, the states were strong and effective while other forces were weak, in the Thai case it seems that the state is becoming weaker but other social and economic forces have yet to consolidate their power. The weakness of the state is due to the decline of security threats and the legitimacy of the military leaders who staged the 1991 coup but were unable to govern.

The Thai case is a test case for current thinking on soft and hard authoritarian regimes and their role in industrialization. In comparison with other East or South-East Asian countries, industrial development in Thailand has involved relatively little direct government intervention (Medhi, 1991, p. 3). I wonder whether the Thai state has the capacity to intervene and lead the market in the way in which its Korean counterpart did. From recent experiences concerning dam construction, the planting of eucalyptus forests and the Land Redistribution Project for the Poor in Degraded Forest Areas, the state has already come into sharp conflict with poor farmers. In all cases the state's projects were strongly resisted by the people and it had to resort to intimidation and violence to implement them.

Although the Thai state is far less interventionist than its Korean and Taiwanese counterparts in promoting industrialization, its rent-seeking behaviour is articulated in resource allocation. Since Thailand's industrial base is not in heavy industry, the state has only degraded forest land to deliver to the industrial sector. The state has legal control over natural resources and it uses its power to determine how natural resources are to be exploited. In the case of eucalyptus plantations, the state is indirectly supporting the wood-chips and paper and pulp industries by levying very low charges. It has just issued concessions to private companies at a cost of US$1 per acre per year, and has granted special privileges under the Board of Investment law. The Royal Forestry Department (RFD) which has been the main bureaucratic instrument for rent-seeking since the nineteenth century, is staffed with technocrats with little regard for poor people. Most of the RFD officials see the forests in terms of trees, not in terms of people. In granting concessions to private companies to rent degraded forest land, the RFD officials consider they have carried out their stewardship, and in a way are exercising their authority to control forest land that had been lost to encroachers (Usher, 1990).

The rent-seeking behaviour of the state has met with strong opposition from non-governmental organisations that have formed a close alliance with poor farmers. The NGOs in Thailand, which are mostly ecological movements, gained their momentum in the late 1980s due to a combination of factors. Most important of these was the return to normalcy in the countryside after the communist insurgency. This enabled the NGOs to work more closely and freely with poor farmers without being accused of acting as conduits for the CPT. International environmental movements also contributed greatly by giving financial and moral support to the Thai NGOs. Because the United Nations, the United States and other European countries are now promoting the ecological cause, NGOs in Thailand have become 'legitimate' as their movement is seen as part of the international concern for a common global future. Although many former radical activists are now working for NGOs, their activism can no longer be suppressed by the military. The environmental movement in Thailand is also able to rally support from all sectors in society because it presents the issue of environmental protection as being non-ideological and above politics. The NGOs quickly became the most active and effective opposition outside the formal political process. In the past five years the strongest opponents of industrialization have been the NGOs and the environmental movement, which have put direct pressure on the government, bypassing political parties and the parliamentary process. This phenomenon reflects the fact that elements in the military, the bureaucracy, the business sector and political parties have vested interests in logging and reforestation, as well as in other industries involved in the exploitation of natural resources in rural areas. The active role of the NGOs also reflects the failure of the formal political process effectively to link the state and society. Political parties provide partial channels for the demands and grievances of the disadvantaged rural sector, but when it comes to the fundamental conflict between the industrial and agricultural sectors, the urban–industrial interests that control the party machine usually act against the interests of small farmers.

It seems that in the Thai case statism and pluralism are coexisting rather than cancelling each other out. This is due to the multistructural nature of the current Thai political system. The state (bureaucratic and military) power structure is strongly entrenched. The formal party and parliamentary political structures are performing only partial functions of interest-articulation and aggregation and are doing so more on behalf of urban–industrial interests. The NGOs act as pressure groups and choose not to ally themselves with parties in the formal political process. Political elites are split in their strategies and behaviour towards bureaucratic and military elites. Some are in close alliance with them but others are trying to become independent of the bureaucratic and military influence in politics. Pluralism is emerging but, due to the capacity of the state to adjust its alliances, it remains a rare phenomenon rather than a sustained, potent force to reduce the political effectiveness of the established bureaucracy.

There is a dilemma here. Military governments in Thailand come and go, but they never succeed in institutionalising their political control over society. In Taiwan and Indonesia the ruling groups created mechanisms to link state and society, but in the Thai case the military has been influential but has not developed into a ruler army. In fact most so-called military dictatorships have been rather fragile when faced with mass movements, as evidenced in the fall of the Thanom–Prapass clique in October 1973 and the inability of the military to control peacefully the May 1992 mass uprising.

Prior to the Anand government (March 1991 to March 1992), the economic decision-making process was highly secretive and technocratic. The Anand government encouraged greater transparency, but this was to combat corruption and reduce monopolistic and oligopolistic tendencies rather than to promote popular participation. The technocrats in the government pushed through a regulation on large-project bidding in order to create a more competitive, open and clean business environment. Poor farmers continued to protest to gain government attention, while industrialists were given access to the high-level decision-making process. However the Anand government lasted just one year and it is doubtful whether their many reforms will be continued by succeeding governments.

The Thai case can be called *institutionalized anarchy or uninstitutionalized soft authoritarianism*. There is no single dominant power centre, not even the most powerful military. Above the military is the monarchy which is still considered the foundation stone of legitimacy. The king's personal comments and speeches on farmers in the reserved forests – that they were there long before the forests were legally reserved – have often been used by environmental groups to counterbalance government actions. It is therefore impossible for the elites to govern the market, let alone to rule in the real sense of the word. The ungovernability syndrome is most manifest in the area of resource management – government policies on forestry and land repeatedly change in response to shifting situations.

11.5 CONCLUSION

In conclusion, democracy in Thailand is not yet institutionalized, neither is public authority. There is coexistence of the opposing forces of industrialization, democratization, technocratization and militarization. These forces interact but each has its own values, structure and processes. So both statism and pluralism are evolving. The only cementing force or reference framework has been the monarchy. As long as the monarchy continues to be legitimate and strong, it will act as the centre holding these opposing forces together. The lack of democratic or authoritarian institutionalization has been offset by the deep institutionalization of the monarchy. In recent years the monarchy has performed its non-political role by solving or minimizing many political crises. It is not an exaggeration to say that, in Thailand, politics is the art of being above politics, and through this posture politics could become the art of the possible.

The Thai Riddle will grow even more perplexing as Thailand becomes more industrialized. However this does not mean that Thailand will mimic Argentina's reversed development. Thailand is capable of self-organisation. Industrialization and democracy are driving forces creating turbulence and fluctuations in the social, economic and political spheres. But fluctuations do not necessarily cause political decay; on the contrary they are signs of dynamism and life.

12 Changes in Social Values in the Thai Society and Economy: A Post-Industrialization Scenario

Suntaree Komin

12.1 INTRODUCTION

Every development has its own price, and so have industrialization and modernisation. Industrialization, defined as the increasing utilization of machines as the primary means of increasing productivity to foster economic growth and development, is not a simple means to an end. It is a complex phenomenon with a culture of its own. As a result, industrialization in Thailand has brought about changes, explicit and implicit, to various aspects of human life, from personal, family and community to the social system and society as a whole. These changes have been both direct and indirect, and have had both positive and negative impacts. On the positive side there have been remarkable increases in productivity, improvements in the standard of living of the average individual, the possibility of affluent and abundant lifestyles, widespread educational and employment opportunities, improved health care, modern transportation and communication systems, countless goods and services, more upward mobility, and equilibrium of birth and death rates. On the other hand, there have been a weakening of kinship and family ties, a reduction in the size and function of families and an increasing divorce rate. There has been a growing emphasis on self-indulgence, which has led to the exploitation of whatever resources are available to achieve material success. It has also led to the discarding of religious and spiritual belief, to a higher incidence of drug abuses, alcoholism and crime, and to a host of spiritual and psychological problems. Last but not least are environmental pollution and the man-made, chemically induced health hazards associated with industrialization.

It should be borne in mind that industrialization in the West started almost two centuries ago and did not occur overnight. Rather it went through an evolutionary process based on technological advancement, maturity of polity and sociocultural systems and structures. Developing countries such as Thailand, with it different sociocultural system and its attempt to industrialize as a shortcut to prosperity, should be cautious of the various social and cultural effects associated with the process. Pushing for abnormally rapid industrialization could trigger off serious problems of imbalance in various areas. Therefore it is very important that Thai development planners and policy makers should have a clear view of the real phenomenon and what lies ahead before charting the developmental road map of the country, so that we can enjoy the benefits of industrialization without repeating all the negative consequences experienced by advanced industrial societies.

The primary purpose of this chapter is to discuss some changes in the social structure (meaning organized patterns of behaviour and social relationships) and social values of Thai society during the rapid industrialization of this past decade. It will also look ahead and project a post-industrialization scenario in Thailand. The chapter concentrates on issues relevant to a post-industrial society, such as democratic and egalitarian trends in the society, the role of religion, family structure and family relations, the aging population and the role of the media, and attempts to assess the nature and characteristics of these changes and how they are affecting Thai society in general.[1]

12.2 DEMOCRATIC AND EGALITARIAN TRENDS

The outcome of the development efforts of a society depends to a great extent on the political system adopted by the government when charting and apportioning benefits, because the government controls the country's budget and has a say in determining who pays for public services and who gets what from public expenditure. With industrialization, coupled with widespread education, today all industrial societies are democratic societies in which freedom and equality are espoused, and in which there is access to the power of government to benefit the masses of ordinary people in countless ways. When the members of a society are skilled and educated, industrialization flourishes. Instead of being politically apathetic, these citizens tend to be self-assertive, jealous of their rights and politically demanding. Such characteristics are essential in a democracy if society is to be made less unequal. In other words, there are changes in values – the drive for equality as the major 'irresistible' force that transforms society into a more egalitarian one.

This is a tremendous change from the practices of governments during the agrarian era, which tended to benefit the governing class. This is also the reason why income inequality in industrial societies is not as great as in agrarian societies, because democratic governments correct the excessive inequality generated by industrialization and the capitalistic economic system through means such as social-security programmes, welfare benefits, housing subsidies, medical aid, unemployment compensation, food stamps and so on. Since distribution of income among a society's members is one of the best measures of the level of social inequality in a society, a brief comparison between the income gaps in industrial societies and that of Thailand is quite revealing. In most industrial societies the top 10 per cent receives about a quarter of the country's total income and the bottom 20 per cent receives around 6–7 per cent, with a top to bottom ratio of around 3–4. In comparison with comparable Asian NIC such as Taiwan, Taiwan's richest top 20 per cent receives 38.2 per cent of the total income while Thailand's richest 20 per cent receives 55 per cent of the country's total income, leaving the bottom 20 per cent with only 4.5 per cent, resulting in a top to bottom ratio of 12.4. The result shows that Thailand has the highest income inequality, and thus the highest societal inequality (Suntaree, 1989).

Democracy in Thailand still has quite a way to go. Thailand has been ruled by a series of authoritarian governments, and even though the composition of the present government has changed it still represents a replacement of one kind of authoritarian government (government officials and the military) with another (businessmen). It is true that most members of the present government have been elected, but one can hardly say that there is a true representation of the people in parliament because of the practice of 'vote-buying'. Without sufficient money, one can hardly get elected. It is said that a great number of MPs have bought their way into parliament, and into the cabinet. It has always been the interests of 'self', 'in-group', personal relationships or personal conflicts that explain the vote-switching, party-switching behaviour of MPs. There are numerous irregularities that can be cited. Of course there are good MPs, but they seem not to be the norm.

Therefore how can one expect those who bribed themselves into parliament to fight for the majority poor and pass laws correcting the excessive inequality of society?

At the national level, given the superstructure of development policies and the type of people holding cabinet positions, one can quite confidently predict not much will be done to reduce inequality. With businessmen now running the government, industrialization will be accelerated and economic and social inequality will be even greater. With the shallow industrial base, coupled with the basic Thai social system of relationships and cliques that are very susceptible to corruption, democracy and the country's economy may easily collapse. President of the Thailand Development Research Institute (TDRI) warned that 'if cronyism was allowed to develop, the Thai economy would go down the drain in the same way as the Philippines under President Marcos' (*Bangkok Post*, 6 July 1989).

Lack of democracy and egalitarian concern can be seen in the government's and MPs' lack of sincere concern over such issues as the plight of industrial workers (Suntaree, 1989), particularly over female- and child-labours problems, let alone taking remedial action to bring about a more egalitarian society that promises a better quality of life.

12.2.1 Female Labour

Industrialization should mean the provision of jobs and therefore an improvement in the standard of living of the people, but for Thai industrial workers the opposite is true. Workers are often exploited and do not receive all that they are entitled to, such as a minimum wage, paid leave and safe working conditions. Surveys showed that most are paid less than the minimum wage; more than 50 per cent of factories failed to provide paid leave, 70 per cent violated sick-leave regulations and 75–95 per cent violated maternity-leave regulations. While industrial workers are exploited in general, women and children are the worst hit.

Today women comprise half the active labour force of the country. There were 1.9 million women workers in 1992, most of whom were employed in the rural agricultural sector. The majority were poorly educated, with primary education or lower. A great number of rural women labourers have migrated to Bangkok to find work in factories, where they are more likely to be exploited by employers than are male workers. The plight of Thai women workers never ceases to make newspaper headlines, both inside and outside the country, to the point where people have started to take their exploitation for granted. This is not to mention those who have been pushed or lured into prostitution as a result of the rapid expansion of tourism and service industries in Bangkok and tourist spots such as Pattaya, Chiang Mai and Phuket.

12.2.2 Child Labour

Various studies have pointed to the increasing phenomenon of child labour in the organized and unorganized sectors. Labour-force statistics show that only 30 per cent of children are enrolled in secondary education, and only 10 per cent of children from rural areas enter secondary schools after completing six year's compulsory primary education, usually at the age of 11. In the Bangkok area as many as 70–90 per cent go on to secondary education. What happens to the 90 per cent of rural children who did not enter secondary school? As a result of rural poverty and large families these rural children are sent to work in cities to supplement the family income. In many cases they have to support the entire family.

The existence of illegal child labour is well-known and can be attributed to several factors. Among them are insufficient government labour inspectors, laxity of law enforcement, the low penalties imposed on those caught violating the Child Labour Law, and the vagueness and loopholes of the Child Labour Law (National Youth Bureau, 1985). This is not to mention unscrupulous employers and businessmen, whose main concern is to make a profit. The problem of child labour in Thailand deserves serious and continuous attention, not least because it is a violation of human rights.

Children who do not work in factories have often ended up as street children, or even worse as prostitutes (both girls and boys). A survey of 300 prostitutes out of the estimated 500 000 prostitutes of the country, found that 0.5 per cent were under 15 years, which amounted to about 2500 child prostitutes in 1982 (Dheppanom and Nunta, 1982). Fifty per cent were between 15 and 19 years, with the majority (62 per cent) coming from the north. Altogether 90 per cent had migrated from rural areas. Some had entered the profession with parental consent or through parental pressure, others tricked into it. Cases exposed by national and international newspapers testify to the problems of this group.

Given the increasing income gap, increasing rural poverty and the rapid rate of industrial expansion, one can predict that more rural poor will be lured to cities to join these disadvantaged and exploited groups.

It is obvious that there is no future for such child workers and the unskilled adult workers who have come to work in order to survive.

12.2.3 Sex Stratification

In general terms the situation of women in industrial societies today has definitely improved as a result of industrialization. With equal educational and occupational opportunities women in industrial societies should have the same pay and political and legal rights as men (Ruble *et al.*, 1976). However in Thailand, there is still a long way to go. Although equal educational opportunity is available and there are roughly equal numbers of educational enrolment, women have consistently maintained a higher rate of illiteracy over the last 40 years, with a growing male–female gap. In the agriculture sector women participate in agricultural activities more than men and they are the major workforce in the rice fields. However when agricultural training or demonstrations are available it is usually men who are called upon to take part.

As for promotion to administrative, executive and managerial positions, the opportunities for women are very limited. Higher administrative positions are dominated by men, as seen in Table 12.1, which indicates that, while women constitute half the country's labour force, they occupy only 19.8 per cent of administrative positions, slightly more in Bangkok (26.2 per cent) than in rural areas (14.9 per cent). Evidently, although economic participation by women is greater than by men in several sectors, administration and decision making tend to be in the hands of men. Sex discrimination is clearly marked by differential pay scales, as many studies have pointed to the fact that women workers doing the same jobs as men are paid much less.

Table 12.1 Administrative, executive and managerial workers

	Male	*Female*
Whole kingdom	326.1 (80.22%)	80.4 (19.78%)
Bangkok	129.5 (73.75%)	46.0 (26.20%)
Up-country	196.6 (85.15%)	34.4 (14.90%)

Source: NSO, Report of Labour Force Survey, Round 2, July–September, 1982.

12.3 RELIGION: THE INCREASING TREND TOWARDS SECULARIZATION

In industrial societies the most important effect that industrialization has had on religion and religious beliefs is the trend towards secularization. As a result of advancement in the fields of science and social science, new ways of thinking about man and society have often shaken traditional belief in the great historic faiths – Judaism, Christianity, Buddhism, Confucianism and so on – and the institutional systems based on them. These beliefs have tended to become alien, obsolete or old-fashioned for members of industrial societies creating an acute theological crisis. Religious leaders have tried to translate important traditional religious elements into modern terms in an attempt to make established religions more relevant, but religion has instead become more private and individualized. There has been a proliferation of new sects and cults, which could reflect the growing spirits of neophilia or novelty, or it could also be reflecting the growing psychological needs of modern people living in societies oriented towards materialism and consumerism. In short, existing religious institutions and teachings have been challenged by social changes.

Buddhism, which is the dominant religion of 95 per cent of the Thai population, is not without problems. It has not kept pace with the social changes that have developed during the past decades, particularly among urban people. The reduction in religious influence on the everyday lives of urban people is quite alarming. Thai studies have shown that while rural Thais continue to place religion at the top of their priorities, for Bangkok people the importance of religion has dropped to an insignificant level (Suntaree and Sanit, 1979; Suntaree, 1990a and 1990b). The research revealed two totally different worldviews between urban and rural Thais. That of rural Thais was characterized by 'other-oriented' mutually helpful community values and a characteristically profound religious faith and spiritual life, with inner harmony and contentedness. In contrast urban Thais were found to be self-oriented and concerned with personal happiness, material comforts, pleasure and social recognition, with a drastic reduction in religious values.

This could be both a result of today's materialistically oriented society and the inefficacy of the clergy in dealing with changing perceptions. Evidently the clergy has done little to counter the alienation of young people; instead, as Sulak Sivarak, an expert on Thai culture and religion, pointed out (*Bangkok Post*, 23 July 1988), the clergy has confined itself to performing rites and rituals while itself turning towards materialism and capitalism. Some are telling fortunes, giving lottery tips, and behaving in a way contrary to religious precepts. Materialism is sweeping through Buddhism in the form of luxurious monasteries and materialistic behaviour. Therefore Buddhism is viewed by many as a mere tradition. For many others, Buddhism has been reduced to a psychological refuge.

As already stated, the significant decline in religious influence can be attributed to an inability to make Buddhist teaching more relevant to modern society: 'the inability to make Buddhist teachings socially relevant accounts for the decline in its influence in the face of the current tidal wave of consumerism and materialism' (Sulak Sivarak, *Bangkok Post*, 16 March 1989). On the other hand, dissatisfaction within the Sangha itself has triggered the emergence of different groups of thinking, three prominent schools of Buddhism having emerged in the past two decades. They are Phra Buddhadasa of Suan Mokh or the Garden of Liberation, Phra Bodhirak of Santi Asoke and Phra Dhammachaiyo of the Dhammakaya Temple. The first two are reformists and the last is traditional. Their conflicting views, as analyzed by some social scientists (for example Jackson, 1989), reflect conflicts in Thai society as a whole. Each group's value system has been influenced by its own social background and aspirations.

Without doubt, industrialization and materialism have brought spiritual emptiness to the people, and a profound challenge to mainstream Buddhism, with the latter being unable to retain its relevance for the people while struggling for its own survival against pressures for change and reform from within.

12.4 FAMILY STRUCTURE AND FAMILY RELATIONS

Industrialization has brought about a change in family structure. The traditional kinship system has been totally transformed and in the United States the nuclear family now accounts for only 25 per cent of families – the rest being one-parent families – due to the high divorce rate and the premarital residential independence (PRI) patterns (offspring leaving the parental home before marriage). The latest is the phenomenon of homelessness (Blau, 1992). Evidently the family core has been reduced to a minimum, and families today are much less cohesive than their agrarian predecessors. Japan and Singapore experienced the breakdown of the extended-family structure decades ago, leading to the establishment of old people's homes, which has undermined traditional Asian cultural patterns. Now their governments have started to take measures to reverse this trend.

In Thailand, family patterns cover the full spectrum. In rural agricultural communities the kin group remains the basic integrative force of people's lives. The traditional Thai family system is that of an extended family, with at least some relatives living in the same compound and some others living nearby. And the average family size in rural areas is much larger than in industrial societies. The peasant family is almost invariably a work unit – place of work and place of residence are the same, and all members of the family, including the children, share in the work. The rural community is like one big family, in which non-blood-related villagers address each other as brother, sister, uncle, aunt, grandfather/mother, son/daughter, nephew/niece and so on. Mutual assistance and obligation are the basic norms and cultural values.

However this system is shattered when farmers, or worse still their children, move to Bangkok for economic reasons. Those who move their whole family are able to face the tough life together, but for those who migrate separately, no matter whether the father, the mother or the children, the psychological impact is tremendous. Being separated affects family relationships and the socialization of the children. In particular, when young people migrate, as is mostly the case, they break loose of any social control and became subject to whatever influence they may encounter in the city. They are ill-equipped to deal with social ills and became trapped by them.

For urban people the trend of change has more or less followed that of the West. Extended-family households are diminishing in Bangkok. Newly married couples are more likely to leave their parents' household to set up their own family. Family size is usually smaller than in rural areas, and one of the reasons for this could be the increased earning power of women. Men are no longer the sole breadwinners and women now make up half the active workforce. With higher education and the resulting economic independence, after marriage women continue to work, making it economically possible to set up their own household. As a result the traditional extended-family structure, where grandparents are surrounded by their children, in-laws and grandchildren has been replaced by a smaller family unit. The disintegration of the extended family has led to a situation where old people have no one to look after them – a problem that does not exist in rural communities – and thus to a formerly unknown institution: old folks homes.

The decline of the family is clearly visible in Bangkok. Now that more women are going out to work some of their former function are being carried out by specialist organizations, from nursery services, to child-care centres, to catering services (pinto), to ready-made food, and so on. Almost all kinds of education (that is, academic, religious, moral and social) are being left to teachers, peers and television. Parents are spending more time with their peers and television. Therefore peer groups and the mass media have become much more powerful influences than families for many teenagers, and serious conflicts often result. Similarly husbands and wives are seeing less of one another, with a consequent effect on family relations. The reduced interactions, in quantity and quality, are creating a larger generation gap between parents and children, as well as a gap between husbands and wives.

12.5 THE CHANGING ROLE OF WOMEN

Nowhere can the effects of industrialization on society's norms, values and sanctions be seen more clearly than in the changing role of women (Lenski and Lenski, 1987; Huber, 1976a, 1976b). Industrialization has provided greater employment opportunities for women and for the first time one can say that women have a secure base for economic independence. One see this in the steadily rising curve of women's participation in the labour force, in the number of families that have more than one regular wage earner (over 70 per cent of the total), and in the rising incidence of divorce as women increasingly feel less economically dependent on men.

The changing role of women in industrialized societies, from that of uneducated housewife, child-carer, nurse, cook and servant to that of an educated woman working outside the home, has led to a more democratic spirit of equal rights, duties and responsibilities, and to women becoming respected members of society. Today, in Western societies women are participating in the labour force in various sectors and at various levels. Inevitably, the role of women in Bangkok has also undergone large changes in the last decades. Gone are the days when girls merely learned domestic and culinary skills and waited to be married off and bear children. Now women are working outside the home side by side with men. Regrettably it is very unusual for Thai men to share household chores as it would be considered 'unmanly', so women now have a double workload as they are still expected to take full responsibility for child rearing and all domestic work. Although no figures are available with regard to the time husbands and working wives spend on work and on family care, it can be hypothesized that the workload is highly skewed. This situation has significantly affected the decline of the family, as well as relations between husband, wife and children.

While the role of women in terms of labour-force participation has dramatically changed, particularly in urban areas, the generally low status of women has remained unchanged, as discussed earlier. Women are able to express their discontent only at the family level, and a logical result of this is family disruption or divorce. Formerly, family unity was maintained at all costs, and the social stigma of 'divorce' was and is still very strong, particularly for women. There was no role for women outside the home. But today the concept of 'marriage is forever' has started to change and divorce is on the increase. Divorce women tend to be aged about 30, educated and economically independent. In Asian societies today there may be cultural variations with regard to the reason for divorce, but the sharp increase is evidently following the trend in Western industrial societies.

Table 12.2 shows the rate of divorce in several countries in Asia and the West. In the United States there are almost three divorces for every four marriages. In England one in three marriages ends in divorce. Japan is catching up, with one divorce for every four or five marriages. It is believed that if it were not for the strong social stigma of divorce, the divorce rate in Asia would be on a par with that of most Western societies (Leigh, 1989). An earlier report stated that Japan had the highest divorce rate in Asia, followed by South Korea (UN Population Report, 1982). Although Chinese women are a lot more conservative, the divorce rate among highly educated Hong Kong Chinese and Singapore Chinese has more than doubled in the last seven years or so, indicating a repeat of the Western trend. Evidently the situation is the same in all the Asian NICs.

In Thailand, although statistics are anything but complete, existing crude figures are sufficient to show a sharp increase in divorce in Bangkok and the surrounding provinces as opposed to rural areas. Infidelity (almost always of the husband) and incompatibility are often the grounds for divorce. Family discords thus often arise, and separation or divorce, although formerly frowned upon, have started to become more common in Bangkok. The national divorce rate has increased sharply over the last decade, jumping from 4.5 per cent to

Table 12.2 Divorce rate in selected Asian countries, Britain and the United States

	Percentage of marriages ending in divorce	*Ratio*
United States	50–70	> 1:2 or 3:4
Great Britain	35	1:3
Japan	20–25	1:4/5
Malaysia		
Muslims	16	1:6.25
Indians	12	1:8.33
Chinese	3	1:33.3
Thailand		
Whole kingdom	11	1:9
Bangkok	25	1:4

Japan: 158 000 cases in 1987
Singapore: 1721 cases in 1980; 2916 cases in 1988
Hong Kong: 2060 cases in1981; 5055 cases in 1987

Sources: Adapted from Bourne and Levin, 1983; Leigh, 1989; Chen, 1980.

11.0 per cent, or from one divorce in 22.2 marriages in 1979 to one in nine in 1986. In Bangkok in 1986 one in four marriages ended in divorce. In the central region and the north, where industrial growth has started to spread, there has also been a sharp increase, although not as sharp as in Bangkok. The north-east, the poorest region, has the lowest divorce rate.

While marital disharmony has various causes, one major cause in Thailand has clearly been the changing role of women as opposed to the unchanged role and values/attitudes of men. The conflicting needs and expectations of many couples have rendered them incompatible, and the effect on their children has been enormous. Psychological studies have shown that it is usually discord and parental quarrelling, rather than divorce itself, that drive children out of the home and into a variety of diversionary outlets that make them prone to delinquency and deviant behaviour.

12.6 THE AGING POPULATION

In industrial societies the highly mobile nuclear family is a norm, as is elderly people living alone or in old-folks homes, in tune with Western cultural values derived from rugged individualism and Social Darwinism, upon which industrialization flourished. This has a strong element of ruthlessness – disregard of the plight of the poor and disadvantaged has been part of the history of industrialization in the West. Influenced by the West's rational-utilitarian orientation, in industrialized and newly industrialized Asian nations such as Japan and Singapore an increasing proportion of the country's aging population have been placed in retirement homes. This reflects changing Asian family-oriented moral values of filial piety and respect for the elderly. Survey results showed that 60 per cent of those over 60 in Japan said they would prefer living with their children. In the United States and Britain only 6 per cent voiced this preference (*Bangkok Post*, 16 September 1988). The value difference is clear but the new generation of Japanese prefer to lead their own lives for they find that living separately from their parents helps to avoid family friction. Now the government wants to put a halt to this trend, not so much out of respect for the elderly, but for the increasing burden incurred by the government in supporting them. Elderly people will make up 23.6 per cent of the population in the next 20 years, meaning that there will be 2.5 people aged between 15 and 65 to care for each person over 65. This is because Japan has the highest life expectancy in the world – 79.8 years for women and 74.2 years for men (Leigh, 1989). To help alleviate the burden on the state Japan passed a law that obliges lineal blood relatives to support each other. Similarly the Singapore government, which over the last decade has deliberately encouraged the development of the nuclear family and a new, aggressive, achievement-oriented generation, which has driven elderly people into welfare homes, is now providing various financial incentives to encourage families to take care of their aging parents.

In Thailand, from a family-oriented Asian viewpoint, institutionalization is usually solely for the destitute. Placing an older person in a home is frowned upon as showing a lack of compassion. Even where nuclear families have evolved, parents would have gone to stay with one of their children, but there is no data to show whether this continues to be true. It is hoped that Thailand will not replicate the experience of the Asian NICs and industrial societies.

12.7 COMMERICALIZED LIFE-STYLE AND IMPERSONALIZATION

Industrialization goes hand in hand with materialism, and an impersonalization of human relations. Thai values and behavioural patterns are highly susceptible to materialism and consumerism, but the family-oriented Thai social system conflicts with cold and impersonal human relations. To what extent this will change remains to be seen.

Of great concern are the pervasive and widespread materialistic values and consumption patterns of Thai people nowadays. According to research findings, Thai people place a high value on form (over content) and material possessions (Suntaree, 1990a, 1990b) as these are instrumental in preserving face, status and social relations. They are important because possession of 'forms' (that is, royal decorations, honorary doctoral degrees, expensive cars, designer labels, mobile telephones, pocket-colour televisions, microwaves, and all the latest electrical gadgets) identifies their owners as belonging to a higher social class. Therefore the flaunting of material possessions is evident among all Thai social classes. When social control becomes more and more lax, and possessions become more and more important, all kinds of irregularities can occur, as exemplified by a series of scandals that have cropped up over the last few years.

Thai people tend to buy things they do not really need in order to show that they possess them, and living beyond one's means is common place. One foreigner in Thailand did not understand why his Thai friend decided had decided to buy a 3 million baht, high-power Mercedes-Benz, even though it was way beyond his means. The answer received was that he was the managing director of a company. As for the lower class, over-spending has become the core cause of the endless circle of poverty, now that everything can be bought on hire-purchase. Added to this is eating at fast-food restaurants and shopping at large shopping centres.

To date the impersonalization of human relations that often characterizes the cold, and business-like Western human interactions does not seem to have afflicted Thais, although such behavioural patterns have already been observed in Asian NICs such as Singapore (Chen, 1980) and Taiwan (Tsow, 1989). It seems that everybody in Taiwan and Singapore today is always in a hurry, and human contact is kept to the bare minimum. The effects of impersonalization have also penetrated Japan, the country that people admire for its ability to retain its social and cultural patterns. Japanese social scientists have noted changed thinking among the new generations. Group-oriented values – particularly the spirit of self-sacrifice and loyalty to company and nation, which have contributed so much to the nation's economic success – are fading out. Instead young Japanese are becoming more like Americans – they are more and more self-centred and 'me-tooism' has seeped into Japanese society (Lohr, 1984).

Traditionally Thailand has been characterized by its hierarchical and highly relationship-oriented social system, and compassion towards others is a strong trait. But even this has started to change in Bangkok. We have heard of cases where doctors in private hospitals have refused to treat accident victims because they were unable to prove they could pay for their treatment. To what extent Thailand's relationship-oriented social system will change remains to be seen.

12.8 LEISURE AND THE MASS MEDIA

With industrialization, the influence of technology on the growth of leisure and recreational activities is huge. With the aid of electronic devices one can now 'command' performances by the world's greatest symphony orchestras or experience the sights and sounds of distant places, all into the comfort of one's own home. Recreation has been commercialized, which has added to the importance of the entertainment industry and manufactures of equipment for leisure activities. Related to this is the role of the advertising industry in the selling of all kinds of consumer goods.

Likewise the mass media has become a powerful force in modern life. More and more people read newspapers and magazines and watch television for news, information and entertainment. In particular, television has transformed modern life. In the United States the average family spends almost 50 hours a week in front of the television (*UPI*, 2 May 1985), while in Japan, it is around 57 hours (*New York Times*, 25 July 1982). Violence on television may have contributed significantly to the increase in violent crimes: it was found that crime rates have increased fivefold since the beginning of the television era (Lenski and Lenski, 1987, using data from US Historical Statistics, and Statistical Abstract, 1985). And today there is sufficient evidence to establish a relationship between violence on television and in films and the aggressive behaviour by a minority of viewers (Phillips, 1986; Huesmann *et al.*, 1984; National Institute of Mental Health, 1982). Usually, media elites resist efforts to tone down the content of programmes because they believe violent portrayals maximize their profits. Thai urban children are subject to similar influences, but the extent to which crimes in Thailand are related to violence on television has not been researched. However there have been occasional reports of children jumping to their death imitating Kung Fu movies and the like.

In the process of presenting news, information and so on the media can change and influence the public's ideas or even society's standards, depending on the degree of bias or distortion and the degree of professionalism, conscience and ethics. The media can work for the benefit of all – it is a very powerful instrument. With regard to freedom of expression, despite occasional political repression and media bans, Thailand has somehow stood out as the country with the highest degree of press freedom in South-East Asia. And the Thai press has more or less developed into a watchdog against wrongdoing.

12.9 CONCLUDING REMARKS

There is no doubt that industrialization has both direct and indirect effects on various social, cultural and human factors. Sometimes it causes changes to social, cultural and human-relations systems, but sometimes industrialization is the result of such changes. Against the backdrop of industrial and post-industrial societies we can see where Thailand stands, where it has changed, and where it is heading. Many aspects of rapid industrialization have made Thai society very vulnerable, yet it has brought benefits to various groups of people. It is the possibility of polarisation – between winners and losers, haves and have-nots, the old and the new, and so on – that we must beware of, and the government should take action to ensure that such harmful polarization does not occur.

Note

1. There are of course more areas that could be discussed in the context of the changes in social values in a rapidly industrializing society such as Thailand, but limited space prevents that. First of all, it must be realized that a post-industrial society is a service society, not an agricultural or even a manufacturing society. In this service society there will be increased dependence upon science and technology, to which an improvement in human resources is of utmost importance. As a result there will be a rise in the preeminence of professional and technical people. These scenarios have not yet taken place in Thailand, but at least they provide us with a framework within which to begin our analysis.

13 The Environmental Costs of Industrialization

Helen Ross and Suwattana Thadaniti

13.1 INTRODUCTION

Development experts and economists are revising their thinking about the environment. Where once they may have regarded the world we all inhabit as consisting of 'natural resources', raw materials to be transformed through labour and capital towards a nation's economic growth, the environment is beginning to be considered more as a capital stock. Many environmental economists argue that using up natural resources should be counted as a reduction in capital stock, not 'growth'. New methods such as natural-resource accounting, hedonic pricing, contingent valuation and inclusion of the costs of 'externalities' such as pollution in production costs have been proposed for valuing the environment (see Pearce *et al.*, 1989 for descriptions of these methods). One of the problems with recognition of the environmental effects of development is that environmental goods such as air and water are 'public goods', so that their costs do not enter directly into the costs of commodity production (Falkus, 1990, p. 67).

The inclusion of environmental and social qualities alongside economic performance, for a holistic view of quality of life (for other species and generations besides our own), is central to the new concept of sustainable development (WCED, 1987). Economic growth is becoming recognized as a clumsy indicator of national well-being, which should not – as has tended to happen – be seen as an end in itself. It is a question of how the growth is achieved, and its effects on environmental qualities, public health and intangible social qualities such as cultural richness and social harmony. Spectacular rates of economic growth are commonly sought through the drawdown of natural resources such as forests or minerals, and rapid industrialization, which is typically introduced in ways that have dramatic social and environmental impacts. Environmental controls are often weak in the early years of a country's industrialization.

Similarly, industrialization and modernization should not be seen as ends in themselves, but as possible means to the real goal of quality of life, achieved on an equitable, environmentally and socially sustainable basis. Industrialization tends to transform the social organization and behaviour patterns of the societal groups participating, leading to cultural as well as economic change (see Suntaree, 1989). The dislocations to agriculture and the Thai people engaged in it have yet to be estimated. In Thailand, 'modernization' has become interpreted as 'Westernization' (Suntaree, 1990a, 1990b; Anuchat and Ross, 1992).

Shalardchai (1989, pp. 39–40) criticizes Thailand as having a dependent economy, in which exports, imports, capital and technology are all dependent on foreign trading partners. This leads to inappropriate, Western-styled policies in which widespread destruction is carried out in the name of economic development. An alternative development agenda within Thailand is based on the concept of 'community development'. This takes a more qualitative social view, concentrating as much on the cooperation and bonds between members of a society as on observable physical improvements such as new infrastructure. Environmental impacts are taken into account because they directly affect local production and well-being. Community development focuses on processes rather than products: the members of a society should themselves decide what sort of development they want! It is a democratic approach that works best in small societal units such as villages.

The concept of 'sustainable development', like 'development', has many possible interpretations, but recognizes that development, the environment and human conditions such as poverty and population are interdependent. It also looks beyond the current generation to consider the needs of future generations (WCED, 1987).

So far, there has been far more emphasis on the natural resource aspects of the concept of 'sustainable development' than on cultural aspects. Industries and governments talk in terms of using ('developing') natural resources more sustainably than in the past. There is still an implicit interpretation of humans as individual consumers, needing their food or their paper, than as spiritual, cultural and social beings valuing certain types of relationship with their gods, the natural world and other people. The production – consumption view of sustainable development is really still the growth ethic, undertaken with a little more care! Indigenous peoples are among the first to point out that sustainable development should be about sustaining societies, sustaining the diversity of cultures, as well as using the environment more considerately. This message is also important to the Thai people, who need to consider how much Westernization, and how much pressure of working lifestyles, and rural–urban migration, is consistent with their most cherished cultural values. Fortunately, the 'community development' approach has had a considerable impact on sustainable-development thinking (IUCN/UNEP/WWF, 1991).

13.2 ECOSYSTEMS AFFECTED BY THAI ECONOMIC GROWTH

To recognize environmental qualities and ensure their protection from damage through industrial development, it is necessary to understand ecosystems. While most of us are trained in disciplines that recognize 'systems' of one sort or another, environmental systems are not widely understood. Soil, water, air, energy from the sun, vegetation and animal life are interdependent. Poison a small species through its air, water or food intake, and toxicity may build up in larger animals further up the food chain. Remove one species from an ecosystem, such as by over-harvesting or 'pest control', and populations of other species that depend on it may also collapse. Populations upon which it preyed may increase out of control. This applies to vegetation as well as animals – forests are habitats that provide food and shelter for many animals. It is no use introducing regulations to protect an endangered animal species if one allows its habitat to be destroyed.

This chapter will describe the ecosystems that are suffering environmental impacts due to Thailand's economic growth and industrialization, then describe the impacts of Bangkok's expansion, arising from its central economic and organizational role. Our description deals with the environmental effects of exploiting the raw materials of Thailand's primary, secondary and tertiary industries, not strictly the processing aspects of industrialization.

13.2.1 Forests

Forests, with water, are critical to all of Thailand's ecosystems. Tree roots help prevent erosion of valuable topsoil. Erosion causes siltation in river systems, threatening fish habitats and irrigation. Forests contribute to water quality and water cycles. They help to keep water pure, and they ensure that rain sinks deep into the ground to be drawn upon later, rather than disappearing rapidly as 'run-off'. Forest shade also helps to reduce evaporation and create favourable microclimates. The failure of forest water storage is popularly blamed for local droughts in the dry season. Forests are the habitat of rich communities of plant and animal life. They are also important sources of subsistence, fuel and medicines for local populations – uses that are not measured in GDP but contribute real income to local communities. Many tropical forest species have immense and as yet unknown economic potential. Loss of forest cover, particularly on hillsides, therefore puts several other systems at risk. Falkus (1990, p. 70), citing Adas, mentions that deforestation also had an impact on the spread of malaria in Burma in the nineteenth century.

Deforestation thus may have long-term and long-distance repercussions for other communities whose subsistence, agriculture or drinking water are affected. The most graphic example is the landslides and floods that followed heavy rains in southern Thailand in November 1988, when large areas were devastated and hundreds of lives lost. This event led to the immediate imposition of a logging ban, which served to displace logging activities across the border into Burma and Laos.

Falkus (1990, pp. 68, 75) reports that in 1938 forest covered 78 per cent of Thailand. By 1968 this was reduced to 53 per cent, and 38 per cent in 1980. By 1985 only 93 million rai, or 29 per cent of the land, had forest cover, and only 10 per cent of this was in river headwaters, which are vital to protect (Anat *et al.*, 1988, p. 154). More recent press reports (Apisak, 1990; Handley, 1991) give the figure of 28 per cent forest remaining. Even less of this may be original forest, as satellite photos cannot necessarily distinguish natural from plantation forest. Falkus (1990, p. 66) remarks that at the recent rate of deforestation, virtually all of Thailand's natural forests will disappear by the end of this decade. Thailand was forced to begin importing timber in 1967 (Anat *et al.*, 1988, p. 173).

The causes of this destruction include excessive commercial exploitation and encroachment by landless peasants. The two often go hand in hand, as commercial interests give financial backing or guarantee bail to villagers willing to encroach on forests (Hirsch, 1990a, p. 39). Once forests are designated as 'degraded' they may be opened up for logging or land rights may be granted to villagers, who may then sell their interests. The settlement of forest areas is related historically to the expansion of the agricultural economy and the development of the wider political economy throughout Thailand (Hirsch, 1990a, p. 39ff).

A recent factor is aid to hill tribes to encourage them to switch from opium growing to cash crops (see, for example, Kaye, 1990). The publicity accorded to one particular conflict may have exaggerated its overall importance. In certain localities, substantial areas of crucial watershed forest on high mountain ridges have been cleared, and pesticides used excessively. Lowland rice growers complain of changes in water regimes and toxic run-off. The minority groups known as 'hill tribes' have been made a scapegoat of deforestation because of their slash and burn agriculture. This method is ecologically sensible, at least at low population densities: the real culprits are logging and increasingly the cash crops pressed upon the hill tribes with international aid support.

Eucalyptus plantations

Under the guise of reforestation the Royal Forestry Department has encouraged the establishment of eucalypt plantations. Eucalypts have become commercially popular as a fast-growing tree since seed became cheap in 1978. They have been promoted vigorously as a source of pulp and chipwood for export, especially to Japan and Taiwan. The export orientation is underlined by the choice of locations, including near the new Eastern Seaboard port where growing conditions are far from optimum (Apichai *et al.*, 1992). Eucalypt and other introduced species are no replacement for natural forests and have a severe environmental impact. They are not attractive to wildlife or other plant species, and they provide no subsistence uses to local communities (Apichai *et al.*, 1992, p. 202). They have a severe impact on underground water because they are capable of absorbing large quantities of water at a deeper level than other trees. They also contaminate soil to the detriment of neighbouring cropland, and pose a greater fire danger than indigenous or fruit trees. Campaigns against eucalypt plantations by villagers and environmentalists have been prominent in recent years. The government has recently imposed a ban on the eviction of people from prospective plantation areas.

Many of those involved in the industry have a view to developing their own pulp mills in time, depending on domestic production capacity and levels of demand (Apichai *et al.*, 1992, p. 190).

Mangroves

Mangrove forests are a very special ecosystem linking land and sea resources. Their ecological value is only just becoming recognized.

They provide a breeding ground for many fish, shrimp, crab and mollusc species, as well as habitat for birds, mammals and reptiles (Anat *et al.*, 1988, pp. 290–1). Many coastal communities derive an important part of their subsistence from mangroves (Thasanee Chantadisai, personal communication; [1] Anat *et al.*, 1988, p. 298). Mangroves are important economically as a source of charcoal, wood products, tannin and natural medicines.

The widespread clearing of mangroves for shrimp farms, mining and salt farms thus threatens sea fisheries. Salt water also encroaches on nearby rice paddies forcing their farmers to sell up. In a 'human ecology' causal chain, Thasanee (personal communication) has discovered that this displacement of rice farmers leads to deforestation as they start new farms elsewhere.

While there are various measures to regulate the clearing of mangroves (Anat *et al.*, 1988, p. 372ff), the active promotion of shrimp culture in particular threatens this crucial resource.

13.2.2 Water Resources

Rivers and marine systems are affected in numerous ways by growing industries and their associated demands. Humans are dependent on rivers for drinking, washing and agricultural water and for transport. Water flow and navigation are affected by siltation following deforestation, and by dams built for irrigation, electricity generation or water supplies for the growing cities. This in turn affects agriculture and fish stocks. Dams also help prevent the annual flooding that is so important to rice growing and the flushing out of pollutants. Up to 11 dams are planned for the Mekong River system – one of the most biologically diverse water catchments in Asia – partly to meet the doubling of Thai electricity demand forecast by the Electricity Generating Authority of Thailand (EGAT). These dams have been predicted to displace up to 350 000 people and disrupt the habitats of more than 100 known species of migratory freshwater fish, which are an important food source to the 52 million inhabitants of the lower Mekong basin (Goldsmith and Hildyard, 1992, p. 106).

The use of pesticides in agriculture, which has been excessive owing to commercial pressures and lack of education among those using them, has led to the poisoning of rivers, fish and irrigated areas. Many farmers are poisoned directly by pesticide misuse, with alarming health effects among present and possibly future generations.

On the central plain water pollution by industry and urban households is an increasing concern, and is transmitted to agricultural areas by the connecting canals and annual floods. The use of artesian bores as a water source by industry has contributed to Bangkok's subsidence problem – one study calculates that 85 per cent of the water used by the 25 000 factories in Bangkok, Nonthaburi and Samut Prakan is from artesian wells (Sopida, 1992, p. 36). Conflicts may be anticipated over plans to meet Bangkok's water needs in future, which may entail the use of the waters of the Mekong (Sopida, 1992, p. 37). The Gulf of Thailand is threatened by increasing pollution and reduced water flows from the Chao Phraya River (Alford, 1992, p. 259).

The management of Thailand's water systems is hampered by lack of understanding. Alford (1992, pp. 258–9) points out that the Thai government possesses a great deal of hydrological, climatic and land-use information, but this is largely unorganized and unanalyzed so does not contribute to a proper understanding of processes. Alford remarks that decisions affecting water resources appear to be made on an ad hoc basis, with limited regard for the ecological systems associated with the Chao Phraya river basin.

13.2.3 Tourism

Tourism accounts for 5 per cent of GDP and is Thailand's single largest foreign-exchange earner (Friedland, 1992). It is an industry that relies heavily on an appealing natural environment and local culture, yet it has been managed (or left largely unmanaged) in a way that has despoiled both. Tourist infrastructure such as hotels and access roads, and recreation facilities such as golf courses, contribute to the clearing of land and entail a very high per-capita consumption of water. Because of the lack of planning and controls, particularly in Pattaya and Phuket, untreated sewerage discharge has been allowed to pollute beaches, rivers and the corals at Phuket (NEB staff, personal communication). This in turn has affected tourist numbers.

13.2.4 Mines and Quarries

The minerals sector in Thailand is relatively small, accounting for around two per cent of GDP (Praipol, 1988, p. 311). Tin has long held the dominant economic role, but over 30 minerals are extracted in

Thailand (Anat *et al.*, 1988, p. 230). Cost factors are slowing the rate of tin production as the prices of tin and some other metals have been low in recent years, and the most accessible known deposits will soon have been exhausted. Many other mineral-based resources are quarried for domestic use, for instance limestone and shale for the cement industry (Gillian Burke, personal communication). [2] In 1989 there were some 850 active mines in Thailand, of which about 40 per cent were tin mines (NSO, 1989b, p. 186).

The environmental impacts are localized, in that 80 per cent of the value comes from small to medium-sized mines, with an emphasis on hand sorting and appropriate technology (Anat *et al.*, 1988, p. 249). The types of environmental impact vary with the specific mineral and its mode of recovery and processing, and with the ecosystem in which it takes place – forest, agricultural or marine. Clearance of forest may be necessary. Erosion, sedimentation and contamination of water systems are potential effects. These impacts are common in developing countries where environmental controls and management may be weak or absent. Enters (personal communication) [3] notes that some 30 per cent of erosion in northern Thailand is attributable to mining, and that roads (an important infrastructure) also account for a high proportion.

The quarrying of minerals and rocks such as barite, clays, dolomite, kaolin, limestone, shale, felspar and talc distributes dust that is damaging to the environment and hazardous to workers. An Indonesian study of small limestone quarries found that dust had spread over a wide area, damaging agriculture (Untung, 1991, Gillian Burke personal communication). Quarrying also causes land degradation, which is not subsequently rehabilitated.

Larger-scale salt mining has had more serious effects than smaller mines. Agriculture has been affected by the increased salinity of waterways and soil (Gillian Burke, personal communication).

Marine dredging for tin has had an impact on marine fishing owing to the disturbance of breeding grounds, food sources and floor sediment. It has also affected coastal water quality. These effects have declined with reduced production, which has also reduced the use of suction boats (Praipol, 1988, p. 320). Typical impacts of tin mining inland include forest clearance, erosion and other forms of land degradation, pollution of groundwater and river systems, and air pollution from dust and fumes (see Gupta 1988, p. 26).

Mining for metals and gems has been carried out by small local operations as a consequence of government policy to restrict foreign ownership. Primitive methods have led to land degradation and pollution from spoil tips. The introduction of larger-scale mining now that the government is encouraging foreign investment is unlikely to improve this situation, because of the lack of regulation and enforcement (Gillian Burke, personal communication).

The human impacts of the mining and processing of some minerals are a concern (Peter Hancock, personal communication).[4] Throughout many developing countries failure to set up and apply adequate safety standards has resulted in collapsed workings, deaths from gas inhalation and suffocation owing to poor ventilation, and flooding. Some primitive blasting, crushing, grinding and hard-rock mining techniques produce dusts that causes diseases such as silicosis ('miners lung') (Gupta, 1988, p. 48).

The Thai government's efforts to avoid environmental impacts have led to cumbersome and time-consuming procedures for obtaining licences. The result is that illegal mining flourishes (Praipol, 1988, pp. 349–50).

13.2.5 The Manufacturing Industry

The impacts of the manufacturing industry depend on the type of industry, the processes it adopts, the efficiency of its technology and its location in relation to agricultural and urban centres. Thailand's notorious inability to agree upon or enforce planning controls has led to the uncontrolled siting of factories in areas where great danger is presented to local ecosystems (particularly through the water systems) and nearby populations. This is particularly serious in Bangkok and its vicinity, where 64 per cent of the country's total industrial production is concentrated (Anuchat, 1991, p. 92). In 1988 a quarter of the new factories approved nationally were to be located in Bangkok.

As inputs, raw materials (such as wood from natural or plantation forests, or minerals) and rates of water and energy use have important and widespread environmental effects. Thailand now imports over a third of its energy sources. A high proportion of the usage is now related to industry: in 1988, 27 per cent of oil equivalent was used in manufacturing and mining, and a further 39 per cent was used in transportation (calculated from NEA, 1989, p. 1). The NEA quotes 30 per cent of the energy consumed as coming from renewable sources. While hydro electricity accounted for only 4 per cent of Thailand's domestic production of energy in 1988 (calculated from NEA 1989, p. 1), plans to expand this sector to meet the growing demand have posed severe environmental threats (see Section 13.2.2 above).

Among the outputs, air and water pollution are currently causing the greatest concern, particularly in and around Bangkok where factories are concentrated amongst the urban population, and the floodplain ecology makes water pollution all-pervasive. While the domestic and service sectors outweigh industry as a cause of measured water pollution, chemical pollution of the waterways is rife (see Anuchat, 1991; Anuchat and Ross, 1992). Similarly traffic is the major cause of air pollution and noise, but industrial causes are nevertheless serious. People's health is affected unnecessarily by the distribution of factories within residential areas, and factories' ability to transgress environmental controls with ease (see Anuchat and Ross, 1992).

The National Environment Board (NEB) has attempted to control industrial pollution by concentrating new industries in industrial estates, establishing emission standards, and requiring environmental impact statements.

We now present a case study of the primacy and industrialization of Bangkok, to illustrate some of the causes and effects of environmental problems related both directly and indirectly to industrialization and economic growth.

13.3 THE ENVIRONMENTAL COSTS OF URBANIZATION: THE CASE OF BANGKOK

The industrialization and consequent urbanization of Bangkok illustrate some of the causes and effects of environmental problems related both directly and indirectly to economic growth. Bangkok is logistically as well as geographically central to Thailand's economic growth. It is the key location for the manufacturing and service industries, transport and communications, and administration. Urban growth has therefore followed from the country's industrialization. In Thailand's case, the degree of concentration in the capital city and relative neglect of the rural hinterland, together with an extreme lack of planning controls, has led to Bangkok becoming what is known as a 'primate city', totally dominating the country's urban hierarchy. The environmental, public-health costs and related economic costs of this rapid and uncontrolled urban growth are now becoming apparent. One reason for the extremeness of the environmental problem is that the form of urban development has in many respects been contrary to the opportunities and constraints presented by the flood-plain/agricultural ecosystem it inhabits.

13.3.1 Bangkok's Urban Growth

Bangkok's growth has two aspects: the growth of built-up areas, and population growth. Built-up areas have been expanding for three decades, according to a pattern of ribbon development and urban sprawl. The effects of this growth pattern include:

- The intrusion of development onto highly productive farm land (the rich flood plain of the Chao Phraya River);
- The provision of infrastructure to service the new populations lagging well behind the frontiers of growth;
- An increasing amount of non-productive, vacant land awaiting development within and around the built-up areas.

The ribbon development is proceeding along seven growth corridors, created by the main roads – a case of transport infrastructure leading urban development (Demaine, 1986). Bangkok has expanded far beyond its generous administrative boundaries, covering extensive areas of the surrounding provinces: Samut Prakan, Nonthaburi, Pathum Thani, Samut Sakhon and Nakhon Pathom. Bangkok and these five provinces are emerging as an economically and spatially integrated 'mega-urban region', known as the Bangkok Metropolitan Region (BMR).

This region is likely to continue to dominate Thailand's economic development in the near future, despite national efforts to encourage decentralization. The region's share of national GDP (at constant 1972 prices) rose from 43 per cent in 1986 to 48 per cent in 1991, and is projected to reach 49 per cent by 1996 (Table 13.1). The region's economic performance is growing slightly faster than the national average, and its population is also increasing faster than the national average. The demand for development land is increasing substantially, and much of the agricultural land preserved in the 'green belt' area is in danger of being lost to residential, commercial and industrial developments. The failure of infrastructure to keep pace with growth (particularly in the form of roads), coupled with mismanagement of land use, has created congestion and environmental deterioration.

13.3.2 Environmental Problems

The haphazard growth of Bangkok has led to numerous problems, exacerbated by the weakness of urban planning controls (see Anuchat and Ross, 1992).

Table 13.1 Population and economy of the Bangkok Metropolitan Region (BMR) during the Seventh National Economic and Social Development Plan.

	Bangkok	*Rest of BMR*	*BMR*	*Kingdom*
Population (million)				
1992	6.4	1.7	8.0	57.8
1996	6.8	2.0	8.8	61.0
Population, % of kingdom				
1992	11.0	2.9	13.9	100.0
1996	11.1	3.3	14.4	100.0
Population growth 1992–96, % p.a.	1.6	5.0	2.3	1.4
GDP, billion baht, 1972 constant prices				
1991			333.0	688.3
1996			504.5	1020.8
GDP, % of kingdom				
1991			48.4	100.0
1996			49.4	100.0
GDP growth, % p.a.				
1991			10.0	9.0
1996			8.3	7.9

Source: Thailand Development Research Institute and National Economic and Social Development Board, cited in Urban Forestry Subteam, 1993.

Traffic

As Bangkok expands, the main land use on its fringes is residential. Road development and transport services are insufficient to service the growing population. Residents of these fringe areas commute to and from the city centre each day, adding greatly to the volume of traffic and putting additional pressure on the limited road space available there. The result is chronic traffic congestion over a wide area and for long periods during the day. Traffic speeds in the inner zone of Bangkok during peak hours have decreased to between five and eight kilometres per hour. The morning peak hour already lasts two to three hours, and congestion continues with only slight relief throughout the day. This congestion is affecting all forms of traffic, though buses are now protected to a limited extent by bus lanes.

Public transport in Bangkok is generally slow and exceedingly uncomfortable, particularly where long distances are involved. People will not leave their cars at home and take a bus, because no matter how bad the congestion the car always seems preferable. Households are stretching their finances extraordinarily to purchase cars (Anuchat and Ross, 1992). The number of cars on the road is predicted to increase at the rate of 35 000 cars per year. The cost to individuals, businesses and the city in fuel and other vehicle operating costs, wasted time and frustration is immense. Travel times are reducing business efficiency and personal well-being by competing with the time available for work, family and leisure. Travel stresses are equally impairing people's productivity (Anuchat and Ross, 1992). Many trips are cancelled on account of the congestion, even if the distances to be travelled are small. The use of motor cycles has increased as a strategy to slip through traffic jams.

Water supply

The water supply for both domestic and industrial uses in Bangkok is provided by a combination of underground and surface sources. The outer zone relies mainly on groundwater. Groundwater resources have been overused, resulting in significant land subsidence, particularly in central and eastern Bangkok. The slowness to provide a fully integrated water-supply system over a large area, combined with rapid urban expansion into areas that lack an existing water supply, has encouraged the continued exploitation of groundwater. The alternatives, however, also carry significant environmental costs. Water supplies for Bangkok are in competition with other water uses, such as irrigation for agriculture. One option under consideration is diverting waters from the Mekong into the Chao Phraya to serve the Central Plain (*The Nation*, 4 January 1993).

Flooding

Ground levels in the city core range between 0.5 and 1.7 metres above mean sea level. Floods in August and September are mostly due to rainfall, whereas those in October and November are due to river overflow. The natural drainage provided by canals (*klongs*) into the Chao Phraya ceases to function because river levels are already high owing to a combination of seasonal water rises in the Gulf of Thailand and high run-off from the north.

The extent and duration of flooding is aggravated by the poor drainage system, which has not kept pace with the rapid urbanization of Bangkok. The once extensive system of *klongs* has been filled in many places to make way for roads. Storm sewers and the remaining canals, which in many parts are poorly maintained or blocked, cannot compete with the runoff from the ever-increasing and impervious surface area. Poor land-use controls have contributed to the blocking of *klongs*, as illegally constructed houses have encroached on or even blocked the flow of *klongs* entirely.

Measures to divert floodwaters away from the inner city, where many businesses and higher-income residents are located, have been taken at the expense of neighbouring provinces, particularly to the west of Bangkok.

Water pollution

Domestic households and restaurants account for about 75 per cent of the pollution of the Chao Phraya River (measured by biochemical oxygen demand), while industrial sources account for the remainder. The high proportion of domestic contribution reflects the lack of a sewerage-treatment system for Bangkok – waste is discharged directly into the *klongs,* which flow into the river. Measures of the pollution levels in *klongs* are difficult to obtain, but most are so severely polluted that they carry no oxygen and give off offensive odours. Industrial sources contribute to the pollution of many *klongs* – local people allege that factories only run their compulsory waste-water-treatment plants when inspections are due, because of the running costs (Anuchat and Ross, 1992). The high rate of pollution in *klongs* disadvantages and threatens the health of local residents, as it is no longer safe to use the *klong* water for domestic purposes. Water pollution is also affecting the viability of farms in the green belt, providing an added incentive to owners to sell their land for urban development.

Air pollution

The problem of air pollution, which is closely related to the traffic problem but also to factories, is becoming increasingly serious. Ambient monitoring data indicate substantial increases in all major pollutants. Lead emissions from petrol are increasing, despite measures to reduce the proportion of lead permitted. When other sources of lead contamination are considered, lead is potentially the most serious urban environmental health hazard. Air pollution is particularly hazardous to those living close to major roads and those exposed for long periods, such as traffic police and street hawkers.

These environmental problems have serious socioeconomic and health consequences for local residents. Avoiding or adapting to adverse environmental conditions affects the behaviour patterns of residents, and when many residents change their behaviour in a similar way the shape of the city is transformed. For instance, those escaping pollution in the inner city by moving to outer areas contribute to the loss of agricultural land, and to the traffic and air-pollution problems suffered by others as well as themselves: the rapidly expanding middle-class strive to purchase cars, thus adding to the congestion and pollution they are trying to escape. Inevitably the poorest people have the least means to adapt, and suffer the inconveniences, health threats and stresses of environmental problems most intensely. The lack of attention to environmental problems is thus a serious equity issue as well as a health and an environmental issue.

Bangkok's environmental problems have reached the point of impairing Thailand's economic efficiency. Traffic particularly interferes with the productivity of the workforce and the transport of goods. Flooding also affects productivity at certain times of year. The cost of health impacts on the urban population, and the costs of clean-up (if attempted) would surely add enormously to the economic costs of the environmental problem. If the social and ecological costs of Bangkok's problems could be taken into account, one might view the apparent economic achievements more sceptically.

13.4 SUSTAINABILITY

So how sustainable is Thailand's society and use of natural resources? The following assessment is based on a set of principles by the Second World Conservation Strategy Project (IUCN/UNEP/WWF, 1991) (see Figure 13.1).

13.4.1 Respect and Care for the Community of Life

This ethical and practical principle assumes a responsibility to other species and future generations to manage development so that it does not threaten the survival of other species or eliminate their habitats.

Buddhist philosophy notwithstanding, the rate of destruction of wildlife and native plant populations in Thailand has paralleled its economic development. Thailand constitutes only 0.36 per cent of the Earth's surface but its forests shelter 2.6 per cent of all vertebrates and more than 10 per cent of the world's bird species (Kumthorn Thirakupt, quoted in *The Nation*, 21 January 1990). Most species that

1. Respect and care for the community of life
2. Improve the quality of human life
3. Conserve the Earth's vitality and diversity
   - conserve life-support systems
   - conserve biodiversity
   - ensure that uses of renewable resources are sustainable
4. Minimize the depletion of non-renewable resources.
5. Keep within the Earth's carrying capacity
6. Change personal attitudes and practices
7. Enable communities to care for their own environments
8. Provide a national framework for integrating development and conservation
9. Create a global alliance

Source: IUCN/UNEP/WWF, 1991.

Figure 13.1 Principles of a sustainable society

depend on forests will soon survive only in protected areas – and some are declining even there. Knowledge of indigenous flora and fauna is very incomplete, but the TDRI has identified five fish, seven reptile, 46 bird and eight mammal species that are expected to become extinct within a few years (Anat *et al.*, 1988, pp. 198–206). This is related to the rapid destruction of natural forest cover, as tropical forests are particularly important sources of biodiversity; to the siltation and pollution of waterways and marine environments; and to severe hunting pressures on some species.

While local communities have some vested interest in maintaining and enjoying the fruits of complex local ecosystems, population growth and land pressures have created societal and economic pressures that have encouraged forest encroachment and caused related damage to waterways. Effects on other species and their habitats have been barely taken into account (if at all) in the shaping of Thailand's economy since the problem began to emerge after the Second World War. It took the severe ecological consequences of the 1988 landslides and floods before a ban on logging was instituted, but this has proved easy to circumvent. Some encouraging signs are that public pressure has led to the cancellation of some dam proposals in protected areas, though it is a sign of the predominantly commercial orientation of government that such projects were proposed at all.

13.4.2 Improve the Quality of Human Life

Development is intended to improve the quality of human life, enabling people to realize their potential, build self-confidence and lead lives of dignity and fulfilment.

Thailand's growth pattern has led to increasing disparities between rich and poor (Anuchat, 1991, which drew on several sources). Even the growing Bangkok middle class, stuck in its traffic jam, has doubts about whether economic improvement has necessarily increased its quality of life! Social problems such as the sex industry and AIDS, which are related to rural poverty, consumerism, the tourist industry and the status of women, denote a decline in some aspects of the quality of life. While Thai standards and values towards political involvement remain rather conservative (Suntaree, 1990a), the crisis point for democracy that was reached in 1992 reflected a new demand for democratic opportunities commensurate with Thailand's economic modernization (for example Sondhi, 1992; Virat *et al.*, 1992).

13.4.3 Conserve the Earth's Vitality and Diversity

This principle demands deliberate action to protect the structure and functions of the world's natural systems, upon which humans and other species utterly depend (IUCN/UNEP/WWF, 1991, p. 9). This includes protecting the ecological processes that shape climate, cleanse air and water, regulate water flow, recycle essential elements, create and regenerate soil, and enable ecosystems to renew themselves. It means conserving the variety of ecosystems and the gene pools of all species, and ensuring that the use of renewable resources is sustainable.

Thailand's economy is still bent on destroying life-support systems and biodiversity, scarcely restrained by the conservation measures attempted by governmental arms such as the Wildlife Conservation and National Park Divisions of the Royal Forests Department and the National Environment Board. Even the vital national parks and wildlife sanctuaries are sometimes placed under threat by illegal forestry, dams, mining and tourist infrastructure. Efforts to redress past damage are often mistaken, such as 'reforestation' by eucalypt plantations. These do not replace natural ecosystems and in reality are another environmentally damaging form of cash crop (Apichai *et al.*, 1992).

13.4.4 Minimize the Depletion of Non-renewable Resources

Minerals, oil, gas and coal are not renewable, but their use can be extended with careful use, recycling for reuse, and switching to renewable substitutes where possible. The TDRI has attempted to estimate the size and likely life of Thailand's mineral reserves, concluding that reserves of several key minerals are sufficient for the near future although the high-grade offshore tin deposits have largely been depleted (Anat *et al.*, 1988, pp. 250–2).

The recycling of all materials is minimal amongst the rich but prevalent among the poorer sections of society. Concessions for the recovery and recycling of metals and glass from Bangkok's tips, for instance, are quite sought after.

The growing affluence among the urban population, and growing industrial demands for energy, have increased energy consumption dramatically in recent years. Energy use in the transportation sector nearly doubled between 1980 and 1988. The residential and commercial, and manufacturing sectors are the next largest consumers (NEA, 1989, p. 10). The majority of this consumption is concentrated in Bangkok. Thailand depends on imported petroleum products as its major energy source; its highly inefficient consumption nevertheless contributes to global concerns such as the greenhouse effect, and to local health and environmental concerns due to air pollution. The Electricity Generation Authority of Thailand has been criticized for its plans for major dams to provide electricity, threatening damage to sensitive forest systems and wildlife and displacement of local populations (Handley and Awanohara, 1991, p. 98). Critics advocate demand management as a priority for transport systems and electricity generation (Project for Ecological Recovery, 1991).

13.4.5 Keep within the Earth's Carrying Capacity

'Carrying capacity' refers to the impact that the Earth's ecosystems and the biosphere can withstand without dangerous deterioration (IUCN/UNEP/WWF, 1991, p. 10). The rates of destruction of natural resources, especially forests and water systems (both of which are important plant and wildlife habitats), and the rates of atmospheric and water pollution are far outstripping this portion of the Earth's carrying capacity. Population pressures are less important than in many other countries, as Thailand had spectacular success with its family-planning policies. Santhad (1989, p. 81) finds social norms and values concerning forests and natural resources, economic expansion and modernization, and commercial logging to be far more important factors. Inequities in land and resource rights have contributed to encroachment on forests. Thailand has historically encouraged extensive rather than intensive increases in agriculture, and the resulting deforestation has caused deterioration of old as well as newer agricultural lands (Hirsch, 1990a, p. 40). Income and developmental inequities have also contributed to urban migration, and thus to urban environmental concerns.

The exportation of natural resources to meet the demands of more developed countries (including the Asian NICs) is carried out irrespective of the carrying capacity of Thailand's ecosystems. Worse still, Thai firms are now contributing to the deforestation of Myanmar and Laos. The increasing affluence and Westernization of the growing middle class is also encouraging consumption and polluting behaviours that ignore Bangkok's and the nation's renewal capacities.

13.4.6 Change Personal Attitudes and Practices

Westernization and material consumption are influencing the values of newly affluent urban elites and increasingly consumer-oriented villagers. These cultural influences support values which are exploitative of the environment, contrary to supposed Buddhist values about living in harmony with nature. (There is an interesting debate about interpretations of Buddhism, with references to 'State Buddhism'.) Falkus (1990, p. 78) cites Terwiel to argue that Thais were 'relentlessly exploiting their environment' even before the Bowring Treaty last century, so destructive values and practices cannot be blamed entirely on the recent drive for economic growth and western-influenced development.

On the other hand there is a minority trend among urban intellectuals towards recognition that quality of life and the health of people and the environment are suffering as a result of Thailand's current path of development (Anuchat and Ross, 1992). In rural areas there is a strong community development movement towards what we would now call 'sustainable agriculture', supported by Buddhist leaders, NGOs and environmental groups (for example Seri and Bennoun, 1988).

13.4.7 Enable Communities to Care for Their Own Environments

One of the promising political trends is the success of local communities, with the support of a strong coalition of other groups, in resisting environmentally damaging proposals designed to benefit elites and foreign interests. The World Bank has been persuaded to refuse funding for several large dams proposed by EGAT (Handley and Awanohara, 1991), and protests against eucalyptus plantations have been widespread. This principle for sustainable development is advocated by environmental and rural development NGOs as an alternative agenda to the centrally oriented forms of development promoted under measures of economic growth (for example Alternative Agriculture Group, 1991, Pornthip *et al.*, 1991; Yos *et al.*, 1991; Charit, 1989, p. 456). The effectiveness of protest as a political tool in Thailand is surprising, given the cultural reluctance to challenge authority and the lack of responsiveness to the electorate in Thailand's quasi-democracy (see Hewison, 1993).

13.4.8 Provide a National Framework for Integrating Development and Conservation

The authors of these principles for sustainable development argue that 'all societies need a foundation of information and knowledge, a framework of law and institutions, and consistent economic and social policies if they are to advance in a rational way' (IUCN/UNEP/WWF 1991, p. 11). They outline subprinciples towards an integrative, systems-oriented and democratic approach to environment and development.

The TDRI documents how the Thai framework of law and institutions actively mitigates against sustainable development (Anat *et al.*, 1988). Coordination of aims, let alone performance, between organizations is an impossibility, for longstanding historical reasons (see Hirsch, 1990a, p. 18). Lack of accurate and comprehensive information, for instance on water pollution resulting from industrial effluents, makes the environmental consequences of industrial actions difficult to monitor. Local observation, for instance of the impacts of eucalypt plantations, has been significant in resistance movements, but environmental measures are essential in a society taking serious development decisions.

The planning activities of the NESDB, which are evolving in a more socially and environmentally responsive direction, provide a brighter outlook on economic and social policies. There is an interesting trade-off between the NESDB's and other agencies' attempts at rational planning, and the realities of development in Thailand whereby political and financial influence buy enough exceptions to undermine any plan (witness the Suan Kitti forests scandal of 1990, after the national logging ban, and the total inefficacy of urban planning in Bangkok).

13.4.9 Create a Global Alliance

The final principle advocated by the Second World Conservation Strategy urges international cooperation to assist lower-income countries to develop sustainably. Little of this influence has been extended to Thailand so far, though it should become a priority for the conservation of tropical rainforests.

Western countries, including Australia, need to adopt a sustainability ethic that changes the ethos of international trade and development away from the persisting colonial form (Goldsmith and Hildyard, 1992, p. 52). This is a cultural as well as an economic matter: as long as Westerners continue to embrace consumerism, and 'Westernization' proves attractive to other cultures, there is little hope of changing environmental trends in any country. This change of ethic necessitates changes in the forms of development advice and aid given to developing countries, which mainly relate to large environmentally damaging projects, and projects that emphasize growth rather than quality-of-life goals.

13.5 CONCLUSION

Stephens (1991) presents three scenarios for the environmental future of Bangkok:

- Bangkok will become increasingly inhospitable and its excesses will leak into the surrounding countryside. Foreign companies will leave and investment will dry up. Tourism will turn down.
- The Thais, with their ingenuity and capacity for hard work, will step back from the edge – but they do not have much time left.
- Bangkok and Thais will muddle through. They will recognize their errors and do enough to stop falling over the edge, but not enough to restore Thailand as a desirable country in which to live.

These scenarios can be extended to the whole country. If Thailand resists the world pressure towards sustainable development, it risks losing development investment from international agencies such as the

World Bank and donor countries, as these tighten up their environmental standards. The 'ethical investment' movement has not, to our knowledge, yet extended to major sources of private capital, but this could ultimately happen. As environmental quality increasingly comes to be measured as an indicator of development performance and an essential component of economic growth, Thailand may come to realize that the economy of which it is so proud has shaky ecological foundations.

Notes

1. Thasanee Chantadisai is an employee of the Office of Environmental Policy and Planning. She conducted a landmark study of mangrove forests and the shrimp-farming industry in the late 1980s.
2. Gillian Burke is visiting fellow at the Research School of Pacific and Asian Studies, Australian National University, and a specialist in the mining industry.
3. Thomas Enters completed his PhD in forestry at the Australian National University, based on field studies in northern Thailand.
4. Peter Hancock is a visiting fellow at the Centre for Resource and Environmental Studies, and a specialist in the mining industry.

14 Thailand's Industrialization: Implications for Health, Education, and Science and Technology

Sirilaksana Khoman

14.1 INTRODUCTION

Thailand's economic growth during the past decade is often cited as a success story, the result of years of industrialization, structural shifts in production and significant advances in real incomes. From an economy dominated by agriculture, Thailand has been so transformed that in 1991 the share of GDP from agriculture registered a mere 12 per cent. Manufactured exports and tourism are clearly responsible for much of the growth, and indeed industry and services have become major sources of employment and income.

At the same time significant strides have been made in health and education. Severe malnutrition has been eliminated, average life expectancy increased from 60 to 65 years between 1980 and 1990, mean caloric consumption has equalled caloric requirements, and population growth has slowed to a rate of 1.3 per cent per annum. With respect to education, expansion of school enrolment has been rapid, and literacy rates are among the highest in the region.

Yet amidst the affluence generated by industrialization, complex problems have emerged. Thailand is currently plagued with infrastructure bottlenecks, environmental degradation, occupational health hazards, widening disparities between urban and rural areas, and the inequitable distribution of wealth. Income distribution has not improved, despite achievements in the provision of social services. Pockets of poverty and inaccessibility to basic services remain. All this points to underlying problems capable of derailing the buoyant economy.

The favourable world environment that allowed high growth in the late 1980s began to falter in 1990 and continues to deteriorate. The year 1992 was a particularly sobering one for Thailand, with political upheavals that required a rethinking of policy and an overhauling of power structures. More imperative than at any other time in recent history is the need to counterbalance the drive towards high growth with the need for sustainability and a more equitable distribution of wealth and opportunity. In this process, human-resource development can be singled out for its crucial contribution to economic and social development and Thailand's capacity to adjust to rapid changes. The quality of the workforce will determine the economy's future competitiveness. Greater equity in human development will affect the social structure, improve income distribution, and enhance the overall quality of life.

The objective of this chapter is to provide a cursory view of the main issues and problems in health and education that have arisen with Thailand's industrial progress, and the situation in terms of manpower for science and technology (S&T). The chapter also explores mechanisms for the development of human resources as users and generators of technological progress for the purpose of achieving sustained and balanced economic and social development. Emphasis is placed on correcting market failures in the economy to encourage those industries that are 'environmentally friendly' and 'health-friendly', and instituting the minimum amount of regulatory machinery that would encourage suitable human-resource training in industry as well as awareness and accountability for health and environmental impacts. The chapter does not claim to be exhaustive, and is necessarily selective in emphasis due to its wide-ranging scope.

14.2 INDUSTRIALIZATION AND HEALTH

Industrialization and high income growth have no doubt made possible the substantial health improvements that Thailand has seen over the last three decades. Better sanitation, better nutrition and improved medical care are the obvious products of higher incomes. The standard of medical care is indeed one of the highest in the region, and the Ministry of Public Health has ensured a fair amount of equity in the distribution of services and health personnel in the rural areas. However specific problems arise with the rapid growth of industries.

That industrial expansion and heavy concentration in Bangkok have taken a heavy toll in terms of pollution and traffic congestion is clearly evident in Thailand's capital city. Less obvious however is the inexorable toll on health and well-being. Bangkok and its satellite provinces account for over 50 per cent of the 52 000 factories and 23 industrial estates in the country, generating three quarters of manufacturing GDP and industrial waste. Although heavy concentration of industry also implies heavy concentration of industry-related health problems, certain environmental consequences have far-reaching implications for the rest of the country.

Three major health concerns can be identified: environment-related health, occupational health hazards, and health problems related to the service sector, particularly tourism.

14.2.1 Environment-Related Health Problems

The benefits of industrialization, in terms of employment opportunities, increased incomes, consumption, and higher living standards, are largely private; the costs, on the other hand, in terms of congestion, pollution and waste, are largely social. The lack of a system of 'environmental accountability', whereby generators of the negative spillover effects of industrialization are made to bear those costs directly or proportionately, means that such costs do not enter into profit calculations and no incentive exists to minimize them.

Thailand's industrial-promotion policies have further encouraged the accelerated introduction of technology-based industries. A wide range of privileges and incentives are given to attract foreign investors, but pollution intensity per unit of GDP has not been included among the selection criteria. The generation of industrial waste and the environmental impact has therefore not been kept in check. Like the NICs until recently, the regulatory framework to safeguard the environment and ensure safe waste disposal is weak or non-existent.

An important concern is over hazardous industrial waste. Analysis of promoted industries shows that the share of hazardous-waste-generating industries increased from 25 per cent in 1987 to almost 60 per cent in 1990. The largest quantity of hazardous waste originates from the manufacturing sector, which accounts for 90 per cent of all such waste in the country. Industrial hazardous waste was estimated to be about two million tons in the early 1990s and is projected to grow to six million tons by the year 2000 (Dhira and Panayotou, 1990).

The basic metals industry generates two-thirds of the hazardous waste, with small amounts being produced by various industries such as fabricated products, transport equipment, electrical machinery, chemical products, textiles, and printing and publishing (Table 14.1). With the exception of a pilot treatment facility for the electroplating industry, which treats about 40 000 tons of waste a year, industrial waste is dumped freely and often haphazardly into rivers and landfills or stored in drums on site with little or no treatment.

Heavy metal sludges and solids, followed by acid waste, pose the greatest environmental risks to humans, fish and wildlife. Harmful effects can spread through direct contact, fire and explosion, groundwater pollution, surface-water pollution through run-off, air pollution through combustion, evaporation, sublimation and erosion by winds, as well as intoxication through the food chain (Kasemsri *et al.*, 1991).

With respect to biodegradable waste, the bulk of it is generated by sugar factories (29 per cent), pulp and paper industries (20 per cent) and the rubber industry (18 per cent). The rest emanates from the beverage industry, tapioca mills, slaughterhouses, canneries and tanneries. Current biochemical oxygen demand (BOD) from industrial sources is estimated at 0.5 million tons and is expected to reach two million tons by the year 2010 (Dhira and Panayotou, 1990). The projections are presented in Table 14.2. Most of this waste is discharged untreated in the form of effluent into public water bodies, where it combines with waste water from households to reduce the dissolved oxygen (DO) in rivers below acceptable standards in many of the canals and tributaries. The main rivers are currently at risk of becoming anaerobic in certain sections at certain times of the year. Biodegradable waste can cause ailments ranging from digestive disorders to neurological problems, and can be fatal to marine life.

Other pollutants in the form of air pollutants, gas emissions, noise levels, dust and particles have localized effects, but these can become quite serious. A high concentration of lead in the air, for example, can pose considerable health dangers. The latest figures obtained by the Ministry of Public Health (MOPH, 1992) show that at three monitoring stations the worst cases of lead concentration in the air were measured as being between 0.29 and 0.40 mg/cu.m, which is well above Thailand's standard of 0.10 mg/cu.m, and far exceeds the US standard of 0.05 mg/cu.m.

As for noise pollution, all 14 MOPH monitoring stations in Bangkok recorded decibel levels that exceeded the limit of 70 decibels in the course of 24 hours, ranging from 79.6–82.9 decibels (MOPH, 1992).

Table 14.1 Hazardous waste quantity, 1986

Industry	*Oils*	*Liquid organic*	*Organic sludge*	*Inorganic sludge*	*Heavy metal sludge*	*Solvent*	*Acid waste*	*Alkaline waste*	*Off spec. prod.*	*PCB*	*Aqueous organic residues*	*Photo waste*	*Total*
Basic metal industry	–	–	–	–	732 508	–	–	–	–	–	–	–	732 508
Fabricated products	1303	–	–	4116	55 854	760	56 272	14 563	–	–	–	–	132 868
Transport equipment	58 509	–	–	1078	3521	501	384	–	–	–	–	–	63 993
Electrical machinery	701	–	–	1491	20 096	591	20 407	5246	–	2458	–	–	50 990
Chemical products	15 455	187	2751	1003	10 034	3250	3266	1843	12	–	116	–	37 916
Machinery	25 150	–	–	132	–	4715	3	158	–	–	–	–	30 158
Textiles	17 362	–	–	–	–	–	–	–	–	–	–	–	17 362
Printing, publishing, allied	–	–	642	–	–	5405	–	–	–	–	–	8820	14 867
Rubber and rubber products	3923	–	–	–	–	4350	–	–	–	–	–	–	8273
Paper and paper products	1325	–	42	1370	–	–	–	–	–	–	–	–	2737
Petroleum products	454	–	302	509	508	205	–	–	–	–	–	–	1978
Miscellaneous nec.	12	–	–	393	549	7	719	142	–	–	–	–	1821
Furniture and fixtures	–	–	2	1092	–	–	–	–	–	–	–	–	1092
Wood and cork	–	–	–	515	–	–	–	–	–	–	–	–	515
Non–metallic minerals	–	–	–	–	–	–	–	–	–	–	–	–	–
Tobacco	–	–	–	–	–	–	–	–	–	–	–	–	–
Leather prod. and footwear	–	–	–	–	–	–	–	–	–	–	–	–	–
Beverages	–	–	–	–	–	–	–	–	–	–	–	–	–
Food	–	–	–	–	–	–	–	–	–	–	–	–	–
Clothing	–	–	–	–	–	–	–	–	–	–	–	–	–
	–	–	–	–	–	–	–	–	–	–	–	–	–
Total	124 194	187	3737	11 698	823 070	19 783	81 051	21 952	12	2458	116	8820	1097 078

Source: Engineering Science *et al.*, 1989.

Table 14.2 Projection of industrial biochemical oxygen demand (BOD), 1990–2010

Industry	*BOD load (thousand tons)*										
	1990	*1991*	*1992*	*1993*	*1994*	*1995*	*1996*	*1997*	*1998*	*1999*	*2000*
Sugar	140.7	153.7	168.2	183.3	199.2	215.6	232.4	249.5	266.7	284.2	302.2
Pulp and paper	93.2	102.7	113.3	124.6	136.5	149.0	162.0	175.4	189.1	203.2	217.9
Rubber[1]	89.7	96.5	104.4	112.5	120.8	129.2	137.5	145.7	153.8	161.6	169.6
Beverages[2]	84.0	91.3	99.0	106.7	114.7	122.8	130.9	139.0	147.0	155.0	163.0
Tapioca	36.7	40.2	44.2	48.3	52.6	57.1	61.8	66.5	71.3	76.2	81.3
Slaughterhouses[3]	14.9	15.5	16.1	16.7	17.3	17.8	18.2	18.6	18.9	19.2	19.4
Canned fish and crustaceans[4]	10.1	10.9	11.8	12.7	13.7	14.6	15.6	16.6	17.5	18.5	19.4
Tannery	9.6	10.6	12.0	13.8	15.8	18.2	20.9	23.9	27.3	31.1	35.4
Canned pineapple[5]	3.5	3.7	3.9	4.1	4.3	4.5	4.6	4.8	4.9	5.1	5.2
Total	482.5	525.2	573.0	622.7	674.8	728.8	784.0	840.0	896.6	954.0	1013.4
	2001	*2002*	*2003*	*2004*	*2005*	*2006*	*2007*	*2008*	*2009*	*2010*	
Sugar	321.1	341.1	362.4	385.2	409.9	436.4	465.2	496.2	529.7	565.8	
Pulp and paper	233.5	250.1	268.0	287.3	308.3	331.1	355.9	382.8	412.1	444.0	
Rubber[1]	177.7	186.1	195.0	204.4	214.5	225.2	236.7	248.9	262.0	276.0	
Beverages[2]	171.3	180.0	189.2	198.9	209.4	220.5	232.5	245.3	259.0	273.7	
Tapioca	86.7	92.3	98.4	104.9	112.0	119.6	127.9	136.8	146.5	157.0	
Slaughterhouses[3]	19.6	19.8	20.0	20.2	20.4	20.7	21.0	21.3	21.6	22.0	
Canned fish and crustaceans[4]	20.4	21.5	22.6	23.7	25.0	26.3	27.7	29.3	30.9	32.6	
Tannery	40.3	46.0	52.4	59.9	68.4	78.4	89.8	103.1	118.5	136.3	
Canned pineapple[5]	5.3	5.4	5.5	5.7	5.8	6.0	6.1	6.3	6.4	6.6	
Total	1075.8	1142.3	1213.5	1290.2	1373.7	1464.1	1562.8	1670.1	1786.8	1913.9	

Notes:
1. Rubber sheet processing only.
2. Beer, distillery and soft drink processing.
3. Beef and pork only.
4. Exported products only.
5. Exported products only.

Source: Dhira and Panayotou, 1990.

On the other hand recorded levels of nitrogen dioxide, sulphur dioxide, and carbon monoxide in the air were generally found not to exceed danger levels (MOPH, 1992). However recent sulphur-dioxide emissions from a lignite-fuelled electricity generating plant in the north became a major health hazard – causing sickness and damaging crops and livestock – and has been dubbed a 'mini-Chernobyl'. Lignite-fuelled power has increased from 9 per cent to 27 per cent between 1980 and 1992 and the possibility of leakages of toxic fumes has not been adequately attended to, or even admitted.

In terms of dust particles, the severest incidence (1137 mg/cu.m) was found to be in Saraburi province (north of Bangkok), with the eastern province of Chon Buri experiencing the greatest exposure to lead (0.15–0.20 mg./cu.m on average).

The kind of industrialization that seeks to upgrade agriculture through agro-industries also leads to dangers from productivity-augmenting chemicals. A survey by the Agriculture Toxicology Division in 1982–5 found that out of 606 rice and cereal specimens on the market, 90 per cent contained organochlorins – chemicals that cannot be broken down or digested. Large build-ups in the human body can cause cancer. Statistics from the Ministry of Agriculture also link illnesses and even death among farmers to heavy use of chemical pesticides and herbicides.

Further, with structural changes in industry and changes in production materials, there is an increasing shift away from traditional pollutants, such as waste-water pollution in the form of BOD, to more complex toxic forms including heavy metals, toxic air and water pollutants, and hazardous wastes. The share of factories generating hazardous waste increased from 29 per cent in 1979 to 60 per cent in 1990, and the trend is expected to continue. Tables 14.3 and 14.4 show that major generators of hazardous waste are in fact among the fastest-growing industries, so that their share is inevitably increasing.

What is important for policy is that waste treatment is possible, based on the principle that the polluter should pay. It is estimated that treatment of all treatable hazardous waste from all industries except the basic metal industry would cost about 600 million baht annually, or 0.3 per cent of the GDP produced by these industries (Table 14.5). Seventy per cent treatment of the current level of BOD would cost about 1 per cent of the GDP generated by the BOD-generating industries (Table 14.6). These are all affordable costs requiring only the necessary machinery to be put in place. Industrial estates also have a potential for pollution control. Currently, while all 23 estates have

Table 14.3 Manufacturing industry: GDP share and growth, 1960–89

Industry group	*1960–5*		*1970–4*		*1975–9*		*1980–4*		*1985–9*	
	Share	*Growth*	*Share*	*Growth*	*Share*	*Growth*	*Share*	*Growth*	*Share*	*Growth*
Food	34.5	25.7	15.3	8.2	15.6	10.0	15.4	8.8	14.9	9.0
Beverages	10.6	10.6	9.4	8.0	10.2	17.4	10.3	9.3	9.5	9.6
Tobacco	13.0	12.1	7.7	7.0	6.4	4.6	5.6	−1.3	4.2	6.7
Textiles*	5.2	10.6	11.5	18.5	13.6	12.4	14.0	4.4	14.1	12.7
Clothing	8.0	5.5	9.2	11.5	8.7	7.2	9.3	7.1	10.9	15.8
Leather products and footwear	0.7	0.6	2.1	4.6	1.9	0.8	2.2	11.9	2.8	19.3
Wood and cork	4.8	5.2	3.6	6.9	2.9	3.2	1.7	−1.4	1.2	−1.4
Furniture and fixtures	1.2	1.4	1.6	0.7	1.3	7.6	1.2	4.4	1.2	14.1
Paper and paper products	0.2	0.4	1.4	10.9	1.3	24.8	1.7	3.1	1.6	11.0
Printing and publishing*	3.2	2.6	1.4	10.8	1.5	10.8	1.7	8.6	1.5	3.2
Chemical products*	6.8	5.8	3.6	8.7	3.6	13.6	4.2	7.3	4.4	9.7
Petroleum products	0.0	4.5	7.5	17.5	6.7	4.9	5.1	2.8	4.3	7.3
Rubber and plastic products*	0.6	0.7	2.6	11.2	2.7	11.4	2.5	1.6	2.6	15.4
Non-metal products	2.9	4.0	4.0	10.5	3.7	9.3	3.8	9.0	4.1	15.1
Basic metal industries*	0.4	0.5	2.3	1.4	1.7	13.4	1.4	−4.7	1.4	4.3
Fabricated products*	0.4	0.7	2.7	3.5	2.0	6.4	1.8	5.3	1.9	13.8
Machinery*	0.6	1.3	2.8	7.6	1.9	10.2	4.2	12.5	3.7	14.7
Electrical machinery*	0.6	0.8	1.8	8.9	2.4	18.7	3.0	9.0	3.3	18.4
Transport equipment *	5.4	5.9	7.2	19.7	7.9	16.3	6.5	−1.3	5.7	26.8
Miscellaneous	0.9	1.1	2.3	25.0	2.9	15.1	4.6	11.3	6.6	22.3
Average		5.0		10.1		10.9		5.4		12.4

Notes: Growth rates are computed as follows: growth rate = 1/t*ln(Yn/Yo)*100.
* = Top generator of hazardous waste

Source: National Economic and Social Development Board (new series).

Table 14.4 Major industries registered with the Department of Industrial Works

Major industry group	*End 1969*	*End 1979*	*End 1989*
Food[1]	112	4200	10099
Beverages	3	60	232
Tobacco[2]	0	146	108
Textiles[3]	30	764	1793
Wearing apparel	4	226	1989
Leather products and footwear	5	97	771
Wood and cork	59	1713	3353
Furniture and fixtures	11	405	1586
Paper and paper products	7	162	537
Printing, publishing and allied[3]	21	817	1674
Chemical products[3]	38	632	1061
Petroleum products	2	21	32
Rubber and rubber products[3]	35	1089	2643
Non-metallic mineral products	20	635	2798
Basic metal industries[3]	6	347	530
Fabricated products[3]	98	2859	6107
Machinery[3]	69	2422	6141
Electrical machinery[3]	9	409	1121
Transport equipment[3]	30	1028	6553
Miscellaneous nec.	72	1659	2370
Total	631	19691	51500

Notes:
1. These figures are an analysis of data from the Department of Industrial Works.
2. Tobacco factories at that time registered under the Department of Excise, Ministry of Finance.
3. Top generators of hazardous waste.
Source: Dhira and Panayotou, 1990.

waste-water-treatment facilities, not one operates facilities to treat hazardous waste.

As for the use of chemicals in agriculture to feed agro-industries, organic production or 'alternative agriculture' has been proposed. If consumer knowledge about the relative merits of organic and chemical production becomes more widespread, the health benefits and dangers would be reflected in market prices, so that environmentally friendly and health-friendly products could also become profitable to produce. Government intervention here could take the form of information

Table 14.5 Cost of treatment at 70 per cent level (million baht)

Industry	*1991*	*1996*	*2001*	*2006*	*2010*
Sugar	107.6	162.7	224.8	305.5	396.1
Pulp and paper	71.9	113.4	163.4	231.7	310.8
Rubber	67.6	96.3	124.4	157.6	193.2
Beverages	63.9	91.7	119.9	154.3	191.6
Tapioca	28.2	43.2	60.7	83.7	109.9
Slaughterhouses	10.8	12.7	13.7	14.5	15.4
Canned fish and crustaceans	7.6	10.9	14.3	18.4	22.8
Tannery	7.4	14.6	28.2	54.8	95.4
Canned pineapple	2.6	3.2	3.7	4.2	4.6
Total	367.7	548.8	753.1	1024.8	1339.7

Source: see text.

Table 14.6 Cost of treatment per industrial GDP (per cent)

Industry	*1991*	*1996*	*2001*	*2006*	*2010*
Sugar	3.33	3.35	3.37	3.39	3.40
Pulp and paper	2.82	2.82	2.82	2.82	2.82
Rubber	1.42	1.23	1.06	0.91	0.81
Beverages	0.44	0.44	0.44	0.44	0.44
Tapioca	5.29	5.29	5.29	5.29	5.29
Slaughterhouses	0.60	0.60	0.60	0.60	0.60
Canned fish and crustaceans	0.12	0.12	0.12	0.12	0.12
Tannery	0.57	0.57	0.57	0.57	0.57
Canned pineapple	0.17	0.17	0.17	0.17	0.17
Average	1.05	1.05	1.04	1.03	1.02

Note: Assuming that a waste stabilization pond system is employed with a cost of 1000 baht/ton BOD.
Sources: Table 14.5 and industrial GDP from NESDB (new series).

dissemination, product grading, testing and certification, as well as fiscal incentives.

14.2.2 Occupational Health Hazards

Industrial development has brought into use several newly synthesized chemicals and industrial processes. Workers are thus subject to ever-increasing exposure to toxic chemicals and unfamiliar production routines. In addition, working conditions may be poor and workers may be forced to endure dust and particles, poor ventilation, inadequate lighting and squalid living conditions at factory sites.

An increasing proportion of poisoning incidences is found to be occupation-related, and the incidence of industrial accidents and injury, though underreported, has shown a marked upward trend. Table 14.7 shows that reported cases of industrial injury increased in total by almost three times between 1981 and 1990, with the largest percentage increases in the chemicals-related industries and in textiles, wood and wood products, where the number of injuries have more than doubled. Table 14.8 also shows a substantial increase in the incidence of occupational health problems – from two to nine per 100 000 people between 1978 and 1987.

One of the most important occupational ailments is lead poisoning. It causes neuro-physiological diseases whose incidence may soon reach alarming proportions. Even data from several years ago showed that the lead-in-blood level had reached as high as 48 mg/100 ml among some workers in battery plants, which was much higher than the International Labour Organisation standard of 25–30 mg/100 ml. A later study by the Ministry of Public Health (MOPH, 1987) showed that more than 14 per cent of cases of occupational exposure to lead recorded lead-in-blood levels exceeding 60 mg/100 ml, with 0.5 per cent of the sample reaching the critical risk level of more than 100 mg/100 ml. As for concentration of lead in urine samples, a staggering 20 per cent of the sampled workers in lead-associated plants registered above-normal concentration levels.

This points to the need for greater selectiveness in industrial promotion and a more developed information and institutional infrastructure to manage the undesirable effects of an expanding industrial sector with its health effects and ecologically disruptive by-products. In practice this would mean taxing the polluters in proportion to their waste generation, and expanding the health-insurance aspect of the Social Security Fund through increased premiums and increased compensation in high-risk industries.

14.2.3 Service-Industry Health Problems

The most important health problem relating to the service sector and the tourism industry in particular is the AIDS nightmare. The link between AIDS and industrialization has not been clearly investigated,

Table 14.7 Occupational injuries in whole kingdom by industry, 1981–90.

Industry	*1981*	*1982*	*1983*	*1984*	*1985*	*1986*	*1987**	*1988*	*1989*	*1990*
Agriculture	85	49	67	25	106	29	24	155	–	5
Mining	399	532	565	594	623	605	15	438	489	678
Manufacturing	21 642	22 370	27 124	31 200	31 099	30 045	10 450	40 418	51 700	62 145
Manufacture of food, beverages and tobacco	–	–	6174	7596	7303	6428	1140	8394	10 001	10 415
Textiles, clothing	–	–	3435	4150	4291	4197	1313	5345	6604	8302
Wood and wood products including furniture	–	–	2203	2857	3026	3535	1655	4932	5602	5814
Paper and paper products, printing and publishing	–	–	791	700	816	767	297	953	999	1266
Chemicals, petroleum, coal, rubber and plastic products	–	–	2091	2376	2688	2544	1073	3455	4752	6189
Non-metallic mineral product except petroleum and coal	–	–	2245	2372	2015	1960	395	2003	2276	3183
Basic metal industries	–	–	1997	2336	2181	2322	530	2730	3244	3318
Fabricated metal products, machinery and equipment	–	–	8105	8691	8693	8124	3946	12 377	17 710	15 334
Other manufacturing industries	–	–	83	122	86	168	101	229	512	8324
Electricity, gas and water	401	408	729	982	591	367	325	361	547	635
Construction	3008	3560	2948	4086	3881	2889	1820	3451	4925	8403
Wholesale and retail trade, restaurants and hotels	1210	1408	1716	1946	1958	2297	1510	2561	3205	3868
Transport, storage and communication	1051	991	968	1230	1208	1083	757	1212	1408	1679
Services	686	671	811	1024	955	1095	724	1278	1583	2374
Total	28 482	29 989	34 928	41 087	40 421	38410	15 625	49 874	63 857	79 787

* Incomplete information due to reclassification into occupational injuries under Workmen's Compensation Law in whole kingdom and in Bangkok by industry, and unavailability of some data.

Source: Labour Studies and Planning Division, Department of Labour.

Table 14.8 Incidence of occupational diseases, 1978–87 (per 100 000 population)

Type	*1978*	*1979*	*1980*	*1981*	*1982*	*1983*	*1984*	*1985*	*1986*	*1987*
Insecticide poisoning	1.970	4.040	3.980	4.550	4.510	4.76	6.37	5.03	5.90	8.64
Lead poisoning	0.013	0.020	0.020	0.040	0.020	0.03	0.07	0.03	0.10	0.10
Manganese, mercury and arsenic poisoning	0.009	0.002	0.020	0.008	0.006	0.02	0.02	0.02	0.02	0.04
Petroleum products poisoning	–	–	0.004	–	–	–	0.03	0.01	0.01	0.02
Gas, vapour poisoning	0.005	0.020	0.013	–	0.010	0.02	0.04	0.09	0.05	0.06
Caisson's disease	–	0.070	0.070	0.070	0.030	0.01	0.008	0.02	0.02	0.01
Silicosis	0.002	0.013	–	–	–	–	–	–	–	–
Total	2.00	4.14	4.11	4.66	4.58	4.84	6.55	5.21	6.10	8.88

Source: Ministry of Public Health, 1990.

but it is certainly believed that the spread of this disease in Thailand started with the tourist industry.

AIDS may be but one of the many diseases with potentially significant economic effects, but its impact is likely to be greater than that of other (more prevalent) diseases. The ultimate outcome of the HIV virus (or full-blown AIDS) is certain death, given existing medical knowledge. The incubation period ranges from one to twenty years, so that fatality and the duration of illness combine to raise the impact per case relative to other causes of morbidity. The impact of existing levels of infection will be felt far into the future even if all infection ceased today. Studies in Africa show that the benefits of averting one case of HIV in terms of discounted healthy life years ranks second only to neonatal tetanus (Ainsworth and Over, 1992). AIDS may also have a greater economic impact than other diseases because it primarily affects adults in their economically most productive years. Weighting the benefits of averting a case by the productivity of years lost would result in AIDS being ranked highest among all the diseases in terms of the value of preventing a case (Over and Piot, 1992).

A conservative estimate is that by the year 2000 at least two million Thais will be infected with HIV if the annual rate of increase can be slowed by 1994. However if slowing down does not occur until 1996, about 3.4 million Thais can be expected to be infected by the year 2000 (Population and Community Development Association, 1990). The cost in terms of lost productivity is estimated at US$5 billion by the year 2000 if infection peaks in 1992 and US$8 billion if the peak occurs in 1994. Additional costs take the form of health-care costs and macroeconomic impacts such as a decline in tourism, reduced income from labour exports, a decline in foreign investment and so on. The looming threat of an AIDS epidemic requires concerted efforts in information dissemination and direct preventive methods. If unsuccessful, the momentum towards 'fifth-tiger' status will certainly be checked.

14.3 INDUSTRIALIZATION AND EDUCATION

The link between industrialization and education in Thailand seems to be a rather unusual one. Industrialization and higher incomes have made expansion of education possible, and indeed enrolments at all levels have increased manifold during the course of industrial development. The occupational distribution of the labour force has undergone significant change, and this distribution, broken down by educational attainment, clearly attests to the correlation between pay, status and education. The educated, on average, have better jobs, and the share of this group has increased over time. In fact studies invariably show that education is the single most important determinant of income and social mobility.

However the general observation that education augments income and that average educational attainment has increased in the general population does not mean that all segments of the population have benefited from educational expansion. In spite of three decades of rapid expansion of education, the quality of education remains a key concern and improper targeting of beneficiaries has led to problems of regional disparity, inequality of access and inefficiency of resource use. Out of the total number of children and youths not attending school, more than 60 per cent live in rural areas (NSO, 1987), reflecting selective migration in response to the urban bias in school location, and the conditions of production in the rural and urban areas.

The notion that expanded education is both a cause and consequence of economic development only has weak support from the evidence for Thailand. The industrial policy that initially pursued import substitution in earnest had little direct effect on upgrading the skills and capabilities of the general workforce due to the inherent bias in favour of utilizing imported capital. The reversal of policy in the 1970s towards export promotion, on the other hand, hinged upon the ability to utilize the vast supply of low-cost labour, largely with low education.

Thailand's high growth is all the more amazing when international comparisons of enrolment ratios, educational attainments and sectoral employment are made. More than 60 per cent of the labour force is still in the agricultural sector as opposed to 40 per cent in the Philippines or 55 per cent for the Republic of Korea as early as 1965. Almost half of the children who complete primary school do not go on to receive secondary education. In 1990, 83 per cent of Thai workers had completed only primary school or less, compared with 49 per cent and 44 per cent for the Republic of Korea and Taiwan, respectively, even ten years earlier (Table 14.9). The secondary-enrolment ratio is the lowest of all the ASEAN countries, and well below that of the Republic of Korea a decade ago (Table 14.10). Educational inequities abound, with huge regional disparities and differential access based on socioeconomic status. And income distribution has deteriorated. Thus Thailand's statistics can either inspire awe or induce nervous tension.

14.3.1 Industrialization and Low Secondary Enrolment

The first decade of industrialization (1960–70) saw enrolments doubling at the lower-secondary level and tripling at the upper-secondary level, with secondary enrolment as a whole growing at an annual rate of 12 per cent. However secondary gross enrolment ratios have remained low. It was estimated that the enrolment ratios for lower and upper secondary in 1986 were 41 per cent of those aged 14–16 and 28 per cent of those aged 17–18 (NEC, 1986). This implies that more than half of the Thai children in the age group 14-18 were not attending

Table 14.9 Shares of workforce with primary education or less: selected countries

	Percent of work force
Thailand (1990)	83.0
Republic of Korea (1980)	49.1
Taiwan (1980)	44.0
Singapore (1980)	62.7
China (1982)	71.3
Malaysia (1980)	58.4
Philippines (1980)	56.5

Sources: For Thailand, unpublished data; for other countries, Psacharapoulos and Arriagada, 1986, cited in Pernia, 1990.

Table 14.10 Gross enrolment ratios for selected Asian countries, 1988

	Primary	*Secondary*	*Tertiary*
Thailand (1990)	95	29	10
Republic of Korea	104	87	37
Singapore	111	69	12
Hong Kong	106	74	13
Indonesia	119	48	7
Malaysia	102	57	7
Philippines	110	71	28

Note: Data for Indonesia, Singapore and Hong Kong for the tertiary level is for 1985.
Sources: For Thailand, unpublished data; for other countries, World Bank, *World Development Report*, 1991.

school. Statistics on continuation rates by cohort show that, while the percentage of students moving on to the next grade is high (85–98 per cent) in the primary grades, the percentage of those continuing on to secondary school after completion of the final primary grade drops dramatically to around 40–50 per cent. In 1990 this rate was 39 per cent for government schools and 60 per cent for private schools.

Low secondary enrolments are partly due to expansion of primary enrolment; transition rates tend to increase at lower levels first as schooling becomes more universal. But a more important factor is the low continuation rates among children from socially and economically disadvantaged backgrounds. About 88 per cent of youths aged 12–14 are still in school in urban areas, whereas the corresponding figure for rural youths in the same age group is a mere 68 per cent (NSO, 1987). This pattern has remained unchanged throughout the years.

The low secondary enrolment and the high share of the labour force with primary education may be the key constraints to achieving sustained growth and better income distribution in the future. With the economy's dependence on manufactured exports and the need to remain competitive in the world market, there is an additional need to equip the workforce with appropriate skills and capability in science and technology (S&T). The ability of the labour force to adapt to rapidly changing skill requirements becomes more and more crucial as technologically sophisticated sectors play a more and more prominent role. The low continuation rates into secondary school will be a major hindrance in the production of a skilled and adaptable labour force, not to mention the creation of scientific, engineering and technical manpower to enhance Thailand's technological capability.

Low secondary enrolment can be attributed to factors on both the demand and supply side, as well as their interaction. On the demand side several studies have shown that socioeconomic status appreciably affects the probability of continuation to a higher level of education. Tan and Wannasiri (1980) found from their analysis of the Children and Youth Surveys of 1975 and 1976, that for the lowest SES group the probability of continuing on to secondary school was found to be only 14 per cent, while the corresponding probability for the highest SES group was as high as 97 per cent. Supang (1979) also reports that the opportunity to move on to secondary level among the children of farmers and labourers was much lower than for the children of businessmen and government officials. Analysis of the 1981 Socioeconomic Survey (Chalongphob *et al.*, 1988) further confirms that parents' education, household income and wealth are important determinants of continuation to secondary school.

In addition the expected returns to additional schooling depend on the student's eventual occupation. If the prospect of being employed in the formal sector is believed to be low, many children of poor rural families choose not to attend secondary schools because of the high cost and low perceived returns. Members of farm households and labourer households have lower expected returns from schooling and consequently drop out at a younger age.

Various studies also show that a large number of siblings also depresses the chances of a child continuing on to secondary school (for example, Chalongphob *et al.*, 1988). This finding brings out the link between fertility and the demand for education that has been found in other countries. In addition, even when remaining in school is an option and educational opportunities are available, children from poor, large families do not perform as well as other children. High birth-order has been found to have an independent negative effect on school performance and possibly the ability to learn, which further reduces the chance of continuation (Sirilaksana, 1986).

On the supply side, geographically unequal distribution is one of the main causes of non-continuation among disadvantaged groups. Some regions have virtually no upper-level schools or persons educated beyond primary level. Except for the primary schools run by provincial authorities, which are evenly located in the rural areas, a disproportionate number of schools are situated in towns and cities. And of these urban schools a disproportionate number are located in Bangkok. Out of the 2923 private secondary schools in the country, almost half (that is, 1046) are located in Bangkok, and none in the villages (MOE, 1989). For municipal schools, 427 out of a total of 894 schools are situated in Bangkok, with enrolment of 233 321 as opposed to an almost equal number – that is, 238 620 – for the rest of the country. Distance from school means longer travelling times and higher money costs, as well as forgone contributions to family production. For some, such costs can be prohibitive.

Part of the low secondary enrolment also stems from quality variations among primary schools. 'Input' measures such as the availability of textbooks, instructional materials and laboratory equipment, as well as teachers' qualifications show that large differences in quality exist between schools. High continuation rates have been attributed to such variables as the high ratio of teachers holding higher teaching certificates or above, a large educational budget (staff salaries) and low land rents in the provinces (Supang, 1979). Sukanya (1988), using different sources of data, also reports a positive relationship between provincial education budgets and the provincial rate of continuation to secondary level. Low perceived quality no doubt interacts with the expected return on continued education and the added cost of sending children to better schools elsewhere. Chalongphob *et al.* (1988) also find that the lower the student/teacher ratio at the primary and secondary levels in the community, the more likely are the children to continue.

The problem of access to secondary education (and above) is compounded by the financing problem. The education system limits access to all but favoured segments of the population and may, through public financing, tax some groups of the population more heavily to subsidize the education of others. The direct cost of many kinds of public education in Thailand is almost entirely borne by the government. Fees charged, as a percentage of costs, vary from level to level and within levels: ranging from 1.6–21.8 per cent for secondary schools, from 3.3–36.6 per cent in vocational education, from 28.1–41.7 per cent in teacher training and from 7–12 per cent in public, closed-access universities. Consequently all calculations of the rate of return on investment in education have invariably shown private rates of return exceeding social rates at all levels. Tuition fees at the tertiary level on average amount to only 2.5 per cent of the annual family income of the university students.

At the secondary level, the low fees in (heavily subsidized) public schools and the fee controls imposed on private schools prevent school expansion, quality improvements and quality-enhancing competition. The highest fees charged by public schools are usually less than 20 per cent of the maximum fees allowable at the corresponding levels in private schools. Such controls limit the ability of the private sector to expand. The share of private enrolment at most levels below higher education has declined, especially at lower-secondary level and the academic stream of upper-secondary level (Table 14.11). Studies comparing public and private schools show that private schools are more cost effective, but no less effective and no more inequitable than public schools (Jimenez *et al.*, 1988). Expansion of private schools in urban areas would therefore not produce inefficiencies or inequity if it allows more public resources to be devoted to promoting and subsiding secondary enrolment and improving quality in rural areas.

The government is currently conducting pilot projects that offer lower-secondary education in some of the rural primary schools that have excess classroom and teacher capacity, charging no fees or tuition, and issuing free uniforms and textbooks. Experiments with new curricula based on the concept that education should be student-centred rather than teacher-centred, have also begun in the hope of enhancing quality. But the success of this approach hinges on high teacher quality and motivation, and strong teacher-student and school-community relations.

14.3.2 Industrialization and S&T Requirements

Technical human-resource development is seen as a key factor underlying the economic success of the newly industrialized economies of East Asia. All the NICs, except possibly Hong Kong, started massive technical-education programmes in the early 1970s. Technically sophisticated sectors are playing an increasingly important role, and the need to master technology is critical if Thailand is to remain competitive in a world where protectionist sentiment, however veiled, is on the increase. S&T manpower is important for the productivity and competitiveness of services and agriculture, and is vital for Thailand's export industries, which will face increasing competition from developed countries using automated techniques to regain competitiveness in labour-intensive products, and from developing countries with lower labour costs. The ability to compete depends on the availability of (1) a skilled and adaptable workforce and (2) scientific and technological manpower capable of linking Thailand to international technology and generating modifications to suit local conditions.

Table 14.11 Percentage of public and private-school students in Bangkok metropolitan area and other provinces

	1978						*1988*					
	Total		*BMA*		*Other provinces*		*Total*		*BMA*		*Other provinces*	
Level of education	*Public*	*Private*	*Public*	*Private*	*Public*	*Private*	*Public*	*Private*	*Public*	*Private*	*Public*	*Private*
Pre-primary education	40	60	4	96	51	49	76	24	14	86	82	18
Primary education	91	9	48	52	94	6	91	9	52	48	94	6
Lower-secondary education	78	22	66	34	80	20	88	12	78	22	91	9
Academic	77	23	66	34	80	20	88	12	78	22	91	9
Vocational	100	0	100	0	100	0	100	0	100	0	100	0
Upper-secondary education	64	36	48	52	72	28	78	22	55	45	86	14
Academic	77	23	82	18	76	24	92	8	86	14	94	6
Vocational	51	49	28	72	67	33	57	43	28	72	71	29
Higher education	81	19	76	24	93	7	64	36	60	40	72	28
Vocational	87	13	78	22	100	0	64	36	54	46	71	29
Undergraduate and higher	78	22	75	25	85	15	65	35	63	37	73	27

Source: Educational Planning Division, Office of the Permanent Secretary, Ministry of Education.

However, while there is general consensus on the need to develop human resources for technological development, the *kind* of human capital development advocated seems to fall into two extreme, alternative directions. Those concerned with competitiveness and productivity increases in line with modern industrialized economies consider that absorption and adaptation of 'mainstream' technology is crucial to sustained growth. Those concerned with human development, on the other hand, view sustainability as conditional upon social coherence and avoidance of further environmental degradation. Perhaps as technologies become more and more science and knowledge-based and less craft-based, an attempt can be made to honour the principles inherent in both views. The generation and creation of technology, and the ability to incorporate traditional technology into modern processes, calls for high levels of scientific and technological education and specialization, and for special skills in managing creative human resources and institutions.

Some form of S&T development can be seen as crucial for increasing the productivity and competitiveness of services, agriculture, and manufacturing alike. Thus the problem lies in three main areas: (1) inadequate local supplies of appropriate S&T manpower by educational institutions, (2) inadequate research and development (R&D) activity for industrial use, and (3) inadequate upgrading of skills through training and continuing education.

Inadequate local supply of S&T manpower

All projections of supply and demand, for example that by the Human Resources Institute and the Ministry of Science, Technology and Energy (HRI/MOSTE, 1986), point to the imbalance between demand and supply. Analyses of Thailand's development pattern indicate a persistent underinvestment in human-capital development. A common complaint is that there are insufficient linkages and information flows between the predominantly private-sector users and the predominantly public-sector producers of S&T manpower, both quantitatively and qualitatively. Consequently there are serious manpower shortages, especially in the areas of skilled technicians and engineers.

It can be seen from Table 14.12 that although the overall distribution of S&T manpower by degree level has been fairly stable, usage by the private sector has increased. Although the data are not strictly comparable due to some differences in definitions, the trend towards greater employment of S&T manpower in private industry is clear. Use of

Table 14.12 S&T manpower by employer status and degree level

	Bachelor		*Master*		*Doctorate*		*Total*	
	No. of Persons	*%*	*No. of Persons*	*%*	*No. of Persons*	*%*	*No. of Persons*	*%*
1979 (NRC):								
Government	10 025	47.6	1796	28.9	173	18.8	11 994	42.5
Education	5446	25.8	3875	62.3	693	75.4	10 014	35.5
State enterprises	4084	19.4	355	5.7	32	3.5	4471	15.8
Private enterprises	1519	7.2	194	3.1	21	2.3	1734	6.1
Total	21 074	100.0	6220	100.0	919	100.0	28 213	99.9
	(74.7%)		(22.0%)		(3.3%)		(100%)	
1986 (HRI/MOSTE):								
Public sector	33 137	74.1	9726	91.2	1687	91.5	44 550	55.8
Private sector	11 577	25.9	934	8.8	156	8.5	12 667	44.2
Total	44 714	100.0	10 660	100.0	1843	100.0	57 217	100.0
	(78.2%)		(18.6%)		(3.2%)		(100%)	

Sources: National Research Council (NRC), 1979 and HRI/MOSTE, 1986.

44 per cent of the S&T manpower by the private sector in 1986 as opposed to 6 per cent in 1979, points to increasing sophistication in private industry. Moreover if employee qualifications are broken down by field of study, employment of engineers dominate in the private sector, especially below Bachelor level (Table 14.13). The fastest growing industries (see Table 14.3 above), such as textiles, machinery, transport equipment and so on, tend to be large users of S&T manpower, as shown by the coefficients in Table 14.14.

The greater demand by private industry for S&T manpower and concern about imbalances have been expressed since the early 1980s. MOSTE (1981) indicated a shortage of about 3500 graduate engineers, but an oversupply of technicians and craftsmen (36 082 persons in engineering and 13 358 in agriculture).

A rough international comparison of S&T manpower in Table 14.15 shows that the number of scientists and engineers per 10 000 population for Thailand is among the lowest among middle-income Asian countries. And when S&T manpower is broken down by field, a KMIT study (1984) shows the lowest proportions of S&T manpower in total employment even in comparison with economies such as Taiwan a decade earlier. A comparison between the S&T manpower structure of Thailand in 1984 and the Republic of Korea in 1981 (Table 14.16) shows that, while the number of scientists and engineers in Korea was almost double that of Thailand, the number of Korean technicians was larger by more than 700 per cent. Per 10 000 people the number for Thailand was only 69 compared with 584 for Korea. In fact, since 1962 when the education system in Korea was not responding fast enough to the demands created by rapidly changing productive structures, the Korean government promptly instituted various legal, financial and administrative steps to address the problem, ranging from laws to promote S&T manpower development and improve the status of subprofessional manpower, to the establishment of research institutes, vocational institutes, mission-oriented graduate schools to serve the needs of industry, and fiscal incentives for in-house training programmes. The concept of 'relevance' was stressed rather than academic excellence, to ensure linkage with the industrialization process. Kim (1987) however argues that insufficient effort to improve the functioning of the labour market limited the effectiveness of these programmes.

In Thailand there are currently acute shortages in some fields, such as metallurgy and material sciences, electronics and information technology (Yongyuth *et al.*, 1985), and a serious lack of experts (Harit, 1987). However there are excess supplies of some types of technicians due to mismatches, the high expectations of job seekers, imperfect labour markets and inadequate on-the-job training to compensate for the inability of educational institutions to supply S&T manpower in sufficient quantities and skills.

In the educational institutions, there is also a higher proportion of students in non-S&T fields, as compared with the Republic of Korea, pointing to the need to allow market factors to play a greater role in setting tuition fees, incentives and patterns of remuneration.

Though few would support economic planning as a method of resource allocation, education is an area where market failures abound due to the presence of externalities and the long gestation period that would be required for market adjustment.

Both producers and users of S&T manpower in Thailand were found to have a myopic view on education and training. The TDRI survey observed that feedback responses (such as short-term signals in the form of wage rates and unemployment rates, applications and completion rates) were the most common. 'Feed-forward' medium-term consideration and incorporation of macroeconomic forecasts and investment trends into planned allocation of resources for S&T manpower development was hardly observed, and 'foresight', or the long-term vision of 'what technologies the future will hold and what S&T manpower resources will best position the economy to react most

Table 14.13 S&T manpower by employer status, field of study and degree level

	Agriculture	%	*Science*	%	*Engineering*	%	*Total*	%
Below bachelor	17003	100.0	6181	100.0	73991	100.0	97175	100.0
	(17.5%)		(6.4%)		(76.1%)			
Public	14403	84.7	2212	35.8	25055	33.9	41670	42.9
	(34.6%)		(5.3%)		(60.1%)		(100%)	
Private	2600	15.3	3969	64.2	48936	66.1	55505	57.1
	(4.7%)		(7.2%)		(88.2%)		(100%)	
Bachelor degree	16217	100.0	9144	100.0	19353	100.0	44714	100.0
	(36.3%)		(20.4%)		(43.3%)		(100%)	
Public	15187	93.6	5948	65.0	12002	62.0	33137	74.1
	(45.8%)		(17.9%)		(36.2%)		(100%)	
Private	1030	6.4	3196	35.0	7351	38.0	11577	25.9
	(8.9%)		(27.6%)		(63.5%)		(100%)	
Master degree	3945	100.0	3570	100.0	3145	100.0	10660	100.0
	(37.0%)		(33.5%)		(29.5%)		(100%)	
Public	3922	99.4	3381	94.7	2423	77.0	9726	91.2
	(40.3%)		(34.8%)		(24.9%)		(100%)	
Private	23	0.6	189	5.3	722	23.0	934	8.8
	(2.5%)		(20.2%)		(77.3%)		(100%)	
Doctoral degree	653	100.0	735	100.0	455	100.0	1843	100.0
	(35.4%)		(39.9%)		(24.7%)		(100%)	
Public	651	99.7	730	99.3	306	67.3	1687	91.5
	(38.6%)		(43.3%)		(18.1%)		(100%)	
Private	2	0.3	5	0.7	149	32.7	156	8.5
	(1.3%)		(3.2%)		(95.5%)		(100%)	

Total	37 818 (24.5%)	100.0	19 630 (12.7%)	100.0	96 944 (62.8%)	100.0	154 392 (100%)	100.0
Public	34 163 (39.6%)	90.3	12 271 (14.2%)	62.5	39 786 (46.1%)	41.0	86 220 (100%)	55.8
Private	3655 (5.4%)	9.7	7359 (10.8%)	37.5	57 158 (83.8%)	59.0	68 172 (100%)	44.2

Note: Percentages in parentheses show the distribution across three fields of study of employers with different levels of education.
Source: HRI/MOSTE, 1986.

Table 14.14 S&T coefficient and total S&T manpower by type of industry and employer status

	Government and state enterprises		*Private sector*		*Total*	
Type of industry	*Coefficient*	*No.*	*Coefficient*	*No.*	*Coefficient*	*No.*
Agriculture	27.52	6797	0.79	282	1.72	7079
Mining	–	–	1.68	2512	1.68	2512
Manufacturing	15.73	6743	4.75	48 666	5.19	55 409
Food	12.12	311	3.03	5927	3.15	6238
Beverage	5.13	589	1.06	1849	1.31	2438
Tobacco and snuff	32.95	5574	0.58	267	9.28	5841
Textiles	0.22	16	2.23	2926	2.12	2942
Wearing apparel (excluding footwear)	–	–	1.78	271	1.78	271
Leather and leather products	–	–	2.14	276	2.14	276
Wood and cork	–	–	12.62	3339	12.62	3339
Furniture and fixtures	–	–	8.74	4234	8.74	4234
Paper and paper products	–	–	5.31	176	5.31	176
Printing and publishing	–	–	8.71	153	8.71	153
Chemicals and chemical products	1.81	29	7.28	5010	7.16	5039
Petroleum refining	–	–	4.43	176	4.43	176
Rubber and rubber products	–	–	3.94	946	3.94	946
Non-metallic mineral products	–	–	3.67	1838	3.67	1838
Basic metal industries	–	–	14.94	8467	14.94	8467
Metal products	7.04	224	0.36	30	2.21	254

Machinery	–	–	16.97	4549	16.97	4549
Electrical machinery and supplies	–	–	2.72	1455	2.72	1455
Transport equipment	–	–	9.48	6733	9.48	6733
Other industries	–	–	0.89	44	0.89	44
Construction	4.12	253	17.03	9265	15.72	9518
Electricity, gas and water supply	15.47	10 033	11.17	64	15.43	10 097
Wholesale and retail trade	7.36	525	4.48	1437	5.00	1962
Transportation and communications	1.27	2181	5.80	405	1.45	2586
Services	14.38	46 383	7.60	5122	13.21	51 505
Banking and insurance	23.64	10 720	1.29	840	10.47	11 560
Total	9.99	83635	4.81	68 593	6.73	152 228

Note: S&T coefficient equals the ratio of S&T employees to total employment, which amounted to about 2.2 million persons.
Source: HRI/MOSTE, 1986.

Table 14.15 Relative position of technological personnel in selected countries

		Total scientists and engineers		*Scientists and engineers engaged in research and development*	
Country	*Year*	*Per 10 000 population*	*Per 10 000 labour force*	*Per 10 000 population*	*Per 10 000 labour force*
Bangladesh	1979	8.5	15.2	0.2	0.4
China	1979	48.5	85.4	20.6	36.2
India	1979	11.6	21.0	0.4	0.6
Indonesia	1976	7.3	13.8	0.6	1.1
Japan	1979	49.6	77.6	29.4	46.0
Korea	1978	24.4	40.5	5.3	7.1
Malaysia	1978	17.5	28.0	0.6	1.0
Nepal	1979	1.8	3.4	0.4	0.8
Pakistan	1979	15.5	30.2	0.6	1.3
Philippines	1979	26.9	50.5	8.4	15.9
Sri Lanka	1983	5.8	10.0	1.0	1.7
Thailand	1975	4.8	9.1	1.4	2.7

Source: APCTT, 1986a, as derived from UN-ESCAP, 1986.

effectively to changing technical requirements', was virtually non-existent (see TDRI, 1989).

The educational institutions producing S&T manpower remain severely constrained in terms of the resources needed to keep up with advances in knowledge and maintain modern facilities, and in terms of retaining quality staff. The high cost of operating and keeping up with new technologies (new equipment, materials and so on) and the much higher salaries offered to S&T personnel in private industry, thus drawing in qualified educational staff, add to the difficulty experienced by public educational institutions in producing adequate S&T manpower supplies. In general private-sector producers, when unconstrained by regulations and tuition ceilings, are seen to respond fairly well to short-term signals. However the large investments required to implement a long-term S&T manpower production strategy require a clearly committed public sector. The financing of higher education needs to be overhauled so that social benefits and costs are more closely aligned. This would mean a whole package of differential fee structures to reflect social costs and benefits, deregulation, and student loans taking the place of current government control and subsidy.

Table 14.16 S&T manpower and labour force by industry for Korea (1981) and Thailand (1984)

Industry	*Scientists and engineers*	*Technicians*	*Total S&T*	*Total labour force*	*S&T manpower per 10 000 labour force*
Korea:					
Agriculture, forestry and fishing	1404	1797	3201	4 806 000	6.7
Mining	2467	2823	5290	124 000	426.6
Manufacturing	47 893	60 461	108 354	2 873 000	377.1
Electricity, gas and water	2385	3746	6131	70 000	875.9
Construction	33 886	15 411	49 297	875 000	563.4
Wholesale and retail trade	267	17 620	17 887	2 151 000	83.2
Transport, communication and storage	2189	27 296	29 485	649 000	454.3
Finance, insurance and real estate	4257	25 073	29 330	498 000	589.0
Other services	12 566	558 602	571 168	2 003 000	2851.6
Total	107 314	712 829	820 143	14 049 000	583.8
Thailand:					
Agriculture, forestry and fishing	6408	767	7175	13 398 600	5.4
Mining	935	1579	2514	100 200	250.9
Manufacturing	7836	47 420	55 256	2 283 900	241.9
Electricity, gas and water	946	9151	10 097	119 600	844.2
Construction	1938	7349	9287	755 100	123.0
Wholesale and retail trade	594	1379	1973	2468 400	8.0
Transport, communication and storage	683	1903	2586	577 900	44.7
Finance, insurance and real estate	5074	6495	11 569	2 556 300	256.3
Other services	32 805	21 132	53 937		
Total	57 219	97 175	154 394	22 302 500	69.2

Sources: (Korea) Lo, 1985; (Thailand) HRI/MOSTE, 1986; NSO, Labour Force Survey, 1984 (round 1).

Inadequate R&D activity

In the area of R&D, the UNESCO/MOSTE survey (1983) showed that only a very small number of S&T employees (approximately 5.6 per cent) were engaged in R&D activities, with the highest percentage share of R&D manpower working in the rubber and rubber products, machinery, chemicals, agricultural products and food industries. In comparison with other countries Thailand's figures are dismal, even taking into account differences in production structures and requirements.

Inadequate R&D activity is limiting the nation's access to inventions, technology and innovations developed worldwide. It is limiting the country's ability to adapt technologies, to draw upon and assimilate the world's scientific and technological resources, to provide support for new productive activities and upgrade the old, and to accumulate the kind of knowledge that will lead to sustained increases in productivity and international competitiveness. Even advocates of 'appropriate technology' would concede that such capability is essential for the process of drawing upon indigenous knowledge, local materials, processes and know-how. Because the educational institutions are not able to produce an adequate supply of researchers and scientists, the ability to build up an expanding capacity for R&D within the institutions as well as in industry is limited.

In developed countries most of the R&D that results in the generation of technology takes place within industrial enterprises. Only some of the more highly specialized work is undertaken by independent research institutes. In developing countries, however, most R&D activity takes place in nationally funded research institutes and laboratories. The utilization of technologies thus generated has therefore been rather limited. Attention is now being given to the commercialization of such technologies and linkage with industry. Home-grown technology, however, has to confront many problems. A survey by TDRI in 1990 encountered complaints from technology users that indigenously produced technologies in most cases do not fit their needs and are not available when required. The user is also concerned about the risk associated with first use of indigenously produced technologies, and often prefer brand name imports or even non-brand-name imports because of the lower risks involved. There is thus a valid infant-industry-type argument for government incentives (credit, subsidies and so on) to motivate local production units towards greater use of domestically produced technologies, but only where efficient production is envisaged in the long run.

Inadequate upgrading of skills

Data from several employer associations have shown that formal training or the upgrading of workers' skills is rather limited, that most of the formal training undertaken by private industry is confined to larger-sized firms, and that scattered, more intensive, formal training is offered mainly to new workers. Most training is informal and given on the job, as high labour mobility, labour poaching and high costs act as disincentives, especially to small firms. There is therefore less training in industry than is socially optimal.

14.3.3 Industrialization and Labour Force Upgrading

The overall fit between the education and training system and the economy is weak and not improving: secondary enrolment remains low, vocational-school graduates do not have the skills employers seek, worker training and upgrading in industry, services and agriculture is much less than is needed, and the university system cannot produce sufficient numbers of people in the fields the private sector demands. The formal public education system needs to be more flexible and responsive to users (students and employers); private schools need to be less controlled and constrained; intensive worker upgrading needs to be accelerated since increased enrolment at the secondary level, even if successful, will affect the economy only after a lag.

Given this situation, what has been proposed is a conversion of the labour force currently with primary education or less into the equivalent of secondary-school graduates in agriculture as well as in industry, to provide a human-resource base for specialized training. There are new training and information needs in agriculture due to structural changes in the rural economy, including crop diversification, increased mechanization and the use of agro-chemicals. System-based rather than crop-based extension work by the public sector is needed, and should include training that relates to machine maintenance and safety in the application of agro-chemicals, through the use of the mass media in combination with existing training programmes and site visits.

Intensive worker training is needed to upgrade workers with primary education to lower-secondary level so that they become more attractive to the industrial sector and able to benefit from additional training in industry. A minimum level of general and technical education is considered a prerequisite for the development of human resources and for the acquisition of skills for employment or self-employment. This minimum level needs urgently to be attained. For the proportion with only primary education to be reduced to 55 per cent by the year 2000, the upgrading of 7.4 million workers over the next eight years will be required. Research on training in industry, services and agriculture suggests that currently about 300 000 are upgraded per year, meaning that the effort needed is 2.5 to 3.0 times the current level. The estimated total cost of the strategy to the year 2000 is about 42 000 billion baht, but the gains in real GDP will be three times the cost, and there will be significant improvements in income distribution as well (Chalongphob, 1991).

While educational planning by the government is not advocated, government incentives could be provided for training programmes to produce not only high-level scientists, technologists and engineers, but also shop-floor workers, foremen, first-level supervisors, maintenance personnel, electricians, mechanics and technicians at all levels. Otherwise technology options may be overlooked, and many may be prevented from locating in rural settings, for example, despite overwhelming agricultural and rural applications.

Strategies for the development of technological human resources must also emphasize special skill-development programmes for rural and urban informal sectors, small-scale industrial enterprises, women and youth. Biomass and solar energy (in preserving and processing agro-products and meeting energy needs) are of increasing importance to agricultural communities. The use of simple technologies and simple equipment made out of locally available materials has to be explored. In the process, local communities can be involved. Maintenance and repair of simple agricultural equipment, for example, can be the vehicle through which technology is transferred, thereby allowing use of equipment that would otherwise be idle as well as providing opportunities for off-farm employment and management of facilities. Merely making primary and secondary education science-oriented is by itself ineffective, unless students are exposed to a scientific, technological environment, and to the products of applied science and technology. Thus special projects need to be developed such as technology parks that display various scientific and technological devices for the benefit of young minds.

Human settlements provide a wide range of technological possibilities, from the provision of shelter and basic infrastructure, to the construction of complex structures to the installation of transport systems for the movement of people, goods and services. The construction industry alone absorbs workers with different levels of skill and professional know-how. Training is possible in the production, testing and use of building materials, backed by research into improved traditional materials and techniques, as well as materials from agricultural and industrial wastes. The construction sector already employs a large number of workers with primary education. Training could involve participation in activities that range from the provision of shelter to the formulation of legislation, involving practitioners in infrastructure, architecture, planning, project management and investment, and the administration of public and private agencies. What is needed is a policy environment – including a policy framework, a planning apparatus and institutions and mechanisms involved in implementing policies – that provides incentives for such training. The institutional infrastructure needs to be strengthened to support technological generation and application, such as standards institutions, development-finance institutions, consultancy and engineering organizations, industrial-safety institutions and so on, in both private and public sectors.

The whole range of activities and events from inception to use of technology needs to be integrated, and a close link developed between the science and technology systems and the productive sectors. Taking part in the technological decision-making process is an integral part of technological capacity, and the ability to make such decisions has to be enhanced in government, in private production units, and in the scientific and technological community. Involvement in the decision-making process is also conducive to selective use of technology that could stem the adverse environmental and health effects. Many applications of biotechnology and genetic engineering, microelectronics and material sciences are scale-independent and may provide opportunities for more humanized work environments, and training could run the full spectrum from training to operate machinery to taking part in complex processes.

14.4 CONCLUSIONS

The accelerated pace of industrial development in Thailand has so far been unimpeded by human-resource constraints, with demands being met through imported manpower, technology and materials. Having originally followed an import-substitution strategy, for years a large part of the industrial sector was isolated from the international mainstream of technological advance, and the need to upgrade skills did not arise. On the other hand, industries producing for export have generally incorporated technologies that have enabled them to produce goods of an internationally acceptable quality, though much of the technology and personnel were non-indigenous.

However the situation cannot continue. As production technology becomes increasingly more complex and as employment shifts increasingly out of agriculture and into industry, low secondary-school enrolment will become increasingly more problematic. Workers require ever more basic education, technological know-how and specialized skills. There is no way of overcoming disparity in economic status without overcoming disparity in education. Education and technology should go hand in hand; where shortages of qualified teachers occur, distance-education through satellite relays can now be used. Computers will be able to act as tutor and library, interacting with students individually. Education's formal rigidity needs to be broken down to allow students to learn at their own pace. The concept of apprenticeship could be revived to allow young people to divide their time between school and training, with provision for adult education to allow workers to retrain for new jobs, keep up with developments in fast-moving fields and learn new skills.

As long as production for export remains essential to the country's economic viability, it will be vital to develop capabilities for technology assimilation and adaptation, better management of export production units, strict quality control, product design, packaging, finance, credit and export risk guarantees, after-sales service and supply of spare parts. Knowledge of available technology also needs to be improved: often technology is purchased without prior evaluation of available alternatives, or is dictated by donor countries, and acquired technology is frequently transplanted without modification. Competition will increasingly lie in the field of technology, making it imperative to develop local skills for managing technology, to move from purchasing turn-key projects to selecting appropriate plant designs and modifications to suit local conditions. Education and training have to include both 'know-how' and 'know-why'.

The institutional infrastructure for managing technology – providing incentives to use indigenous technology, upgrade skills and produce S&T manpower – needs to be strengthened. This would involve enlisting the greater participation of the private sector and substantial deregulation. Thus tackling the problem calls for three types of public-finance reform: redirecting spending towards activities in which government participation is most critical, increasing reliance on user and other benefit-related charges to finance such spending, and decentralizing some public responsibilities to those in closer touch with industrial needs and conditions.

Public investment and intervention are urgently required to encourage and develop activities and programmes that the market will not undertake. Such intervention should include incentives to retrain and upgrade rural primary-school teachers and rural primary schools; experiments with curricula and teaching methods to promote critical thinking and learning skills; promotion of enrolment of rural children in good-quality secondary schools; incentives to increase private-sector training in industry and services; support for training and information dissemination to farmers; support for a programme to upgrade the productivity and learning skills of workers with only primary education; and measures to increase the incentives for environmental and health consciousness of industry and households.

Whether the issue is fostering environmental awareness, accountability for workers' health or skill upgrading in industry, a common theme can be found. Health, education and skill upgrading contain significant public-goods elements, offering spillover effects to the rest of the community in a way that private benefit calculations tend to ignore. The role of economic policy is to provide systems of incentives – where market failures exist – to internalize both positive and negative externalities, and to reduce knowledge imperfections through information-dissemination regarding product, industrial and input safety, so as to induce socially desirable behaviour in these areas.

This poses a complex challenge for Thailand. The ability of Thailand to replicate the experience of the four Asian NICs to become the so-called fifth tiger is not as straightforward as it may seem. The four Asian NICs achieved accelerated growth through the use of autocratic rule and national discipline to an extent that would not be easily accepted or easily accomplished in Thai society. That path is therefore not a desirable one. On the other hand, the path of development that Thailand has chosen cannot be further pursued without encountering severe stumbling blocks, and appropriate policy directives are now vital.

Part IV

Thai Industrialization in Regional and International Perspectives

15 External Economic Influences, Regional Cooperation and the Role of Thailand as an NIC

Suthiphand Chirathivat[1]

15.1 INTRODUCTION

Thailand no longer stands in isolation from the world economy. Outward-looking policies have benefited the domestic economy through linking its international trade and capital flows to the world economy. The structural changes begun some three decades ago have, up to now, largely served to strengthen this outward orientation of the economy, and the impact of external economic influences on the economy is well recognized. These influences have become more pronounced – in the form of external shocks and subsequent structural adjustments – over the past few years. The recent high growth rate of the economy is a good example of how external influences had impacted upon Thailand. The economy is now led by its external sector, as exports and imports form more than 70 per cent of the country's GDP. The international capital flows since 1987 have surged to an unprecedented level, contributing to a substantial improvement in the performance of the national economy. Indeed Thailand has been placed in the group of 'dynamic Asian economies' by the OECD.

While Thailand is moving towards the NICs' level of growth and development, it is subject to different constraints, considered as a 'price' to pay for prosperity. The external economic influences have increased not just economic opportunities but also economic vulnerability. International economic ups and downs through the international linkage in trade and capital flows have affected the stability of domestic income, output, employment and prices. Sound economic management is often called for to cope with these external influences.

An analysis of external economic influences is therefore important to a better understanding of Thailand's future development potential.

As the Thai economy has become increasingly dependent upon the world economy, structural adjustments are often required to cope with important external fluctuations. The currency appreciation in Japan and other Asian NICs in the late 1980s is one of the most recent examples of how an external economic change can have a tremendous impact on the local economy. In the case of Japan's currency appreciation, enormous capital inflows into Thailand opened up far-reaching opportunities in many sectors. The relevant questions are: how serious are the effects of external economic influences on the Thai economy? Is the domestic economy strong enough to withstand external shocks in general? What policy experiences can be drawn upon while Thailand is becoming an NIC?.

Also pertinent is Thailand's economic relationship with its Asia-Pacific partners and with other developed and developing economies. Are Thailand's trade and investments becoming more regionalized or globalized? What will be the future trends of Thailand's external economic influences when it has attained NIC status? Is the new international economic environment (the end of Cold War, the ascendancy of global regionalism, the economic slowdown in developed countries and so on) conducive to the growth of the Thai economy? Does Thailand need to strengthen its international competitiveness and position itself more strongly in different regions of the world? What form of regional cooperation, if any, could help Thailand to develop further short- and long-term strategies on trade and investment flows?

This chapter will attempt to tackle some of the above questions. Section 15.2 briefly outlines the current profile of the Thai external sector and evaluates its performance. Section 15.3 focuses on the impact of external economic influences on the domestic economy. Certain policy interventions by the government as a result of these influences will also be discussed. Finally, Section 15.4 discusses the integration of these external economic influences within the framework of regional cooperation and the role of Thailand as an NIC.

15.2 FEATURES OF THE THAI EXTERNAL SECTOR

The strong linkage between the domestic economy and the external sector was clearly shown during the high growth period between 1987 and 1990. The domestic economy, which grew at the rate of 9.5 per cent in 1987, enjoyed double-digit growth for three consecutive years (1988–90, see Table 15.1). The degree of openness, measured by imports and exports, also increased rapidly from 51 per cent in 1987 to 69 per cent in 1990 and 76 per cent in 1991. The production base of the manufacturing sector broadened rapidly between 1987 and 1990. [2] It should also be noted that investment in the overall economy has not only increased the scope of national output and employment but has also encouraged large quantities of exports and imports. In terms of value, Thai exports generated more than US$10 billion in 1987, the level attained by Korea 10 years earlier. This figure became US$20 billion in 1989 and almost US$30 billion in 1991 (Table 15.2).[3]

It is quite natural in the Thai case that the country's exports have encouraged foreign imports. The need for export-led production increases created a need for imported machinery, equipment, intermediate products and raw materials. Growth rates of imports were generally higher than growth rates of exports from 1987 to 1990, but not in 1991 (Tables 15.2 and 15.3). This situation led to trade deficits during the high-growth period, which caused some concern

Table 15.1 Key macro-economic indicators for Thailand

	Real GDP growth (%)	*GNP per capita (US$)*	*Inflation (%)*	*Gross national savings (%GNP)*	*Trade/ GDP*[1]	*Gross capital formation (%GNP)*
1980	5.8	683	19.9	22.7	0.49	29.2
1981	6.3	692	13.4	22.2	0.49	29.3
1982	4.1	731	5.4	24.2	0.43	26.8
1983	5.9	796	3.4	22.8	0.42	30.2
1984	5.5	707	0.7	24.6	0.43	29.7
1985	3.2	737	3.2	25.3	0.44	29.3
1986	4.6	796	1.8	27.4	0.43	26.7
1987	9.7	932	2.5	23.6	0.51	28.8
1988	13.3	1095	3.8	26.5	0.63	33.4
1989	12.4	1257	5.4	28.3	0.66	36.5
1990	10.3	1461	6.1	28.4	0.69	42.9
1991	7.7	1698	5.7	34.1	0.63	42.4
1992	7.6	1882	4.1	34.2	0.65	40.0
1993	7.8	2085	3.3	34.7	0.66	40.1

Notes:
1. For basic data, see ADB, *Key Indicators of Developing Member Countries*.
Sources: Bank of Thailand; ADB.

Table 15.2 Value of Thailand's exports, 1980–93

	Value of exports (millions of baht)			*Exports/GDP (%)*			*Growth rate of exports (%)*		
	Merchandise	*Services*	*Merchandise and services*	*Merchandise*	*Services*	*Merchandise and services*	*Merchandise*	*Services*	*Merchandise and services*
1980	133 197	43 529	176 726	20.2	6.6	26.8	23.1	49.3	28.7
1981	152 821	51 399	204 220	20.1	6.8	26.9	14.7	18.1	15.6
1982	159 728	59 269	218 997	19.5	7.2	26.7	4.0	15.3	7.2
1983	146 472	67 136	213 608	16.1	7.4	23.5	−8.3	13.3	−2.5
1984	175 238	72 741	247 979	18.0	7.5	25.5	19.6	8.4	16.1
1985	193 366	85 879	279 245	19.1	8.5	27.5	10.3	18.1	12.6
1986	233 383	87 664	321 047	21.3	8.0	29.3	20.7	2.1	14.1
1987	299 853	107 187	407 040	23.3	8.6	32.5	28.5	22.3	26.8
1988	403 570	150 337	553 907	26.8	10.0	36.8	34.6	40.3	36.1
1989	515 745	182 619	698 364	28.8	10.2	39.0	27.8	21.5	26.1
1990	583 206	216 723	799 930	28.4	10.6	39.0	13.1	18.7	14.5
1991	720 545	243 063	963 608	28.8	9.7	38.5	23.5	12.2	20.5
1992	815 201	277 242	1 092 443	29.0	10.0	39.0	13.1	14.1	13.4
1993	921 402	322 734	1 244 136	29.4	10.3	39.7	13.0	16.4	13.9

Source: Bank of Thailand.

Table 15.3 Value of Thailand's imports, 1980–93

	Value of imports (millions of baht)			*Imports/GDP (%)*			*Growth rate of imports (%)*		
	Merchandise	*Services*	*Merchandise and services*	*Merchandise*	*Services*	*Merchandise and services*	*Merchandise*	*Services*	*Merchandise and services*
1980	188 686	32 383	221 069	28.7	4.9	33.6	29.1	24.9	28.5
1981	216 746	45 357	262 103	28.5	6.0	34.5	14.9	40.1	18.6
1982	196 616	50 474	247 090	24.0	6.2	30.1	–9.3	11.3	–5.7
1983	236 609	50 562	287 171	26.0	5.6	31.6	20.3	0.2	16.2
1984	245 155	57 543	302 698	25.2	5.9	31.1	3.6	13.8	5.4
1985	251 169	70 627	321 796	24.8	7.0	31.7	2.5	22.7	6.3
1986	241 358	72 695	314 053	22.0	6.6	28.7	–3.9	2.9	–2.4
1987	334 209	78 474	412 683	26.7	6.3	32.9	38.5	8.0	31.4
1988	513 114	95 961	609 075	34.1	6.4	40.4	53.5	22.3	47.6
1989	656 428	111 470	767 898	36.7	6.2	42.9	27.9	16.2	26.1
1990	832 139	153 195	985 334	40.6	7.5	48.0	26.8	37.4	28.3
1991	963 347	195 721	1 159 068	38.4	7.8	46.2	15.8	27.8	17.6
1992	1 015 495	249 433	1 264 928	36.2	8.9	45.1	5.4	27.4	9.1
1993	1 136 985	298 141	1 435 126	36.3	1.0	37.3	12.0	19.5	13.5

Source: Bank of Thailand.

among policy makers in 1990. The overall current-account deficit that year reached 9 per cent of GDP. It is believed that as long as this deficit is related to export-oriented activities, it should improve quickly once the first stage of high import content for export production has passed and the demand has shifted to local content. If this is the case, then the current-account deficit of Thailand should improve in the years to come.

As mentioned earlier, the changing structure of the Thai economy has manifested itself in the external sector, especially in international trade in goods and services and international capital flows. In the early 1990s more than three quarters of exports consisted of manufactured products, all with strong growth rates. The structure of imports has also gone through a significant change. Recent experiences have shown that import surges occur when capital goods, intermediate goods and raw materials become necessary to support export-oriented manufacturing production. This has, of course, resulted in trade deficits and trade imbalances between Thailand and the rest of the world. The United States, the EC (now the Economic Union or EU) and Japan are by far the largest import-export markets for Thailand. Exports to these three trading partners accounted for around 60 per cent of the total exports and exports to ASEAN and Asian NICs contributed another 20 per cent, adding up to four fifths of the total exports (Tables 15.4 to 15.6).

While Thailand has managed to keep its export trade in some balance, on the import side there exist bilateral trade imbalances between Thailand and some of its major trading partners. Thailand gained a trade surplus with the United States in the 1980s and this has continued up to the present. Its trade with European countries has been kept at a satisfactory balance, but it has deepened its trade deficit with Japan and is starting to do so with the Asian NICs. This development has encouraged Thailand more than ever to exert pressure for market access to Japan while trying to withstand trade-protection measures by the United States and the EC where it has a favourable trading position.

Apart from trade in goods, there are two other major items in the external sector: trade in services and foreign direct investment. Trade in services as opposed to trade in goods will continue to receive special consideration in the future. In fact the surplus in trade in services has helped to lighten the burden of the overall trade deficit of Thailand. Thailand is quite specialized in tourism and labour exports and these two sectors have contributed a net income in the overall balance of trade in services, as opposed to other service areas such as transport, banking and finance, insurance and telecommunications. A pertinent issue now is how to improve and maintain Thailand's international competitiveness in services in the long run.

One cannot deny the crucial role of direct foreign investment (DFI) in the development of the Thai economy. Trade and investment have been moving closer to each other since Thailand began to diversify its export products, especially those of export-oriented industries promoted by the BOI. Domestic conditions such as attractive investment incentives, relatively acceptable infrastructure and abundant manpower, together with the changes in the international environment, have attracted DFI to Thailand.[4] The Western developed countries have long been major investors in Thailand, but more recently Japan has become a major net investor (Table 15.7).[5] Asian NICs have also emerged as important investors, especially Taiwan and Hong Kong. In fact, Taiwan ranked second in terms of DFI (that is, projects approved) in 1989. DFI activities have been very much associated with the manufactured exports of the countries involved. It was in the 1980s that a wide range of manufacturing activities began, ranging from food processing to the production of scientific and precision instruments. Food, electronics, chemicals, textiles and metals and machinery products constitute the bulk of DFI industries in Thailand.[6] It was precisely these substantial inflows of DFI that helped Thailand's overall balance-of-payments position. Thailand's net international reserves grew to more than US$20 billion in 1991, which was sufficient to finance around six months of imports.

15.3 MAJOR EXTERNAL ECONOMIC INFLUENCES ON THAILAND

The importance of the Thai economy has increased in terms of size and openness over the years, and it has become more deeply integrated with the global economy. The well-being of the Thai economy is being shaped more and more by events in the international environment that are largely beyond its control. The two oil shocks, Japan's currency appreciation and the surge in DFI, all mentioned above, provide ample examples. But despite international fluctuations the Thai economy has remained resilient and the government has managed to come up with appropriate domestic policy responses. A low inflation rate and stable domestic agricultural prices were of course a great help.

Table 15.4 Major importers of Thai products, 1980–93 (per cent)

	1980	*1981*	*1982*	*1983*	*1984*	*1985*	*1986*	*1987*	*1988*	*1989*	*1990*	*1991*	*1992*	*1993*
World[1]	100.0	100.0	100.0	100.0	100.0	100.0	100.0	100.0	100.0	100.0	100.0	100.0	100.0	100.0
(billion baht)	(133.2)	(153.0)	(160.0)	(146.5)	(175.2)	(193.4)	(233.2)	(300.0)	(403.6)	(515.8)	(589.8)	(725.4)	(824.6)	(935.7)
United States	12.6	12.9	12.8	15.0	17.2	19.7	17.8	18.6	20.0	21.7	22.7	21.3	22.4	21.6
EC/EU[2]	25.8	21.7	23.4	21.2	20.7	19.1	21.3	22.2	20.8	19.1	21.6	20.7	19.6	16.7
Germany	4.1	3.2	3.4	3.5	3.3	3.7	4.6	4.9	4.6	4.1	5.2	5.2	4.4	4.0
United Kingdom	1.9	1.6	1.9	2.0	2.2	2.4	3.2	3.6	3.7	3.7	4.1	3.6	3.6	3.2
France	1.7	1.9	1.9	1.9	1.7	1.9	2.3	2.4	2.4	2.2	2.4	2.5	2.3	2.1
Netherlands	13.2	12.2	13.2	10.8	10.0	7.1	7.2	6.7	5.5	4.9	4.8	4.4	4.3	3.1
Italy	2.0	1.4	1.6	1.4	1.8	1.7	1.6	1.9	1.8	1.5	1.8	1.8	1.7	1.3
Japan	15.1	14.2	13.7	15.1	13.0	13.4	13.9	14.9	16.0	17.0	17.2	18.1	17.5	17.0
ASEAN[3]	16.2	14.6	15.7	15.7	14.2	14.5	14.3	13.6	11.7	11.6	11.4	11.8	12.7	16.1
Asian NIEs[4]	7.2	8.2	7.3	7.4	6.8	7.5	8.3	7.0	7.9	7.0	7.8	8.0	8.2	8.5
Middle East[5]	7.2	8.8	7.1	8.0	7.5	7.1	6.0	6.9	5.9	5.9	5.0	4.8	4.7	4.6
China	1.9	2.7	4.4	1.7	2.5	3.8	3.1	3.3	3.0	2.7	1.2	1.2	1.2	1.5
Myanmar	0.1	0.1	0.1	0.1	0.2	0.2	0.2	0.1	0.1	0.1	0.2	0.2	0.2	0.4
Indochina	1.4	0.5	0.5	0.5	0.4	0.3	0.4	0.4	0.4	0.4	0.4	0.5	1.1	2.1
Laos	0.7	0.4	0.5	0.5	0.2	0.3	0.3	0.3	0.3	0.3	0.3	0.4	0.4	0.5
Cambodia	0.5	0.1	–	–	–	–	–	–	–	–	–	–	0.2	0.5
Vietnam	0.2	–	–	–	0.1	–	–	–	–	0.1	0.1	0.1	0.2	0.3
Other Countries in Western Europe[6]	1.2	1.3	1.3	1.7	1.9	1.9	2.1	2.1	2.1	2.2	2.2	2.0	n.a.	n.a.
Oceania[7]	2.9	2.4	2.0	2.0	1.7	1.7	1.8	1.9	2.0	2.1	1.9	1.9	n.a.	n.a.
Eastern Europe[8]	2.9	5.1	3.1	1.7	1.6	1.5	1.5	0.9	0.9	2.0	1.5	2.3	2.2	2.4
Canada	0.4	0.5	0.4	0.8	1.2	1.2	1.4	1.5	1.8	1.5	1.3	1.4	1.3	1.4

Notes:
1. Figures in parenthesis are export value in million baht.
2. Includes Netherlands, Germany, United Kingdom, France, Italy, Belgium, Spain, Denmark, Portugal, Greece, Ireland, Luxembourg.
3. Includes Singapore, Malaysia, Indonesia, Philippines, Brunei.
4. Includes Hong Kong, S.Korea, Taiwan.
5. Includes Saudi Arabia, U.Arab Emirates. Iran, Kuwait, Israel, Syria, Lebanon, Yemen, Bahrain, Jordan, Iraq, Oman, Cyprus, Qatar, Yemen (South).
6. Includes Switzerland, Sweden, Finland, Norway, Malta, Iceland, Andorra, San Marino, Liechtenstein, Monaco, Gibraltar, Greenland (Denmark), Farrow Islands (Denmark).
7. Includes Australia, New Zealand, Papua New Guinea, Fiji, US Pacific Islands, French Pacific, Western Samoa, Tonga, Cook Islands, Solomon Islands.
8. Includes USSR, Austria, Poland, Yugoslavia, German(East), Bulgaria, Czechoslovakia, Hungary, Romania, Albania.

Source: Department of Foreign Trade.

Table 15.5 Major exporters to Thailand, 1980–93

	1980	*1981*	*1982*	*1983*	*1984*	*1985*	*1986*	*1987*	*1988*	*1989*	*1990*	*1991*	*1992*	*1993*
World[1]	100.0	100.0	100.0	100.0	100.0	100.0	100.0	100.0	100.0	100.0	100.0	100.0	100.0	100.0
(billion baht)	(193.6)	(219.0)	(197.2)	(236.6)	(245.2)	(251.2)	(241.4)	(334.2)	(513.1)	(662.7)	(853.0)	(959.4)	(1033.2)	(1116.6)
United States	14.1	12.8	13.3	12.6	13.3	11.3	14.3	12.5	13.6	11.3	10.8	10.6	11.7	11.6
EC/EU[2]	16.6	13.4	13.7	12.6	13.3	11.3	14.3	12.5	13.6	11.3	14.7	14.0	14.4	14.8
Germany	12.8	12.9	11.5	12.7	12.5	14.8	15.1	15.6	15.5	14.0	5.1	5.6	5.3	5.4
United Kingdom	4.3	4.3	3.9	4.7	4.2	5.4	5.8	5.9	5.4	5.1	2.7	2.3	2.3	2.3
France	2.6	2.7	2.6	2.3	2.3	2.5	3.2	3.2	3.0	2.6	2.4	1.4	2.3	2.0
Netherlands	1.0	2.2	1.5	1.5	1.7	2.7	1.6	1.5	2.4	1.6	0.7	0.9	2.0	1.0
Italy	2.4	1.3	1.2	1.1	1.1	1.0	1.0	1.2	1.1	0.9	1.3	1.4	1.6	2.0
Japan	20.7	24.0	23.4	27.4	26.9	26.5	26.4	26.0	29.0	30.3	30.4	29.4	29.3	30.3
ASEAN[3]	9.4	10.0	11.9	13.2	15.8	18.2	14.2	15.3	12.2	12.4	12.2	12.5	12.8	11.8
Asian NIEs[4]	5.1	4.4	5.6	6.4	6.8	6.3	7.5	7.6	8.2	9.2	9.6	11.1	11.1	10.5
Middle East[5]	17.4	18.5	19.0	12.9	9.7	8.0	5.2	4.9	3.8	4.6	4.1	3.2	3.0	3.3
China	3.4	3.1	2.6	2.9	2.5	2.9	3.3	2.8	2.8	2.9	3.3	3.1	3.0	2.4
Myanmar	4.4	3.2	2.7	2.6	3.0	2.4	2.9	3.9	3.4	2.9	0.4	0.5	0.3	0.3
Indochina	0.1	0.1	0.2	0.2	0.3	0.4	0.4	0.3	0.3	0.3	0.4	0.5	0.9	0.9
Laos	–	–	–	–	–	–	–	0.1	0.2	0.4	0.1	0.1	0.1	0.1
Cambodia	–	–	–	–	–	–	–	0.1	0.1	0.2	–	–	0.2	0.2
Vietnam	–	–	–	–	–	–	–	–	–	–	0.3	0.3	0.3	0.2
Other Countries in Western Europe[6]	–	–	–	–	–	–	–	–	0.1	0.2	3.3	3.2	n.a.	n.a.
Oceania[7]	2.2	3.5	2.9	2.3	2.3	2.1	2.4	2.2	2.1	2.4	2.0	2.1	n.a.	n.a.
Eastern Europe[8]	1.0	1.2	0.7	1.3	1.4	1.2	1.5	2.0	2.1	1.8	1.7	2.3	0.8	0.8
Canada	1.4	1.3	1.4	1.4	1.2	1.2	1.2	1.2	1.3	1.4	1.1	0.9	1.0	0.9

Notes:

1. Figures in parenthesis are import value in million baht.
2. Includes Netherlands, Germany, United Kingdom, France, Italy, Belgium, Spain, Denmark, Portugal, Greece, Ireland, Luxembourg.
3. Includes Singapore, Malaysia, Indonesia, Philippines, Brunei.
4. Includes Hong Kong, S.Korea, Taiwan.
5. Includes Saudi Arabia, U.Arab Emirates. Iran, Kuwait, Israel, Syria, Lebanon, Yemen, Bahrain, Jordan, Iraq, Oman, Cyprus, Qatar, Yemen (South).
6. Includes Switzerland, Sweden, Finland, Norway, Malta, Iceland, Andorra, San Marino, Liechtenstein, Monaco, Gibraltar, Greenland (Denmark), Farrow Islands (Denmark).
7. Includes Australia, New Zealand, Papua New Guinea, Fiji, US Pacific Islands, French Pacific, Western Samoa, Tonga, Cook Islands, Solomon Islands.
8. Includes USSR, Austria, Poland, Yugoslavia, German(East), Bulgaria, Czechoslovakia, Hungary, Romania, Albania.

Source: Department of Foreign Trade.

Table 15.6 Major Thai exports

1980		*1985*	
Total principal exports	246 888	Total principal exports	725 888
Rice	19 508	Textile products	23 578
Tapioca products	14 887	Rice	22 524
Rubber	12 351	Tapioca products	14 969
Tin	11 347	Rubber	13 567
Textile products	9643	Integrated circuits	8248
Maize	7299	Maize	7700
Integrated circuits	6156	Precious stones	6350
Precious stones	3240	Sugar	6247
Sugar	2975	Tin	5647
Prawns	1961	Prawns	3439
Total principal exports	89 367	Total principal exports	112 620
Others	43 830	Others	63 617
Total	133 197	Total	175 237
1990		*1991*	
Textile products	84 472	Textile products	109 524
Rice	27 770	Rice	30 516
Rubber	23 557	Prawns	26 681
Tapioca products	23 136	Integrated circuits	25 760
Precious stones	22 045	Rubber	24 953
Integrated circuits	21 580	Tapioca products	24 368
Prawns	20 454	Precious stones	23 438
Sugar	17 694	Sugar	14 782
Maize	4144	Maize	3925
Tin	1880	Tin	877
Total principal exports	246 732	Total principal exports	284 824
Others	343 081	Others	440 806
Total	589 813	Total	725 630

Source: Bank of Thailand, *Monthly Bulletin*, various issues.

Two types of external economic influence on Thailand may be noted. One is the change in macroeconomic variables [7] and the other is the shift in international trends and policy. [8] It is evident from past experience that Thailand is able to respond quite well to the first category of macroeconomic variables. The oil shock actually brought about specific attempts to stabilize the economy, and the international interest-rates hike resulted in exchange-rate adjustments to maintain

Table 15.7 Percentage distribution of net inflows of foreign direct investment by investing country, 1970–90 (per cent)

Country/Region	*1970–9*	*1980–2*	*1983–6*	*1987–9*	*1990*
*APEC member countries	86.22	72.94	79.86	86.38	88.89
North America	35.72	27.03	30.57	12.65	9.50
United States	35.56	27.25	29.71	12.36	9.35
Canada	0.16	−0.22	0.86	0.29	0.15
Japan	29.78	22.89	32.87	44.30	44.50
Asian NIEs	10.32	14.06	11.06	22.70	24.24
Hong Kong	9.59	13.88	9.68	11.25	12.01
Korea, Rep	0.35	0.07	0.09	0.70	0.78
Taiwan	0.38	0.11	1.29	10.74	11.45
ASEAN	6.38	7.57	4.00	6.04	10.30
Brunei	–	–	0.04	–	–
Indonesia	0.10	0.24	0.05	0.05	0.10
Malaysia	0.61	1.12	0.74	0.11	0.73
Philippines	0.28	0.00	−0.12	–	0.01
Singapore	5.11	6.21	3.28	5.87	9.45
Oceania (Australia and New Zealand)	0.46	1.39	0.93	0.22	0.19
China	–	–	0.44	0.48	0.16
Non-APEC countries	17.34	27.06	20.14	13.62	11.11
EC/EU and other European Countries	15.40	19.16	11.73	8.47	6.86

Source: Bank of Thailand.

international competitiveness.[9] As a rule shifts in these macroeconomic variables are difficult to predict, making early domestic policy responses difficult. Also the magnitude of these macroeconomic changes varies: some are quickly and smoothly absorbed into the national economy, while others may present it with a jolt.

On future trends and policy shifts, it is expected that the followings will have an important bearing upon domestic policy responses in Thailand:

- The world economic slowdown and rise in protectionism.
- World economic-management systems after the Uruguay round of GATT and the move towards bilateralism and regionalism in world trade.
- Rapid growth for intra-Asian trade and investments.

- Intensification of worldwide competition in trade and investment.
- Regionalization in ASEAN countries and their eventual emergence as NIEs.

The first major trend is that world economic growth will continue to be sluggish. Intense market competition around the world is causing major trading partners such as the United States and the EC to adopt protectionist measures. By the end of the 1980s almost one third of Thai exports to the United States, the EC and Japan had fallen into managed trade, causing concerns in trade-policy management.[10] A number of agricultural and industrial products have been caught up in non-tariff barriers (NTBs) (Table 15.8).

Although there was increasing use of these NTBs against Thai exports in the 1980s, Thailand was able to maintain its export growth. This has led some to conclude that Thailand has nothing to fear from NTBs. However this belief may not take into account some important facts. First, Thailand is lucky in not having to face the same trade restrictions as many Asian NICs. But this situation may not last long, as Thailand is moving towards NIC status and will become subject to the same sorts of trade restrictions.

Second, one sees continued use of protectionist measures such as Section 301 of the US Trade Act, widely applied quantitative restrictions, and the proliferation of anti-dumping duties (AD) and countervailing duties (CVD). Restrictions on cassava in the EC, rice in the Japanese market, textiles and clothing in the EC and the United States are clear examples of how protective NTBs can affect the export growth of these products. And the list above does not include manufactured products such as footwear, electronic and electrical products such as television tubes, telephones, and fax machine parts and accessories. The list of NTBs is longer if we extend it to trade in services and intellectual property rights, for which Thailand established greater contact with the developed world in the 1990s.

Thirdly, because of its NIC or near-NIC status, Thailand can no longer be certain of retaining unilateral trade preferences, such as those enjoyed under the General System of Preference (GSP). Thus the country must prepare for a new era of international trade negotiations. It can no longer wait to be given preferences, but must be ready to enter into 'give and take' trade deals with a number of its trading partners. This will require an improvement in its negotiating skills and its ability to coordinate trade-related issues that are not yet in place.

Table 15.8 Non-tariff barriers on Thai exports, 1990

Type of NTBs	*Goods or Services Affected*
United States:	
Section 301	Intellectual property rights
Countervailing duties (CVD)	Apparel 1.23 per cent; fittings 2.94 per cent; ball bearings 21.54 per cent;
Anti-dumping (AD)	Steel pipes 15.67 per cent
Multi-Fibre Agreements (MFA)	Textiles
Import restrictions	Canned tuna; raw sugar
Automatic detention	Rice noodles
Farm Act 1990	Export enhancement programs; marketing loan program
Using environmental issues as trade barriers	Marine Mammal Protection Act Amendments of 1988; Public Law 101–162 (sea turtles conservation)
EC/EU:	
Sanitary and phytosanitary	Canned seafood (the use of food additives)
Quota restrictions (VRA)	Tapioca products (pellets)
MFA	Textiles
Discrimination on GSP beneficiaries	Canned pineapple
High tariff rate	Canned tuna
Common Agricultural Policy	Sugar, rice
CVD	Ball bearings 1.76 baht/unit;
AD	lighter (ongoing investigation); glutamic acid 0.0407 ECU/kg (price undertaking at US$1497 per ton); cotton yarn (ongoing investigation)
Japan	
High tariff rate	Sugar; preserved pineapple
Sanitary and psytosanitary	Pork; some fresh fruits and vegetables
Quantitative restrictions	Cassava flour; frozen squid
Import ban	Rice

Source: Department of Business Economics, Ministry of Commerce.

The second major trend is the dispersed and complex world economic management system after the Uruguay Round. The free-trade policy, based on the fixed-rules system of GATT, has done much for world trade expansion. However it is facing increasing protectionism from many parts of the world, especially in markets such as the EC and the United States. In 1994 the EC became EU, a single market, and this is expected to be followed by economic and monetary union (EMU). Intra-trade and investment trends suggest that the EU will be quite preoccupied with its own economic, political and social affairs. This regionalism is unlikely to promote as much openness as before. The United States, with the creation of the North American Free Trade Area (NAFTA), is also trying to strengthen its trading position. It seems that the 1990s will continue to be characterized by structural adjustments to individual economies, each economy concentrating on arrangements that help to guarantee success. Unilateralism, bilateralism and regionalism will continue to manifest themselves throughout the 1990s .

Countries in the Asia-Pacific region, which have been affected by Western policy shifts, have also begun to consider forms of regional cooperation. As far as Thailand is concerned – because it has received massive investment from Japan and the Asian NICs since the mid-1980s onward, and these countries have become an integral part of a production sphere that is emerging in the Asia-Pacific region – the link with the intraregional trade and investment of the Asia-Pacific region has become of paramount importance.

The third major trend, which is a corollary to the second, is the regionalization of the Asia-Pacific economy. The economic growth of the region is predicted to be strong through to the year 2000 vis-à-vis Europe and North America. If this is true, all three regions are likely to have the same GDP by the beginning of the twenty-first century. However, as a result of the economic chaos in the United States and the threat posed by such a powerhouse as the EU, it is no wonder that the Asia-Pacific global market is becoming less dependent on traditional Western markets. In fact the strong growth of the Asia-Pacific region is based more on intra-Asian trade, which is predicted to grow from the present 40 per cent to 60 per cent by the end of the decade. The deeper regionalization of trade and production in Asia will create greater flows of goods, services and capital, and the countries of the region will have to adjust themselves to one another.

The above account demonstrates the importance of regional trade and investment to Thailand and the time has come for Thailand to formulate a regional policy.[11] This regional policy would aim at increasing Thai understanding of important issues such as efficient technology transfer, trends in regional migration, upgrading of physical infrastructure and labour productivity, and so on. It is expected that the regional policy of ASEAN will be important to Thailand. As the ASEAN region is expected to become a growth area in this part of the world with the creation of ASEAN Free Trade Area, many Asian investors may be interested in entering the region, starting with Thailand as a gateway to Indochina. At the same time Thailand is expected to invest more extensively in the region, especially in ASEAN and Indochina.

The fourth major trend is the intensification of worldwide competition in trade and investment, which is forcing individual countries to improve their international competitiveness. Thailand has been affected by this trend and will need to improve its productivity and efficiency if it is to continue to compete. Thailand's exports, after attaining NIC status, will no longer be based only on cheap labour costs, but on new industrial activities that reflect global changes. Textiles and clothing are clear examples of the challenge presented to Thailand by low-labour-cost countries such as China, Indonesia, Vietnam and a number of South Asian countries. The electronic and electrical industries are also facing intensified world competition. Thailand, at present, can attract multinational corporations by offering an attractive investment environment with a low cost structure. However, to remain attractive at the NIC level the country will have to improve its human and physical infrastructure. The pace of change in the international environment requires Thailand to adapt and to formulate domestic policy responses aimed at improving overall competitiveness in the long term.

15.4 REGIONAL COOPERATION AND THE ROLE OF THAILAND AS AN NIC

The section above discussed various trends and policy shifts that are relevant to Thailand's pursuit of trade and investment development. Of course the most important components of any trade and investment strategy are measures aimed at improving international competitiveness. It is recognized that the relative labour-cost advantage of Thai exports will rapidly become a thing of the past. For the moment, importance is being placed more on how Thailand can produce products of greater sophistication and requiring higher technology. In the long term it is vital that the country learns how to maintain and improve its relative competitiveness by improving productivity, and how to conduct trade and investment strategies and policy options in a more efficient way.

It is important at the same time to realize that Thailand's move towards NIC status is not happening in isolation of what is happening around it. The catching-up process in the Asia-Pacific region has caught up Thailand in its flow, providing a balance against the economic slowdown of many developed countries. In this sense any regional cooperation entered into by Thailand will have to be carried out on at least two levels. The first level will be to develop an international economic cooperation that can best serve the national interests and the strength of country's international competitiveness; the second will be to act as part of a group, especially from the ASEAN and Indochina standpoint, in order to handle more efficiently trade and investment negotiations with different economic partners.

Concerning the multilateral framework, Thailand should continue to adhere to the GATT-based, free-trade system. The negotiations in the Uruguay Round have shown Thailand to be aware of the multilateral rules that are significant to future trade and investment expansion. While the negotiations were in progress Thailand showed its willingness to liberalize its trade in over 4000 products. It had expected that a number of rules would have been rewritten in numerous sectors such as trade in services, agricultural trade, textiles and clothing, trade-related intellectual properties (TRIPs) and trade-related investment measures (TRIMs). With the successful conclusion of this round in December 1993, Thailand stood ready to abide by the final agreements. Adjustment periods may be necessary before Thailand can really enjoy the trade and investment benefits in the longer run. Of course participation in the GATT system has allowed Thailand to mature economically and to negotiate on a 'give and take' basis, especially in multilateral fora. It is clear that Thailand will resort more to GATT when facing with constraints on trade by different countries.

On the other hand the dynamics of regional cooperation seem to have become more and more complex since the conclusion of the GATT Uruguay Round. This is particularly true with regard to the rise of regionalism around the world. For many, regionalism appears to have gained favour as a new means of dealing effectively with trading partners, while multilateralism remains as a framework for trade in general. There is a fear that the world may be dividing into inward-looking, protectionist regional blocs, where trade and investment flows between regions will be more regulated and controlled than ever before. As mentioned earlier, should this situation arise Thailand will probably also turn to regional cooperation. As ASEAN is the closest regional organization to Thailand, it could aim at encouraging greater intra- and extra-ASEAN economic cooperation in the 1990s.

The key concern for Thailand is that intra-ASEAN economic cooperation should serve to strengthen the competitiveness of Thailand

and the region, and not to undermine the role of Japan, the Asian NICs and China, who are also major players in the region. The recent agreement on AFTA among ASEAN members was an important exercise of increased cooperation and possible economic integration. Although not all ASEAN members are unanimous about AFTA remaining an important step towards their intensified economic cooperation, Thailand should encourage such a move. Intra-ASEAN economic cooperation would create new opportunities among the countries to discover mutual complementarities and competitiveness, allowing them to respond positively to the changing pattern of comparative advantage in the region and not to depend too much on Japan and the Asian NICs. This path will be important if ASEAN is to gain its own identity and not let its development be overwhelmed by the flow of trade and investment from Japan and the Asian NICs. Thailand should work with ASEAN to extend intra-ASEAN trade to industrial and other areas of cooperation.

As far as extra-ASEAN economic cooperation is concerned, ASEAN should establish an effective mechanism to deal with major economic powers such as the United States, the EU and Japan, and new important partners such as the Asian NICs, China, Indochina and other international organizations and institutions. With the growing regionalism and bilateral agreements, Thailand should advocate economic and trade agreements between ASEAN and its other major trading partners. If Western Europe and North America are resorting more to close trading blocs, Thailand has to cooperate closely not only with ASEAN, but also with Asia-Pacific organizations such as the Asia-Pacific Economic Cooperation (APEC) and the East Asian Economic Caucus (EAEC), initiated by Malaysia in 1991. In fact the wider scope offered by intraregional trade is a way of overcoming the restrictions imposed by small domestic markets, stimulating market expansion and increasing investment. Regionalization will allow members to share resources, including technological, natural and human resources, thus providing a new basis for sustained growth and structural change.

Finally, Thailand will need to strengthen its ability to deal with all forms of trade negotiations. Bilateral and multilateral agreements should provide mechanisms to settle disputes and facilitate economic integration. Unilateral actions, on the other hand, are aimed at strengthening trade and investments in goods and services. Unilateral actions may take different forms, such as a general reduction in the overall protective tariff structure in GATT, special reduction of protective tariff rates in ASEAN, the creation of an office to coordinate international economic affairs, reformulating investment-promotion incentives according to TRIMs, and enforcement of intellectual property rights in the country. At the same time, Thailand has to be prepared constantly for unilateral actions in response to growing protectionism.

15.5 CONCLUSION

There is no doubt that Thailand is moving towards the level of growth and development enjoyed by NICs. It is necessary for the country to find the right balance between different economic and social activities. The external balance and the transformation of the external sector have become inextricable parts of Thailand's economic development. The experiences of more than three decades of economic development have shown that openness or the external sector is a major factor in expanding the rest of the economy. The modern manufacturing sector, for instance, has been able to initiate and keep up with rapid and profound changes in export-led production, allowing Thailand to increase its participation in international trade and investment, and hence become more involved in the world economy.

The country's integration into the world economy has not been without some forced adjustments. In fact Thailand continues to be shaped more and more by events in the international environment that are largely beyond its control. The recent past has shown how vulnerable the Thai economy is to external disturbances. The two oil shocks, high world interest rates, price fluctuations of major commodities and currencies, and increased DFIs are but a few examples of major events having a major economic impact and requiring timely policy responses. Therefore Thailand must be ready to analyze future events as they arise and work towards appropriate domestic and international policy responses . Current issues to which Thailand must respond in order to ensure its strength and competitiveness in a changing world economy include the world economic slowdown, the rise in protectionism, the new world economic management system after the Uruguay Round, the rapid growth in intra-Asian trade and investment, the intensification of worldwide competition in trade and investment, and the regionalization of ASEAN countries and their eventual emergence as NICs.

As a result of Thailand's move towards NIC status, one of the most important questions is how to maintain its international competitiveness. The Asian region, for example, is moving quickly as a major growth centre of the world and Thailand is now seeing the emergence of countries such as China and Vietnam as serious competitors in the markets for labour-intensive manufactured products. This is a good reason for Thailand to produce goods with a greater degree of sophistication and requiring higher technology. To achieve this it will have to upgrade its human-resource base by education and training. Thailand, in this sense, is definitely flowing with the mainstream of the international catching-up process in the Asia-Pacific region.

Concerning regional cooperation, Thailand has to participate in the form of economic cooperation that best serves the national interests and adds to the country's international competitiveness. The country will need to act as one of a group of countries, from the ASEAN and Indochina standpoint, to fulfil trade and investment negotiations with different economic partners. Within the multilateral framework, Thailand should continue to adhere to the GATT-based trading system. Because regionalism, as manifested in NAFTA and the EU is gaining stature as a new means of dealing with trading partners, Thailand will probably turn towards regional cooperation within ASEAN or with Asia-Pacific regional organizations such as the Asia-Pacific Economic Cooperation (APEC) grouping and the East Asian Economic Caucus (EAEC). Finally, Thailand will find it necessary to strengthen its ability to deal with all forms of trade negotiations in its march towards NIC status.

Notes

1. The author would like to thank Professor Peter Drysdale and Dr Andrew Elek for their cogent and constructive comments on this chapter.
2. However the share of agricultural sector in GDP declined over the years to around 12.4 percent in 1990. The service sector is subject to cyclical fluctuations, but the sector has maintained its importance to keep pace with country's rapid economic development.
3. Probably US$40 billion in 1993.
4. Thailand has been one of the greatest beneficiaries of the post-1986 direct-investment boom. Foreign investment rose from around US$260 million up to 1986 to US$ 352 million in 1987, US$1.1 billion 1988, and US$1.7 billion in 1989.
5. From the 25–30 per cent to 44 per cent.
6. Firms associated with foreign-investment subsidiaries of foreign companies and joint ventures now account for a substantial share of Thai manufacturing. They are especially important in advanced manufacturing

subsectors such as chemicals, metals and machinery. Foreign affiliates account for the bulk of output in machinery and electrical machinery and the bulk of exports in chemicals, metals and electrical machinery. See Petri, 1991.

7. Commodity prices, exchange rates, inflation and interest rates and so on. Given these sharp swings in every aspect of the international economy, it is not surprising that the problem of dealing with external shocks has been a central preoccupation of policy in developing countries. See Krugman, 1988, pp. 54–7.
8. Which has become more involved with global issues such as the GATT system, future trading blocs, regionalization in Asia, the end of Cold War and so on. Given the important changes internationally, it is also becoming of interest to academicians to discuss these subjects.
9. The last one, on 22 November 1984, the baht was devalued from 23 baht per US$1 to 27 baht per US$1. Also the baht was pegged to a basket of major currencies.
10. See Suthiphand, 1991, pp. 72–9.
11. This will be elaborated on in Section 15.5.

16 A Japanese Perspective of Thailand's Industrialization

Makoto Sakurai

16.1 INTRODUCTION

Thailand's high economic growth since the second half of the 1980s has attracted much attention in Japan. In part, this interest reflects the strong historical, economic and cultural relations between the two countries. To Japan, the image of Thailand since the 1950s has been that of a Buddhist country with a widely respected royal family and a powerful military regime. Since the 1960s Thailand has remained politically stable in spite of frequent shifts in political power. Although the Thai economy has not grown as fast as that of Korea or Taiwan, most Japanese economists and businessmen agree that, because of low inflation and few balance-of-payments and accumulated-debt problems, the Thais have managed their economy quite well.

At times many economists have believed that the Thai economy is sluggish because it does not have high-valued primary goods and natural resources which could help push up the economy.[1] Yet its efforts in achieving double-digit economic growth in the second half of the 1980s gave rise to the belief that Thailand is the emerging 'fifth tiger'.[2] Moreover, in the 1980s various economic policy packages were implemented, including outward-oriented industrialization programs, drastic changes in the export structure, liberalization of trade policy and deregulation. In other words, the Thai economy during the past decade has succeeded in attaining not only quantitative expansion but also notable qualitative changes.

Naturally Japan is concerned about Thailand because Japan has made substantial direct investments there. The appreciation of the yen in 1985 prompted the expansion of Japanese direct foreign investment in Asia, and Japanese investment in ASEAN countries (except for Singapore) started to boom in 1987. It is interesting to note that this investment boom actually started first in Thailand. Direct foreign investment, once launched, requires medium and long-term production of goods and services in the host country. In this context, foreign direct investment is a highly fixed economic activity, so the decision to invest must be made with the utmost caution. The fact that Japan's direct investment boom in the ASEAN region started in Thailand seems to imply that Japan, which has kept a careful watch over economic development in the region, regards Thailand as a highly suitable destination for investment.

16.2 JAPANESE RESEARCH ON THE THAI ECONOMY

There are extensive Japanese studies on individual Asian economies, and the bulk of these cover the Thai economy. From the 1950s to the early 1960s most research concentrated on India and Pakistan. India, for example, was one of the first nations in Asia to announce a Five Year Development Plan, and also a leading nation of the 'non-alliance conference' at that time, and this helps explain why India was a centre of interest. It was not until the early 1960s that the study of Thailand became widespread. This was the period when the Thai economy embarked upon 'modern economic growth.' Additionally, the Institute of Developing Economies (IDE) was established in Japan in 1960, which helped promote large-scale studies of the countries in the Asian region throughout the decade.[3] The fact that the headquarters of the Economic Commission for Asia and the Far East (ECAFE) of the United Nations was set up in Bangkok helped this process. From the second half of the 1950s, many economists representing Japan went to stay in Bangkok to conduct research, to work for international organizations or to attend international meetings. Through the efforts of these people, studies of the Thai economy flourished. Therefore research on Asian economies in the 1960s would normally include India, Thailand, Indonesia and Taiwan. Compared with the present day, little research was undertaken on Korea and China.

Japan's economic relations with Asia from the 1950s to the 1960s basically reflected the economic conditions of the region at that time. Japan imported raw materials from Asia and exported goods that were strongly related to or were a part of the postwar reparations. However, thereafter Japan's trade with Asian countries gradually shifted from postwar reparations to official development aid (ODA) as they began to embark on their 'modern-economic-growth' programme. Still, their industrialization was at an early stage and the share of agriculture and natural resources in the overall economy was still very high. Therefore most research on Asian economies was concerned with agriculture and primary products. Japanese studies of the Thai economy in the 1960s followed these same general trends.

In the second half of the 1960s, not only trade and postwar reparations but also direct foreign investment made its appearance in Japanese relations with Thailand. Naturally a significant factor in the expansion of such relations was the progress of Thai industrialization. At the beginning of the 1970s the study of the Thai economy had made great strides, and with good reason.[4] During the 1960s the Thai economy had registered the highest economic growth rate (at 8 per cent per annum) among South-East Asian economies, outranking even Singapore. In addition, Thailand's rate of inflation remained low and its process of industrialization progressed smoothly based on import-substitution industries. In the agricultural sector new types of crop for exports, such as maize, had been developed, showing that economic restructuring was taking a noticeable new turn. As a result numerous papers on Thai industrialization and Japan–Thailand relations were published in Japan in the 1970s. By then research on Thailand no longer remained the sole domain of the Institute of Developing Economies and universities – private financial institutions and government sectors also began to carry out their own business or business-related research on Thailand.[5] A typical example of this was a study on large company groups in Thailand (Thai '*zaibatsu*').

Studies in the 1980s may be said to have stuck to the traditional trends of the preceding decade, but they were more systematic and detailed. A number of books on the Thai economy were published, and so were many papers on macroeconomic, trade and industrial policies. From the end of the 1980s to the present, even more interesting changes in the themes of study can be observed. The success of the Thai economy, as shown by its tremendous growth and development since the second half of the 1980s, was analyzed to see whether the keys to success could be applied to other developing countries. The pattern of Thailand's economic growth was also compared with that of Japan, Korea and Taiwan.[6]

16.3 EVALUATION OF GROWTH DEVELOPMENT AND INDUSTRIALIZATION IN THAILAND IN JAPANESE STUDIES OF THE THAI ECONOMY

Japan's image of the Thai economy has greatly changed since the second half of the 1980s. Until the middle of the 1970s Japan still viewed Thailand as an agricultural country, famous for its exported rice and potential resources for tourism. Now this image has shifted to one of a country making rapid progress in industrialization and urbanization, while preserving its cultural traditions. The country's exports increased markedly and increasingly shifted to industrial goods. Also, direct foreign investment from Japan sharply increased. One often wonders whether the image of Thailand presented on TV and in periodicals and other types of publication reflects actual conditions in Thailand. It is undeniable that systematic and detailed Japanese research has helped foster such an image of Thailand in Japan. However, it is not the aim of this chapter to analyze the process of growth and development of the Thai economy, but mainly to introduce some Japanese views on it. Two aspects will be discussed: Thailand's economic policies, namely macroeconomic policy, industrialization policy, trade policy and foreign investment policy; and the economic and social capability of its policy responses and transformation.

16.3.1 Appraisal of Related Economic Policies

Macroeconomic policy

Japanese appraisals of Thailand's macroeconomic policy compare it favourably with those of other developing countries. The Thai economy has been perceived as achieving an excellent macroeconomic performance without incurring rise to such serious problems as inflation, balance-of-payments deficits and external debts.[7] In this respect the Thai economy has succeeded in attaining stable growth. Nevertheless the growth rate did not reach double-digits as it did in the Asian NIEs after the 1960s. In Japan there are two different views of this. One is a favourable evaluation of the Thai economy for its success in attaining stable growth; the other maintains that excessive stress has been placed on stability and because of this the Thai economy has remained conservative.[8] As a result one view would argue that if a more ambitious and aggressive macroeconomic policy had been adopted, the economic growth rate could have been much higher, whereas the other view would argue that if a more aggressive macroeconomic policy had been undertaken, it could have disrupted economic stability. Nevertheless, while these two arguments seem to conflict with each other, they both admit that Thailand's macroeconomic performance has been favourable. It is observed that the Thai economy in the second half of the 1980s was able to achieve double-digit economic growth while maintaining its basic policy stance of stable growth.

Industrialization policy

Thailand's industrialization policy began in the 1950s and was fully fledged by the 1960s. During the 1960s its industrialization policy mainly supported import substitution, based on consumer goods. On entering the 1970s it gradually moved towards export-led industrialization. By the second half of the 1980s this export-led industrialization policy had borne fruit. Thus the Thai economy displays a feature common among those developing economies that have found success by moving away from an import-substitution policy towards an export-oriented one. However we should not overlook various features that are unique to the Thai economy. The most important of these may be the role of the agricultural sector. Thailand is blessed with abundant agricultural resources and it endeavoured to develop new export products in the agricultural sector during the time of import-substitution industrialization, with an eye to diversifying agriculture. Furthermore, in the course of the export-led industrialization of the 1970s, a concept of NAIC (newly agro-industrializing country), replacing NICs, was introduced in an attempt aggressively to tackle industrialization based on agriculture and primary goods. The rising share of manufactured exports, brought about by export-led industrialization in the 1980s, also increased the weight of processed agricultural goods and manufactured primary goods. This was an indication of the importance of the NAIC policy.[9] Another important feature of Thai industrialization policy can be seen in the relationship between the government and the private sector. Compared with those of other countries in East and South-East Asia, Thailand's industrialization policies have respected the independence of the private sector by including measures that have not largely contradicted the market mechanism. A number of countries in East and South-East Asia instead favoured powerful and strong government leadership.[10]

Trade policy

Trade policy and industrialization policy are often two sides of the same coin. This is also true in the case of Thailand, where trade policy is closely and systematically linked to industrial policy. Judging from the changes in the export structure in the 1980s, its effects can be evaluated highly.[11]

Apart from investment promotion, actual policy measures included export credit, tax refunds and tax rebates. In addition, export industries enjoyed concessionary tariffs on electricity. Looking also at the composition of export products in four ASEAN countries (Thailand, Indonesia, Malaysia and the Philippines), it may be seen that the share of primary exports to total exports is currently lowest in Thailand, which shows how impressive its progress has been in this area since the 1970s. The share of industrial goods in the total exports of both Thailand and the Philippines are almost the same (Table 16.1). However, while the Philippines' total exports amounted to only US$8.7 billion, those of Thailand reached US$23 billion.

Table 16.1 Share of manufactured goods in the total exports (per cent)

	1965	*1990*
Thailand	3	64
Indonesia	4	34
Malaysia	6	44
Philippines	6	62

Source: World Bank, *World Development Report*, 1992.

Foreign investment policy

Thailand has been receiving foreign capital since the 1960s. The introduction of direct foreign investment was important to Thailand's economic development because it involved, among other things, the transfer of technology. At present all the ASEAN countries have direct-investment promotion policies, and the difference between the foreign-capital policies of ASEAN countries is narrowing. Nevertheless Thailand led all the others (except Singapore) in liberalizing foreign investment in its policy measures of the 1980s. For example Thailand now allows 100 per cent foreign ownership where total output is exported. Competition for direct foreign investment has become quite keen in all ASEAN countries.[12] Investors are able to examine and compare the investment-promotion measures of each individual country. At the same time they are able to analyze the investment environment and decide on the best destination for their capital. As mentioned earlier, Thailand was the first among the ASEAN-4 to experience a direct-investment boom. In the beginning investment came mainly from Japan, and then from Taiwan. Thailand's macro-economic performance and political–social stability were said to be major factors contributing to accelerated inflows of direct foreign investment.

16.3.2 Economic and Social Ability to Respond and Transform

What is outstanding about the course of growth and development of the Thai economy is that adjustment of the economic structure – including reforms of the industrial and export structures was implemented smoothly. Such efforts were further accelerated in the middle of the 1980s, and were strengthened to achieve the double-digit economic growth rate of the second half of that decade. The fact that economic restructuring has gone so well for the past 30 years indicates that Thailand possesses a strong ability to transform. This stands out in a comparison with other countries in the region. For example, although the Philippines' per capita income was higher than that of Thailand in the 1950s, transformation of its industrial and export structures did not take place so smoothly from the 1970s to the 1980s. In addition, political turmoil aggravated the economic situation and pushed the Philippine economy into serious stagnation during that decade.

Economic growth and development of developing countries generally means a transfer of production factors and resources from the agricultural sector to the industrial sector. Similarly it means that the share of production by industry is shifted to the industrial sector as well, which in turn results in an income gap between rural and urban areas and between different economic sectors. In the case of Thailand, economic growth has been maintained while incurring comparatively few income-distribution problems.[13] Thailand has also been able to promote local entrepreneurship. The formation and operation of large company groups (*zaibatsu*) have been the subject of study in Japan since the 1970s. Recently, however, there have emerged a new group of *zaibatsu*, consisting of relatively young entrepreneurs who have become successful through their aggressive business activities.[14]

In order to transform an economy a number of prerequisites have to be met. In the case of Thailand such prerequisites, to a large extent, have been satisfactorily met. The first is political–social stability. In spite of a number of changes in government administration in the past few years, they have neither caused serious political turmoil nor prolonged instability. This is a highly significant precondition for business activities, especially direct investment from abroad. The second precondition is the stability and continuity of economic policies. Despite changes in the administrations, the underlying principles of Thailand's economic policies have continued, and thus lessened the concern of investors. In addition to these two requirements, a proper level of education, job training and infrastructure (not only physical but also social) are important. To a certain extent these latter requirements have also been satisfied in the Thai economy.

Also worth mentioning is Thailand's ability to promote or foster small and medium-sized companies. In Thailand, subcontracting relations between the leading companies and small and medium-sized companies are relatively weak (compared with Japan, for example), which is a problem. However what is important is that small and medium-sized companies do exist, which has enhanced the linkage effects between various industries in the economy as a whole and strengthened Thailand's ability to transform. In the future, when subcontracting relations between major companies and small and medium-sized ones become stronger, the linkage effect of industries will increase to further enhance the economy's transformation.

16.4 THE MOVEMENT OF THE THAI ECONOMY TOWARDS 'FIFTH TIGER' STATUS

Per capita income among the Asian NIEs ranges from US$5 000 to US$12 000. As Singapore and Hong Kong are considered city states it may be preferable to compare them with Bangkok rather than with the entire country. On the other hand it is appropriate to compare Korea and Taiwan with Thailand as a whole, despite the smaller populations of Korea (43 million) and Taiwan (20 million). We already know that these four countries have attained NIC or NIE status since the close of the 1970s. In 1979 the OECD published a report concerning the impact of production and trade of the NICs.[15] Let us now make a comparative sketch of Thailand as the potential 'fifth tiger' of Asia, using Korea and Taiwan to make the comparison.

The OECD report lists features of NICs as follows:

- Export-led growth and development policy is being implemented in these countries.
- The share of industrial production in GDP increases.

- The share of manufactured products in total exports increases.
- The gap in per capital income with the industrial world is narrowing.

As it is already well known that an export-led development policy is being aggressively pursued in Thailand, we need not dwell further on this point. The share of the industrial sector as a proportion of GDP in Thailand in 1990 was estimated at 39 per cent, which was not very different from Korea's 41 per cent in 1980 or Taiwan's 46 per cent, also in 1980. Actually, in Taiwan the industrial sector had a 40 per cent share in GDP in 1970. Next, in comparing the share of manufactured goods (including the share of processed agricultural goods) in total exports, Thailand's figure indicated 64 per cent in 1990, while Korea registered 90 per cent and Taiwan 96 per cent, marking a substantial difference in this area.[16] However, since Korea produces few primary goods, the difference with Korea could be expected. But, in common with Thailand, Taiwan is richly endowed with primary goods such as sugar and rice, so the difference the two countries provides a useful reference.

In Taiwan the share of manufactured goods in exports had already reached 76 per cent by 1965. Thailand's export-led growth policy was only launched in the 1970s. Moreover, although transformation from import-substitution to export-led policy took place in the 1970s, the real economy persistently retained the characteristic of import substitution. On that premise, we may say that it was only in the 1980s that the full-scale export-led policy package was stabilized and its effects gradually became visible. Consequently, even if Thailand's share of manufactured goods in total exports was lower in comparison with Korea or Taiwan from the second half of the 1970s to 1980, we cannot discount the possibility of Thailand becoming the 'fifth tiger' in Asia.

In the light of the basic common features of NICs noted by the OECD, Thai economy has more or less satisfied the preconditions of an NIC since 1979. However, in order to become the 'fifth tiger' other elements are required, especially social factors and indicators. For example the social indicators of Thailand, such as enrolment in secondary education, infrastructure status and so on, were not satisfactory in comparison with other Asian NICs in 1979. Nonetheless there is a good possibility of Thailand becoming the 'fifth tiger' in the future. Perhaps Thailand will develop as an NAIC and be distinct from Korea or Taiwan.

In closing, it should be pointed out that the economic success achieved so far has produced a new set of problems. These are new growth constraints, such as infrastructure shortages and environmental considerations. Economic growth and development have contributed to an increased income level in Thailand, and have created a growing middle class. In this context economic growth must have balancing domestic and social policies. If Thailand sustains its efforts to overcome the new growth constraints and steadily follows appropriate policy measures as before, it will not have difficulty in emerging as the 'fifth tiger' of Asia.

Notes

1. In the first half of the 1980s some Japanese economists were afraid that the Thai economy might face stagnation. See Ezaki, 1992.
2. Ezaki (1992) and Harada (1988) actually pointed out the all ASEAN-4 countries will become the next group of NIEs.
3. The background of the establishment of IDE was written by Tobata (1979) who was the first President of the IDE.
4. A definitive and comprehensive study on the economy of Thailand in the early 1970s can be found in Shishido, 1973.
5. Many reports and studies were published by the Export–Import Bank of Japan, Bank of Tokyo, JETRO and others.
6. See Ezaki, 1992, Harada, 1988, and Yamazawa and Hirata, 1987.
7. This appraisal has become something of a consensus in the works of Japanese economists since the 1970s.
8. A discussion on the conservativeness of Thai economic policy, as reflected in its stress on the stability of the baht, can be found in Ezaki, 1992.
9. With regard to NAIC, see Suehiro and Yasuda, 1987.
10. The relationship between the private sector and the government was pointed out by Yoshihara (1992a), who also compared the difference in the above relationship in Thailand and the Philippines.
11. For details, see Hirata, 1992, and Yamazawa and Hirata, 1987.
12. See JETRO's white paper on institutional and policy measures on direct investments in the ASEAN countries.
13. See Ikemoto, 1992.
14. See Inoue, 1989, 1991.
15. See OECD, 1979.
16. World Bank, *World Tables 1992;* Council for Economic Planning and Development, Republic of China, *Taiwan Statistical Data Book, 1991.*

Bibliography

AINSWORTH, MARTHA and MEAD OVER (1992) 'The Economic Impact of AIDS: Shocks, Responses and Outcomes', technical working paper no. 1, World Bank, Population, Health and Nutrition Division, June.

ALFORD, D. (1992) 'Streamflow and Sediment Transport from Mountain Watersheds of the Chao Phraya Basin, Northern Thailand: a Reconnaissance Study', *Mountain Research and Development*, vol. 12, no. 3, pp. 257–68.

ALT, JAMES E. and ALEC K. CHRYSTAL (1983) *Political Economics* (New York: Wheatsheaf Books).

ALTERNATIVE AGRICULTURE GROUP (1991) 'Alternative Agriculture: the Survival of Small Peasants', paper presented at People's Forum, Bangkok, Thailand, 8–17 October.

AMMAR SIAMWALLA (1975) 'Growth, Stability and Income Distribution in Thailand', in Prateep Sondysuvan (ed.) *Finance, Trade, and Development in Thailand, Essay in Honour of Khunying Suparp Yossundara* (Bangkok: Sompong Press).

AMMAR SIAMWALLA (1990) 'Land Abundant Agricultural Growth and Some of Its Consequences: The Case of Thailand', paper presented at the International Food Policy Research Institute Conference on Agriculture on the Road to Industrialization held in Taipei, Taiwan, 4–7 September.

AMMAR SIAMWALLA (1992) 'Myths, Demons and the Future of Thai Agriculture', paper presented at the 1992 TDRI Year-End Conference, Chon Buri, 12–13 December.

AMMAR SIAMWALLA and SUTHAD SETBOONSARNG (1989) 'Trade, Exchange Rate, and Agricultural Pricing Policies in Thailand', *The Political Economy of Agricultural Pricing Policy*, Washington, DC, World Bank.

ANAT ARBHABHIRAMA, DHIRA PHANTUMVANIT, JOHN ELKINGTON and PHAITOON INGKASUWAN (1988) *Thailand Natural Resources Profile*, issued by Thailand Development Research Institute (Singapore: Oxford University Press).

ANEK LAOTHAMATAS (1992) *Business Associations and the New Political Economy of Thailand: From Bureaucratic Polity to Liberal Corporatism* (Boulder and Singapore: Westview Press and Institute of Southeast Asian Studies).

ANUCHAT POUNGSOMLEE (1991) 'An Integrative Study of an Urban Ecosystem: the Case of Bangkok', PhD thesis, Centre for Resource and Environmental Studies, Australian National University.

ANUCHAT POUNGSOMLEE and HELEN ROSS (1992) *Impacts of Modernization and Urbanization in Bangkok: an Integrative Ecological and Biosocial Study* (Bangkok: Institute for Population and Social Research, Mahidol University).

APCTT (1986a) *Technology Policies and Planning: Regional Report* (Bangalore: Asian and Pacific Centre for Transfer of Technology).

APCTT (1986b) *Technology Policies and Planning: Republic of Korea* (Bangalore: Asian and Pacific Centre for Transfer of Technology).

APCTT (1986c) *Technology Policies and Planning: Thailand* (Bangalore: Asian and Pacific Centre for Transfer of Technology).

APICHAI PUNTASEN, SOMBOON SIRIPRACHAI and CHAIYUTH PUNYASAVATSUT (1992) 'Political Economy of Eucalyptus: Business, Bureaucracy and the Thai Government', *Journal of Contemporary Asia*, vol. 22, no. 2, pp. 187–206.

APISAK DHANASETTAKORN (1990) 'Going for Self-Sufficiency Through Encroachment', *The Nation*, 8 February.

ARIFF, MOHAMED and HAL HILL (1985) *Export-Oriented Industrialization: the ASEAN Experience* (Sydney: Allen and Unwin).

ASIAN DEVELOPMENT BANK (ADB) (1971) *Southeast Asia's Economy in the 1970s* (London: Longman).

ASIAN DEVELOPMENT BANK (ADB) (1991) *Key Economic Indicators of Developing Member Countries* (Manila: Asian Development Bank).

BANGKOK MASS TRANSIT AUTHORITY (BMTA) (987) *Corporate Plan, 1987–1991* (Bangkok) (in Thai).

BANK OF THAILAND (1990) 'Domestic Financial Institutions and the Conduct of Monetary Policy by the Bank of Thailand', Economic Research Division, December (mimeographed, in Thai).

BANK OF THAILAND (1992) 'Impacts of the Second Stage of Foreign Exchange Liberalization', *Bank of Thailand Monthly Bulletin*, February (in Thai).

BANK OF THAILAND (various years) *Bank of Thailand Monthly Bulletin* (Bangkok).

BAUTISTA, ROMEO M. (1992) *Development Policy in East Asia: Economic Growth and Poverty Alleviation* (Singapore: ASEAN Economic Research Unit, Institute of Southeast Asian Studies).

BECKER, G.S. (1983) 'A Theory of Competition among Pressure Groups for Political Influence', *Quarterly Journal of Economics*, vol. 98, pp. 371–400.

BERTRAND, T. and L. SQUIRE (1980) 'The Relevance of the Dual Economy Model: A Case Study of Thailand', *Oxford Economic Papers*, vol. 32, no. 3 (November), pp. 480–511.

BHANUPONGSE NIDHIPRABHA (1992) 'Fiscal Policy and Economic Stabilization in Thailand', *Thammasat Economic Journal*, vol. 10 (September), pp. 37–54 (in Thai).

BIGGS, T. *et al.* (1990) 'Rural Industry and Employment Study: A Synthesis Report', Rural Industries and Employment Project, TDRI, Bangkok.

BLAU, J. (1992) *The Visible Poor: Homelessness in the United States* (New York: Oxford University Press).

BOURNE, R. and J. LEVIN (1983) *Social Problems: Causes, Consequences, Interventions* (New York: West).

CASTLE, LESLIE V. and CHRISTOPHER FINDLAY (eds) (1988) *Pacific Trade in Services* (Sydney: Allen and Unwin).

CHAI-ANAN SAMUDAVANIJA (1982) *The Thai Young Turks* (Singapore: Institute of Southeast Asian Studies).

CHAI-ANAN SAMUDAVANIJA (1990a) 'Economic Policy-Making in a Liberal Technocratic Polity', in John W. Langford and K. Lorne Brownsey (eds), *Economic Policy-Making in the Asia-Pacific Region* (Halifax: The Institute for Research on Public Policy).

CHAI-ANAN SAMUDAVANIJA (1990b) 'Thailand: A Stable Semi-Democracy', in Larry Diamond, Juan J. Linz and S. M. Lipset (eds), *Politics in Developing Countries: Comparing Experiences with Democracy* (Boulder: Lynn Rienner)

CHALONGPHOB SUSSANGKARN (1991) 'Education, Labor Markets, and Economic Development: Policy Simulations', paper presented at the 1991 TDRI Year-End Conference, December.

CHALONGPHOB SUSSANGKARN *et al.* (1988) 'The Long-Term View on Growth and Income Distribution', paper presented at the 1988 TDRI Year-End Conference on Income Distribution and Long-term Development, December.

CHARIT TINGSABADH (1989) 'Economic Systems and the Environment in Thailand', in *Culture and Environment in Thailand* (Bangkok: Siam Society).

CHEN, P. (1980) 'The Cultural Implications of Industrialization and Modernization: With Special Reference to Southeast Asia', in R. E. Vente and P. S. J. Chen (eds), *Culture and Industrialization: An Asian Dilemma* (Singapore: McGraw-Hill).

CHENG TUN-JEN (1990) 'Political Regimes and Development Strategies: South Korea and Taiwan in Gary Gereffi and Donald L. Wyman (eds), *Manufacturing Miracles: Paths of Industrialization in Latin America and East Asia*, Princeton: Princeton University Press.

CHESADA LOHA-UNCHIT (1989) 'Policies, Instruments and Institutions for Rural Industrial Development', The Rural Industries and Employment Project, Thailand Development Research Institute, August.

CHRISTENSEN, SCOTT R. (1992a) 'Capitalism and Democracy in Thailand', paper presented at the Roundtable Discussion on Capitalism and Democracy in Southeast Asia, AAS Annual Conference, Washington DC.

CHRISTENSEN, SCOTT R. (1992b) 'The Role of Agribusiness in Thai Agriculture: Towards a Policy Analysis', *TDRI Quarterly Review*, vol. 7, no. 4 (December), pp. 3–9.

CHRISTENSEN, SCOTT R., DAVID DOLLAR, AMMAR SIAMWALLA and PAKORN VICHYANOND (1992) 'Institutional and Political Bases of Growth-Inducing Policies in Thailand', paper prepared for the World Bank project on the role of government and East Asian success, October.

CHULACHEEB CHINWANNO and SOMSAK TAMBUNLERTCHAI (1983) 'Japanese Investment in Thailand and Its Prospects in the 1980's', in S. Sekiguchi *et al.* (eds), *ASEAN–Japan Relations: Investment*, East–West Seminar (Singapore: ASEAN Economic Research Unit, Institute of Southeast Asian Studies).

COCHRANE, SUSAN and YAFFA MANCHNES (1982) 'The Determinants of Employment Outside the Family and Off the Farm', World Bank, mimeographed.

COUNCIL FOR ECONOMIC PLANNING AND DEVELOPMENT, Republic of China (1991) *Taiwan Statistical Data Book 1991.*

DAPICE, DAVID and FRANK FLATTERS (1989) 'Thailand: Prospects and Perils in the World Economy', Background Paper no. 1, TDRI 1989 Year-End Conference, Chon Buri, Thailand, 14–15 December.

DEMAINE, H. (1986) 'Kanpattana: Thai Views of Development', in M. Hobart and R. H. Taylor (eds), *Context Meaning and Power in Southeast Asia* (Ithaca, NY: Cornell University, Southeast Asia Program–SEAP).

DEPARTMENT OF LAND TRANSPORT (DLT) Ministry of Communications (1990) 'Land Transport Department Sector Paper', Bangkok, 31 March.

DHEPPANOM MUANGMAN and S. NUNTA (1982) 'Knowledge, Attitudes and Practices Concerning Health, Abortion, Sexually-Transmitted Diseases, and Narcotic Addiction of Prostitutes in Bangkok' (Bangkok: Mahidol University).

DHIRA ASHAKUL (1992) 'Future of Tourism in Thailand', paper presented at Industrial Finance Corporation of Thailand (IFCT), 27 August.

DHIRA PHANTUMVANIT and THEODORE PANAYOTOU (1990) 'Industrialization and Environmental Quality: Paying the Price', synthesis paper no. 3, the 1990 TDRI Year-End Conference, Chon Buri, 8–9 December.

DICKEN, PETER (1992) *Global Shift: The Internationalization of Economic Activity*, 2nd edition (London: Paul Chapman).

DIREK PATMASIRIWAT (1991) 'Fiscal Policy in Thailand 2529–Present', paper presented at the seminar organised by the Institute of Public Policy Studies, the Social Sciences Association of Thailand (in Thai).

DIREK PATMASIRIWAT (1992) 'Tax Reform in Thailand 1991: Comment', *Chulalongkorn Journal of Economics*, vol. 4 (in Thai).

DONNELLY, JACK (1984) 'Human Rights and Development: Complementary or Competing Concerns?' *World Politics*, vol. XXXVI, no. 2 (January).

DONER, RICHARD (1991) Driving a Bargain: Japanese Firms and Automobile Industrialization in Southeast Asia, Berkeley, University of California Press.

EDWARDS, SEBASTIAN (1987) 'Sequencing Economic Liberalization in Developing Countries', *Finance and Development* (March).

ENGINEERING SCIENCE, INC., THAI DCI CO. LTD. and SYSTEM ENGINEERING CO. LTD. (1989) Main Report: 'National Hazardous Waste Management, vol. 2', report submitted to Office of the National Environmental Board.

EZAKI MITSUO (1992) 'Growth and Stagnation in the Southeast Asian Economy', in Kunio Yoshihara (ed.) *The Economy of Southeast Asia* (Tokyo: Koubundo) (in Japanese).

FALKUS, M. (1990) 'Economic History and Environment in Southeast Asia', *Asian Studies Review*, vol. 4, no. 1, pp. 65–79.

FREYN, HUBERT (1961) 'Culture and Economics in Thailand', *Far Eastern Economic Review*, 12 January, p. 53.

FRIEDLAND, J. (1992) 'Cost of a Crisis', *Far Eastern Economic Review*, 4 June, p. 56.

GINSBURG, N., B. KOPPEL and T.G. MCGEE (1991) *The Extended Metropolis: Settlement Transition in Asia* (Honolulu: University of Hawaii Press).

GOLDSMITH, E. and NICHOLAS HILDYARD (eds) (1992) *The Earth Report 3* (London: Mitchell Beazley).

GUPTA, A. (1988) *Ecology and Development in the Third World* (London: Routledge).

HANDLEY, P. (1991) 'The Land Wars', *Far Eastern Economic Review*, 31 October, pp. 15–6.

HANDLEY, P. (1992) 'Twisted Tracks: Bangkok's Rail Projects Pose Numerous Planning Problems', *Far Eastern Economic Review*, 30 April, pp. 50–1.

HANDLEY, P. and SUSUMU AWANOHARA (1991) 'Power Struggles', *Far Eastern Economic Review*, 17 October.

HARADA YUTAKA (1988) *Economic Development in Thailand–the Nation toward the 5th NIE* (Tokyo: Nihon Kodonsha) (in Japanese).

HARIT SUTABUTR (1987) 'Science and Technology Manpower for Development: The Thai Way', paper presented at the Seminar on Technological Considerations in the Development of Thailand, Pattaya, April.

HEWISON, K. (1993) 'Of Regimes, State and Pluralities: Thai Politics Enters the 1990s', in K. Hewison, R. Robinson and G. Rodan (eds), *Southeast Asia in the 1990s: Authoritarianism, Democracy and Capitalism* (Sydney: Allen and Unwin).

HIRATA AKIRA (1992) 'Trade Structure in Southeast Asia', in Yoshihara Kunio (ed.) *The Economy of Southeast Asia* (Tokyo: Koubundo) (in Japanese).

HIRSCH, PHILIP (1990a) *Development Dilemmas in Rural Thailand* (Singapore: Oxford University Press).

HIRSCH, PHILIP (1990b) 'Thai Agriculture: Restructuring in the 1980s and 1990s', RIAP Occasional Paper no. 12, Research Institute for Asia and the Pacific, the University of Sydney.

HUBER, J. (1976a) 'The Future of Parenthood: Implications of Declining Fertility', in D. Hiller and R. Sheets (eds), *Women and Men* (Cincinnati: University of Cincinnati Press), pp. 333–51.

HUBER, J. (1976b) 'Toward a Socio-Technological Theory of the Women's Movement', *Social Problems*, vol. 23.

HUESMANN, L.R. *et al.*, (1984) 'Intervening Variables in the TV Violence-Aggression Relation: Evidence from Two Countries', *Developmental Psychology*, vol. 20, pp. 746–75.

HUGHES, HELEN (1985) 'Asian Pacific Developing Economies: Performance and Issues', *Asian Development Review*, vol. 3, no. 1, pp. 1–23.

HUMAN RESOURCE INSTITUTE (HRI) and Ministry of Science and Technology and Energy (MOSTE) (1986) *Manpower Planning and Survey for Scientists and Technologists*, (Human Resources Institute, Thammasat University, and Ministry of Science, Technology and Energy).

IKEMOTO YUKIO (1992) 'Income Distribution in Southeast Asia', in Yoshihara Kunio (ed.) *The Economy of Southeast Asia* (Tokyo: Koubundo) (in Japanese)

INGRAM, J.C. (1971) *Economic Change in Thailand 1850–1970* (Stanford: Stanford University Press).

INOUE RYUICHIRO (1989) *Big Business in Asia* (Tokyo: Koudansha) (in Japanese).

INOUE RYUICHIRO (1991) *Thailand: Dynamism toward the Industrial Nation* (Tokyo: Chikumashobo) (in Japanese).

INTERNATIONAL CIVIL AVIATION ORGANIZATION (ICAO) (1984) 'On-Flight Origin and Destination Year and Quarter Ending 31 March 1983', no. 301, (Montreal: International Civil Aviation Organization).

INTERNATIONAL CIVIL AVIATION ORGANIZATION (ICAO) (1991) 'On-Flight Origin and Destination Year and Quarter Ending 31 March 1990', no. 378 (Montreal: International Civil Aviation Organization).

IUCN/UNEP/WWF (1991) *Caring for the Earth: a Strategy for Sustainable Living* (Gland, Switzerland).

JACKSON, P.A. (1989) *Buddhism Legitimation and Conflicts: The Political Functions of Urban Thai Buddhism* (Singapore: Institute of Southeast Asian Studies).

JAMES, WILLIAM E., S. NAYA and G.M. MEIER (1987) *Asian Development: Economic Success and Policy Lessons*, International Center for Economic Growth (Madison: University of Wisconsin Press).

JETRO, *White Paper on the World Market: Overseas Investment*, annual edition (in Japanese).

JIMENEZ, EMMANUEL, MARLAINE LOCKHEED and NONGNUCH WATTANAWAHA (1988) 'The Relative Effectiveness of Private and Public Schools in Enhancing Achievement: The Case of Thailand', mimeo (Washington, DC: World Bank).

JITTAPATR KRUAVAN (1991) 'Patterns and Trends of Employment by Location and Sector', Background Report No. 2–3, National Urban Development Framework Project, TDRI, January 1991.

JOHNSTON, B. and J. MELLOR (1961) 'The Role of Agriculture in Economic Development', *American Economic Review*, vol. 54, no. 4, pp. 566–92.

KASEMSRI HOMCHUEN, BOONCHONG KAOSITTHIWONG and BANDID TANTIEN (1991) 'Preliminary Review of Potential Health Hazards from Industrial Activity, Technical Report' (Bangkok: National Epidemiology Board of Thailand) (in Thai).

KATANO H., MURAKAMI A. and IKEMOTO K. (1978) *Japan's Direct Investment to ASEAN Countries* (Kobe: Research Institute for Economics and Business Administration, Kobe University).

KAYE, L. (1990) 'Of Cabbages and Cultures', *Far Eastern Economic Review*, 13 December, pp. 35–7.

KIDIKORO T. (1992) 'Overview of Strategies for Urban Development and Transportation Systems in Asian Metropolises: with Special Focus on Bangkok Metropolitan Area', *Development Digest*.

KIM, Y.B. (1987) 'Evaluation of Manpower Policies in the Republic of Korea', in R. Amjad (ed.) *Human Resource Planning: The Asian Experience* (International Labour Organization, Asian Employment Programme).

KING MONGKUT INSTITUTE OF TECHNOLOGY (KMIT) (1984) 'Status of Science and Technology in Thailand', report submitted to USAID, Thailand, by the Center for Operation for Research and Development, King Mongkut Institute of Technology, Thon Buri Campus.

KOSIT PANPIEMRAS (1990) 'Importance of Income Distribution in Economic Policy and National Economic Planning: Lesson from Thailand', in Colin Durkop (ed.) *Readings in Social Market Economics* (Bangkok: Konrad Adenauer Stiftung).

KOSIT PANPIEMRAS (1991) 'Agricultural Policy and Newly-Industrialized Country Status', Bangkok: Institute of Public Policy Studies (in Thai).

KRAIYUDHT DHIRATAYAKINANT (1990) 'Partnership in Development: An Exploratory Analysis of the Relative Role of the Public and Private Sectors in Economic Progress of Thailand', in Proceedings of the 4th International Conference on Thai Studies, 11–13 May, volume IV (Kunming, China: Institute of Southeast Asian Studies).

KRIRKKIAT PIPATSERITHAM (1981) 'Ownership Analysis of Big Business in Thailand', research report submitted to the Thai Khadi Research Institute, Thammasat University, Bangkok.

KRUEGER, ANNE O., MAURICE SCHIFF and ALBERTO VALDES (1988) 'Impact of Sector-Specific and General Economic Policies toward Agriculture', *World Bank Economic Review* (September).

KRUGMAN, PAUL (1988) 'External Shocks and Domestic Policy Responses', in Rudiger Dornbusch, F. Leslie and C. H. Helmers, *The Open Economy: Tools for Policy makers in Developing Countries* (New York: Oxford University Press), pp. 54–79.

LECRAW, D. (1977) 'Direct Investment by Firms from Less Developed Countries', *Oxford Economic Papers*, vol. 29, no. 3, pp. 442–57.

LEE TSAO YUAN (1990) 'NIC Investment in ASEAN: the Pattern in the Eighties', in Soon Lee Ying (ed.) *Foreign Direct Investment in ASEAN* (Kuala Lumpur: Malaysian Economic Association).

LEIGH, S. (1989) 'Divorce in Asia', *Asia Magazine*, 27 October, pp. 8–14.

LENSKI, G. and J. LENSKI (1987) *Human Societies*, 5th ed. (New York: McGraw Hill).

LO, S. Y. (1985) 'Industrial Technology Development in the Republic of Korea', Asian Development Bank Economic Staff Paper no. 27.

LOHRMANN, LARRY (1991) 'Peasants, Plantations, and Pulp: The Politics of Eucalyptus in Thailand', *Bulletin of Concerned Asian Scholars*, vol. 23, no. 4.

LOHR, S. (1984) 'Me-Tooism Seeps into Japan', *The Straits Times*, 14 May.

MACHIMURA, T. (1992) 'The Urban Restructuring Process in Tokyo in the 1980s: Transforming Tokyo into a World City', *International Journal of Urban and Regional Research*, vol. 16, no. 1, pp. 114–28.

MALEE PLUKSPONGSAWALEE (1982) 'Women and the Law', in Suchart Prasith-rathasint and Suwalli Piampiti (eds), *Women in Development: Implications for Population Dynamics in Thailand*, proceedings of Seminar (Bangkok: National Institute of Development Administration).

MCGEE, T. G. (1991) 'The Emergence of Desakota Regions in Asia', in N. Ginsburg, B. Koppel and T. G. McGee (eds), *The Extended Metropolis: Settlement Transition in Asia* (Honolulu: University of Hawaii Press), pp. 3–26.

MCKINNON, R. J. (1988) 'Financial Liberalization and Economic Development: A Reassessment of Interest Rate Policies in Asia and Latin America', International Center for Economic Growth (September).

MEDHI KRONGKAEW (1979) 'The Distributive Impact of Government's Policies: An Assessment of the Situations in Thailand', research report, Faculty of Economics, Thammasat University, Bangkok (in Thai).

MEDHI KRONGKAEW (1986) 'Imbalance in Agricultural Development and Industrialization and Its Impact on Social Welfare: A Case of Thailand', paper presented at the 8th World Congress of the International Economic Association, New Delhi, 1–5 December.

MEDHI KRONGKAEW (1988) 'The Current Development of Small and Medium Scale Industries (SMIs) in Thailand', *Asian Development Review*, vol. 6, no. 2 (December), pp. 70–95.

MEDHI KRONGKAEW (1991) 'The Making of A Fifth Tiger? Thailand's Industrialization and Its Consequences', a conference proposal, Department of Economics, Research School of Pacific Studies, Australian National University, July.

MEDHI KRONGKAEW (1992a) 'Changing Urban System in a Fast Growing City and Economy: the Case of Bangkok and Thailand', paper presented at the United Nations University Conference on the Asian Pacific Urban System: Towards the 21st Century, held at Hong Kong Institute of Asian-Pacific Studies, the Chinese University of Hong Kong, 11–13 February.

MEDHI KRONGKAEW (1992b) 'Thai Economy at a Crossroads: the Best Years and Beyond', working paper submitted to the Evaluation Division, Australian International Development Assistance Bureau (AIDAB), July.

MEDHI KRONGKAEW and CHINTANA CHERNSIRI (1975) 'The Determination of Poverty Level in Thailand', *Thammasat University Journal*, vol. 5 (June–September), pp. 48–68.

MEDHI KRONGKAEW, DOW MONGKOLSMAI and VARAKORN SAMAKOSES (1988) *Financing Public Sector Development Expenditure in Selected Countries: Thailand* (Manila: Asian Development Bank, Economics Office).

MEDHI KRONGKAEW and PRANEE TINAKORN (1985) 'Poverty Conditions and Income Distribution in Thailand 1975/76 and 1980/81', *Thammasat Economic Journal*, vol. 3, no. 4 (December), pp. 54–99 (in Thai).

MEDHI KRONGKAEW, PRANEE TINAKORN and SUPHAT SUPHACHALASAI (1991) 'Priority Issues and Policy Measures to Alleviate Rural Poverty: The Case of Thailand', research report submitted to the Economics and Development Resources Center, Asian Development Bank, May.

MEDHI KRONGKAEW, PRANEE TINAKORN and SUPHAT SUPHACHALASAI (1992) 'Rural Poverty in Thailand: Policy Issues and Responses', *Asian Development Review*, vol. 10, no. 1, pp. 199–225.

MINGSARN SANTIKARN (1977) 'Technology Transfer: A Case Study', PhD dissertation, Department of Economics, Australian National University.

MINGSARN SANTIKARN KAOSA-ARD and ADIS ISRANGKURA (1988) 'Industrial Policies of Thailand', in Warin Wonghanchao and Yukio Ikemoto (eds), *Economic Development Policy in Thailand, A Historical Review* (Tokyo: Institute of Developing Economies).

MINISTRY OF EDUCATION (MOE) (1987) *Survey of Vocational Graduates Entering into Labor Markets, 1986*, Vocational Department, Ministry of Education.

MINISTRY OF EDUCATION (MOE) (1989) *Education Statistics* (Bangkok).

MINISTRY OF INTERIOR, OFFICE OF THE PERMANENT SECRETARY GENERAL (1992) *The Role of Provincial JPPCC* (Bangkok) (in Thai).

MINISTRY OF PUBLIC HEALTH (MOPH) (1987) Department of Health, 'Survey of Concentration of Lead in Blood and Urine', (Bangkok) (in Thai).

MINISTRY OF PUBLIC HEALTH (MOPH) (1990) Department of Health, Division of Occupational Health, 'Review of the Occupational Health Status and Problems in Thailand' (Bangkok) (in Thai).

MINISTRY OF PUBLIC HEALTH (MOPH) (1992) Department of Health, 'Report from Air Pollution Monitoring Stations', mimeo (Bangkok) (in Thai).

MINISTRY OF SCIENCE, TECHNOLOGY AND ENERGY (MOSTE) (1981) *Survey of Science and Technology Manpower: 1981* (Bangkok) (in Thai).

MUNDELL, ROBERT A. (1962) 'Appropriate Use of Monetary and Fiscal Policy Under Fixed Exchange Rates', *IMF Staff Papers*, vol 9. (March).

NANTHANA VACHIRAPHOL (1991) 'The Making of the Northeastern Entrepreneurs in Bangkok', MA thesis, Faculty of Economics, Thammasat University. May.

NARONGCHAI AKRASANEE (1986) 'Industrial Planing', paper presented at Symposium on Problems and National Planning Process, organised by the Faculty of Economics, Chulalongkorn University, 16 December (in Thai).

NARONGCHAI AKRASANEE and JUANJAI AJANANT (1983) 'Manufacturing Protection in Thailand: Issue and Empirical Studies', sub-project, ASEAN–Australia Joint Research Project.

NARONGCHAI AKRASANEE *et al.* (1983) *Rural off farm Employment in Thailand. Summary Report and Synthesis of the Rural Off Farm Employment Assessment Project*, September.

NATIONAL EDUCATIONAL COUNCIL (NEC) (1986) *Education in Thailand* (Bangkok).

NATIONAL EDUCATIONAL COUNCIL (NEC) (1989) 'Resource Allocation for Educational Investment', a study for the project on a search for new educational development path in the future, March.

NATIONAL ENERGY AUTHORITY (NEA) (1989) 'Thailand Energy Situation 1988' (Bangkok: NEA).

NATIONAL INSTITUTE OF MENTAL HEALTH (1982) *Television and Behaviour* (Washington, DC: U.S. Government Printing Office).

NATIONAL RESEARCH COUNCIL (NRC) (1979) *Survey on University Graduate Manpower in Thailand: 1979* (Bangkok).

NATIONAL YOUTH BUREAU (1985) *Welfare and Development of Child Labour in Production Industries*, WHO-sponsored research project, Office of the Prime Minister, National Youth Bureau.

NESDB (1981) *Framework for Future Science and Technology Development Plan*, Technology and Environment Planning Division (Bangkok).

NESDB (1986a) *Bangkok Metropolitan Development Proposals: Recommended Development Strategies and Investment Programmes for the Sixth Plan (1987–1991)* (Bangkok).

NESDB (1986b) *Compilation of Works by the Joint Public–Private Consultative Committee to Solve Economic Problems* (Bangkok) (in Thai).

NESDB (1986c) *Electronics Industry Development Planning and Employment During the Sixth Plan* (Bangkok) (in Thai).

NESDB (1986d) *The Sixth National Economic and Social Development Plan (1987–1991)* (Bangkok).

NESDB (1987a) *Compilation of Works by the Joint Public–Private Consultative Committee to Solve Economic Problems* (Bangkok) (in Thai).

NESDB (1987b) *Social Indicators 1986* (Bangkok).

NESDB (1988) *Handbook on JPPCC* (Bangkok) (in Thai).

NESDB (1992) *The Seventh National Economic and Social Development Plan, 1992–1996* (Bangkok).

NESDB (various issues) *National Income of Thailand* (Bangkok).

NESDB (various years) *National Economic and Social Development Plans, I–VI* (Bangkok).

NESDB/UNDP/TDRI (1991) *National Urban Development Policy Framework: Final Report*, 2 vols. (Bangkok).

NGAOSILP KRONGKAEW (1991) 'Occupation and Employment in Pornsawan Village', a research report of the Rural Labor Market Project, Thailand Development Research Institute.

NIPON POAPONGSAKORN (1993) 'Economics of Labour Law', in W. A. W. Neilson, J. L. Knetsch and E. Quah (eds), *Law Reform Strategies and Economic Development* (Singapore: Prentice-Hall).

NSO (1987) *The Children and Youth Survey* (Bangkok).

NSO (1988) *The Survey of Migration* (Bangkok).

NSO (1989a) *Report of the Labour Force Survey,* February (Round 1), August (Round 3) (Bangkok).

NSO (1989b) *Statistical Yearbook Thailand Number 36* (Bangkok).

NSO (1990) *Intercensal Survey of Agriculture* (Bangkok).

NSO (various years) *Socioeconomic Survey Report* (Bangkok).

NUTTAPONG THONGPAKDI and BUNLUESAK ISSARANGSI (1992) 'Provincial Industry: Compensating Disadvantage Policy', paper presented at the 1992 TDRI Year-End Conference, Chon Buri, December.

NUTTAPONG THONGPAKDI *et al.* (1991) 'A Study of Industry and Dispersion of Industry to the Provinces', paper prepared for the Seventh National Economic and Social Development Plan. TDRI.

OECD (1979) *The Impact of the Newly Industrialising Countries on Production and Trade in Manufactures* (Paris: OECD).

OEY MEESOOK (1975) 'Income Inequality in Thailand 1962/63 and 1968/69', in Harry T. Oshima and Toshiyuki Mizoguchi (eds), *Income Distribution, Employment and Economic Development in Southeast and East Asia,* vol. 1 (Manila and Tokyo: the Council for Asian Manpower Studies, and the Japan Economic Research Center).

OEY MEESOOK (1976) 'Income Distribution in Thailand', Faculty of Economics, Thammasat University, Discussion Paper Series, no. 50 (Bangkok).

OEY MEESOOK (1979) 'Income, Consumption and Poverty in Thailand, 1962/63 to 1975/76', World Bank staff working paper no. 364 (Washington, DC).

OEY MEESOOK, PRANEE TINAKORN and CHAYAN VADDHANAPHUTI (1988) 'The Political Economy of Thailand's Development: Poverty, Equity, and Growth, 1950–1985', mimeo (Washington, DC: World Bank).

OFFICE OF AGRICULTURAL ECONOMICS (OAE) Ministry of Agriculture and Cooperatives, (1991) *Agricultural Statistics of Thailand Crop Year 1990/91* (Bangkok).

OSHIMA, HARRY T. (1987) *Economic Growth in Monsoon Asia: A Comparative Survey* (Tokyo: University of Tokyo Press).

OVER, MEAD and P. PIOT (1992) 'HIV Infection and Sexually Transmitted Diseases', in D. Jamison and H. Mosely (eds), *Disease Control Priorities in Developing Countries* (New York: Oxford University Press).

PADECO CO. LTD (1990) 'The Survey of Urban Transport Costs and Fares in the SEATAC Region, Phase 1 (REL-14/1): Final Report', Kuala Lumpur, Southeast Asian Agency for Regional Transport and Communications Development.

PAITOON WIBOONCHUTIKULA (1987) 'Second Phase Import Substitution in Thailand,' paper prepared for the ASEAN-US Economic Relationship Conference, San Francisco, 29–30 September.

PANAS SIMASATHIEN and SOMCHAI RICHUPAN (1991) 'A Proposal for Tax Reform in Thailand 1991', *Chulalongkorn Journal of Economics,* vol. 3, no. 1 (April), pp. 1–51 (in Thai).

PASUK PHONGPAICHIT (1990) 'Japanese investment in ASEAN after the yen appreciation', in Soon Lee Ying (ed.) *Foreign Direct Investment in ASEAN,* (Kuala Lumpur: Malaysian Economic Association).

PATIRA SUKSTHIEN (1992) 'The Securities and Exchange Act: Its Impact on Commercial Banks', *Bangkok Bank Monthly Review,* vol. 33 (May).

PATMAWADEE SUZUKI (1993) 'Tax System Reforms and Domestic Industrial Protection', paper presented at the 1993 Annual Symposium of the Faculty of Economics, Thammasat University, Bangkok, 17–18 March.

PEARCE, D., A. MARKANDYA and E.B. BARBIER (1989) *Blueprint for A Green Economy (*London: Earthscan).

PERNIA, ERNESTO (ed.) (1990) *Human Resource Development in Asia* (Manila: Asian Development Bank).

PETRI, PETER (1991) 'Platforms in the Pacific: The Trade Effects of Direct Investment in Thailand', mimeo (Brandeis University, Department of Economics).

PHANU KRITIPORN, THEODORE PANAYOTOU and KRERKPONG CHARNPARATEEP (1990) 'The Greening of Thai Industry: Producing More and Polluting Less', research report no. 5, the 1990 TDRI Year-End Conference, 8–9 December.

PHILLIPS, DAVID P. (1986) 'Natural Experiments in the Effects of Mass Media Violence on Fatal Aggression: Strengths and Weaknesses of a New Approach', *Advances in Experimental Social Psychology,* vol. 19, pp. 207–50.

PHISIT PAKKASEM (1988) *Leading Issues in Thailand's Development Transformation* (Bangkok, National Economic and Social Development Board).

PIROM CHANTHAWORN (1976) 'The Decomposition Analysis of the Source of Income Inequality in Thailand, 1962/63 and 1968/69', MA thesis, School of Economics, University of the Philippines.

POPULATION AND COMMUNITY DEVELOPMENT ASSOCIATION (1990) 'HIV and Its Economic Impact', paper presented at the Chulabhorn Research Institute International Congress on AIDS, Bangkok, 17–21 December.

PORNTHIP BOONCROUP, CHATCHAVARN THONGDEELERD, PRATHOENG NARITTHARANGKUL NA AYUTTHAYA and ORAWAN SRIPIM (1991) 'Water Management by Local Communities', paper presented at People's Forum, Bangkok, 8–17 October.

PRAIPOL KOOMSUP (1988) 'Minerals and Energy in Thailand: Production, Consumption and Trade' in B. McKern and Praipol Koomsup (eds), *The Minerals Industries of ASEAN and Australia: Problems and Prospects* (Sydney: Allen and Unwin).

PRANEE TINAKORN (1988) 'Industrial Development in Thailand', in Rangsun Thanapornpun and Nipon Poapongsakorn (eds), *The Economy of Thailand on the Path of Santi-Prachatham,* collected essays in honour of Dr. Puey Ungphakorn on his 72nd birthday (Bangkok: Faculty of Economics, Thammasat University) (in Thai).

PRASARN TRAIRATVORAKUL (1984) 'The Effects on Income Distribution and Nutrition of Alternative Rice Policies in Thailand', research report no. 46, International Food Policy Research Institute, November.

PROJECT FOR ECOLOGICAL RECOVERY (1991) 'Failures of Hydroelectric Dams', paper presented at People's Forum, Bangkok, 8–17 October.

RACHAIN CHINTAYARANGSAN (1989) 'Industrial Structures and Interindustry Linkages', The Rural Industries and Employment Project, Thailand Development Research Institute, August 1989.

RANGSUN THANAPORNPUN (1987) *The Economics of Rice Premium* (Bangkok: Thammasat University Press) (in Thai).

RIDDLE, DOROTHY I. (1986) *Service-Led Growth: The Role of the Service Sector in World Development* (New York: Praeger).

RIGGS, F.W. (1966) *Thailand: The Modernization of a Bureaucratic Polity* (Honolulu: East–West Center Press).

RIMMER, P.J. (1986) *Riksha to Rapid Transit: Urban Public Transport Systems and Policy in Southeast Asia* (Sydney: Pergamon).

RIMMER, P.J. (1988a) 'Buses in Southeast Asian Cities: Privatization without Deregulation', in J. S. Dodgson and N. Topham (eds), *Bus Deregulation and Privatization: An International Perspective* (Aldershot: Avebury) pp. 185–208.

RIMMER, P.J. (1988b) 'Restructuring Transport Parastatals: Case Studies from Southeast Asia', in P. Bell and P. Cloke (eds), *Deregulation and Transport: Market Forces in the Third World* (London: David Fulton) pp. 156–180.

RIMMER, P.J. (1991) 'A Tale of Four Cities: Competition and Bus Ownership in Bangkok, Jakarta, Manila and Singapore', *Transportation Planning and Technology*, vol. 15, no. 2/4, pp. 231–52.

RIMMER, P.J., ABDUL RAHIM OSMAN and H.W. DICK (1989) 'Priming the Parastatals; Improving the Efficiency of State–Owned Transport Enterprises in the Asia–Pacific Region', regional seminar on transport policy, vol. I (Manila, Asian Development Bank and Economic Development Institute), pp. 133–84.

ROBINSON, D., YONGHO BYEON and RANJIT TEJA, with WANDA TSENG (1991) 'Thailand: Adjusting to Success, Current Policy Issues', International Monetary Fund, Occasional Paper no. 85 (August).

RUBLE, D.N., L.H. FRIEZE and J.E. PARSONS (eds) (1976) 'Sex Roles: Persistence and Change', *Journal of Social Issues*, vol. 32, no. 3.

RUECHADA BUDDHIKARANT (1973) 'A Case Study on the Economic Contribution of Private Direct Foreign Investment in the Textile Industry', MA thesis, Faculty of Economics, Thammasat University, Bangkok.

SAENG SANGUANRUENG, NISA XUTO, PREEYANUCH SAENGPASSORN and CHUCHEEP PIPUTSITEE (1978) *Development of Small and Medium Manufacturing Enterprises in Thailand* (Singapore: International Development Research Centre, Singapore).

SAENG SANGUANRUENG, SOMSAK TAMBUNLERTCHAI and NIT SAMMAPAN (1977) *A Study of Small and Medium Scale Industries in Thailand* (Bangkok: National Institute of Development Administration and Thammasat University) (in Thai).

SAISUREE CHUTIKUL (1986) 'Children in Especially Difficult Situation I (Thailand)' (National Youth Bureau, Office of the Prime Minister).

SANTHAD SERMSRI (1989) 'Population Growth and Environmental Protection', in *Culture and Environment in Thailand* (Bangkok: Siam Society).

SAROTE AUNGSUMALIN (1989) 'Finance and Service of Development of Rural Industry', paper presented at the seminar on Provincial Industry and Employment, organised by TDRI, Chon Buri, 19–20 August.

SAVIT BHOTHIVIHOK (1990) 'The Eastern Seaboard Development Programme: Revisited', in Suchart Prasith-rathasint (ed.) *Thailand on the Move: Stumbling Blocks and Breakthroughs* (Bangkok: Thai University Research Association and Canadian International Development Agency).

SAWAENG RATTANAMONGKOLMAS (1986) 'Status, Role, Problems and Solutions Related to Public–Private Cooperation', an evaluation report submitted to NESDB, May, Bangkok (in Thai).

SERI PHONGPHIT and ROBERT BENNOUN (eds) (1988) *Turning point of Thai farmers* (Bangkok: Thai Institute for Rural Development).

SHALARDCHAI RAMITANONDH (1989) 'Forests and Deforestation in Thailand: a Pandisciplinary Approach' in *Culture and Environment in Thailand* (Bangkok: Siam Society).

SHISHIDO TOSHIO (ed.) (1973) *Conditions of Economic Development in Thailand, 1973* (Tokyo: Institute of Developing Economies) (in Japanese).

SILCOCK, THOMAS H. (ed.) (1967) *Thailand: Social and Economic Studies in Development* (Canberra: Australian National University Press).

SIRILAKSANA CHUTIKUL (1986) 'Malnourished Children: An Economic Approach to the Causes and Consequences in Northeastern Thailand', East-West Population Institute, paper series no. 102 (Honolulu: East–West Center).

SIRILAKSANA CHUTIKUL (1987a) 'The Economics of Education Subsidies and the Effect of Fee Increases: A Case Study, discussion paper series, no. 93, Faculty of Economics, Thammasat University.

SIRILAKSANA CHUTIKUL (1987b) 'Education Policy in Thailand: Promises and Problems', paper presented at the International Conference on Thai Studies at the Australian National University, July.

SOMBOON SUKSAMRAN (1990) 'Socio-Political and Cultural Constraint on the Decision-making Process in Thailand', in Samart Chiasakul and Mikimasa Yoshida (eds), *Thai Economy in the Changing Decade and Industrial Promotion Policy* (Tokyo: Institute of Developing Economics).

SOMCHAI RATANAKOMUT (1990) 'Tourism Impact of Thailand', report of study prepared for the UN-ESCAP, Bangkok, May.

SOMLUCKRAT GRANDSTAFF (1989) 'The Role of Demand in Provincial Industry', The Rural Industries and Employment Project, Thailand Development Research Institute, August.

SOMLUCKRAT WATTANAVITUKUL (1978) 'Income Distribution of Thailand', in Harry T. Oshima and Toshiyuki Mizoguchi (eds), *Income Distribution by Sectors and Overtime in East and Southeast Asian Countries* (Quezon City: Council for Asian Manpower Studies).

SOMSAK TAMBUNLERTCHAI (1987) 'Development of the Manufacturing Sector in Thailand', paper presented at International Conference on Thai Studies, Australian National University Canberra, 3–6 July.

SOMSAK TAMBUNLERTCHAI (1989) 'Overview of the Provincial Industry', paper presented at the seminar on Provincial Industry and Employment, organised by TDRI at the Ambassador City Jomthien Hotel, Chon Buri, 19–20 August (in Thai).

SOMSAK TAMBUNLERTCHAI and CHESADA LOHAWENCHIT (1985) 'Rural Industries in Thailand', mimeo (April).

SONDHI LIMTHONGKUL (1992) 'The Thai State and Freedom of Information', presentation at the Conference on Thailand: the State and Civil Society, Australian National University, 18 October.

SOPIDA WERAKULTAWAN (1992) 'On the Water Front' *The Manager*, no 43, pp. 34–39.

STAPLE, G.C. (1990) 'The Global Telecommunications Traffic Boom: A Quantitative Brief on Cross-Border Markets and Regulation', IIC research report (London, International Institute of Communications).

STEPHENS, T. (1991) 'The Toxic Growing Pains of Thailand', *Sydney Morning Herald*, 22 June.

SUEHIRO AKIRA (1989) *Capital Accumulation in Thailand, 1855–1985* (Tokyo: Centre for East Asian Cultural Studies).

SUEHIRO AKIRA and YASUDA OSAMU (eds) (1987) *Industrialization of Thailand: A Challenge to NAIC* (Tokyo: Institute of Developing Economies) (in Japanese).

SUGANYA HUTASERANI and SOMCHAI JITSUCHON (1988) 'Thailand Income Distribution and Poverty Profile and Their Current Situation', paper presented at the 1988 TDRI Year-End Conference, 17–18 December.

SUKANYA NITUNGKORN (1988) 'The Problems of Secondary Education Expansion in Thailand', *Journal of Southeast Asian Studies*, vol. 26, no. 1 (June), pp. 24–41.

SUNTAREE KOMIN (1989) *Social Dimensions of Industrialization in Thailand* (Bangkok: National Institute of Development Administration).

SUNTAREE KOMIN (1990a) *Psychology of the Thai People: Values and Behaviour Patterns* (Bangkok: National Institute of Development Administration).

SUNTAREE KOMIN (1990b) 'Culture and Work-Related Values in Thai Organizations', *International Journal of Psychology*, vol. 25, no. 5/6, pp. 681–704.

SUNTAREE KOMIN (1991) 'Psychology of the Thai People: Values and Behavioural Patterns of Thai People' (Bangkok: NIDA Research Center).

SUNTAREE KOMIN and SANIT SMUCKARN (1979) *Thai Value Systems: The Measurement Instrument* (Bangkok: National Institute of Development Administration, Research Center) (in Thai).

SUPANG CHANTAVANICH (1979) 'Equality of Opportunity of Continuation to Secondary Education', *Journal of National Education*, vol. 14, no. 1 (in Thai).

SUTHIPHAND CHIRATHIVAT (1989) 'The Changing World Economy and Its Implications for Japan-Thailand Economic Relations', paper prepared for ASEAN-Japan Dialogue Project on 'Structural Changes in the World Economy and their Implications to the ASEAN-Japan Relations', organised by JCIE, East-West Seminar, ISEAS and NIRA, Bangkok, February.

SUTHIPHAND CHIRATHIVAT (1991) 'Managing Thai Trade Policy to Better Access Developed Countries'Markets', *ASEAN Economic Bulletin*, vol. 8, no. 1 (July), pp. 72–79.

SUTHIPHAND CHIRATHIVAT (1992a) 'International Service Trade: Concept and Issues for Thailand', paper presented at International Economic Forum, Economic Research Center, Faculty of Economics, Chulalongkorn University, 7 April.

SUTHIPHAND CHIRATHIVAT (1992b) 'Southeast Asia: What Next Move to Take With the Changing International Economic Environment', paper submitted to the Conference on New International Context of Development, Madison, Wisconsin, 24–25 April.

SUTHIPHAND CHIRATHIVAT (1992c) 'AFTA–A Step Towards Intensified Economic Integration?' ASEAN–Future Economic and Political Cooperation, Kuala Lumper, 13–15 November.

SUTHIPHAND CHIRATHIVAT, CHUMPHORN PACHUSANOND AND TANASAK WAHWISAN (1989) 'The Management Systems of the World Economy and the Response of Thailand's External Sector', background paper no. 2, TDRI 1989 Year-End Conference, Jomtien, Chon Buri, Thailand, 14–15 December.

TAN, EDITA A. and WANNASIRI NAIYAVITIT (1984) 'The Distribution Flow of Education in the Formal School System: An Analysis on Distribution of Educational Attainment', *Journal of the National Research Council of Thailand*, vol. 16, no. 2 (July–December).

TDRI (1989) 'The Development of the Thailand Technical Capability in Industry: Overview and Recommendation, STD Project.

TEERANA BHONGMAKAPAT (1990) 'Structural Changes and Industrial Promotion Policy', in Samart Chiasakul and Mikimasa Yoshida (eds), *Thai Economy in the Changing Decade and Industrial Promotion Policy* (Tokyo: Institute of Developing Economies), pp. 1–22.

THAMMANUN PONGSRIKUL and SOMCHAI RATANAKOMUT (1989) 'Trade in Services', background paper no. 5, the 1989 TDRI Year-End Conference, Jomtien, Chon Buri, Thailand, 14–15 December.

THAMMASAT UNIVERSITY, FACULTY OF ECONOMICS (1989) *What to be Gained from being a NIC?* (Bangkok, February).

THANISR CHATURONGKUL (1992a) 'BIBF: Essence and Impacts' unpublished paper, Bangkok Bank.

THANISR CHATURONGKUL (1992b) 'Net Capital Inflow and the Money Supply of Thailand', *Bangkok Bank Monthly Review*, vol. 33 (April).

TOBATA SEIICHI (1979) *Autobiography* (Tokyo: Nihon Keizai Shimbun) (in Japanese).

TOURISM AUTHORITY OF THAILAND (several years) 'Annual Statistical Report on Tourism in Thailand'.

TSENG, W. and R. CORKER (1991) 'Financial Liberalization, Money Demand, and Monetary Policy in Asian Countries' (International Monetary Fund, July).

TSOW, S. (1989) 'Reflections on a Newly Industrialised Country', *Bangkok Post*, 14 May.

TURTON, ANDREW (1978) 'The Current Situation in the Thai Countryside', in Andrew Turton, Jonathan Fast and Malcolm Caldwell (eds), *Thailand: Roots of Conflict* (Nottingham: Spokeman).

UN *Population Report, 1982* (UN).

UN-ESCAP (1986) *Human Resources Development: Its Technological Dimensions* (Bangkok).

UNESCO/MOSTE (1983) *Survey of Science and Technology Manpower and Research and Development (R&D) in the Private Sector in Thailand* (Bangkok: Ministry of Science, Technology and Energy and the Science Committee of the Thailand National Commission for UNESCO).

UNIDO (1985) 'Thailand', Industrial Development Review Series (Rome: UNIDO).

UNTUNG, DRA SITI RAFIAH (1991) 'Environmental Problems in the Limestone Industry, Citatah, West Java, Indonesia', Master of Environmental Studies thesis, University of Adelaide.

URBAN FORESTRY SUBTEAM (1993) 'Urban Forestry' (Bangkok: Royal Forestry Department, Ministry of Agriculture and Cooperatives).

URQUHART, MICHAEL (1981) 'Is Services Industry Recession–Proof?', *Monthly Labor Review* (October), pp. 12–18.

USHER, ANN DANAIYA (1990) 'A Forest Policy Sadly Gone Awry', *The Nation*, 10 May.

VILLANUEVA, D. and A. MIRAKHOR (1990) 'Strategies for Financial Reforms: Interest rate Policies, Stabilization and Bank Supervision in Developing Countries', *IMF Staff Papers*, vol. 37, no. 3 (September).

VIRABONGSA RAMANGKURA and PAKORN VICHYANON (1988) 'Three Decades of Fiscal and Monetary Policy in Thailand' in Rangsun Thanapornpun and Nipon Poapongsakorn (eds), *The Economy of Thailand on the Path of Santi-Prachatham*, collected essays in honour of Dr. Puey Ungphakorn on his 72nd birthday (Bangkok: Faculty of Economics, Thammasat University).

VIRAT SAENGTHONGKHAM, VISHNU CHOLITKUL, SOMPOONG SUWANJITKUL and BRET THORN (1992) 'Coming of Age', *The Manager*, no 43, pp. 20–25.

WADE, ROBERT (1990) *Governing the Market: Economic Theory and the Role of Government in East Asian Industrialization* (Princeton, NJ: Princeton University Press).

WATTANA NA RANONG (1989) 'Dissemination of Data and Data Service to Provincial Industry', paper presented at seminar on Provincial Industry and Employment, organised by TDRI at the Ambassador City Jomthien Hotel, Chon Buri, 19–20 August.

WILSON, G.W. (1986) 'Privatization in Transportation: the Case of Thailand', paper presented at the Fourth World Conference on Transport Research, Vancouver, Canada.

WINCKLER, E. (1981) 'Institutionalization and Participation on Taiwan: from Hard to Soft Authoritarianism?', *China Quarterly*, 9 September.

WIRAT WATTANASIRITHAM *et al.* (1988) 'Thailand Socio Economic Development Planning', in Warin Wonghanchao and Yukio Ikemoto (eds), *Economic Development Policy in Thailand: A Historical Review* (Tokyo: Institute of Developing Economies).

WORLD BANK (1959) *A Public Development Program in Thailand* (Baltimore: The Johns Hopkins Press).

WORLD BANK (1972) 'Current Economic Position and Prospects of Thailand, vol. 1: The Main Report' (Washington, DC: World Bank).

WORLD BANK (1978) 'Thailand: Toward a Development Strategy of Full Participation', report no. 2059-TH (Washington, DC: World Bank).

WORLD BANK (1980a) *Thailand: Income Growth and Poverty Alleviation*, A World Bank Country Study (Washington, DC: World Bank).

WORLD BANK (1980b) 'Agricultural Development Strategy Review', report no. 3108-TH (Washington, DC: East Asia and Pacific Regional Office, World Bank).

WORLD BANK (1980c) 'Thailand: Coping with Structural Change in a Dynamic Economy', report no. 3067a-TH (Washington, DC: East Asia and Pacific Region, World Bank).

WORLD BANK (1982) 'Thailand: Program and Policy Priorities for an Agricultural Economy in Transition', report no. 3705a-TH in 4 volumes (Washington, DC: East Asia and Pacific Regional Office, World Bank).

WORLD BANK (1983) *Growth and Employment in Rural Thailand*, A World Bank Country Study (Washington, DC: World Bank).

WORLD BANK (1984) Thailand: *Managing Public Resources for Structural Adjustment*, A World Bank Country Study, Washington, DC: World Bank).

WORLD BANK (1985) *Thailand: Pricing and Marketing Policy for Intensification of Rice Agriculture*, A World Bank Country Study (Washington, DC: World Bank).

WORLD BANK (1986) 'Thailand: Growth with Stability A Challenge for the Sixth Plan Period. A Country Economic Report', vol. 2, the Main Report, (Washington, DC: World Bank).

WORLD BANK (1989) 'Thailand: Country Economic Memorandum. Building on the Recent Success. A Policy Framework', report no. 7445-TH, (Washington, DC: World Bank).

WORLD BANK (1992) *World Tables 1992* (Washington, DC: World Bank).

WORLD BANK (various years) *World Development Report* (Washington, DC: World Bank).

WORLD COMMISSION ON ENVIRONMENT AND DEVELOPMENT (WCED) (1987) *Our common future* (Oxford: Oxford University Press).

YAMAZAWA IPPEI and HIRATA AKIRA (eds) (1987) *Industrialization and Export Promotion Policy in Developing Countries* (Tokyo: Institute of Developing Economies) (in Japanese)

YONGYUTH YUTHAVONGS (1989) 'Science and Technological Capability in Thailand Being A NIC', paper presented at the Symposium on What to be Gained if Thailand becomes a NIC? Faculty of Economics, Thammasat University, February (in Thai).

YONGYUTH YUTHAVONGS *et al.* (1985) 'Key Problems in Science and Technology in Thailand', *Science*, vol. 227.

YOS SANTASOMBAT, WICHEAN SAENGCHOT and THERAPON SAWANRUENGRANG (1991) 'Community Forestry: a Dimension of Alternative Development', paper presented at People's Forum, Bangkok, 8–17 October.

YOSHIDA MIKIMASA (1990) 'Foreign Direct Investment in Thailand', in Samart Chiasakul and Mikimasa Yoshida (eds), *Thai Economy in the Changing Decade and Industrial Promotion Policy* (Tokyo: Institute of Developing Economies), pp. 1–22.

YOSHIHARA KUNIO (1992a) 'Overview of the Southeast Asian Economy' in Yoshihara Kunio (ed.) *The Economy of Southeast Asia* (Tokyo: Koubundo) (in Japanese).

YOSHIHARA KUNIO (ed.) (1992b) *The Economy of Southeast Asia* (Tokyo: Koubundo) (in Japanese).

ZIMMERMAN, CARLE C. (1932) *Siam: Rural Economic Survey, 1930–1* (Bangkok: Bangkok Times).

Index